THE

BEST

OF

Gourmet

THE BEST OF *Gourmet*

1996

FROM THE EDITORS OF GOURMET

PHOTOGRAPHS BY ROMULO A. YANES

CONDÉ NAST BOOKS · RANDOM HOUSE, NEW YORK

Copyright © 1996
The Condé Nast Publications Inc.
All rights reserved under International and
Pan-American Copyright Conventions.
Published in the United States by
Random House, Inc., New York, and
simultaneously in Canada by Random
House of Canada Limited, Toronto.

LIBRARY OF CONGRESS
CATALOGING-IN-PUBLICATION DATA

(Revised for vol. 11)
Main entry under title:
The Best of Gourmet: 1996 /from the editors of
Gourmet;/ photographs by Romulo A. Yanes
    p.   cm.
"Condé Nast books"
Includes indexes.
   1. Cookery, English. 2. Cookery, Irish.
3. Cookery, Scottish. 4. Quick and Easy
Cookery. 5. Soups. 6. Sandwiches. I. Gourmet
TX717.B532 1996
641.5-dc20   95-41183
ISBN 0-679-44936-1 (hardcover: alk. paper)
ISSN 1046-1760

Most of the recipes in this work were published previously in *Gourmet* Magazine.

Manufactured in the United States of
America on acid-free paper.

98765432
First Edition

All the informative text in this book was
written by Diane Keitt and Judith Tropea.

The text of this book was set in Times
Roman by Carl Jablonski and Media
Projects Incorporated. The four-color
separations were done by The Color
Company, Seiple Lithographers, and
Applied Graphic Technologies. The book
was printed and bound at R. R. Donnelley
and Sons. Stock is Citation Webb Gloss,
Westvaco.

Front Jacket: "Baked Scrod in Cider"
(page 268).

Back Jacket: "Tomato and Onion Tart"
(page 179).

Frontispiece: "Fancy Sandwich Cake"
(page 261).

For Condé Nast Books

Jill Cohen, President
Ellen Maria Bruzelius, Direct Marketing
   Director
Pat Van Note, Production Development
   Manager
Lucille Friedman, Fulfillment Manager
Tom Downing, Direct Marketing Manager
Jennifer Metz, Direct Marketing Associate
John Crutchfield, Direct Marketing
   Assistant
Diane Pesce, Prepress Services Manager
Serafino J. Cambareri, Quality Control
   Manager

For *Gourmet* Books

Diane Keitt, Director
Judith Tropea, Editor
Caroline A. Schleifer, Associate Editor

For *Gourmet* Magazine

Gail Zweigenthal, Editor-in-Chief

Zanne Early Zakroff, Executive Food
   Editor
Kemp Miles Minifie, Senior Food Editor
Alexis M. Touchet, Associate Food Editor
Amy Mastrangelo, Food Editor
Lori Walther, Food Editor
Elizabeth Vought, Food Editor
Peggy Anderson, Assistant Food Editor

Romulo A. Yanes, Photographer
Marjorie H. Webb, Style Director
Nancy Purdum, Senior Style Editor

Produced in association with
Media Projects Incorporated

Carter Smith, Executive Editor
Anne B. Wright, Project Editor
John W. Kern, Production Editor
Marilyn Flaig, Indexer
Carl Jablonski, Art/Production Director

ACKNOWLEDGMENTS

The editors of *Gourmet* Books would like to thank everyone who contributed to *The Best of Gourmet, 1996.*

As always, this annual would not be possible without Zanne Zakroff, Executive Food Editor; all the food editors; Romulo A. Yanes, photographer; and Marjorie Webb and Nancy Purdum, stylists — all of whom create, month after month, most of the material that appears in this collection.

This year our Cuisines of the World section features The Flavors of England, Ireland, and Scotland. Menus were created and styled by *Gourmet* food editors Liz Vought (English Afternoon Tea), Lori Walther (An Irish Country Supper), and Alexis Touchet (A Scottish Dinner). Lori also developed and styled the Baked Scrod in Cider featured on our jacket, and Liz developed and styled the Fancy Sandwich Cake that appears on page 2. Gerald Asher, *Gourmet*'s Wine Editor, expertly chose the wines for each menu. Food photographs were shot by Romulo A. Yanes and prop styled by Jeannie Oberholtzer. Regional photographs by Adam Woolfitt, Mathias Oppersdorff, and Julian Nieman, and line drawings by Laura Hartman Maestro complement the text. And, special thanks to Judy Hyde of the British Trade Office for her knowledgeable input.

Leslie Glover Pendleton created recipes for this year's addendum — Quick and Easy Soups and Sandwiches, to which light-hearted drawings by Suzanne Dunaway add a whimsical touch.

The Recipe Compendium is graced with the line drawings of many talented artists, including: Carla Borea, Jean Chandler, Beverly Charlton, Suzanne Dunaway, Barbara Fiore, Vicky Harrison, Susie Howard, Lauren Jarrett, Young Kim, Elisa Mambrino, Zoe Mavridis, Jeanne Meinke, Bob Palevitz, Agni Saucier, Jim Saucier, Alexis Seabrook, and Meg Shields.

Finally, we give thanks to our book designer, Carl Jablonski; to Anne Wright and John Kern of Media Projects; to Mark Ferri for his lovely food photographs; to colleagues Kemp Minifie, Elaine Richard, and Hobby McKenney for their editorial contributions; and to Karen Salsgiver for her artistic suggestions.

CONTENTS

INTRODUCTION

The best solution is often the simplest one. Last year, when we set out to develop a leaner/lighter column for *Gourmet* magazine, we kept this little adage in mind. The simplest solution to a sensible diet, we concluded, is to consume healthy, flavorful foods while keeping an eye on fat and calories. *Gourmet*'s "Less Is More" column does just that. Our delicious menus contain 500 or fewer calories per serving, with the total fat content per serving running no more than 15 grams (or 30% of calories, in agreement with FDA guidelines). Our single-theme recipes maintain the same low-fat criteria as well as a reduced calorie count. Your response to this column has been overwhelming, proving that this balanced approach to eating fits into your lifestyle infinitely better than a complicated diet. Naturally, you will find our favorite "Less Is More" menus and recipes in *The Best of Gourmet, 1996*. Look for the leaner/lighter symbol in our general index, and be sure to give these recipes a try.

As always, our annual is packed with exceptionally beautiful full-color food photographs by Romulo Yanes. This year they are noticeably bigger, bolder, and brighter; and there are more of them to enjoy than ever before. You'll want to take plenty of time to savor The Menu Collection for year-round entertaining ideas: From a relaxed party for New Year's Eve featuring Chipotle Cheese Fondue, to a lovely Easter dinner complete with Rosemary Garlic Pork Rib Roast with Roasted Carrots and Onions (and Honey-Glazed Bunny Rolls), to a refreshing grilled lobster buffet at poolside, to a very special Southern Christmas boasting Ham with Apple Mustard Glaze and fabulous trimmings ... inventive ideas abound.

Because we know that you have enjoyed our quick and easy dishes all year long, we've collected more than 200 of them in The Recipe Compendium. Then, to add some new speedy recipes to your repertoire, we've included 24 marvelous Quick and Easy Soups and Sandwiches especially created for this year's Addendum. We hope, too, that you will explore The Flavors of England, Ireland, and Scotland with three all-new menus in our Cuisines of the World section. A food awakening is under way throughout the British Isles with renewed interest in traditional fare, and here we present many longtime favorites with exciting *Gourmet* touches.

It's all here in *The Best of Gourmet, 1996*. I encourage you to have a look, then sample all that this volume has to offer.

Gail Zweigenthal, Editor-in-Chief

Month after month *Gourmet* magazine brings the art of good living to life through its exceptional menus. Arriving at bound glossy menu pages is the result of a creative collaboration of food editors, prop stylists, and photographer. Themes, locations, and menus are debated, then, after weeks of recipe development, weeks of hunting for just the right setting and props, and several days of styling and photography, a menu comes to life. Here we present the 29 best menus of 1995.

To meet your on-going demand for relaxed fare, we offered several alfresco menus throughout the year. These require dishes that can be prepared ahead of time, needn't be reheated, and are easily transported. Seaworthy treats are the mainstay of our America's Cup Countdown Picnic: an impressive Pizza Rustica accompanied by Fennel-Marinated Vegetables in Lettuce Cones, and Carrot Cupcakes with Molasses Cream Cheese Icing for an exhilarating finish. For another easy mini-meal, turn to our Cycling Picnic: Prosciutto and Brie Sandwiches with Rosemary Fig Confit, and Smoked Chicken and Sun-Dried Tomato Sandwiches with Basil Olive Pesto will surely impress your biking companions. But for a glorious outdoor meal, splurge on a Picnic among the Vines. With Spiced Poussins, a luscious Tomato and Onion Tart, memorable salads, and a Plum and Almond Cobbler, who could ask for more?

During the autumn, turn to our Weekend in the Country, a collection of five menus that helps you organize all the food planning for a relaxed three-day visit with friends. From a welcoming Friday night dinner of Grilled Garlic Lime Pork Tenderloin, to a leisurely Sunday send-off brunch complete with egg tostadas and yummy cinnamon buns, you'll be assured of luscious eating and contented guests.

In yet another *Gourmet* innovation, leaner/lighter menus that promise to be both flavorful and filling (without the calories and fat) are introduced. We've included one delicious meal of Roast Pork Loin with Shiitake and Leek Compote and another that highlights memorable Saffron Linguine with Spicy Shrimp and Vegetables.

Come and enjoy the variety, the creativity, and the magic of this year's Menu Collection. Over 75 pages of exciting full-color menu possibilities await.

Mixed Bitter Greens with Sautéed Mushrooms

A FONDUE PARTY

Chipotle Cheese Fondue, p. 153

Mixed Bitter Greens with Sautéed Mushrooms, p. 190

Preston Vineyards Dry Creek Valley Marsanne '93

•

Baked Pears on Sugared Puff Pastry with Caramel Sauce, p. 227

•

Serves 4

Chipotle Cheese Fondue

DINNER FROM
THE WEST INDIES

Black Bean Soup with Lime, p. 113

•

Braised Beef, Peppers, and Onions, p. 130

Yellow Rice with Toasted Cumin, p. 131

Fried Plantains, p. 182

*Avocado, Hearts of Palm, and Red Onion Salad
with Coriander Vinaigrette*, p. 190

Viña Pedrosa '90 Hermanos Pérez Pascuas Ribera del Duero

•

Fried Custard Squares with Rum Sauce, p. 230

•

Serves 8

Fried Custard Squares with Rum Sauce

Braised Beef, Peppers, and Onions; Yellow Rice with
Toasted Cumin; Fried Plantains; Avocado, Hearts of Palm,
and Red Onion Salad with Coriander Vinaigrette

17

Panettone Bread and Butter Pudding

SUPPER IN THE KITCHEN

Minted Orange, Fennel, and Red Onion Salad, p. 196

•

Braised Veal Shanks with Green Olives and Capers, p. 134

Parmesan Sage Polenta Sticks, p. 163

Geyser Peak California Semchard '93

•

Panettone Bread and Butter Pudding, p. 232

•

Serves 6

Minted Orange, Fennel, and Red Onion Salad

Braised Veal Shanks
with Green Olives and Capers;
Parmesan Sage Polenta Sticks

VALENTINE'S DAY
DINNER

Halibut with Olive Tarragon Bread Crumbs
on Roasted Tomato and Garlic Coulis, p. 120

Braised Leeks with Lemon, p. 173

Wild Rice with Fennel and Porcini, p. 166

Langwerth von Simmern Erbacher Marcobrunn Riesling Spätlese '92

•

Bittersweet Chocolate Mousse in Phyllo
with Raspberry Sauce, p. 234

St. George Spirits Framboise Eau de Vie

•

Serves 2

Halibut with Olive Tarragon Bread Crumbs
on Roasted Tomato and Garlic Coulis;
Braised Leeks with Lemon;
Wild Rice with Fennel and Porcini

Carrot Cupcakes with Molasses Cream Cheese Icing

AMERICA'S CUP

COUNTDOWN PICNIC

Pizza Rustica, p. 110

Fennel-Marinated Vegetables in Lettuce Cones, p. 180

Swanson Napa Valley Sangiovese '92

•

Carrot Cupcakes with Molasses Cream Cheese Icing, p. 208

•

Serves 6

Pizza Rustica; Fennel-Marinated
Vegetables in Lettuce Cones

Warm Lentil Salad with Mustard Vinaigrette

A WINE CELLAR DINNER

Salade Chaude aux Lentilles avec Vinaigrette à la Moutarde, p. 192
(Warm Lentil Salad with Mustard Vinaigrette)

•

Potée, p. 117
(Smoked Pork, Sausage, and Vegetable Soup)

Aligot Gratin, p. 176
(Potato and Cheese Purée)

Kunde Sonoma Valley Shaw Vineyard Zinfandel '92

•

Grape Milliard, p. 211
(Grape Custard Cake)

•

Serves 6

Grape Custard Cake

Smoked Pork, Sausage, and Vegetable Soup;
Potato and Cheese Purée

29

Honey-Glazed Bunny Rolls

EASTER DINNER

Rosemary Garlic Pork Rib Roast with Roasted Carrots and Onions, p. 135

Balsamic Rhubarb Compote, p. 201

Spring Vegetables with Shallots and Lemon, p. 181

Honey-Glazed Bunny Rolls, p. 106

Franz Künstler Hochheimer Hölle Riesling Auslese '90

•

Ginger Crunch Cake with Strawberry Sauce, p. 214

Geyser Peak Late Harvest Riesling '93

•

Serves 6

Rosemary Garlic Pork Rib Roast with Roasted Carrots and Onions;
Balsamic Rhubarb Compote; Spring Vegetables with Shallots and
Lemon; Honey-Glazed Bunny Roll

Ginger Crunch Cake
with Strawberry Sauce

Octopus, Cannellini, and Arugula Salad

ANTIPASTO BUFFET

Tomato and Olivada Crostini, p. 99

Orange, Fennel, and Garlic Marinated Olives, p. 96

•

Turkey Breast Braciola, p. 151

Octopus, Cannellini, and Arugula Salad, p. 186

Zucchini and Spinach Frittata, p. 156

Roasted Peppers and Potatoes with Bagna Cauda, p. 175

Columbia Crest Chardonnay '93

•

Panna Cotta with Praline Caramel Sauce, p. 233

•

Serves 12

Tomato and Olivada Crostini;
Orange, Fennel, and Garlic Marinated Olives

Turkey Breast Braciola; Orange, Fennel, and Garlic
Marinated Olives; Roasted Peppers and Potatoes with
Bagna Cauda; Octopus, Cannellini, and Arugula
Salad; Grissini; Zucchini and Spinach Frittata

PICNIC AMONG THE VINES

Spiced Poussins, p. 141

Tomato and Onion Tart, p. 179

Green Bean and Fingerling Potato Salad, p. 191

Eggplant Salad, p. 193

Fig, Ham, and Nectarine Salad in Wine Syrup, p. 196

Cornmeal Harvest Loaves, p. 108

•

Plum and Almond Cobbler, p. 228

•

Joseph Phelps Vin du Mistral Syrah '91

Joseph Phelps Vin du Mistral Viognier '93

•

Serves 12

DINNER
AT A GRAND HOUSE

Crisp Scallops with Horseradish Lime Sauce, p. 96

Sterling Vineyards Napa Valley Estate Chardonnay '93

•

*Blue Cheese and Walnut Soufflés and Mesclun
with Red Pepper Vinaigrette, p. 152*

Clos du Bois Sonoma County Merlot '92

•

Grilled Veal Chops with Morel Sauce, p. 133

New Potatoes in Chive Butter, p. 175

Warm Cherry Tomato Salad, p. 196

Heitz Cellars Martha's Vineyard Cabernet Sauvignon '87

•

Strawberry Rhubarb Napoleons and Lemon Cream, p. 228

Grgich Hills Late Harvest Napa Valley Johannisberg Riesling '93

•

Serves 6

Blue Cheese and Walnut Soufflés and
Mesclun with Red Pepper Vinaigrette

Grilled Veal Chop with Morel Sauce; New Potatoes in Chive Butter; Warm Cherry Tomato Salad

Blue Cheese and Walnut
Soufflé and Mesclun with
Red Pepper Vinaigrette

Strawberry Rhubarb Napoleon and Lemon Cream

Raspberry Lime Rickeys; Spiced Curly Tortilla Chips; Tomatillo Salsa

POOLSIDE LOBSTER BUFFET

Raspberry Lime Rickeys, p. 237

Spiced Curly Tortilla Chips, p. 103

Tomatillo Salsa, p. 103

•

Grilled Lobster with Orange Chipotle Vinaigrette, p. 128

Potato and Toasted Corn Salad with Buttermilk Dressing, p. 194

Melon with Feta, Red Onion, and Pine Nuts, p. 196

Grilled Bread and Guacamole "Butter", p. 110

Truchard Napa Valley Carneros Chardonnay '93

•

Cornmeal Cake with Sweet Rosemary Syrup and Blackberries, p. 214

•

Serves 8

Grilled Lobster with Orange Chipotle
Vinaigrette; Melon with Feta, Red Onion,
and Pine Nuts; Potato and Toasted
Corn Salad with Buttermilk Dressing

Herb Salad Spring Rolls with Spicy Peanut Sauce;
Squid Salad with Tamarind Sauce

VIETNAMESE SALAD
SUPPER

Herb Salad Spring Rolls with Spicy Peanut Sauce, p. 194

Squid Salad with Tamarind Sauce, p. 185

Chappellet Old Vine Cuvée '93

•

Grilled Lemongrass Beef and Noodle Salad, p. 184

Green Papaya Salad with Shrimp, p. 186

Cline Cellars Oakley Cuvée '90

•

Jasmine Tea Sorbet, p. 222

Minted Lemongrass Sorbet, p. 223

•

Serves 4

Minted Lemongrass Sorbet;
Jasmine Tea Sorbet

Grilled Lemongrass Beef and Noodle Salad;
Green Papaya Salad with Shrimp

A CYCLING PICNIC

Ratatouille Dip, p. 100

Assorted Olives

*Prosciutto and Brie Sandwiches with
Rosemary Fig Confit, p. 154*

*Smoked Chicken and Sun-Dried Tomato Sandwiches with
Basil Olive Pesto, p. 146*

White Bean and Red Onion Salad, p. 191

Joseph Phelps Vin du Mistral Grenache Rosé '94

·

Chocolate Chip Apricot Bars, p. 216

Fresh Fruit

·

Serves 4

Prosciutto and Brie Sandwich with Rosemary Fig Confit;
Smoked Chicken and Sun-Dried Tomato Sandwich
with Basil Olive Pesto; Assorted Olives;
White Bean and Red Onion Salad; Ratatouille Dip

Ham and Fresh Peach Chutney on Corn Bread;
Smoked Salmon "Tartare" on New Potato Slices

FOURTH OF JULY DINNER

Smoked Salmon "Tartare" on New Potato Slices, p. 97

Ham and Fresh Peach Chutney on Corn Bread, p. 98

Watermelon Vodka Coolers, p. 237

•

Grilled Leg of Lamb with Hot Red Pepper Relish, p. 139

Lemon Tarragon Green Beans, p. 168

Toasted Bulgur Salad with Corn and Tomatoes, p. 198

Stonestreet Alexander Valley Cabernet Sauvignon '91

•

Individual Berry Cobblers with Lemon Buttermilk Ice Cream, p. 226

•

Serves 8

Grilled Leg of Lamb with Hot Red
Pepper Relish; Lemon Tarragon
Green Beans; Toasted Bulgur
Salad with Corn and Tomatoes

Grilled Leg of Lamb with Hot Red Pepper Relish; Lemon Tarragon
Green Beans; Toasted Bulgur Salad with Corn and Tomatoes

Individual Berry Cobblers
with Lemon Buttermilk Ice Cream

LUNCH ON THE PORCH

*Cold Cucumber and Yellow Pepper Soup
with Crab Meat and Chives,* p. 115

•

Grilled Chicken with Tomato and Bread Salad, p. 143

De Loach Russian River Valley Sauvignon Blanc '93

•

Spiced Strawberry Sorbet, p. 222

Toasted Almond Phyllo Crisps, p. 222

•

Serves 6

Cold Cucumber and Yellow Pepper Soup
with Crab Meat and Chives

Spiced Strawberry Sorbet;
Toasted Almond Phyllo Crisps

Grilled Chicken with Tomato and Bread Salad

59

CAMPSITE COOKOUT

Garlic-and-Chili-Rubbed Steaks, p. 130

Smoky Potato Salad, p. 194

Grilled Corn on the Cob, p. 172

Two-Bean Salad with Vegetables, p. 192

Lolonis "Orpheus" Mendocino County Petite Sirah '91

•

S'mores, p. 217

•

Serves 4

A WEEKEND IN THE COUNTRY

FRIDAY SUPPER

Grilled Garlic Lime Pork Tenderloin, p. 136

Jalapeño Onion Marmalade, p. 136

Cashew Sesame Noodles, p. 161

Snow Pea and Napa Cabbage Slaw, p. 195

A. & P. de Villaine La Digoine Bourgogne Rouge '92

·

Mascarpone Cheesecake Tart with Nectarines, p. 220

·

Serves 6

SATURDAY BREAKFAST

Plum Streusel Coffeecake, p. 157

Red and Green Grapes

Orange Juice

Coffee

·

Serves 6

Friday Supper: Mascarpone
Cheesecake Tart with Nectarines

SATURDAY LUNCH

Chilled Herb Soup, p. 115

Mediterranean Couscous and Lentil Salad, p. 198

Assorted Meats, Cheeses, and Breads

Château de la Chaize Brouilly '94

•

Miniature Double-Chocolate Cakes, p. 211

Cherries

•

Serves 6

SATURDAY DINNER

Roasted Zucchini and Yogurt Spread, p. 104

Pita Toasts, p. 104

•

Shrimp and Peppers in Spicy Tomato Sauce, p. 126

Basmati Rice with Mustard Seeds and Golden Raisins, p. 126

Watercress and Romaine Salad with Ginger Vinaigrette, p. 188

Shafer Napa Valley Chardonnay '93

•

Raspberry Frozen Yogurt Cake with Raspberry Amaretto Sauce, p. 223

•

Serves 6

SUNDAY BRUNCH

Sangrita Bloody Marys, p. 237

·

Scrambled Egg, Potato, and Bacon Tostadas, p. 155

Red and Green Tomato Salsa, p. 155

Corn and Avocado Relish, p. 155

Sour Cherry Pecan Cinnamon Buns, p. 106

Errazuriz Chilean Merlot '93

·

Melon and Pineapple with Lemon Mint Syrup, p. 226

·

Serves 6

Friday Supper: Grilled Garlic Lime Pork Tenderloin; Jalapeño
Onion Marmalade; Cashew Sesame Noodles; Snow Pea and
Napa Cabbage Slaw

Saturday Breakfast: Plum Streusel Coffeecake; Red and Green Grapes

Saturday Lunch: Chilled
Herb Soup; Mediterranean
Couscous and Lentil Salad;
Assorted Meats, Cheeses,
and Breads

66

Saturday Dinner: Shrimp and Peppers in Spicy Tomato Sauce; Basmati Rice with Mustard Seeds and Golden Raisins; Watercress and Romaine Salad with Ginger Viniagrette

Sunday Brunch: Sangrita Bloody Marys; Scrambled Egg, Potato, and Bacon Tostadas; Red and Green Tomato Salsa; Corn and Avocado Relish; Sour Cherry Pecan Cinnamon Buns

Roasted Squash, Red Pepper, and Jack Cheese Quesadillas
with Chipotle Lime Sour Cream Dip

COCKTAILS IN THE SKY

*Roasted Squash, Red Pepper, and Jack Cheese Quesadillas
with Chipotle Lime Sour Cream Dip, p. 95*

*Middle Eastern Sesame Lamb Meatballs
with Minted Yogurt Dip, p. 94*

Caviar, Cream Cheese, Scallion, and Egg Towers, p. 93

Miniature Crab Cakes with Mustard Mayonnaise, p. 92

*Coconut Curry Scallop, Kumquat, and
Asian Pear Canapés, p. 99*

Parmesan Walnut Salad in Endive Leaves, p. 95

Worcestershire Mushroom Rolls, p. 94

*Smoked Salmon and Chive Mascarpone Mousse
with Pink Pickled Onions, p. 102*

•

Martinis, Manhattans, Old Fashioneds

Champagne Veuve Clicquot Yellow Label Brut Non-Vintage

Joseph Faiveley Clos Rochette Mercurey Blanc '92

•

Serves 20 to 30

Witches' Brew; Poppy Cheddar Moon Crackers

A HAUNTED HOUSE DINNER

Witches' Brew, p. 238

Poppy Cheddar Moon Crackers, p. 110

•

Black Linguine with Orange and Red Peppers, p. 160

•

Braised Short Ribs, p. 132

Duchesse Potato Ghosts, p. 176

Roasted Golden Nugget Squash, p. 178

López de Heredia Viña Tondonia Rioja '87

•

Devil's Food Cake with Chocolate Spider Web, p. 210

•

Serves 6 to 8

Black Linguine with
Orange and Red Peppers

Braised Short Ribs; Roasted Golden Nugget Squash

Duchesse Potato Ghosts

Devil's Food Cake with Chocolate Spider Web

Curried Squash Soup with Frizzled Leeks

A COUNTRY THANKSGIVING

Curried Squash Soup with Frizzled Leeks, p. 119

•

Roast Turkey with Sausage Fennel Stuffing and Madeira Gravy, p. 150

Cranberry, Shallot, and Dried-Cherry Compote, p. 202

Balsamic-Glazed Beets, p. 169

Roast "Chrysanthemum" Onions, p. 174

Root Vegetable Purée, p. 180

Green Beans with Hazelnuts and Lemon, p. 168

Chaddsford Proprietor's Reserve Red '93

•

Sweet Potato Meringue Pie, p. 219

Candied Quince Tart, p. 220

Essensia California Orange Muscat Sweet Dessert Wine '94

•

Serves 8

Roast Turkey with Sausage Fennel Stuffing and
Madeira Gravy; Balsamic-Glazed Beets; Green Beans
with Hazelnuts and Lemon; Roast "Chrysanthemum"
Onions; Cranberry, Shallot, and Dried-Cherry
Compote; Root Vegetable Purée

Grilled Turkey

THANKSGIVING
CALIFORNIA STYLE

Grilled Turkey with Cranberry Gravy, p. 148

Three-Onion Stuffing, p. 149

Whipped Chipotle Sweet Potatoes, p. 179

Date, Goat Cheese, and Mesclun Salad, p. 189

Eberle Paso Robles Sauret Vineyard Zinfandel '93

•

Apple Walnut Upside-Down Cake with Calvados Caramel Sauce, p. 206

Newlan Napa Valley Late Harvest Johannisberg Riesling '93

•

Serves 8

Almond and Chocolate Dacquoise with Cranberry Sauce

ROCKY MOUNTAIN
CHRISTMAS

*Smoked Salmon with Cognac Caraway Mayonnaise
and Toasted French Bread, p. 96*

S. Anderson Napa Valley Brut '90

•

Rosemary-Roasted Buffalo Tenderloin with Gorgonzola Butter, p. 140

Parsley Leaf Potatoes, p. 177

Stir-Fried Broccoli with Pickled Red Onions, p. 170

Whole-Grain Mustard Pan Rolls, p. 105

Almond and Chocolate Dacquoise with Cranberry Sauce, p. 207

Rosemount Estate Balmoral McLaren Vale Syrah '92

•

Dried Fruits and Nuts, p. 229

Noval 10-Year-Old Tawny Port

•

Serves 8

SOUTHERN CHRISTMAS

Oyster Spinach Bisque with Corn Bread Croutons, p. 116

Bollinger Grande Année '88

•

Ham with Apple Mustard Glaze, p. 137

Pear Apple Chutney, p. 202

Collard Greens with Red Onions and Bacon, p. 171

Honey Ginger-Glazed Carrots, p. 171

Corn Chive Pudding, p. 172

Green Onion Casserole, p. 174

Benne Seed Angel Biscuits, p. 108

Robert Sinskey Vineyards Carneros Chardonnay '93

•

Coconut Cake with Lime Curd, p. 212

Gold-Dusted Bourbon Pecan Balls, p. 229

Chocolate Orange Fudge, p. 230

BV Muscat de Beaulieu

•

Serves 8

Oyster Spinach Bisque with Corn Bread Croutons

Ham with Apple Mustard Glaze; Pear Apple Chutney; Collard Greens
with Red Onions and Bacon; Corn Chive Pudding; Green Onion
Casserole; Honey Ginger-Glazed Carrots; Benne Seed Angel Biscuits

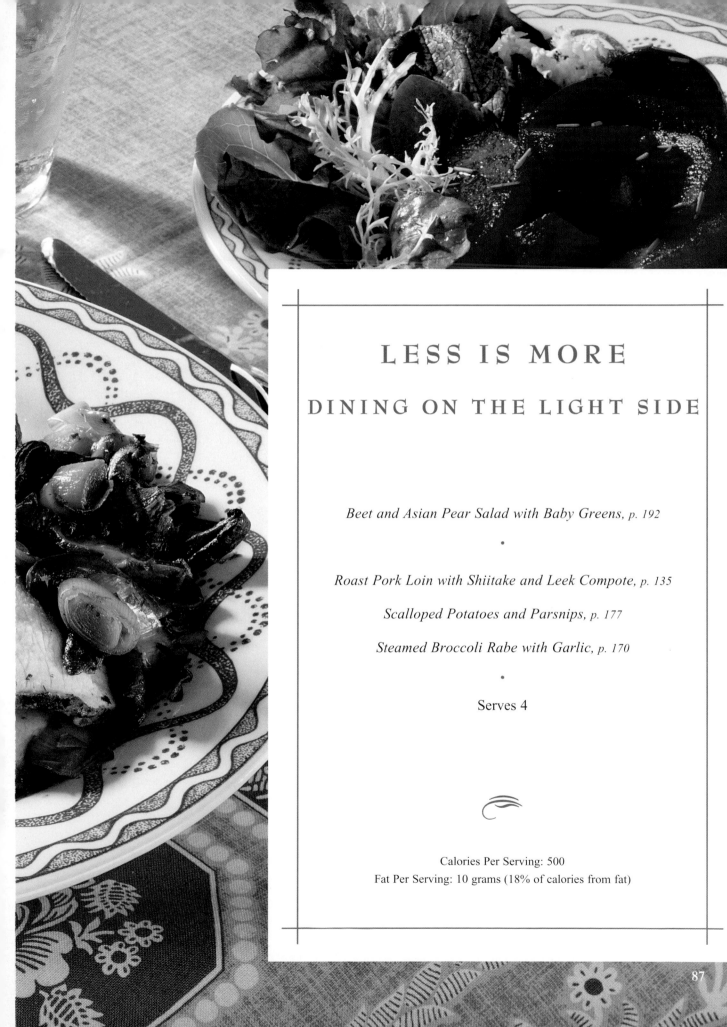

LESS IS MORE

DINING ON THE LIGHT SIDE

Beet and Asian Pear Salad with Baby Greens, p. 192

•

Roast Pork Loin with Shiitake and Leek Compote, p. 135

Scalloped Potatoes and Parsnips, p. 177

Steamed Broccoli Rabe with Garlic, p. 170

•

Serves 4

Calories Per Serving: 500
Fat Per Serving: 10 grams (18% of calories from fat)

LESS IS MORE

DINING ON THE LIGHT SIDE

Breadsticks

Saffron Linguine with Spicy Shrimp and Vegetables, p. 160

Caesar-Style Salad, p. 188

•

Serves 4

Calories Per Serving: 494
Fat Per Serving: 7.7 grams (14% of calories from fat)

A RECIPE COMPENDIUM

Over 400 of the very best recipes that appeared in *Gourmet* Magazine during 1995 are gathered here in time for you to plan your next dinner party, weekend gathering, weeknight meal, or just a simple tasty snack. Each has been carefully selected from *Gourmet*'s monthly food and entertainment columns to ensure an eclectic recipe collection full of welcome surprises. Diverse choices range from fanciful hors d'oeuvres, warming soups and breads, succulent fish and shellfish, hearty meats and poultry, and nourishing breakfast and brunch dishes to innovative pastas, crunchy vegetables and salads, luscious sauces (both sweet and savory), dreamy desserts, and playful beverages.

All the dishes that appear in The Menu Collection are included. As part of a special menu these dishes play a supporting role, but they are also exceptional on their own. When you're in the mood for lighter dishes, look for "Less is More" recipes — indicated by the 🍃 symbol.

And, because we know that sometimes you don't have much time to spend cooking, half of the recipes in this collection can be prepared in 45 minutes or less: From our "In Short Order" columns come quick snacks (Scallion and Anise Pita Toasts), hearty one-dish meals (Black-Eyed Pea and Ham Salad), lovely little desserts (Baked Pear and Orange Crisp), and much, much more. Speedy recipes from the "Last Touch" column offer easy thematic ideas including: tasty shrimp hors d'oeuvres, flavor-packed dips, spicy barbecue sauces, and fruity iced teas.

You'll find plenty of seasonal dishes to enjoy year-round from *Gourmet*'s kitchens as well as from contributing chefs. So, when the first thin stalks of asparagus appear at your greenmarket, will it be Steamed Asparagus with Ginger Garlic Sauce; Asparagus with Hazelnut Vinaigrette; or Asparagus, Leek, Shiitake, and Potato Ragout? And for special occasions our "Forbidden Pleasures" column comes through with such irresistable indulgences as Braised Pheasant with Red Cabbage Wild Rice.

The next thirteen chapters are packed with *Gourmet*'s newest and best ideas. Give yourself plenty of time to peruse them. We guarantee that you'll have a fascinating and delectable journey along the way.

HORS D'OEUVRES, CANAPÉS, DIPS AND SPREADS

Miniature Crab Cakes with Mustard Mayonnaise

For crab mixture
½ cup minced red bell pepper (about 1 small)
1 teaspoon vegetable oil
⅓ cup mayonnaise
1 large egg yolk
1½ tablespoons stone-ground mustard
1 to 2 teaspoons fresh lemon juice
¾ teaspoon dried tarragon, crumbled
1 pound jumbo lump crab meat, picked over
1½ cups *panko** (Japanese flaked bread crumbs)
For mustard mayonnaise
¼ cup mayonnaise
2½ teaspoons stone-ground mustard
¼ teaspoon fresh lemon juice,
   or to taste

½ stick (¼ cup) unsalted butter, melted

*available at Japanese markets, some specialty
   foods and seafood shops, and by mail order
   from Uwajimaya, tel. (800) 889-1928

Make crab mixture:
In a small non-stick skillet sauté bell pepper in oil over moderately high heat, stirring, 2 minutes, or until softened and golden. In a bowl whisk together mayonnaise, yolk, mustard, lemon juice, tarragon, and bell pepper and stir in crab and salt and pepper to taste gently but thoroughly. *Chill crab mixture, covered, at least 1 hour and up to 1 day.*
Preheat oven to 350° F.
In a large shallow baking pan spread *panko* in an even layer. Toast *panko*, stirring occasionally, until golden, about 10 minutes, and cool. *Panko may be toasted 1 week ahead and kept in an airtight container at room temperature.*

Form rounded teaspoons of crab mixture into slightly flattened 1-inch rounds and gently coat with *panko*, transferring to a shallow baking pan. *Chill crab cakes, loosely covered with wax paper, at least 2 hours and up to 4.*
Make mustard mayonnaise:
In a small bowl whisk together mayonnaise, mustard, and lemon juice. *Mayonnaise may be made 3 days ahead and chilled, covered.*
Preheat oven to 450° F.
Drizzle a scant ¼ teaspoon butter on each crab cake and bake in middle of oven until crisp and cooked through, about 15 minutes.
Serve crab cakes with mustard mayonnaise. Makes about 42 miniature crab cakes.

PHOTO ON PAGE 69

Olive and Anchovy Stuffed Eggs

6 hard-cooked large eggs
3 tablespoons sour cream
6 Kalamata or other brine-cured black olives,
   pitted and minced
½ teaspoon anchovy paste
½ teaspoon white-wine vinegar
2 to 3 tablespoons minced fresh flat-leafed
   parsley leaves

Garnish: black olive slivers and chopped
   parsley leaves

Cut a paper-thin slice off both ends of eggs and halve eggs crosswise. Force yolks through a sieve into a bowl (or mash with a fork) and stir in remaining ingredients and salt and pepper to taste. Transfer filling to a pastry bag fitted with a large plain or decorative tip and pipe into whites, mounding it. *Stuffed eggs may be made 6 hours ahead and chilled, covered.*
Just before serving, garnish eggs with olives and parsley. Makes 12 stuffed eggs.

Smoked Salmon, Cream Cheese, and Dill Stuffed Eggs

6 hard-cooked large eggs
3 ounces thinly sliced smoked salmon
2 ounces cream cheese, softened
2 tablespoons sour cream
½ teaspoon fresh lemon juice
2 tablespoons minced fresh dill

Garnish: fresh dill sprigs

Cut a paper-thin slice off both ends of eggs and halve eggs crosswise. In a small food processor blend yolks, salmon, cream cheese, sour cream, lemon juice, and salt and pepper to taste until smooth. Add minced dill and blend until mixture is just combined. Transfer filling to a pastry bag fitted with a large leaf or other decorative tip and pipe filling into whites, mounding it.

Garnish eggs with dill. Makes 12 stuffed eggs.

Caviar, Cream Cheese, Scallion, and Egg Towers

For filling
8 ounces cream cheese, softened
2 hard-cooked large eggs
1 cup finely chopped scallion greens

8 egg sheets (recipe follows)
2 ounces beluga or sevruga caviar*

*available at some specialty foods shops and by
    mail order from Petrossian, tel. (800) 828-9241

Make filling:

In a bowl beat cream cheese until fluffy. Quarter eggs and with back of a spoon force through a sieve into cream cheese. Add scallion and stir well. *Filling may be made 1 day ahead and chilled, covered. Bring filling to room temperature before proceeding.*

On a work surface arrange 2 egg sheets, side by side and overlapping by 1 inch. Put a dab of filling between sheets where they overlap (to act as glue) and press sheets together gently. Spread ½ cup filling on overlapping egg sheets, leaving about a ½-inch border on each long side. Fold in border of long side nearest you and tightly roll up sheets jelly-roll fashion into one 11-inch-long roll. Wrap egg sheet roll in plastic wrap and chill 1 hour, or until firm. Make 3 more egg sheet rolls with remaining egg sheets and filling in same manner. *Egg sheet rolls may be made 1 day ahead and chilled, wrapped well.*

Discard plastic wrap and trim ends of egg sheet rolls. Cut rolls crosswise into ¾-inch pieces. Arrange pieces, cut ends up, on a platter and top each with about ¼ teaspoon caviar. Makes 40 hors d'oeuvres.

PHOTO ON PAGE 69

Egg Sheets
(Paper-Thin Omelets)

1 teaspoon cornstarch
1 tablespoon cold water
4 large eggs, beaten lightly
¼ teaspoon salt
vegetable oil for brushing skillet

In a bowl dissolve cornstarch in water and whisk in eggs and salt until smooth. Brush a 6-inch non-stick skillet lightly with oil and heat over moderately high heat until hot but not smoking. Half-fill a ¼-cup measure with egg mixture. Remove skillet from heat and pour in ⅛ cup egg mixture, swirling skillet to coat evenly. Return skillet to heat and cook egg sheet until set, 10 to 15 seconds. Loosen edges with a heatproof rubber spatula and turn sheet over. Cook sheet until set, 5 to 10 seconds more, and slide onto a plate. Make more sheets with remaining mixture in same manner, brushing skillet lightly with oil each time. *Sheets may be made 1 day ahead and chilled, wrapped in plastic wrap.* Makes 8 or 9 sheets.

*Middle Eastern Sesame Lamb Meatballs
with Minted Yogurt Dip*

⅓ cup minced onion
1 large garlic clove, minced
1½ teaspoons olive oil
½ teaspoon dried mint, crumbled
½ teaspoon salt
¼ teaspoon ground allspice
a pinch cinnamon
1 pound ground lamb (10% fat)
1 cup fine fresh bread crumbs
1 large egg, beaten lightly
2 tablespoons dried currants
¼ cup black sesame seeds*
¼ cup white sesame seeds, toasted lightly

Accompaniment: minted yogurt dip
   (recipe follows)

*available at Asian markets and some specialty
   foods shops and supermarkets

In a small non-stick skillet cook onion and garlic in oil over moderately low heat, stirring, until softened. Transfer mixture to a bowl and stir in mint, salt, allspice, and cinnamon. Add lamb, bread crumbs, egg, and currants and combine well. Form level tablespoons of lamb mixture into 1¼-inch meatballs, arranging on a tray as formed.

In a small bowl roll half of meatballs, 1 at a time, in black sesame seeds until coated, transferring to a rack set in a shallow baking pan. Coat remaining meatballs with white seeds in same manner, transferring to rack. *Meatballs may be prepared up to this point 1 day ahead and chilled, covered loosely.*

Preheat oven to 450° F.

Bake meatballs in upper third of oven 8 to 10 minutes, or until golden and just cooked through.

Serve meatballs with dip. Makes 32 meatballs.

PHOTO ON PAGE 69

Minted Yogurt Dip

2 cups plain yogurt
¼ cup packed fresh mint leaves, chopped
½ teaspoon salt, or to taste

In a fine sieve set over a bowl drain yogurt, covered and chilled, 3 hours. Discard whey in bowl and transfer yogurt cheese to bowl. *Yogurt cheese may be made 2 days ahead and chilled, covered.*

Into yogurt cheese stir mint and salt. Makes about 1½ cups.

Worcestershire Mushroom Rolls

¾ pound mushrooms, trimmed and quartered
¼ pound shallots (about 3), minced
5 tablespoons unsalted butter
¼ cup Worcestershire sauce
¼ cup grated Cheddar
14 very thin slices firm white sandwich bread

Garnish: 28 long fresh chives

In a food processor mince mushrooms in 2 batches. In a 10-inch non-stick skillet cook shallots in 2 tablespoons butter over moderate heat, stirring, until golden. Add mushrooms with salt to taste and cook over moderate heat, stirring occasionally, until dark brown and very dry, about 15 minutes.

Add Worcestershire sauce and simmer, stirring occasionally, until sauce is evaporated and mixture is very dry, about 5 minutes. Remove skillet from heat and stir in Cheddar. *Filling may be made 3 days ahead and chilled, covered.*

Discard crusts from bread and with a rolling pin flatten each slice into a rectangle. In a small saucepan melt remaining 3 tablespoons butter.

On a work surface arrange a bread slice with a long side facing you and mound a level tablespoon filling along long side. Roll up bread jelly-roll fashion. Arrange roll, seam side down, in a shallow baking pan. Make more rolls with remaining bread and filling in same manner, arranging in pan in one layer, touching each other, and keeping covered with plastic wrap.

Brush mushroom rolls all over with melted butter and rearrange, seam sides down and barely touching, in pan. *Chill mushroom rolls, covered, at least 1 hour and up to 1 day.*

Preheat oven to 425° F.

Bake rolls in upper third of oven 15 minutes, or until golden. Halve rolls crosswise and tie a chive around each half. Makes 28 hors d'oeuvres.

Parmesan Walnut Salad in Endive Leaves

1 small garlic clove, minced and mashed to a
    paste with ½ teaspoon salt
1 tablespoon mayonnaise
2 tablespoons fresh lemon juice
2 tablespoons olive oil
a ¼-pound piece of Parmesan, sliced ⅛ inch thick
    and cut into ⅛-inch dice (about 1 cup)
½ cup finely chopped celery
4 Belgian endives
1 cup walnuts, toasted lightly and chopped fine
¼ cup finely chopped fresh flat-leafed parsley
    leaves

In a bowl whisk together garlic paste, mayonnaise, lemon juice, and oil and stir in Parmesan and celery. *Salad may be prepared up to this point 1 day ahead and chilled, covered.*

Trim endives and separate leaves. *Endive leaves may be prepared up to this point 1 day ahead and chilled, wrapped in dampened paper towels, in a plastic bag.*

Stir walnuts and parsley into salad. Dip wide end of each endive leaf into salad, scooping 1 tablespoon of salad onto it. Makes about 40 hors d'oeuvres.

Roasted Squash, Red Pepper, and Jack Cheese Quesadillas with Chipotle Lime Sour Cream Dip

a ¾-pound seedless piece butternut squash, peeled
    and cut into ¾-inch dice (about 5 cups)
1 medium onion, unpeeled, cut into eighths
1 large garlic clove, unpeeled

1 tablespoon vegetable oil
eight 5- to 6-inch flour tortillas
1 cup chopped red bell pepper (about 1 large)
1 cup coarsely grated jack cheese
½ stick (¼ cup) unsalted butter, softened

*Accompaniment: chipotle lime sour cream dip
    (recipe follows)*

Preheat oven to 400° F.

In a shallow baking pan arrange squash, onion, and garlic in one layer and drizzle with oil, tossing to coat. Roast mixture in oven 15 minutes, or until garlic is tender, and transfer garlic to a work surface. Roast squash and onion until tender, about 15 minutes more. Discard peels from onion and garlic.

In a food processor purée squash, onion, and garlic with salt and pepper to taste until smooth. *Squash purée may be made 2 days ahead and chilled, covered.*

Spread about one fourth squash purée on each of 4 tortillas and sprinkle each with about one fourth bell pepper and about one fourth cheese. Top each with a plain tortilla, pressing gently together. Spread each side of *quesadillas* with ½ tablespoon butter.

Heat a griddle or 7-inch non-stick skillet over moderately high heat until hot and cook *quesadillas,* 1 at a time, until golden, about 3 minutes on each side, transferring to a cutting board.

Cut each *quesadilla* into 6 or 8 wedges and serve warm with *chipotle* lime sour cream dip. Makes 24 to 32 hors d'oeuvres.

PHOTO ON PAGE 68

Chipotle Lime Sour Cream Dip

1 canned *chipotle* chili in *adobo**, minced
2 teaspoons fresh lime juice
1 cup sour cream

*available at Hispanic markets, some specialty
    foods shops, and by mail order from Adriana's
    Caravan, tel. (800) 316-0820

In a small bowl stir chili and lime juice into sour cream until combined well. *Dip may be made 2 days ahead and chilled, covered.* Makes about 1 cup.

Orange, Fennel, and Garlic Marinated Olives

4 cups mixed Italian olives* such as Alfonse,
　　Gaeta, and Sicilian, drained
¼ cup caper berries*, drained
2 tablespoons extra-virgin olive oil
1 tablespoon julienne strips orange zest
1 teaspoon fennel seeds, crushed
1 large garlic clove, sliced

*available at specialty foods shops

In a bowl combine all ingredients. *Marinate olive mixture, covered and chilled, stirring occasionally, at least 1 day and up to 3.* Makes about 4¼ cups.

PHOTO ON PAGE 35

*Smoked Salmon with Cognac Caraway Mayonnaise
and Toasted French Bread*

1 teaspoon caraway seeds
½ cup mayonnaise
3 tablespoons sour cream
1 tablespoon chopped fresh dill
2 teaspoons Cognac
a side of smoked salmon (about 2 pounds)

Garnish: fresh dill sprigs and lemon wedges
Accompaniment: toasted French bread

With a mortar and pestle or in an electric spice grinder grind caraway seeds fine and in a small bowl stir together with mayonnaise, sour cream, dill, and Cognac.

Arrange salmon on a cutting board or platter and garnish with dill sprigs and lemon wedges. Serve salmon, sliced thin, with mayonnaise and French bread. Serves 8 generously.

Crisp Scallops with Horseradish Lime Sauce

For sauce
½ cup mayonnaise
2 tablespoons drained bottled horseradish
1½ teaspoons fresh lime juice
½ teaspoon freshly grated lime zest
⅛ teaspoon freshly ground black pepper

For scallops
six 5- by 2½-inch graham crackers
1 teaspoon coarse salt
1 pound sea scallops (about 24)
vegetable oil for deep-frying
1 large egg, beaten lightly

Make sauce:
In a bowl whisk together sauce ingredients and chill, covered.
Make scallops:
Put graham crackers in a sealable plastic bag and with a rolling pin lightly crush until crumbs are coarse. In a bowl stir together crumbs and salt. Discard small tough muscle from side of each scallop and halve any large scallops. Pat scallops dry.

In a 4-quart heavy saucepan or heavy kettle heat 1½ inches oil to 365° F. on a deep-fat thermometer. Working in batches of 6, dip scallops in egg to coat, letting excess drip off, and roll in crumb mixture. Fry scallops, stirring gently, 2 minutes, or until browned and cooked through. Transfer scallops as cooked with a slotted spoon to paper towels to drain and season with salt and pepper.

Serve scallops with horseradish lime sauce. Makes about 24 hors d'oeuvres.

Coriander Lime Shrimp

½ cup fresh lime juice
¼ cup orange marmalade
3 large garlic cloves, minced and mashed to a
　　paste with 1 teaspoon salt
½ cup fresh coriander sprigs, washed well, spun
　　dry, and chopped fine
4 tablespoons olive oil
1 tablespoon soy sauce
½ teaspoon dried hot red pepper flakes
1 pound large (21 to 24 per pound) shrimp,
　　shelled, leaving tail and first shell section
　　intact, and if desired deveined

Garnish: fresh coriander sprigs

In a measuring cup whisk together lime juice, marmalade, garlic paste, coriander, 3 tablespoons oil, soy sauce, red pepper flakes, and salt and pepper to taste and reserve ⅓ cup mixture in a small bowl or ramekin for dipping. In a large sealable plastic bag combine shrimp with remaining mixture and marinate, chilled, tossing occasionally to coat shrimp, 45 minutes.

Drain shrimp and lightly pat dry between paper towels. In a large non-stick skillet heat 1½ teaspoons oil over moderately high heat until hot but not smoking and sauté half of shrimp until golden brown and cooked through, about 1½ minutes on each side. Sauté remaining shrimp in remaining 1½ teaspoons oil in same manner.

Garnish shrimp with coriander sprigs and serve with reserved sauce. Makes about 24 hors d'oeuvres.

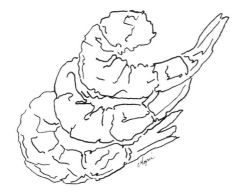

Spiced Shrimp

1 tablespoon chili powder
1½ teaspoons paprika
1½ teaspoons firmly packed brown sugar
1 teaspoon salt
¾ teaspoon ground cumin
½ teaspoon dry mustard
½ teaspoon freshly ground black pepper
¼ teaspoon dried oregano, crumbled
¼ teaspoon cayenne
1 pound large (21 to 24 per pound) shrimp, shelled, leaving tail and first shell section intact, and if desired deveined
2 tablespoons olive oil

Accompaniment: lemon wedges

In a small bowl stir together all ingredients except

shrimp and oil. Arrange shrimp in one layer on a baking sheet and sprinkle with half of spice mixture. Turn shrimp over and sprinkle with remaining mixture.

In a heavy skillet (preferably cast-iron) heat 1 tablespoon oil over moderately high heat until hot but not smoking and sauté half of shrimp until golden brown and cooked through, about 1½ minutes on each side. Sauté remaining shrimp in remaining 1 tablespoon oil in same manner.

Serve shrimp with lemon wedges. Makes about 24 hors d'oeuvres.

CANAPÉS

Smoked Salmon "Tartare" on New Potato Slices

6 red potatoes, 1½ to 2 inches in diameter (about ¾ pound)
For "tartare"
¼ pound smoked salmon, chopped fine
2 tablespoons finely chopped red onion
1 tablespoon chopped fresh chives

1 tablespoon fresh lemon juice
¼ cup sour cream

Slice red potatoes into twenty-four ¼-inch-thick rounds. In a vegetable steamer set over boiling water steam one layer of potato slices, covered, until tender, 5 to 10 minutes, and cool completely. Steam remaining slices in same manner. *Potato slices may be steamed 1 day ahead and chilled in a sealable plastic bag. Bring potato slices to room temperature before proceeding.*
Make "tartare":
In a bowl stir together "tartare" ingredients and salt and pepper to taste.
To assemble hors d'oeuvres:
Brush tops of potato slices with lemon juice and season with salt and pepper. Top each slice with a heaping ½ teaspoon "tartare" and a small dollop sour cream. Makes 24 hors d'oeuvres.

PHOTO ON PAGE 52

Sesame Shrimp Toasts

1 tablespoon Asian sesame oil
1 tablespoon soy sauce
1 tablespoon cornstarch
1 large egg white
2 scallions, chopped
1 large garlic clove, chopped
2 teaspoons grated peeled fresh gingerroot
1¼ teaspoons salt
1 pound shrimp, shelled and if desired deveined
12 slices firm white sandwich bread, crusts discarded
2 tablespoons sesame seeds
about 6 cups vegetable oil for deep-frying

In a food processor blend sesame oil, soy sauce, cornstarch, egg white, scallions, garlic, gingerroot, and salt. Add shrimp and pulse until mixture is like paste but not completely smooth.

Divide mixture among bread slices, spreading it evenly to edges, and sprinkle with sesame seeds. Cut each bread slice into 4 triangles.

In a 6-quart heavy saucepan heat 1½ inches oil to 360° F. on a deep-fat thermometer and fry shrimp toasts in batches, coated sides down first, about 1 minute on each side, or until golden. Transfer shrimp toasts with a slotted spoon to paper towels to drain and serve warm. Makes 48 hors d'oeuvres.

Ham and Fresh Peach Chutney on Corn Bread

For corn bread
½ cup all-purpose flour
½ cup yellow cornmeal
¾ teaspoon baking powder
1 teaspoon salt
1 cup grated sharp Cheddar
1 large egg
2 tablespoons unsalted butter, melted and cooled
½ cup sour cream
¼ cup milk

24 slices cured ham such as Westphalian or prosciutto, or cooked country ham such as Smithfield
about ½ cup fresh peach chutney (recipe follows)

Make corn bread:
Preheat oven to 350° F. and generously butter a jelly-roll pan, 15½ by 10½ by 1 inch.

In a bowl whisk together flour, cornmeal, baking powder, salt, and Cheddar. In a small bowl whisk together egg, butter, sour cream, and milk. Stir egg mixture into flour mixture until just combined and spread evenly in pan. (Spread batter evenly or corn bread will be too thin and crisp in places.) Bake corn bread in middle of oven 15 to 20 minutes, or until sides pull away from pan and top is golden.

While corn bread is hot, with a sharp knife loosen corn bread edges and cut into twelve 2½-inch squares, preferably with a square cutter. With a metal spatula carefully transfer corn bread to a cutting board to cool and trim if necessary.

Halve each square diagonally to form 24 triangles. *Corn bread triangles may be made 2 days ahead and kept in a sealable plastic bag, chilled. Corn bread will soften slightly. If crisper bread is desired, reheat in a 350° F. oven until crisp before proceeding.*

To assemble hors d'oeuvres:
Top each triangle with a folded ham slice and 1 teaspoon chutney. Makes 24 hors d'oeuvres.

PHOTO ON PAGE 52

Fresh Peach Chutney

1 firm-ripe peach
¼ cup golden raisins, chopped fine
1 fresh *serrano* or *jalapeño* chili, seeded and chopped fine (wear rubber gloves)
1 tablespoon finely chopped peeled fresh gingerroot
1½ teaspoons finely chopped shallot
¼ teaspoon ground cumin
1 tablespoon sugar
1 tablespoon fresh orange juice
1 teaspoon fresh lemon juice

Halve and pit peach and cut into ⅛-inch dice.

In a bowl combine peach, raisins, chili, gingerroot, shallot, and cumin. *Chill chutney, covered, at least 1 hour and up to 2.*

About 1 hour before serving, stir in remaining ingredients and salt and pepper to taste. Serve chutney at room temperature. Makes about 1½ cups.

Tomato and Olivada Crostini

a 16-inch thin loaf Italian or French bread, cut
    into ¼-inch-thick slices
⅓ cup freshly grated Parmesan
two 28-ounce cans Italian whole tomatoes, seeded
    and drained
¼ cup extra-virgin olive oil
1 small garlic clove, chopped and mashed to a
    paste with ½ teaspoon salt
2 teaspoons minced fresh parsley leaves
½ teaspoon sugar
about ⅓ cup *olivada* or other bottled black olive
    paste*

Garnish: about 50 small fresh parsley leaves

*available at specialty foods shops and some
    supermarkets

Preheat oven to 350° F.

Arrange bread slices in one layer on 2 baking
sheets and sprinkle slices on one sheet with Parmesan. Toast slices in upper and lower thirds of oven
until crisp and golden, 8 to 12 minutes, and cool.
*Crostini may be made 2 weeks ahead and kept in an
airtight container at room temperature.*

In a colander or sieve drain tomatoes well, pressing gently on solids to squeeze out as much liquid as
possible, and blot with paper towels. Chop tomatoes
fine. In a bowl stir together tomatoes, extra-virgin
olive oil, garlic paste, parsley, sugar, and salt and
pepper to taste.

Put a heaping teaspoon tomato mixture on each
Parmesan *crostino* and top with ¼ teaspoon olive

paste. Spread each plain *crostino* with ½ teaspoon
olive paste and top with a heaping ½ teaspoon tomato mixture.

Garnish *crostini* with parsley leaves. Makes about
50 *crostini*.

PHOTO ON PAGE 35

Coconut Curry Scallop, Kumquat, and Asian Pear Canapés

1 teaspoon curry powder
1 cup canned unsweetened coconut milk,*
    stirred well
¼ cup fresh lime juice, or to taste
½ teaspoon salt, or to taste
½ pound bay or sea scallops
2 Asian pears**
8 to 10 kumquats**
about 40 fresh coriander leaves, washed well
    and spun dry

*available at Asian markets and some specialty
    foods shops and supermarkets
**available at specialty produce markets

In a heavy 1-quart saucepan stir curry powder into
about 1 tablespoon coconut milk until dissolved. Stir
in 1 teaspoon lime juice, salt, and remaining coconut
milk and simmer over moderately low heat 10 minutes, or until thickened.

Remove tough muscle from side of each scallop if
necessary. If using sea scallops, cut into ½-inch
pieces. Add scallops to coconut milk mixture and
poach at a bare simmer until just cooked through but
still tender, 2 to 3 minutes. Remove pan from heat
and cool mixture. Transfer scallops with poaching
liquid to a small bowl. *Scallops may be poached 1
day ahead and chilled, covered.*

Cut pears crosswise into ¼-inch-thick rounds and
discard seeds and core. Cut rounds into 1-inch
wedges and in a small bowl toss with remaining lime
juice. *Macerate pears, covered and chilled, at least
15 minutes and up to 3 hours.*

Just before serving, cut kumquats crosswise into
thin slices. Top each pear wedge with 1 kumquat
slice, 1 coriander leaf, and 1 piece of scallop coated
with poaching liquid. Makes about 40 canapés.

Chick-Pea, Garlic, and Parsley Dip

a 19-ounce can chick-peas,
  rinsed and drained
  (about 2 cups)
2 garlic cloves, chopped and mashed
  to a paste with ½ teaspoon salt
½ cup packed fresh parsley leaves
¼ cup water
3 tablespoons fresh lemon juice
¼ cup extra-virgin olive oil

Accompaniment: toasted pita wedges or
  toasted French bread slices

In a food processor blend all ingredients except oil until smooth. With motor running add oil in a slow stream. Season dip with salt.
Serve dip with toasts. Makes about 2 cups.

Herbed Eggplant Dip

1 medium onion, chopped
⅓ cup olive oil
a 1-pound eggplant, cut into ¼-inch dice
1 teaspoon salt
2 plum tomatoes, seeded and diced
3 tablespoons fresh lemon juice
¼ cup fresh basil leaves, washed well,
  spun dry, and minced
2 tablespoons minced fresh parsley leaves

Accompaniment: garlic-flavored Melba toasts
  or assorted crudités

In a large heavy skillet cook onion in oil over moderate heat, stirring, until softened. Add diced eggplant and salt and cook, stirring, until eggplant begins to brown, about 10 minutes. Cover skillet and cook eggplant, stirring occasionally, 5 minutes, or until tender. Remove skillet from heat and cool eggplant. Stir in remaining ingredients and salt and pepper to taste.
Serve dip with toasts or crudités. Makes 2⅓ cups.

Ratatouille Dip

a 1- to 1¼-pound eggplant
2 tablespoons olive oil plus additional
  for coating eggplant
1 medium-large onion, chopped fine
  (about 1½ cups)
2 garlic cloves, minced
2 medium red bell peppers, chopped fine
  (about 1½ cups)
1 medium zucchini, cut into
  ½-inch cubes
1 medium yellow squash,
  cut into ½-inch cubes
1½ tablespoons minced fresh thyme leaves
½ cup finely chopped seeded vine-ripened
  tomato or drained canned tomatoes
2 tablespoons finely chopped fresh
  parsley leaves

Accompaniment: thin French bread slices,
  toasted, or crackers

Preheat oven to 400° F.
Prick eggplant with a fork several times and coat lightly with additional oil. In a shallow baking dish roast eggplant in middle of oven, turning once, 1 hour, or until collapsed and very soft, particularly at stem end. Cool eggplant slightly and halve lengthwise. Scoop out flesh into a bowl, scraping as close to skin as possible, and cool. Pour off any liquid that accumulated in bowl and in a food processor purée eggplant. *Eggplant purée may be made 1 day ahead and chilled, covered. Bring purée to room temperature before proceeding.*
In a large heavy skillet cook onion in 2 tablespoons oil over moderate heat, stirring, until softened. Add garlic and cook, stirring, 1 minute. Add bell peppers, zucchini, yellow squash, thyme, and salt and pepper to taste and cook, stirring occasionally, until tender, 8 to 10 minutes. Add tomato and cook, stirring, 3 minutes. In a bowl stir together eggplant purée, vegetable mixture, and parsley and season with salt and pepper. *Dip may be made 1 day ahead and chilled, covered.*
Serve dip at room temperature with toasts or crackers. Makes about 2 cups.

PHOTO ON PAGES 50 AND 51

Creamy Clam Dip

8 ounces cream cheese, softened
¼ cup sour cream
two 6½-ounce cans minced clams, drained,
 reserving 3 tablespoons liquid
⅓ cup finely chopped red bell pepper
1 shallot, minced
2 tablespoons minced fresh parsley leaves
¾ teaspoon Worcestershire sauce
⅛ teaspoon cayenne

Accompaniment: toasted pita wedges or potato chips

In a bowl whisk together cream cheese and sour cream until smooth. Stir in remaining ingredients and salt to taste.

Serve dip with toasts or chips. Makes about 2 cups.

Smoked Fish and White Bean Brandade

a 19-ounce can cannellini beans, rinsed
 and drained
a 1-pound piece smoked whitefish,
 skin and bones discarded and
 fish flaked (about 3 cups)
1 garlic clove, chopped and mashed to a paste
 with ½ teaspoon salt
¾ cup milk
2 teaspoons fresh thyme leaves, minced

Accompaniment: Melba toasts or red bell pepper,
 cut into wide strips

In a food processor blend beans, fish, and garlic paste until smooth. With motor running add milk in a slow stream. Stir in thyme and salt to taste.

Serve *brandade* with toasts or bell pepper strips. Makes about 3½ cups.

Red Pepper Dip with Walnuts

1 small onion, chopped
2 large garlic cloves, sliced
¼ cup olive oil
a 12-ounce jar roasted red peppers, rinsed and
 drained (about 1¾ cups)
½ cup walnuts, toasted and cooled
⅓ cup packed fresh basil leaves, washed well and
 spun dry
1 slice firm white sandwich bread, chopped
2 tablespoons fresh lemon juice

Accompaniment: toasted pita wedges

In a small skillet cook onion and garlic in oil over moderate heat, stirring, until softened. In a food processor blend remaining ingredients until nuts are chopped fine. With motor running, gradually add onion mixture and blend until incorporated. Season dip with salt.

Serve dip with toasts. Makes about 1½ cups.

101

Smoked Salmon and Chive Mascarpone Mousse
with Pink Pickled Onions

1 teaspoon unflavored gelatin
2 tablespoons fresh lemon juice
1½ cups *mascarpone* cheese* (about ¾ pound)
¾ cup sour cream
2 hard-cooked large eggs
1 tablespoon drained bottled horseradish,
   or to taste
¾ pound sliced smoked salmon*
½ cup chopped fresh chives
about 2 cups pink pickled onions
   (recipe follows)

Garnish: chive blossoms
Accompaniment: Melba toasts and/or sesame
   flatbread

*available at specialty foods shops and some
   supermarkets

In a small saucepan sprinkle gelatin over lemon juice and soften 10 minutes. In a bowl with an electric mixer beat together *mascarpone* and ½ cup sour cream until combined well. Quarter eggs and with back of a spoon force through a coarse sieve into *mascarpone* mixture. Add drained horseradish and stir well.

Add remaining ¼ cup sour cream to gelatin mixture and heat over moderately low heat, stirring, just until gelatin is dissolved. Add gelatin mixture to *mascarpone* mixture and stir well.

Cut about one third salmon into strips and arrange 1 in every other ridge of a 3-cup brioche or other mold, letting ends hang over edge. Chop remaining salmon into ½-inch pieces and fold with chives into *mascarpone* mixture. Spoon mousse into mold and fold ends of salmon strips over top. *Chill mousse, covered, at least 2 hours, or until firm, and up to 2 days.* Run a thin knife along inside of each ridge of mold and dip mold into a bowl of hot water a few seconds. Invert a plate over mold and invert mousse onto it.

With a slotted spoon arrange pickled onions decoratively on and around mousse and garnish with chive blossoms. Serve mousse with Melba toasts and/or flatbread. Serves 20 as an hors d'oeuvre.

The following recipe is adapted from Rick and Deann Bayless's cookbook, Authentic Mexican.

Pink Pickled Onions

2 medium red onions, chopped
½ cup cider vinegar
1½ teaspoons salt

In a saucepan barely cover onions with cold water. Bring water to a boil and simmer 1 minute. Drain onions in a colander and return to pan with vinegar, salt, and cold water to just cover. Bring liquid to a boil and simmer 3 minutes. Remove pan from heat and cool onions in liquid. *Pickled onions may be made 1 week ahead and chilled in liquid, covered.* Makes about 2 cups.

Potted Shrimp

½ cup finely chopped shallots
1 bay leaf
¾ stick (6 tablespoons) unsalted butter, softened
½ pound shrimp, shelled and if desired deveined
3 tablespoons medium-dry Sherry
4 ounces cream cheese (about ½ cup), softened
1 tablespoon fresh lemon juice
2 tablespoons minced fresh chives

Accompaniment: crackers or Melba toast

In a large skillet cook shallots with bay leaf in 1 tablespoon butter over moderate heat, stirring, until soft. Add shrimp and salt and pepper to taste and cook, stirring occasionally, until shrimp are pink and cooked through, about 3 minutes. Add Sherry and boil mixture until almost all liquid is evaporated. Cool mixture and discard bay leaf. Transfer shrimp with tongs to a cutting board, reserving shallot mixture, and chop fine.

In a bowl stir together remaining 5 tablespoons butter and cream cheese until smooth. Stir in shrimp, shallot mixture, juice, chives, and salt and pepper to taste and transfer to a 1½-cup crock. *Chill potted shrimp, covered, at least 4 hours and up to 24.*

Serve potted shrimp with crackers or Melba toast. Makes about 1½ cups.

Tomatillo Salsa

1 large fresh *jalapeño* chili
1 pound tomatillos*, husks discarded
1 tablespoon minced fresh coriander sprigs
½ cup finely chopped red onion
½ cup sour cream

Garnish: small coriander sprig
Accompaniment: spiced curly tortilla chips
   (recipe follows) or plain tortilla chips

*available at specialty produce markets and many
   supermarkets

Cut 2 or 3 thin slices from tip of *jalapeño* (wear rubber gloves) and reserve for garnish. In a saucepan simmer tomatillos and remaining *jalapeño* in water to cover until tomatillos are tender, about 5 minutes, and transfer tomatillos, *jalapeño*, and ¼ cup cooking liquid to a blender or food processor. Blend salsa until chopped but not completely smooth and transfer to a serving bowl. Cool salsa and chill, covered, until cold. *Salsa may be prepared up to this point 2 days ahead and chilled, covered.*

Just before serving, stir coriander, all but 1 teaspoon onion, and salt to taste into salsa. In a small bowl stir sour cream until smooth and spoon into center of salsa. Garnish sour cream with coriander sprig, reserved *jalapeño,* and remaining onion and serve with chips. Makes about 2½ cups.

PHOTO ON PAGE 44

Spiced Curly Tortilla Chips

sixteen 6-inch corn tortillas
about ¼ cup vegetable oil
1½ tablespoons chili powder
¾ teaspoon salt
½ teaspoon sugar

Preheat oven to 350° F.
Brush both sides of tortillas with oil and with scissors cut each tortilla into about 5 randomly shaped wavy strips. In 2 large shallow baking pans arrange half of strips in one layer. (Strips should curl up, but if necessary gently twist or fold them over.)

In a small bowl combine chili powder, salt, and sugar and through a small sieve sprinkle half of mixture over tortilla strips in pans. Bake tortilla strips in upper and lower thirds of oven until just crisp, 6 to 8 minutes, and transfer to paper towels to cool. Make more chips in same manner with remaining tortilla strips and chili mixture. Serves 8 as an hors d'oeuvre.

PHOTO ON PAGE 44

Tuna Dip with Lemon and Capers

two 6-ounce cans solid white tuna packed in oil,
   drained well
a 10¼-ounce package soft tofu, drained
3 scallions, minced
1 carrot, shredded fine
2 tablespoons minced fresh parsley leaves
2 tablespoons drained capers, chopped
3 tablespoons fresh lemon juice

Accompaniment: crackers or assorted crudités

In a bowl stir tuna with a fork until finely flaked. In another bowl whisk tofu until smooth. Stir tofu and remaining ingredients into tuna until combined and season with salt and pepper.

Serve dip with crackers or crudités. Makes about 3 cups.

Roasted Zucchini and Yogurt Spread

2 pounds zucchini (about 6 medium), washed
    well, halved lengthwise, and cut crosswise
    into ⅛-inch-thick slices
2½ tablespoons olive oil
2 teaspoons salt
½ cup plain yogurt
4 scallions, chopped fine

Accompaniment: pita toasts (recipe follows)

Preheat oven to 500° F.
In a large shallow roasting pan toss zucchini with
oil and salt and roast in middle of oven, stirring
once, until browned and falling apart, about 25 minutes. Cool zucchini and in a bowl mash coarse with a
potato masher. Stir in yogurt, scallions, and salt and
freshly ground black pepper to taste. *Spread may be
made 1 week ahead and chilled, its surface covered
with plastic wrap.*
Serve spread at room temperature with toasts.
Makes about 2 cups.

Pita Toasts

four 6-inch pita loaves
2 tablespoons olive oil

Preheat oven to 350° F.
Halve loaves horizontally to form 8 rounds. Brush
rough sides of rounds with oil and season with salt.
Cut each round into 8 wedges and bake in 2 batches
on a baking sheet in middle of oven until golden,
about 10 minutes. Cool toasts on a rack. *Toasts may
be made 1 week ahead and kept in sealable plastic
bags at room temperature.* Makes 64 pita toasts.

BREADS

Whole-Grain Mustard Pan Rolls

1¼ cups milk
¾ stick unsalted butter, cut into pieces
¼ cup pure maple syrup
two ¼-ounce packages active dry yeast
   (5 teaspoons)
6 cups all-purpose flour
1 tablespoon salt
1 large whole egg
1 large egg yolk
½ cup whole-grain or coarse-grained Dijon
   mustard
For glaze
2 tablespoons unsalted butter, melted and cooled
1 tablespoon pure maple syrup
1 large egg, beaten lightly

1 teaspoon mustard seeds for sprinkling

In a saucepan heat milk, butter, and syrup just until warm (about 105° F.) and butter begins to melt and remove pan from heat. Stir in yeast and let stand until foamy, about 5 minutes.

In bowl of a standing electric mixer (or a large bowl if kneading by hand) whisk together flour and salt. In a small bowl lightly beat together whole egg, yolk, and mustard.

With dough hook stir milk mixture and egg mixture into flour mixture to form a sticky dough. With dough hook knead dough 5 minutes, or until smooth and elastic (dough will be soft). (Alternatively, dough may be mixed with a wooden spoon and kneaded on a floured surface with floured hands until smooth and elastic, 10 to 15 minutes.)

Transfer dough to a lightly oiled large bowl and turn to coat with oil. Let dough rise, covered loosely, in a warm place 1 hour, or until doubled in bulk.

Make glaze:
In a small bowl with a fork stir together butter, syrup, and egg.

Grease a 13- by 9-inch roasting or baking pan.

Punch down dough and divide into 20 pieces. Form each piece into a smooth ball and transfer to pan. Brush rolls with about half of glaze and let rise, covered loosely with plastic wrap, in a warm place about 1 hour, or until doubled in bulk.

Preheat oven to 400° F.

Brush rolls with remaining glaze and sprinkle with mustard seeds. Bake rolls in middle of oven 20 minutes, or until golden brown, and cool in pan on a rack 20 minutes. *Rolls may be made 1 day ahead and kept, covered, in a cool dry place. (Alternatively, rolls may be made 2 weeks ahead and frozen in pan, wrapped well. Thaw rolls at room temperature.)* Serve rolls warm or at room temperature. Makes 20 rolls.

Sour Cherry Pecan Cinnamon Buns

For dough
a ¼-ounce package active dry yeast
    (2½ teaspoons)
¼ cup warm water (105° to 115° F.)
¼ cup granulated sugar
2½ cups all-purpose flour
½ cup milk at room temperature
1 teaspoon salt
2 large egg yolks
½ stick (¼ cup) unsalted butter, cut into
    pieces and softened
For filling
½ cup dried sour cherries, dried cranberries,
    or raisins
¾ cup pecans, toasted until golden brown
    and chopped fine

¼ cup granulated sugar
1¼ teaspoons cinnamon
2 tablespoons unsalted butter, melted and
    cooled slightly
For glaze
1 cup confectioners' sugar
2 tablespoons water

Make dough:

In bowl of a standing electric mixer fitted with paddle attachment sprinkle yeast over water with ¼ teaspoon sugar and let stand until foamy, about 5 minutes. Add remaining sugar, flour, milk, salt, and yolks and beat on low speed until combined well. Beat in butter, a few pieces at a time, and beat on medium speed until smooth and elastic, about 5 minutes. (Dough will be soft.) Scrape dough from side of bowl and let rise, covered with plastic wrap and a kitchen towel, in a warm place 1 hour, or until doubled in bulk.

Make filling while dough is rising:

In a bowl soak dried fruit in warm water to cover 15 minutes. Drain fruit, discarding water, and chop fine. In a small bowl stir together fruit and pecans.

In a small bowl stir together well sugar and cinnamon.

Grease a 13- by 9-inch baking pan.

Punch down dough and on a floured surface roll out into a 16- by 12-inch rectangle. Brush dough with melted butter, leaving an unbuttered ½-inch border on long sides, and sprinkle filling evenly over buttered dough. Sprinkle cinnamon sugar evenly over filling.

With a long side facing you, roll up dough jelly-roll fashion, brushing off any excess flour, and pinch long edge together firmly to seal. Cut rolled dough crosswise into 12 pieces with a sharp knife and arrange pieces, cut sides down, in pan. Let buns rise, covered loosely, in a warm place 45 to 50 minutes, or until doubled in bulk.

Preheat oven to 350° F. while buns are rising.

Bake buns in middle of oven until golden, about 25 minutes. *Alternatively, buns may be made 1 week ahead: Bake buns in middle of oven until pale golden, about 15 minutes (buns will not be completely baked), and transfer pan to a rack to cool completely. Freeze buns in pan, covered tightly with foil. To serve, thaw buns at room temperature 1 hour and bake in a preheated 350° F. oven until golden, about 10 minutes.* Transfer buns to a rack and cool slightly.

Make glaze while buns are cooling:

In a small bowl whisk together confectioners' sugar and water until smooth. Transfer glaze to a small sealable plastic bag and snip off tip of 1 corner to make a hole for piping glaze.

Pipe glaze onto cinnamon buns and let stand until set, about 15 minutes. Makes 12 cinnamon buns.

PHOTO ON PAGE 67

Honey-Glazed Bunny Rolls

1 cup milk
¼ cup honey
a ¼-ounce package active dry yeast
½ stick (¼ cup) unsalted butter, melted
2 large egg yolks
4 cups bread flour
2 teaspoons salt
For glaze
2 tablespoons honey
½ stick (¼ cup) unsalted butter
⅔ cup confectioners' sugar

12 dried currants, halved

In a small saucepan heat milk with honey over low heat, stirring, just until lukewarm and remove pan from heat. Stir in yeast and let stand until foamy, about 5 minutes. Add butter and yolks, whisking until combined well.

Transfer milk mixture to bowl of a standing electric mixer (or to a large bowl if kneading by hand). Add flour and salt gradually to milk mixture, stirring until incorporated. With dough hook knead dough until smooth, about 2 minutes. (Alternatively, dough may be kneaded by hand on a lightly floured surface until smooth, 10 to 15 minutes.)

Transfer dough to a lightly oiled large bowl and turn to coat with oil. *Let dough rise, covered with plastic wrap, in refrigerator overnight, or until doubled in bulk.* (Alternatively, dough may be allowed to rise in a warm place about 2 hours, or until doubled in bulk.)

Make glaze:

In a small saucepan heat glaze ingredients over low heat, stirring occasionally, until butter is melted. Remove pan from heat and keep glaze warm, covered.

Grease 2 baking sheets. Punch down dough and divide into 12 pieces. Form each piece into an egg shape and transfer pieces to prepared baking sheets. Form a bunny tail on each by holding scissors, points down, perpendicular to baking sheet and making a ½-inch-long snip at base of wide end (see drawing A). Form 2 bunny ears on each piece by making a narrow 2-inch-long snip on each side, starting near wide end and cutting toward narrow end (see drawing B). Form eyes on each piece by making 2 holes in narrow end with a wooden pick and pressing a currant half firmly into each hole with pick.

Brush half of warm glaze on rolls and let rise, covered loosely with plastic wrap, in a warm place 45 minutes, or until doubled in bulk (rising will take longer if dough is cold).

Preheat oven to 400° F.

Heat remaining glaze over low heat just until warm and brush rolls. Bake rolls in upper and lower thirds of oven, switching position of sheets in oven halfway through baking, 20 minutes, or until golden, and transfer to racks to cool.

Serve rolls warm or at room temperature. Makes 12 rolls.

PHOTO ON PAGE 30

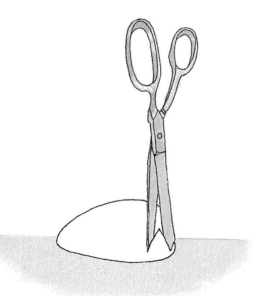

a.

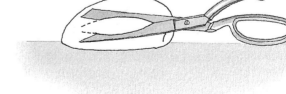

b.

Benne Seed Angel Biscuits

a ¼-ounce package active dry yeast
    (2½ teaspoons)
¼ cup warm water (about 105° F.)
3 tablespoons sugar
5½ cups White Lily flour* or cake flour
    (not self-rising)
1 tablespoon baking powder
1 teaspoon baking soda
2 teaspoons salt
½ cup chilled vegetable shortening
1 stick (½ cup) cold unsalted butter, cut
    into pieces
1¼ cups buttermilk plus additional for
    brushing biscuits
3 tablespoons benne (sesame) seeds, toasted
    lightly and cooled

*available by mail order from The White Lily
    Foods Company, P.O. Box 871, Knoxville, TN
    37901, tel. (423) 546-5511

In a small bowl stir together yeast, water, and a pinch sugar and let stand until foamy, about 5 minutes.

In a large bowl whisk together flour, baking powder, baking soda, salt, and remaining sugar. With your fingertips blend in shortening and butter until mixture resembles coarse meal. Add yeast mixture and 1¼ cups buttermilk, stirring until a dough just forms, and gather into a ball (dough will be sticky). On a lightly floured surface with floured hands knead dough gently 6 times and pat out into a 10-inch round (about ½ inch thick). *Chill biscuit dough, wrapped in plastic wrap, at least 8 hours and up to 2 days.*

Preheat oven to 425° F. and lightly butter a large baking sheet.

With a 2½-inch round cutter dipped in flour cut out as many rounds as possible and arrange, sides just touching, on baking sheet. Gather scraps into a ball and pat out dough. Cut out more rounds in same manner. Brush biscuits with additional buttermilk and sprinkle with benne seeds. Bake biscuits in middle of oven 10 minutes, or until golden, and cool on racks. *Biscuits may be made 1 week ahead and frozen in sealable plastic bags. Thaw biscuits and reheat in a preheated 350° F. oven 5 to 10 minutes or until heated through.* Makes about 24 biscuits.

PHOTO ON PAGES 84 AND 85

Cornmeal Harvest Loaves

2 cups lukewarm water
¼ cup firmly packed light brown sugar
two ¼-ounce packages (5 teaspoons)
    active dry yeast
1 cup plus 2 tablespoons yellow cornmeal
about 4¾ cups bread flour
5 teaspoons salt

In bowl of a standing electric mixer (or a large bowl if kneading by hand) stir together lukewarm water, sugar, yeast, and 1 cup cornmeal and let stand until foamy, about 5 minutes. In another bowl stir together flour and salt and gradually stir enough flour mixture into cornmeal mixture to form a soft dough. With dough hook knead dough, adding any remaining flour mixture if dough is too sticky, 5 minutes, or until smooth and elastic. (Alternatively, dough may be kneaded on a floured surface with floured hands until smooth and elastic, 10 to 15 minutes.)

Put dough in an oiled deep bowl, turning to coat with oil. Cover bowl loosely and let dough rise in a warm place 2 hours, or until doubled in bulk. (Alternatively, dough may be allowed to rise, covered, in refrigerator overnight.)

Punch down dough and divide into 4 pieces. Roll each piece between hands to form a 14-inch loaf and put 2 loaves on each of 2 large baking sheets. With a knife or kitchen scissors make eight to ten 2-inch-long diagonal cuts down length of each loaf and pull open to make decorative holes (exaggerate openings as they will shrink during rising and baking).

Cover loaves loosely and let rise in a warm place until doubled in bulk, about 45 minutes.

Preheat oven to 400°F.

Sprinkle loaves with remaining 2 tablespoons cornmeal and bake in upper and lower thirds of oven 25 minutes, or until golden, switching baking sheets between upper and lower oven racks halfway through baking. Cool loaves on racks. Makes 4 loaves.

PHOTO ON PAGE 38

JEANNE

QUICK BREADS

Silver Dollar-Size Biscuits

2 cups all-purpose flour
1 tablespoon baking powder
1 teaspoon salt
1 tablespoon sugar
¼ cup lard
½ to ¾ cup milk

Preheat oven to 400° F.
In a bowl whisk together flour, baking powder, salt, and sugar and with a fork or pastry blender blend in lard until mixture resembles coarse meal. Add milk, a little at a time, stirring until dough just pulls away from side of bowl.
Roll out dough ½ inch thick on a lightly floured surface. Cut out biscuits with a 1½-inch round cutter and transfer to an ungreased baking sheet. Reroll scraps and cut out more biscuits in same manner.
Bake biscuits in middle of oven until pale golden, 10 to 15 minutes. Makes 20 biscuits.

Blueberry Maple Oatmeal Muffins

1 cup heavy cream
1 cup pure maple syrup
2 large eggs
½ cup firmly packed dark brown sugar
1 teaspoon vanilla
1¾ cups all-purpose flour
1½ cups old-fashioned rolled oats
2 teaspoons baking powder
1 teaspoon baking soda
¾ teaspoon salt
2 cups picked-over blueberries

Preheat oven to 375° F. and generously butter eighteen ½-cup muffin tins.
In a bowl whisk together cream, maple syrup, eggs, brown sugar, and vanilla.
In another bowl whisk together flour, oats, baking powder, baking soda, and salt and reserve ¼ cup.
Stir remaining flour mixture into cream mixture until just combined. In a bowl toss blueberries with reserved flour mixture and stir mixture into batter.
Divide batter evenly among muffin tins and bake in middle of oven 20 to 25 minutes, or until a tester comes out clean. Let muffins stand in tins 5 minutes and turn out onto a rack to cool completely. *Muffins may be made 2 days ahead and kept in an airtight container.* Makes 18 muffins.

CRACKERS AND TOASTS

Scallion and Anise Pita Toasts

1 tablespoon unsalted butter
1 scallion, minced
¼ teaspoon anise seeds, crushed
two 6-inch pita loaves,
    halved horizontally

Preheat broiler.
In a small saucepan heat butter over moderate heat until foam subsides. Add scallion and anise seeds and cook, stirring, until scallion is slightly softened. Arrange pita halves, rough sides up, on a baking sheet and brush with butter mixture. Season pita halves with salt and pepper. Broil pita halves about 4 inches from heat 30 seconds, or until golden. Transfer pita toasts to a cutting board and immediately cut each into 6 wedges. Makes 24 toasts.

Grilled Bread and Guacamole "Butter"

a 16- to 18-inch *ficelle* (very thin French bread)
about ¼ cup olive oil
2 ripe avocados (preferably California)
2 tablespoons chopped onion
1½ tablespoons fresh lemon juice
1 garlic clove, chopped
¾ teaspoon ground cumin

Cut bread diagonally into ¼-inch-thick slices and brush both sides of each slice with oil.

Prepare grill (or preheat oven).

Grill bread in batches on a rack set 5 to 6 inches over glowing coals, turning once, until toasted on both sides, about 3 minutes. (Alternatively, bread may be toasted in batches on a baking sheet in a 350° F. oven until crisp, 10 to 12 minutes.) *Grilled bread may be made 1 week ahead and cooled completely before keeping in an airtight container at room temperature.*

Halve avocados and discard pits. Spoon flesh into a food processor. Add remaining ingredients and blend just until smooth. *Guacamole "butter" may be made 1 day ahead and chilled, its surface covered with plastic wrap.*

Serve bread topped with dollops of *guacamole "butter."* Serves 8.

Poppy Cheddar Moon Crackers

¾ cup all-purpose flour
¼ cup yellow cornmeal
1 tablespoon poppy seeds
¼ teaspoon salt
¼ teaspoon baking powder
½ stick (¼ cup) cold unsalted butter, cut into bits
1 cup coarsely shredded extra-sharp Cheddar
4 to 5 tablespoons cold water
an egg wash made by beating 1 large egg with
    1 tablespoon water
coarse salt for sprinkling

In a bowl with a pastry blender or in a food processor blend or pulse together flour, cornmeal, poppy seeds, salt, and baking powder. Add butter and blend or pulse until mixture resembles coarse meal. Add Cheddar and 4 tablespoons water and toss with a fork or pulse just until water is incorporated, adding enough of remaining tablespoon water if necessary to form a soft dough.

On a work surface smear dough in 3 or 4 forward motions with heel of hand to develop gluten in flour slightly and make dough easier to work with. Form dough into 2 balls and flatten into disks.

Preheat oven to 400° F. and lightly grease 2 large baking sheets.

On a lightly floured surface roll out half of dough with a lightly floured rolling pin into a 12-inch round (about ¹⁄₁₆ inch thick) and with a 2¾-inch crescent-moon cutter cut out shapes, transferring them to lightly greased baking sheets. Gather scraps and reroll dough. Cut out more crescent shapes in same manner and transfer to baking sheets.

Brush crescents lightly with egg wash and prick all over with a fork. Sprinkle crescents with salt and bake in upper and lower thirds of oven, switching position of sheets halfway through baking, until golden, 12 to 14 minutes. Transfer crackers with a metal spatula to racks and cool. Make more crackers with remaining dough in same manner. *Crackers may be made 3 days ahead and kept in an airtight container at room temperature.* Makes about 75 crackers.

PHOTO ON PAGE 70

PIZZA

Pizza Rustica

2 pounds Swiss chard, washed well, stems
    removed and sliced thin, and leaves
    chopped separately
2 tablespoons olive oil
4 large eggs, beaten lightly
a 15- to 16-ounce container whole-milk ricotta
    cheese
4 large red bell peppers (about 1½ pounds),
    roasted (procedure follows) and chopped
2 garlic cloves, minced and mashed to a paste
    with 1 teaspoon coarse salt
1 recipe *pizza rustica* pastry dough (page 111)
¼ pound Parmesan, grated (about 1 cup)
½ pound thinly sliced prosciutto, chopped

6 ounces provolone cheese, cut into
  ¼-inch dice (about 1 cup)
an egg wash made by beating 1 large egg with
  2 tablespoons milk

In a large heavy saucepan cook chard stems in oil over moderately low heat, stirring occasionally, until crisp-tender, about 3 minutes. Add chard leaves with water clinging to them and cook, covered, over moderate heat, stirring occasionally, until stems are tender, about 8 minutes. Drain chard well in a colander and squeeze out as much moisture as possible.

In a large bowl combine well eggs and ricotta. In a bowl combine roasted bell peppers and garlic paste.

Preheat oven to 375° F.

On a lightly floured surface roll out two thirds pastry dough ⅛ inch thick into a round about 18 inches in diameter. Fit dough into a 9-inch springform pan and trim edge, leaving a 2-inch overhang. Into shell layer evenly half chard, half ricotta mixture, all roasted bell pepper mixture, half Parmesan, all prosciutto, all provolone, remaining ricotta mixture, remaining chard, and remaining Parmesan.

On a lightly floured surface roll out remaining dough ⅛ inch thick into a round about 11 inches in diameter. Brush edge of shell in pan with some egg wash and fit dough on top of filling. Trim top crust flush with bottom crust and crimp edges together decoratively. Cut four 3-inch-long vents in top crust and brush top crust with more egg wash.

Bake *pizza rustica* in middle of oven 1½ hours, or until top crust is deep golden, and cool completely in pan on a rack. *Pizza rustica may be made 2 days ahead and chilled in pan, covered.*

Serve *pizza rustica* warm or at room temperature, cut into wedges. Serves 6.

PHOTO ON PAGE 25

To Roast Peppers

Using a long-handled fork, char peppers over an open flame or on a rack set over an electric burner, turning them, until skins are blackened, 4 to 6 minutes. (Or broil peppers on rack of a broiler pan under a preheated broiler about 2 inches from heat, turning them every 5 minutes, 15 to 20 minutes, or until skins are blistered and charred.) Transfer peppers to a bowl and let stand, covered, until cool enough to handle. Keeping peppers whole, peel them, starting at blossom end. Cut off pepper tops and discard seeds and ribs.

Pizza Rustica Pastry Dough

4 cups all-purpose flour
2 teaspoons sugar
1 teaspoon salt
2 sticks (1 cup) cold unsalted butter,
  cut into bits
4 large eggs, beaten lightly

In a bowl with a pastry blender or in a food processor mix or pulse together flour, sugar, and salt. Add butter and blend or pulse until mixture resembles coarse meal. Add eggs and toss or pulse until eggs are incorporated and a dough is formed. Form dough into a disk and chill, wrapped in wax paper, 1 hour. *Dough may be made 1 day ahead and chilled, covered.*

Three-Cheese Cornmeal Pizzette

cornmeal for sprinkling baking sheet
For dough
2 cups all-purpose flour
a ¼-ounce package fast-acting yeast
   (2½ teaspoons)
1 teaspoon sugar
1 cup hot water (130° F.)
1 cup yellow cornmeal
2 tablespoons olive oil
1 teaspoon salt

olive oil for brushing *pizzette*
⅓ cup crumbled Gorgonzola cheese
   (about 1½ ounces)
⅔ cup finely diced mozzarella cheese
   (about 3 ounces)
½ medium red onion, sliced thin
   (about ⅔ cup)
1 teaspoon finely chopped fresh rosemary
   leaves or ½ teaspoon dried rosemary,
   crumbled
⅓ cup freshly grated Parmesan

Preheat oven to 500° F. Lightly grease a large baking sheet and sprinkle with cornmeal.

Make dough:

In a food processor combine 1 cup flour, yeast, and sugar and with motor running add water. Turn motor off and add remaining dough ingredients. Process mixture until it forms a ball and process 15 seconds more to knead it.

Turn dough out onto a lightly floured surface and knead 10 times. Reserve half of dough for making 2 more *pizzette* another time, wrapping it in a sealable plastic bag, pressing out excess air, and chilling or freezing. *Reserved dough keeps, chilled, 1 day or, frozen, 1 month.*

Halve remaining dough and on lightly floured surface roll out each half into an 8-inch round. Transfer rounds to baking sheet and brush lightly with oil. Top rounds evenly with remaining ingredients and season with salt and pepper.

Bake *pizzette* in lower third of oven 10 to 12 minutes, or until crusts are golden and cheese is golden and bubbling. Serves 2, with enough leftover dough for 2 more *pizzette.*

SOUPS

Black Bean Soup with Lime

1 large ham hock (about ¾ pound)
3 quarts plus 1 cup water
1 pound dried black beans, picked over
1 red onion, chopped
  (about 2 cups)
1 bay leaf
a 28- to 32-ounce can whole tomatoes
  with juice, chopped
¾ teaspoon salt, or to taste
1 to 2 tablespoons fresh lime juice

Garnish: lime slices

In a 5-quart kettle simmer ham hock in 3 quarts water, covered, 1 hour. Add beans, onion, and bay leaf and simmer, uncovered, 1 hour, or until beans are just tender. Stir in tomatoes with juice, salt, and remaining cup water and simmer soup 45 minutes, or until beans are tender. *Soup may be made 1 day ahead, cooled completely, and chilled, covered.*

Remove ham hock and reserve for another use. Discard bay leaf and stir in lime juice to taste.

Divide soup among 8 bowls and garnish with lime slices. Serves 8.

PHOTOS ON PAGES 14 AND 15

Cauliflower, Swiss Chard, and Chicken Soup

⅔ cup chopped onion
1 teaspoon caraway seeds, crushed lightly
1 teaspoon olive oil
3 cups chicken broth
3 cups water
3 cups 1-inch cauliflower flowerets
  (about 1 small head)
½ cup *orzo* (rice-shaped pasta)
1 pound skinless boneless chicken breast,
  cut into 1-inch pieces
4 cups chopped red Swiss chard leaves,
  washed well and drained

In a 4-quart heavy saucepan cook onion and caraway seeds in oil over moderately low heat, stirring, until onion is softened. Add broth and water and bring to a boil. Stir in cauliflower and *orzo* and simmer, stirring occasionally, 7 minutes. Stir in chicken and Swiss chard and simmer until chicken is cooked through, about 3 minutes. Season soup with salt and pepper. *Soup may be made 3 days ahead, cooled, uncovered, and chilled, covered.* Makes about 8 cups, serving 4.

Each serving: 250 calories,
4.27 grams fat (15% of calories from fat)

Chilled Pea and Spinach Soup

1 pound fresh green peas, shelled (about
    1½ cups), or 1½ cups thawed frozen
6 ounces spinach leaves (2 cups packed),
    washed well and spun dry
1 tablespoon sugar
1 teaspoon dried tarragon
½ teaspoon salt
2 cups chicken broth
1 cup ice
⅔ cup plain yogurt

In a saucepan simmer peas, spinach, sugar, tarragon, and salt and freshly ground black pepper to taste in broth 15 minutes, or until peas are very tender. Purée soup in a blender until smooth and transfer to a bowl. Stir in ice and ½ cup plain yogurt, stirring until ice is melted and soup is chilled. Divide soup between 2 bowls and top with remaining yogurt. Serves 2.

White Gazpacho

For croutons
1 slice firm white sandwich bread, cut into
    ½-inch cubes
1 teaspoon olive oil
For gazpacho
1 slice firm white sandwich bread, soaked in
    cold water to cover 5 minutes
½ medium cucumber, peeled and chopped
    (about 1 cup)
½ medium green bell pepper, chopped
    (about ¾ cup)
white part of 1 scallion, chopped
1 garlic clove, chopped
2 tablespoons olive oil
2 tablespoons mayonnaise
1 tablespoon white-wine vinegar (preferably
    tarragon-flavored)
⅛ teaspoon dried tarragon, crumbled
¾ cup ice water

Make croutons:
Preheat oven to 350° F.
In a bowl toss bread cubes with oil and salt to

taste and spread on a small baking sheet. Bake cubes in oven until golden and crisp, 8 to 10 minutes.
    Make gazpacho:
    Drain soaked bread and squeeze out water. In a blender blend bread with remaining ingredients until smooth. Season gazpacho with salt and pepper and transfer to a metal bowl set in a larger bowl of ice and cold water. Stir gazpacho occasionally until chilled, about 10 minutes.
    Serve white gazpacho topped with croutons. Makes about 2 cups.

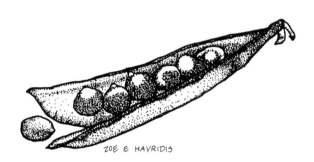

ZOE E HAVRIDIS

Escarole Soup with Turkey Meatballs

For soup
1 onion, chopped fine
1 teaspoon chopped fresh rosemary leaves or
    ½ teaspoon dried rosemary, crumbled
1 tablespoon olive oil
½ pound escarole (about ½ head), cut crosswise
    into ½-inch strips, washed well, and spun dry
    (about 6 cups packed)
3½ cups low-salt chicken broth
¼ cup *orzo* (rice-shaped pasta) or other small
    pasta
For meatballs
¼ pound ground turkey
3 tablespoons fine fresh bread crumbs
1 large egg yolk
1 scallion, minced
1 tablespoon freshly grated Parmesan
1 tablespoon olive oil

1 garlic clove, minced and mashed to a paste with
    ⅛ teaspoon salt
2 teaspoons fresh lemon juice

Make soup:

In a large heavy saucepan cook onion and rosemary in oil over moderate heat, stirring, until onion is softened. Add escarole, stirring to coat with oil, and cook, covered, 1 minute. Add broth and *orzo* and simmer, partially covered, stirring occasionally, 10 minutes.

Make meatballs while soup simmers:

In a bowl combine well all meatball ingredients except oil and season with salt and pepper. Form mixture into meatballs about 1 inch in diameter. In a heavy 9-inch skillet heat oil over moderately high heat until hot but not smoking and brown meatballs about 3 minutes (meatballs will not be cooked through).

Add meatballs to soup and simmer, partially covered, 5 minutes. Stir in garlic paste, lemon juice, and salt and pepper to taste. Serves 2.

Cold Cucumber and Yellow Pepper Soup with Crab Meat and Chives

For soup
2 medium cucumbers, peeled, seeded, and chopped (about 3 cups)
2 medium yellow bell peppers, chopped (about 1 cup)
2 cups 1-inch cubes honeydew melon
1½ tablespoons finely chopped shallot (about 1 large)
1 fresh *jalapeño* chili, or to taste, seeded and chopped (wear rubber gloves)
½ cup plain yogurt
3 tablespoons fresh lemon or lime juice, or to taste

½ pound lump crab meat, picked over
1 tablespoon extra-virgin olive oil
2 teaspoons white-wine vinegar, or to taste
3 tablespoons finely chopped fresh chives, or to taste

Garnish: finely diced yellow bell pepper and 2-inch pieces fresh chives

Make soup:

In a blender purée soup ingredients with salt and pepper to taste until smooth. Force soup through a fine sieve into a bowl and chill, covered, 4 hours, or until very cold. *Soup may be made 1 day ahead and chilled, covered.*

Just before serving, in a small bowl toss crab with oil, vinegar, and salt and pepper to taste.

Divide crab mixture among 6 soup bowls, mounding it in center, and ladle soup around it. Sprinkle each serving with finely chopped chives and garnish with diced bell pepper and chive pieces. Serves 6.

PHOTO ON PAGE 57

Chilled Herb Soup

1¼ pounds sweet onions such as Vidalia, chopped (about 4 cups)
½ stick (¼ cup) unsalted butter
¼ cup all-purpose flour
4 cups chicken broth
2 cups water
3 cups loosely packed fresh flat-leafed parsley leaves, washed well and spun dry
1 cup chopped fresh chives (about 3 bunches)
6 tablespoons fresh tarragon leaves
3 tablespoons fresh thyme leaves (preferably lemon thyme)
¾ cup sour cream
1½ tablespoons fresh lemon juice, or to taste

Garnish: sour cream, finely chopped fresh chives, and fresh thyme sprigs

In a 4- to 5-quart saucepan cook onions in butter with salt and pepper to taste over moderately low heat, stirring, until softened. Add flour and cook, stirring, 3 minutes. Stir in broth and water and simmer, stirring, 2 minutes, or until slightly thickened. Add herbs and simmer 1 minute.

Remove pan from heat and let mixture cool slightly. In a blender purée mixture in small batches until very smooth, forcing as puréed through a fine sieve into a bowl. Whisk in sour cream and salt and pepper to taste. *Chill soup, covered, until very cold, at least 4 hours and up to 24.*

Just before serving, stir in lemon juice and season with salt and pepper. Garnish soup with sour cream and herbs. Makes about 8 cups.

PHOTO ON PAGE 66

Oyster Spinach Bisque with Corn Bread Croutons

36 shucked oysters in their liquor
2 tablespoons unsalted butter
2 large shallots,
    chopped fine
½ cup medium-dry Sherry
3 cups milk
1 cup heavy cream
1 cup packed spinach leaves, washed well,
    drained, and shredded fine

Garnish: 24 small spinach leaves, washed
    well and spun dry, and ¼ cup finely chopped
    red bell pepper
Accompaniment: corn bread croutons
    (recipe follows)

Drain oysters in a fine sieve set over a glass measure, adding enough water to liquor to measure 1 cup, and reserve liquid. Rinse oysters under cold water and drain. Transfer oysters to a bowl and chill, covered.

In a large saucepan melt butter over moderate heat until foam subsides and cook shallots, stirring, until softened. Add Sherry and cook until almost all liquid is evaporated. Stir in reserved oyster liquid and 1½ cups milk and bring barely to a simmer (do not let boil). Stir in 12 oysters and poach until edges begin to curl, about 2 minutes. (Liquid may separate but will come together once blended.) In a blender purée mixture in batches until smooth and strain into a kettle, skimming froth. Stir in remaining 1½ cups milk and cream and bring barely to a simmer (do not let boil). Stir in remaining 24 oysters, spinach, and salt and pepper to taste and poach oysters until edges begin to curl, about 2 minutes.

Ladle bisque into 8 heated soup plates and garnish with spinach leaves and bell pepper. Serve bisque with croutons. Makes about 6 cups, serving 8.

PHOTO ON PAGE 83

Corn Bread Croutons

1 tablespoon olive oil
2 Thomas' corn Toast-R-Cakes or 1 corn muffin,
    cut into ⅓-inch cubes

In a skillet (preferably non-stick) heat oil over moderately high heat until hot but not smoking and toast corn bread until golden brown and crisp. Season croutons with salt and pepper. *Croutons may be made 1 day ahead and kept in a sealable plastic bag at room temperature.* Makes about 1 cup.

Tomato and Bacon Clam Chowder

2 slices bacon, chopped
1 small onion, chopped fine
1 celery rib, chopped
1 garlic clove, minced
1½ dozen small hard-shelled clams, shucked,
    reserving ½ cup liquor, and chopped
⅓ cup dry white wine
1 cup water
2 teaspoons tomato paste
1 small boiling potato
2 medium vine-ripened tomatoes, seeded and
    chopped
2 tablespoons finely chopped fresh parsley leaves

In a 1½-quart saucepan cook bacon over moderate heat until crisp and transfer with a slotted spoon to paper towels to drain. In fat remaining in pan cook onion, celery, and garlic with salt and pepper to taste over moderately low heat, stirring, until softened.

In a bowl whisk together reserved clam liquor, wine, water, and tomato paste and add to onion mixture. Peel potato and cut into ½-inch pieces. Add potato and tomatoes to pan and simmer, covered, until potato is tender, about 15 minutes. Add clams and parsley and simmer, covered, 2 minutes.

Serve chowder sprinkled with crumbled bacon. Makes about 3½ cups.

Red Lentil and Carrot Soup

¾ pound red lentils*, picked over
7 cups water
1 cup chopped onion
3 garlic cloves, minced
1 teaspoon ground coriander
1 teaspoon ground cumin
¼ teaspoon turmeric

5 carrots (about 10 ounces), halved lengthwise
and sliced thin crosswise
1 cup finely chopped red bell pepper
¼ cup packed fresh coriander sprigs, washed
well, spun dry, and chopped fine
¼ cup chopped scallion greens
cayenne to taste

Garnish: fresh coriander sprigs

*available at natural foods stores and specialty
foods shops

In a 4-quart saucepan bring lentils and water to a
boil and skim froth. Stir in onion, garlic, ground
coriander, cumin, and turmeric and simmer, partially
covered, 15 minutes. Stir in carrots and bell pepper
and simmer until carrots are tender, about 10
minutes. *Soup may be prepared up to this point 3
days ahead, cooled, uncovered, and chilled, covered.*
Stir in coriander, scallion greens, cayenne, and salt
and pepper to taste.

Serve soup garnished with fresh coriander sprigs.
Makes about 8 cups, serving 4.

Each serving: 339 calories,
.67 grams fat (1% of calories from fat)

Potée
(Smoked Pork, Sausage, and Vegetable Soup)

1½ tablespoons vegetable oil
1 onion with skin, halved
3 pounds boneless smoked pork such as ham
or pork butt
5 quarts cold water
1 bay leaf
½ teaspoon whole black peppercorns
1 fresh thyme sprig or ½ teaspoon dried thyme
3 fresh parsley sprigs plus ½ cup finely chopped
leaves
6 fresh pork sausage links (not breakfast links)
3 celery ribs, cut crosswise into 3 sections and
each section cut lengthwise into 3 sticks
6 Savoy cabbage leaves, halved along center rib,
discarding rib
4 leeks, white and pale green parts cut crosswise
¼ inch thick, washed well, and drained

6 white turnips, trimmed and cut into ½-inch
wedges
6 carrots, halved and cut lengthwise into
½-inch-wide sticks

In a heavy skillet heat 1 tablespoon oil over moderately high heat until hot but not smoking and
brown onion, cut sides down. In a 7- to 8-quart heavy
kettle combine onion, smoked pork, water, bay leaf,
peppercorns, thyme, and parsley sprigs and simmer,
covered, 1 hour.

Prick each sausage in several places to prevent
skins from bursting when browning. In skillet heat
remaining ½ tablespoon oil over moderately high
heat until hot but not smoking and brown sausages.
Transfer sausages to paper towels to drain. Stir celery into soup and put cabbage leaves on top. Simmer
soup, covered, 15 minutes.

Lifting cabbage leaves, stir sausages, leeks, turnips, and carrots into soup and simmer, covered,
until carrots are tender, about 10 minutes. *Soup may
be prepared up to this point 1 day ahead. Cool soup,
uncovered, and chill, covered. Reheat soup before
proceeding with recipe.*

Transfer smoked pork to a cutting board and slice.
Arrange cabbage leaves in bottoms of 6 large soup
bowls and stir chopped parsley and salt and pepper
to taste into soup. Arrange vegetables, smoked pork,
and sausages in bowls and ladle desired amount of
broth over mixture. Serves 6.

PHOTO ON PAGE 28

Transfer cooked squash to a bowl. Add remaining tablespoon oil to pan and cook onion, stirring occasionally, until just tender. Reduce heat to moderate. Stir in garlic and curry powder and cook, stirring, 1 minute.

Add lentils, water, and broth and simmer 20 minutes, or until lentils are tender. Add squash and remaining ingredients and simmer 3 minutes. Season soup with salt and freshly ground black pepper. Serves 2 generously.

Red Snapper Chowder

1 large leek, white and pale green part only
½ pound red snapper fillets, cut crosswise into
   1½-inch-wide strips
½ teaspoon salt
1 tablespoon olive oil
1 large garlic clove, minced
½ teaspoon ground coriander
⅛ teaspoon cayenne
1 large boiling potato (about ½ pound)
a 16-ounce can whole tomatoes including juice
1¼ cups water
2 tablespoons fresh orange juice
½ extra-large vegetarian vegetable bouillon cube
1 tablespoon minced fresh parsley leaves
¼ teaspoon freshly grated orange zest

Cut leek crosswise into ½-inch slices and in a bowl soak in water to cover, agitating occasionally to dislodge any sand, 5 minutes. Lift leek out of water and drain in a colander.

In a bowl toss snapper gently with salt and chill, covered.

In a saucepan cook leek with salt to taste in oil over moderately high heat, stirring occasionally, until softened, about 5 minutes. Add garlic, coriander, and cayenne and cook, stirring, 1 minute.

Peel potato and cut into ¾-inch cubes. To leek add potato, tomatoes with juice, water, orange juice, and bouillon cube, stirring and crushing tomatoes against side of pan, and simmer until potatoes are almost tender, about 10 minutes. Stir in snapper, parsley, zest, and salt to taste and cook until snapper is opaque, about 5 minutes. Serves 2 generously as a main course.

Vegetable Lentil Soup

2 tablespoons olive oil
1 medium yellow squash, cut into
   ½-inch cubes
1 medium onion, chopped
1 garlic clove, chopped
¼ teaspoon curry powder
½ cup lentils, picked over and rinsed
3 cups water
1½ cups chicken broth
1 cup packed escarole or spinach leaves, washed
   well, spun dry, and chopped
2 plum tomatoes, peeled and chopped
¼ cup chopped fresh parsley leaves
1 teaspoon red-wine vinegar

In a large saucepan heat 1 tablespoon oil over moderately high heat until hot but not smoking and sauté squash, stirring occasionally, until golden.

Curried Squash Soup with Frizzled Leeks

For soup
white and pale green parts of 1 pound leeks
    (about 4 medium), chopped
1 medium onion, chopped
2 tablespoons unsalted butter
1½ teaspoons curry powder
3½ pounds butternut squash, peeled,
    seeded, and cut into 1-inch pieces
    (about 8 cups)
1 medium carrot, chopped
4 cups chicken broth
4 cups water
For frizzled leeks
white and pale green parts of ½ pound leeks
    (about 2 medium), cut crosswise into
    2-inch pieces
vegetable oil for deep-frying

Make soup:
In a large bowl of water wash leeks and drain in a colander. In a kettle cook onion in butter over moderately low heat, stirring, until softened. Add leeks and salt to taste and cook, stirring, until softened. Add curry powder and cook, stirring, 1 minute. Add remaining soup ingredients and simmer, covered, 30 minutes, or until vegetables are soft.

Cool soup slightly and in a blender purée in batches, transferring as puréed to a bowl. Season soup with salt and pepper. *Soup may be made 5 days ahead and cooled, uncovered, before chilling, covered. Reheat soup, thinning with water if desired.*

Make frizzled leeks:

Cut leeks lengthwise into thin strips. In a bowl of water wash leeks and drain in a colander. Dry leeks very well between layers of paper towels.

In a saucepan at least 3½ inches deep heat 1 inch oil to 375° F. on a deep-fat thermometer. Working in very small batches fry leeks (oil will bubble up quite high) until golden, about 10 to 15 seconds, transferring with a slotted spoon to paper towels to drain. Season frizzled leeks with salt. *Leeks may be fried 1 day ahead and kept in an airtight container at room temperature.*

Serve curried squash soup topped with frizzled leeks. Makes about 12 cups.

PHOTO ON PAGE 74

FISH AND SHELLFISH

Halibut with Olive Tarragon Bread Crumbs on Roasted Tomato and Garlic Coulis

For bread crumbs
½ cup fresh bread crumbs (from about 1 slice)
1 tablespoon finely chopped fresh tarragon leaves
2 tablespoons chopped pitted Kalamata or other brine-cured black olives (about 5)
For coulis
1 tablespoon extra-virgin olive oil plus additional for brushing pan
¾ pound plum tomatoes (about 6), cut into ¼-inch-thick slices
4 large garlic cloves, unpeeled
½ teaspoon balsamic vinegar, or to taste
about ¼ cup water for thinning coulis

1 tablespoon mayonnaise
½ teaspoon Dijon mustard
two 1-inch-thick halibut or other firm-fleshed fish fillets such as scrod (each about 6 ounces)

Preheat oven to 450° F.
Make bread crumbs:
In a small bowl combine bread crumb ingredients. Bread crumbs may be made 1 day ahead and chilled, covered.
Make coulis:
Lightly brush a shallow baking pan with additional oil and in it arrange tomatoes in one layer. Brush tomatoes with remaining tablespoon oil and season with salt and pepper. Wrap garlic tightly in foil and roast tomatoes and garlic in pan in middle of oven about 20 minutes, or until tomatoes are lightly browned and garlic is tender when pierced with a knife. Peel garlic and in a blender purée with tomatoes and vinegar until smooth, adding some water if coulis is too thick. Season coulis with salt and pepper. Coulis may be made 1 day ahead and chilled, covered.

In a saucepan heat coulis over low heat, thinning with more water if too thick, and season with salt and pepper. Keep coulis warm.

In a small bowl stir together mayonnaise and mustard. Arrange fish fillets in a lightly oiled shallow baking pan and season with salt and pepper. Spread mayonnaise mixture evenly on top of fillets and pat bread crumbs evenly on top. Roast fillets in middle of oven until just cooked through, 7 to 10 minutes.

Serve fillets on top of coulis. Serves 2.

PHOTO ON PAGE 23

Spinach-Wrapped Flounder and Warm Lentil Salad with Cucumber Yogurt Sauce

1½ pounds fresh spinach (about 2 medium bunches), stems discarded and leaves washed, rinsed thoroughly, and drained
4 cups water
1 cup dried lentils, picked over
1 small red onion, chopped (about 1 cup)
3 tablespoons olive oil
1 tablespoon red-wine vinegar
1 cup plain yogurt
2 garlic cloves, minced and mashed to a paste with ¼ teaspoon salt
½ large seedless cucumber (about ¾ pound)
six 6- to 7-ounce flounder fillets
½ cup loosely packed fresh mint leaves (about 1 bunch), chopped
½ cup crumbled feta cheese (about 2 ounces)

Garnish: mint sprigs

Line 2 baking sheets with paper towels. In a kettle of boiling salted water blanch spinach in small batches 2 seconds and transfer with tongs to paper towels, laying leaves flat to drain.

In a saucepan bring water to a boil with lentils. Simmer lentils, covered, 15 minutes and add salt to taste. Simmer lentils, covered, until just tender, 3 to 5 minutes more, and drain well. Transfer cooked lentils to a bowl.

While lentils are cooking, in a heavy skillet cook onion in 1 tablespoon oil over moderate heat, stirring, until softened, about 5 minutes. Stir in lentils, red-wine vinegar, and salt and pepper to taste. Cook lentil mixture, stirring, until just heated through and keep warm.

In a bowl whisk together yogurt and garlic paste. Peel cucumber and remove any seeds. Cut cucumber into 1-inch pieces and in a blender blend until smooth. Whisk cucumber into yogurt mixture with salt and pepper to taste and let sauce come to room temperature.

Preheat oven to 400° F. and lightly oil a shallow baking pan.

Pat flounder fillets dry and season with salt and pepper. Divide spinach among fillets, overlapping leaves to cover each fillet completely on one side, and transfer fillets, spinach sides down, to oiled pan. Sprinkle top of fillets with half of mint and wrap with remaining spinach, overlapping leaves until fillets are completely covered. Brush tops of fillets with remaining 2 tablespoons oil and bake fillets in middle of oven until cooked through, about 10 minutes.

Stir remaining mint into yogurt sauce and stir feta into lentil mixture.

Divide lentil mixture among 6 plates and top with fillets. Spoon some of sauce onto each plate and garnish fillets with mint sprigs. Serves 6.

Cod with Mediterranean Salsa

⅓ cup Kalamata or other brine-cured black olives, pitted and diced
1 plum tomato, seeded and chopped
1 shallot, minced
1 tablespoon julienne fresh basil leaves
1 tablespoon drained capers
¼ teaspoon freshly grated orange zest
1 teaspoon fresh lemon juice
2 tablespoons olive oil
two 6-ounce pieces cod fillet

Garnish: fresh basil sprigs

In a bowl stir together olives, tomato, shallot, basil julienne, capers, zest, lemon juice, and 1 tablespoon oil to make salsa and season with salt and freshly ground black pepper.

Season cod with salt. In a non-stick skillet heat remaining tablespoon oil over moderately high heat until hot but not smoking and cook cod about 4 minutes on each side, or until golden and cooked through.

Spoon salsa over cod and garnish with basil sprigs. Serves 2.

Salmon Burgers with Ginger Mustard Mayonnaise

For mayonnaise
2 tablespoons mayonnaise
1½ teaspoons Dijon mustard
¾ teaspoon finely grated peeled fresh gingerroot
½ teaspoon soy sauce
For salmon burgers
¾ pound salmon fillet, skin discarded
1 tablespoon Dijon mustard
2 teaspoons finely grated peeled fresh gingerroot
1 teaspoon soy sauce

2 teaspoons vegetable oil
2 hamburger buns, cut sides toasted lightly
2 thin slices sweet onion
2 slices vine-ripened tomato

Make mayonnaise:
In a bowl whisk together mayonnaise ingredients.
Make salmon burgers:
Discard bones in salmon and finely chop salmon by hand. In a bowl stir together salmon, mustard, gingerroot, soy sauce, and salt and pepper to taste and form into two 3-inch patties.

In a non-stick skillet heat oil over moderate heat until hot but not smoking and sauté patties 4 minutes on each side, or until just cooked through.

Transfer burgers to buns and top with mayonnaise, onion, and tomato. Serves 2.

Leek-Wrapped Pompano with Roasted Beet Sauce

4 medium leeks
5 garlic cloves, unpeeled
3 medium beets, scrubbed and trimmed, leaving
    about 1 inch of stems attached
¼ cup water
1 tablespoon fresh lemon juice, or to taste
2 teaspoons balsamic vinegar, or to taste
six 6- to 7-ounce pompano or sole fillets, skinned
3 teaspoons freshly grated lemon zest,
    or to taste
1 tablespoon olive oil

Cut off root ends of leeks and trim tops so that leeks are 8 to 10 inches long. Discard tough outer

leaves. Separate leaves and soak in a large dish filled with water, rubbing to remove any sand.

Fill a large bowl with ice and cold water.

Drain leeks and in a kettle of boiling salted water blanch in batches, stirring, 1 to 2 minutes, or until tender, transferring leeks as cooked with tongs to ice water. Drain cooled leeks on paper towels, arranging them in one layer and stacking more paper towels and leeks as needed. *Leeks may be prepared 1 day ahead, rolled in damp paper towels, and chilled in a sealed plastic bag.*

Preheat oven to 450° F. and lightly oil a shallow baking pan.

Separately wrap garlic and beets tightly in foil and on a baking sheet roast in middle of oven 30 minutes, or until garlic is tender. Transfer garlic to a plate and roast beets until tender, about 30 minutes more. Unwrap garlic and beets carefully and cool until they can be handled. Squeeze garlic out of peel into blender. Peel and cut beets into 2-inch pieces, discarding stems. In blender blend garlic with beets, water, lemon juice, vinegar, and salt and pepper to taste until smooth. *Sauce may be made 1 day ahead and chilled, covered.* Reheat sauce over low heat and season with salt and pepper.

Season tops of pompano or sole fillets with salt and pepper and half of zest. Wrap about 5 leek strips completely around each fillet, overlapping them slightly and leaving ends of fillet exposed. Transfer fillets as wrapped to oiled pan and brush tops with oil. Roast fillets in middle of oven 8 minutes, or until cooked through.

Serve fillets over sauce and garnish with remaining zest. Serves 6.

Sautéed Salmon with Dill Lemon Pesto

a 1½-pound piece salmon fillet with skin
1 tablespoon extra-virgin olive oil
½ cup dill lemon pesto (recipe follows)
1 to 2 tablespoons hot water

Pat salmon dry between paper towels and sprinkle with coarse salt and freshly ground black pepper to taste. In a 12-inch non-stick skillet heat oil over moderately high heat until hot but not smoking and sauté salmon, skin side down, 3 minutes. Reduce heat to moderate and cook salmon 4 minutes more. Turn salmon and sauté over moderately high heat 2 minutes. Reduce heat to moderate and cook until just cooked through, about 3 minutes more.

In a food processor blend pesto with 1 tablespoon hot water, adding additional hot water if necessary to reach desired consistency.

Serve pesto over salmon. Serves 6.

Dill Lemon Pesto

3 slices homemade-type white bread, torn into
   small pieces
2 tablespoons fresh lemon juice
3 tablespoons water
¾ cup packed fresh dill (feathery leaves)
¾ cup packed fresh flat-leafed parsley leaves,
   washed well and spun dry
2 teaspoons Dijon mustard
½ teaspoon freshly grated lemon zest
⅛ teaspoon sugar
⅓ cup olive oil

In a bowl soak bread in lemon juice and water 10 minutes and squeeze out excess liquid between hands. In a food processor blend together bread and remaining ingredients with salt and pepper to taste until smooth. *Pesto keeps, surface covered with plastic wrap, chilled, 1 week.* Makes about ¾ cup.

Broiled Salmon with Spicy Maple Basting Sauce

6 tablespoons maple syrup, or to taste
½ cup water
2 tablespoons minced peeled fresh gingerroot
2 garlic cloves, minced
1 teaspoon dried hot red pepper flakes,
   or to taste
¼ teaspoon salt
four 1-inch-thick pieces salmon fillet
   (about 6 ounces each)

In a small heavy saucepan combine maple syrup, water, gingerroot, garlic, red pepper flakes, and salt and simmer until reduced to about ½ cup. Cool basting sauce.

Preheat broiler.

Arrange salmon, skin sides down, on oiled rack of broiler pan and season with salt. Broil salmon about 4 inches from heat 4 minutes. Brush salmon with sauce and broil until just cooked through, about 6 minutes more. Serves 4.

Pan-Roasted Sea Bass with Lemon Fennel Oil

two 5- to 6-ounce fillets of sea bass or other
   firm-fleshed white fish, with skin
4 teaspoons olive oil
2 teaspoons fresh lemon juice
¼ teaspoon fennel seeds, chopped fine

Preheat oven to 425° F.

Rinse fillets and pat dry. Season fillets with salt and freshly ground black pepper. In a 9- to 10-inch cast-iron skillet (or non-stick skillet with handle wrapped in foil) heat 1 teaspoon oil over moderately high heat until hot but not smoking and sear fillets skin sides down, pressing flat with a metal spatula to prevent curling, 2 minutes. Transfer skillet to middle of oven and roast fillets 5 minutes, or until just cooked through.

While fish is roasting, in a small skillet whisk together remaining 3 teaspoons oil, lemon juice, fennel seeds, and salt and pepper to taste and heat over moderately low heat until hot but not boiling.

Serve fillets skin sides up and spoon sauce over them. Serves 2.

Zucchini-Wrapped Red Snapper with Tomato, Cumin, and Orange Sauce

2 teaspoons cumin seeds
4 tablespoons olive oil
1 large onion, sliced
⅛ teaspoon cinnamon
4 garlic cloves, sliced thin
1½ pounds plum tomatoes, cut into chunks
two 3-inch strips fresh orange zest, removed
    with a vegetable peeler
¼ cup dry white wine
¼ cup fresh orange juice
¼ cup chopped fresh flat-leafed parsley leaves
four 6- to 7-ounce red snapper fillets, skinned
two 7-inch-long zucchini (each about ½ pound)

Garnish: flat-leafed parsley sprigs

Preheat oven to 450° F.

In a small dry heavy skillet toast seeds over moderate heat, shaking skillet, until fragrant, being careful not to burn them, and cool.

Brush an ovenproof skillet large enough to hold red snapper fillets in one layer with 3 tablespoons oil and cook onion over moderate heat, stirring, 5 minutes, or until softened and slightly golden.

Stir in seeds, cinnamon, and garlic and cook, stirring, 1 minute. Add tomatoes and zest and cook, stirring, 5 minutes, or until tomatoes are slightly softened. Stir in wine and cook, stirring, until most of liquid is evaporated. Remove pan from heat and stir in orange juice, chopped parsley, and salt and pepper to taste.

Pat fillets dry and season with salt and pepper.

Trim ends of zucchini and with a *mandoline* or other hand-held slicing device slice zucchini lengthwise into about twenty-eight ⅛-inch-thick strips.

On a work surface arrange fillets in one layer and place about 7 zucchini strips crosswise on top of each fillet, overlapping them slightly and leaving ends of fillet exposed. Carefully tuck ends of zucchini strips under each fillet and with a long spatula transfer zucchini-wrapped fillets to tomato sauce (fillets should be in one layer). Brush tops of zucchini with remaining tablespoon oil and bake fillets in skillet in middle of oven 15 to 20 minutes, or until just cooked through.

Discard zest and divide fillets and sauce among 4 plates. Garnish fillets with parsley. Serves 4.

Spiced Tuna Steaks with Fennel and Red Peppers

two 6-ounce tuna steaks, each 1 inch thick
1½ tablespoons olive oil plus additional oil
    for brushing
1 tablespoon fennel seeds
1½ teaspoons black peppercorns
1 medium fennel bulb (about 1 pound), trimmed
    and cut into ¼-inch crosswise slices
1 medium red bell pepper, quartered and cut
    into ¼-inch slices
2 large garlic cloves, sliced thin
½ cup water
1 tablespoon fresh lemon juice

Lightly brush tuna steaks with some additional oil and season with salt. Crush fennel seeds and peppercorns coarse in a mortar with a pestle and press onto both sides of tuna steaks. Let tuna steaks stand on a plate 10 minutes.

In a heavy non-stick skillet sauté fennel bulb in 1½ tablespoons oil over moderately high heat, stirring, until golden. Add bell pepper and garlic and sauté 1 minute. Add water and simmer vegetables, covered, 10 minutes, or until fennel is tender. Remove lid and, if necessary, boil mixture until liquid is nearly evaporated. Add lemon juice and salt and pepper to taste and keep warm.

While fennel mixture is cooking, brush a heavy skillet, preferably cast-iron, with some additional oil and heat over moderately high heat until hot but not smoking. Sauté tuna steaks 2 minutes on each side, or until barely pink in center, for medium meat. Transfer tuna steaks to plates and spoon fennel-pepper mixture over and around them. Serves 2.

Baked Sea Bass in Herbed Salt Crust

a 2-pound sea bass, cleaned, leaving head and tail
    intact
2 tablespoons plus ½ teaspoon dried tarragon,
    crumbled
¼ teaspoon freshly ground black pepper

1 lemon
3½ cups coarse salt (about 1¼ pounds)
1½ cups all-purpose flour
1 cup warm water plus additional if necessary

Accompaniment: lemon wedges

Rinse sea bass under cold water and pat dry inside and out. Sprinkle cavity of bass with ½ teaspoon tarragon and pepper.

With a sharp knife trim ends of lemon to expose flesh and, standing lemon on one end, cut from top to bottom to remove peel and pith. Cut lemon crosswise into ¼-inch-thick slices and arrange in cavity.

Preheat oven to 450° F. and oil a baking pan.

In a bowl whisk together remaining 2 tablespoons tarragon, coarse salt, and flour. Stir in 1 cup warm water plus additional as necessary to form a slightly stiff paste (paste should resemble wet sand).

Arrange bass in oiled pan. Coat top of bass completely with half of salt mixture, patting it on, and turn bass over. Coat other side in same manner (bass should be completely covered).

Bake bass in middle of oven 30 minutes. Crack salt crust with a sharp knife or hammer and remove top crust, discarding it. To serve, lift bass in pieces off bones and discard bones. Lift out remaining bass. Serve bass with lemon wedges. Serves 4.

Grilled Swordfish with Coriander Lime Butter

1½ tablespoons unsalted butter, softened
1 teaspoon freshly grated lime zest
1 tablespoon fresh lime juice
1 small garlic clove, minced
1 tablespoon minced fresh coriander leaves
two 6- to 8-ounce swordfish steaks

Accompaniment if desired: grilled spiced red
    onions (recipe follows)

Prepare grill.

In a small bowl stir together butter, zest, 1 teaspoon lime juice, garlic, coriander, and salt and pepper to taste.

Rub both sides of swordfish steaks with remaining 2 teaspoons lime juice and season with salt and pepper. Grill swordfish on an oiled rack set 5 to 6 inches over glowing coals until just cooked through, 3 to 4 minutes on each side. (Alternatively, swordfish may be grilled in a hot well-seasoned ridged grill pan over moderately high heat.)

Top each swordfish steak with a dollop of coriander lime butter and serve with grilled onions. Serves 2.

Grilled Spiced Red Onions

1 tablespoon olive oil
½ teaspoon ground cumin
cayenne to taste
1 large red onion, cut crosswise into four
    ½-inch-thick slices
1 teaspoon fresh lime juice if desired

Prepare grill.

In a small bowl stir together oil, cumin, cayenne, and salt and pepper to taste.

Brush both sides of onion slices with oil mixture and grill on an oiled rack set 6 inches over glowing coals until well-charred and tender, 2 to 3 minutes on each side. (Alternatively, onion slices may be grilled in a hot well-seasoned ridged grill pan over moderately high heat.)

Separate onion slices into rings. In a bowl toss onion rings with lime juice and season with salt and pepper.

Serve onions with grilled fish, meat, or poultry. Serves 2.

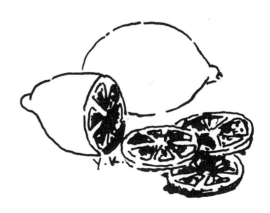

SHELLFISH

Shrimp and Peppers in Spicy Tomato Sauce

3 tablespoons olive oil
2½ tablespoons all-purpose flour
1½ cups chopped onion (about 1 large)
3 large garlic cloves, minced
4 cups hot water
an 8-ounce can tomato sauce (about ¾ cup)
2 tablespoons chili powder
1 tablespoon sugar
1 tablespoon Worcestershire sauce
2 teaspoons salt
½ teaspoon Angostura bitters
½ teaspoon cayenne
1 teaspoon black pepper
3 yellow bell peppers, cut into ½-inch-wide strips
3 red bell peppers, cut into ½-inch-wide strips
2½ pounds jumbo shrimp (about 36), shelled,
    leaving tail and last shell section intact, and
    deveined
¼ cup fresh lemon juice

Accompaniment: basmati rice with mustard seeds
    and golden raisins (recipe follows)
Garnish: 2 tablespoons minced fresh parsley
    leaves

In a deep 12-inch heavy skillet stir together oil and flour and cook roux over moderate heat, stirring constantly, until color of peanut butter, about 10 minutes. Add onion and cook, stirring occasionally, until softened. Stir in garlic and cook, stirring, 1 minute. Add hot water, tomato sauce, chili powder, sugar, Worcestershire sauce, salt, bitters, cayenne, and black pepper and simmer, uncovered, stirring occasionally, until reduced to about 2½ cups, about 35 minutes. Season sauce with salt. *Sauce may be made 1 week ahead and chilled, covered. Reheat sauce in skillet before proceeding.*

Stir bell peppers into sauce and cook, covered, over moderate heat, stirring often to avoid scorching, until crisp-tender, about 10 minutes. Transfer peppers with a slotted spoon to a large bowl, letting excess sauce drip into skillet, and cover. Stir shrimp into sauce and cook, covered, over moderate heat,

stirring occasionally, until cooked through, about 5 minutes. Transfer shrimp with slotted spoon to bowl and cover. Boil sauce, stirring, until thickened. Pour sauce, lemon juice, and salt to taste over shrimp mixture and stir to combine well.

Serve shrimp and bell peppers over rice and sprinkle with parsley. Serves 6.

PHOTO ON PAGE 67

*Basmati Rice with
Mustard Seeds and Golden Raisins*

2⅔ cups water
1⅓ cups Texmati rice* (American *basmati*) or
    brown *basmati* rice**
¼ cup golden raisins
1 cinnamon stick
1 teaspoon mustard seeds
¾ teaspoon salt
½ cup thinly sliced scallion greens

*available at specialty foods shops and some
    supermarkets
**available at Indian markets, natural foods
    stores, and some specialty foods shops

In a 3-quart heavy saucepan stir together all ingredients except scallion and bring to a boil. Reduce heat to low and cook, covered, until rice is tender and liquid is absorbed, about 20 minutes. Fluff rice with a fork and stir in scallion. Serves 6.

PHOTO ON PAGE 67

*Glazed Sea Scallops with
Wilted Napa Cabbage Slaw*

1½ teaspoons soy sauce
1½ tablespoons white-wine vinegar
½ teaspoon sugar
2 tablespoons olive oil
1 tablespoon Asian sesame oil
3 cups thinly sliced Napa cabbage
1 medium carrot, shredded
1 scallion, sliced thin
½ pound sea scallops

Garnish: thinly sliced scallion greens

In a small bowl whisk together soy sauce, vinegar, sugar, 1½ tablespoons olive oil, sesame oil, and salt and pepper to taste.

In a bowl toss cabbage, carrot, and scallion with 2 tablespoons soy sauce mixture.

Remove tough muscle from side of each scallop if necessary. Pat scallops dry with paper towels and season with salt and pepper. In a heavy non-stick skillet just large enough to hold sea scallops in one layer heat remaining ½ tablespoon olive oil over moderately high heat until hot but not smoking and sauté scallops until golden and cooked through, about 2 minutes on each side. Transfer scallops to a bowl. Add remaining soy sauce mixture to skillet and boil until reduced to a glaze. Add glaze to scallops and toss to coat well. Keep scallops warm.

Add slaw to skillet and cook over moderately high heat, stirring, just until cabbage is wilted, 1 to 2 minutes. Season slaw with salt and pepper.

Serve slaw topped with scallops and garnished with scallion greens. Serves 2.

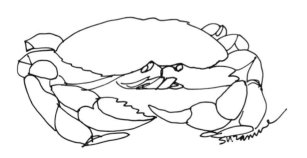

Crab-Meat Gratin

2 tablespoons minced carrot
2 tablespoons minced celery
2 tablespoons minced red bell pepper
1 tablespoon unsalted butter
½ cup chicken broth
¼ cup dry vermouth or dry white wine
¼ teaspoon dried tarragon, crumbled
½ cup heavy cream
½ pound fresh lump crab meat, picked over (about 1½ cups)
fresh lemon juice to taste
¼ cup freshly grated Parmesan

Accompaniment: lightly toasted thin French bread slices

Preheat broiler.

In a small heavy saucepan cook carrot, celery, and bell pepper in butter over moderate heat, stirring, 1 minute. Add broth, vermouth or wine, and tarragon and boil mixture until liquid is reduced to about 1 tablespoon. Add cream and boil sauce until thickened, 1 to 2 minutes. Stir in crab meat, lemon juice, and salt and pepper to taste and divide mixture between two 1-cup shallow baking dishes. Sprinkle Parmesan over crab mixture and set dishes in shallow baking pan. Broil gratin about 4 inches from heat 2 minutes, or until bubbling and golden, and serve with toasts. Serves 2.

Shrimp Sandwiches with Barbecue Sauce

1 tablespoon olive oil
¾ pound medium shrimp (about 24), shelled and deveined
2 teaspoons mayonnaise
3 tablespoons ketchup
1 tablespoon Worcestershire sauce
½ teaspoon Tabasco, or to taste
4 sesame seed hamburger buns, halved
1 cup prepared coleslaw

In a large non-stick skillet heat oil over moderately high heat until hot but not smoking and sauté shrimp with salt and pepper to taste 2 to 3 minutes, or until just cooked through. Transfer shrimp with a slotted spoon as cooked to a plate and cool. Cut each shrimp in half horizontally and in a bowl toss with mayonnaise and salt and pepper to taste.

In a small bowl whisk together ketchup, Worcestershire sauce, and Tabasco and spread evenly on cut sides of buns. Make sandwiches on buns with shrimp and coleslaw. Makes 4 sandwiches.

Grilled Lobster with Orange Chipotle Vinaigrette

¾ teaspoon finely grated fresh orange zest
1 cup fresh orange juice
¼ cup white-wine vinegar
2 canned *chipotle* chilies in *adobo* sauce*,
    or to taste
2½ teaspoons salt
1 teaspoon firmly packed brown sugar
1 cup olive oil
eight 1½-pound live lobsters
2 tablespoons chopped fresh basil leaves

Garnish: basil sprigs

*available at Hispanic markets, some specialty
    foods shops, and by mail order from Los
    Chileros de Nuevo Mexico, P.O. Box 6215,
    Santa Fe, NM 87502, tel. (505) 471-6967, or
    Adriana's Caravan, tel. (800) 316-0820

Bring a large kettle (at least 8-quart capacity)
three-quarters full of water to a boil for lobsters.

In a blender blend zest, juice, vinegar, *chipotles* in
adobo sauce, salt, and brown sugar until *chipotles*
are chopped fine. With motor running add oil in a
slow stream. *Vinaigrette may be prepared up to this
point 3 days ahead and chilled, covered. Bring
vinaigrette to room temperature before serving.*

In boiling water partially cook lobsters, 2 at a
time, over high heat 3 minutes and transfer with
tongs to a colander to drain and cool. (Make sure
water returns to a full boil before adding each batch
of lobsters.)

When lobsters are cool enough to handle, remove
tails and claws and discard bodies. With kitchen
shears halve tails (including shells) lengthwise, cutting off swimmerets on underside of tails if desired.
*Lobsters may be prepared up to this point 1 day
ahead and chilled, covered.*

Prepare grill.

Grill claws, in batches if necessary, on a rack set 5
to 6 inches over glowing coals, turning occasionally,
until liquid bubbles at open end, 5 to 7 minutes, and
transfer to a platter.

Stir basil leaves into vinaigrette and reserve 1¼
cups in a small pitcher. Brush meat in lobster tails
with some vinaigrette. Grill tails, meat side down, in
batches if necessary, 3 minutes. Turn tails meat side
up, brushing with more vinaigrette, and grill until
juices are bubbling and meat is plump and opaque,
3 to 5 minutes. Transfer tails to platter. *Lobster may
be grilled 2 hours ahead and cooled, uncovered,
before chilling, covered.*

Serve lobster warm or chilled with reserved vinaigrette and garnish with basil sprigs. Serves 8.

PHOTO ON PAGE 45

MEAT

Braised Cube Steaks with Orange

2 cube steaks (about ¾ pound total)
1½ tablesoons vegetable oil
1 large onion, sliced thin
½ teaspoon freshly grated orange zest
1 garlic clove, minced
⅓ cup low-salt beef broth
1½ teaspoons soy sauce

Pat steaks dry between paper towels and season with salt and pepper. In a heavy skillet heat oil over moderately high heat until hot but not smoking and brown steaks. Transfer steaks with tongs to a plate and in drippings remaining in skillet cook onion over moderate heat, stirring, until softened. Stir in zest and garlic and cook until fragrant, about 30 seconds. Add broth, soy sauce, and steaks and simmer, uncovered, until steaks are tender, about 5 minutes. Serves 2.

Grilled Sirloin Steak with Anise Basil Butter

For butter
1½ tablespoons unsalted butter,
    softened
1 tablespoon minced fresh basil leaves
½ teaspoon anise seeds, ground coarse with a
    mortar and pestle or in an electric coffee
    grinder
¾ teaspoon fresh lemon juice
For steak
2 teaspoons black peppercorns
1 teaspoon anise seeds
a 1-pound boneless sirloin steak
    (about 1 inch thick)
olive oil for brushing steak

Prepare grill.
Make butter:
In a small bowl stir together butter ingredients with salt and pepper to taste until well blended and juice is incorporated.
Grill steak :
In a heavy-duty sealable plastic bag or between 2 sheets of wax paper crush peppercorns and anise seeds with bottom of a heavy skillet. Pat steak dry and coat both sides with spice mixture, pressing it in.

Season steak with salt to taste and brush both sides with oil. Grill steak on an oiled rack set 5 to 6 inches over glowing coals 4 to 5 minutes on each side for medium-rare meat. (Alternatively, steaks may be grilled in a hot well-seasoned ridged grill pan over moderately high heat.) Transfer steak with tongs to a platter and let stand 10 minutes.

Top steak with dollops of anise basil butter. Serves 2.

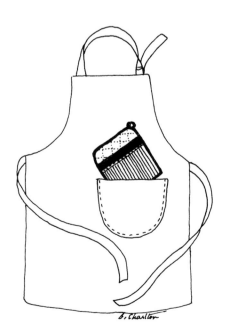

Filets Mignons with Port Wine Glaze

2 filets mignons, each about
    1¼ inches thick
½ cup Tawny Port
¼ cup red-wine vinegar
½ teaspoon Dijon mustard
1½ teaspoons olive oil

Pat filets dry and season with salt and pepper. In a small bowl whisk together Port, vinegar, and mustard until combined well.

In a non-stick skillet heat oil over moderately high heat until hot but not smoking and cook filets 4 minutes. Turn filets and cook 4 minutes more for medium-rare. Transfer filets to a warm platter. Pour Port mixture carefully down side of skillet and boil, stirring, until reduced to about 2 tablespoons. Serve filets with glaze. Serves 2.

Garlic-and-Chili-Rubbed Steaks

2 tablespoons chili powder
2 large garlic cloves, chopped and mashed
    to a paste with 1 teaspoon salt
1 teaspoon ground cumin
¾ teaspoon sugar
3½ tablespoons Worcestershire sauce
four 1-inch-thick strip or
    shell steaks

In a small bowl stir together chili powder, garlic paste, cumin, and sugar and stir in Worcestershire sauce to make a paste.

Arrange steaks on a plate large enough to hold them in one layer and rub both sides of steaks with chili paste. Transfer steaks to a large sealable plastic bag. *Marinate steaks, chilled, at least 4 hours and up to 2 days.*

Prepare grill.

Grill steaks on an oiled rack set 5 to 6 inches over glowing coals 5 minutes on each side for medium-rare. (Alternatively, steaks may be grilled in a hot well-seasoned large ridged grill pan over moderately high heat.) Transfer steaks to plates and let stand 5 minutes. Serves 4.

PHOTO ON PAGE 61

Ropa Vieja
(Braised Beef, Peppers, and Onions)

For braising beef
3 pounds skirt or flank steak, trimmed
2 quarts water
2 carrots, chopped coarse
1 large onion, chopped coarse
2 celery ribs, chopped coarse
1 bay leaf
3 garlic cloves, crushed lightly
1 teaspoon dried oregano
1 teaspoon ground cumin
1 teaspoon salt
¼ teaspoon whole black peppercorns

2 green bell peppers, cut into ¼-inch strips
1 red onion, cut into ¼-inch strips
4 tablespoons olive oil
2 cups braising liquid plus additional
    if desired
a 14- to 16-ounce can whole tomatoes
    with juice, chopped
3 tablespoons tomato paste
3 garlic cloves, minced
1 teaspoon ground cumin
¼ teaspoon dried oregano
2 red bell peppers, cut into ¼-inch strips
2 yellow bell peppers, cut into ¼-inch strips
1 cup frozen peas, thawed
½ cup pimiento-stuffed Spanish olives,
    drained and halved

Accompaniment: yellow rice with toasted cumin
    (recipe follows)

Braise beef:
In a 5-quart kettle combine all braising ingredients and simmer, uncovered, 1½ hours, or until beef is tender. Remove kettle from heat and cool meat in liquid 30 minutes. Transfer meat to a platter and cover. Strain braising liquid through a colander, pressing on solids, into a bowl. Return braising liquid to kettle and boil until reduced to 3 cups, about 30 minutes. *Stew may be made up to this point 1 day ahead. Cool braising liquid completely and chill it and the beef separately, covered.*

In kettle cook green bell peppers and onion in 2

tablespoons olive oil over moderate heat, stirring, until softened.

While vegetables are cooking, pull meat into shreds about 3 by ½ inches. To onion mixture add shredded meat, 2 cups braising liquid, tomatoes with juice, tomato paste, garlic, cumin, oregano, and salt and black pepper to taste and simmer, uncovered, 20 minutes.

While stew is simmering, in a large skillet cook red and yellow bell peppers in remaining 2 tablespoons oil over moderate heat, stirring occasionally, until softened. Stir peppers into stew with enough additional braising liquid to thin to desired consistency and simmer, uncovered, 5 minutes. Stir in peas and olives and simmer, uncovered, 5 minutes.

Serve *ropa vieja* with yellow rice. Serves 8.

PHOTO ON PAGE 16

Yellow Rice with Toasted Cumin

2 tablespoons olive oil
2 teaspoons cuminseed
¼ teaspoon crumbled saffron threads
2 cups unconverted long-grain rice
4 cups water
¾ teaspoon salt

In a heavy 3-quart saucepan heat oil over moderately high heat until hot but not smoking and sauté cuminseed 10 seconds, or until it turns a few shades darker and is fragrant. Stir in saffron and rice and sauté, stirring, 1 to 2 minutes, or until rice is coated well. Stir in water and salt and boil rice, uncovered and without stirring, until surface of rice is covered with steam holes and grains on top appear dry, 8 to 10 minutes. Reduce heat to as low as possible and cook rice, covered, 10 minutes more. Remove pan from heat and let rice stand, covered, 5 minutes. Fluff rice with a fork. Serves 8.

PHOTO ON PAGE 16

Barbecued Beef Ribs

3 pounds beef ribs from the loin
  (about 7 meaty ribs)
1 large garlic clove, minced
1 tablespoon vegetable oil
⅓ cup ketchup
2 tablespoons Worcestershire sauce
1 teaspoon curry powder

Prepare grill.

On a steamer rack set over simmering water steam beef ribs, covered, 20 minutes.

While ribs are steaming, in a small saucepan cook garlic in oil over moderately low heat, stirring, until golden. Stir in ketchup, Worcestershire sauce, and curry powder and simmer, stirring, until thickened slightly, about 1 minute.

Transfer ribs to a large plate and sprinkle with salt and pepper to taste. Grill ribs on a rack set 5 to 6 inches over glowing coals, meat sides down, until golden, 2 to 3 minutes. Grill ribs on edges until golden, about 2 minutes on each edge, and grill, bone sides down, until golden, about 3 minutes.

Brush ribs with barbecue sauce and grill, continuing to baste, until barely charred, about 1 minute on each side. Serves 2.

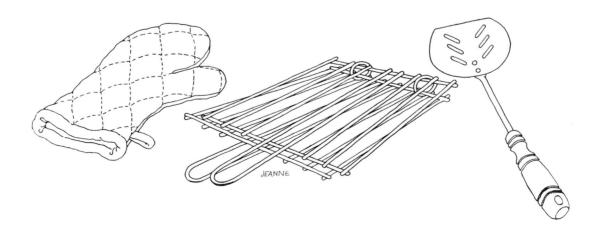

Braised Short Ribs

6 pounds beef short ribs, cut into 1-rib pieces
1 tablespoon olive oil
3 medium onions, chopped
4 large garlic cloves, minced
1½ cups dry red wine
a 28- to 32-ounce can whole tomatoes including
  liquid, coarsely puréed in a blender
1½ cups beef broth
2 tablespoons Worcestershire sauce
six 3- by 1-inch strips fresh orange zest removed
  with a vegetable peeler
2 teaspoons chopped fresh rosemary leaves or
  1 teaspoon dried rosemary, crumbled
½ teaspoon salt
10 ounces pearl onions (about 2 cups), blanched
  in boiling water 2 minutes and peeled
a 1-pound bag peeled baby carrots

Garnish: finely chopped fresh parsley leaves

Pat short ribs dry and season with salt and pepper. In a heavy kettle (at least 6 quarts) heat oil over moderately high heat until hot but not smoking and brown ribs in batches, transferring with tongs to a large bowl.

Add chopped onions to kettle and cook over moderate heat, stirring, until golden. Add garlic and cook, stirring, 1 minute. Add wine, tomatoes, broth, Worcestershire sauce, zest, rosemary, and salt and bring to a boil. Add ribs including any juices that have accumulated in bowl and simmer, covered, 30 minutes.

Add pearl onions and carrots, stirring and pushing down to make sure they are covered by liquid, and simmer, covered, 1 to 1½ hours, or until meat is tender. Transfer meat, pearl onions, and carrots with a slotted spoon to a large bowl. Discard zest and boil braising liquid, stirring occasionally, until slightly thickened and reduced to about 5 cups. Return meat and vegetables to kettle and cook over low heat, stirring occasionally, until heated through. *Stew may be made 3 days ahead and cooled, uncovered, before chilling covered. Reheat stew, adding water as necessary to thin sauce.*

Serve stew sprinkled with parsley. Serves 6 to 8.

PHOTO ON PAGE 72

Roast Beef Sandwiches with Roquefort and Caramelized Shallots

3 tablespoons unsalted butter
12 large shallots (about ¾ pound), sliced thin
4 kaiser rolls (5 inches in diameter), halved
1 pound thinly sliced medium-rare roast beef
6 ounces chilled Roquefort cheese, crumbled

In a heavy skillet melt butter over moderate heat and stir in shallots with salt and pepper to taste. Cook shallots, stirring occasionally, about 15 minutes, or until golden brown.

Preheat oven to 375° F.

Make sandwiches on rolls with roast beef, shallots, and Roquefort. Bake sandwiches on a baking sheet in middle of oven until Roquefort is melted and sandwiches are hot, about 10 minutes. Makes 4 sandwiches.

Grilled Mozzarella Cheeseburgers with Dried Tomato and Arugula Pesto

1 large red onion
2 pounds ground beef
¾ cup dried tomato and arugula pesto
  (recipe follows), or to taste
6 ounces mozzarella cheese, cut into 6 slices
olive oil for brushing onion
6 hamburger buns, grilled lightly if desired

Prepare grill.

Cut six ¼-inch-thick slices from center of onion and reserve. Divide beef into 6 portions. Press small indentation in each portion and spoon rounded teaspoon pesto into each indentation. Form beef portions into six ¾-inch-thick patties, enclosing pesto completely. Grill patties on an oiled rack set 5 to 6 inches over glowing coals 5 minutes. Turn burgers and grill 3 minutes more. Top burgers with mozzarella and grill 2 minutes more, or until just cooked through. Transfer burgers to a platter and let stand, loosely covered, while grilling onion. Brush onion on both sides with oil and grill until softened and browned, about 3 minutes on each side.

Spread pesto on both sides of buns and make sandwiches with onion and burgers. Serves 6.

Dried Tomato and Arugula Pesto

1½ cups packed arugula, washed well and
    spun dry
⅓ cup drained bottled dried tomatoes packed
    in oil
¼ cup olive oil
3 tablespoons freshly grated Parmesan
2 tablespoons pine nuts, toasted golden and
    cooled
1 large garlic clove, chopped and mashed
    to a paste with ½ teaspoon salt
a pinch sugar

In a food processor blend together all ingredients with salt and pepper to taste until smooth. *Pesto keeps, surface covered with plastic wrap, chilled, 1 week.* Makes about 1 cup.

VEAL

Grilled Veal Chops with Morel Sauce

For sauce
¼ cup water
¼ cup sugar
¼ cup red-wine vinegar
1 tablespoon balsamic vinegar plus additional
    to taste if desired
24 fresh morels* (about 1 pound), washed well,
    patted dry, and trimmed, or 1 ounce dried
    morels*, soaked (procedure page 134),
    reserving ½ cup soaking liquid
3 tablespoons unsalted butter
⅓ cup finely chopped shallots
2 cups dry red wine
2 cups rich veal stock** or *demiglace***
fresh lemon juice to taste if desired

six 1½-inch-thick veal chops
    (about 4 pounds total)
vegetable oil for rubbing on chops

*available at specialty foods shops and
    by mail order from Aux Délices des Bois,
    tel. (800) 666-1232 or fax. (212) 334-1231

**available at specialty foods shops and by mail
    order from D'Artagnan, tel. (800) 327-8246
    or, in New Jersey, (201) 792-0748

Make sauce:
In a small heavy saucepan boil water with sugar, without stirring, until a golden caramel. Remove pan from heat and carefully add red-wine vinegar and 1 tablespoon balsamic vinegar down side of pan (mixture will bubble and steam). Stir mixture over moderate heat until caramel is dissolved, about 3 minutes. Remove pan from heat.

In a heavy saucepan cook morels in butter, stirring, over moderate heat until liquid from morels is evaporated, about 5 minutes. Transfer morels with a slotted spoon to a bowl and reserve. Add shallots to pan and cook, stirring, until golden. Stir in wine and boil until reduced to about 1 cup, about 15 minutes. Add stock or *demiglace* and reserved morel soaking liquid (if using dried morels) and reduce to about 1¼ cups, about 15 minutes. Remove pan from heat and stir in caramel mixture. *Sauce may be prepared up to this point 2 days ahead and chilled, covered. Chill morels separately, covered. Reheat sauce over moderate heat before proceeding with recipe.* Add morels to sauce with salt and pepper to taste. If desired stir in additional balsamic vinegar, 1 teaspoon at a time, and lemon juice.

Prepare grill and preheat oven to 425° F. Bring veal chops to room temperature (about 20 minutes).

Rub chops lightly with oil and season with salt and pepper. Grill chops on a rack set about 5 to 6 inches over glowing coals until evenly browned, 3 to 4 minutes on each side. (Alternatively, chops may be grilled in a hot well-seasoned ridged grill pan over moderately high heat). Arrange chops in one layer in a shallow baking pan. Roast chops in middle of oven 15 to 20 minutes for medium, barely pink meat.

Serve chops with sauce. Serves 6.

PHOTO ON PAGE 42

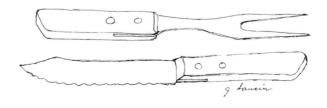

To Soak Dried Morels

Dried morels should be rehydrated in twice their volume of warm water until tender, 10 to 30 minutes. Lift morels out of soaking liquid and strain liquid through a fine sieve into a bowl, reserving it if desired. Pat drained morels dry with paper towels. (Do not eat raw morels as they can cause digestive disorders.)

Braised Veal Shanks with
Green Olives and Capers

¾ cup unpitted brine-cured green olives
    (preferably cracked)*, rinsed well
5 pounds 2-inch-thick veal shanks (6 to 8 shanks),
    each tied securely with kitchen string to keep
    meat attached to bone
all-purpose flour for dredging
2 tablespoons olive oil
1 tablespoon unsalted butter
1 medium-large onion, halved lengthwise and
    sliced thin
2 large garlic cloves, minced
1 anchovy fillet, chopped
five 3- by ½-inch strips fresh lemon zest
1½ tablespoons drained bottled capers
1 tablespoon finely chopped fresh rosemary
    leaves or 1 teaspoon dried, crumbled
1½ cups dry white wine
1½ cups low-salt chicken broth

Accompaniment: gremolata (recipe follows)
Garnish: drained caper berries**

*available at specialty foods shops and
    Mediterranean markets
**available at specialty foods shops and by
    mail order from Grace's Marketplace,
    tel. (800) 325-6126 or, in New York City,
    (212) 737-0600

Preheat oven to 425° F.
Pit ¼ cup olives and chop fine. Lightly crush remaining ½ cup olives with side of a large knife.
Pat veal shanks dry between paper towels and season with salt and pepper. Dredge top and bottom (not side) of each shank in flour, knocking off excess. In a 12-inch heavy skillet heat 1 tablespoon oil and butter over moderately high heat until foam subsides and brown tops and bottoms of shanks in batches, about 2 minutes on each side. Transfer shanks as browned to a flameproof roasting pan.

Wipe out skillet and add remaining tablespoon oil. Heat oil over moderate heat until hot but not smoking and cook onion, stirring, until golden. Add garlic and anchovy and cook, stirring, 1 minute. Add chopped olives, zest, capers, rosemary, and wine and boil 5 minutes. Add broth and crushed olives and bring to a boil.

Pour broth mixture over shanks and cover tightly with foil. Braise shanks in oven 2 hours, or until meat is tender. *Shanks may be prepared up to this point 2 days ahead and cooled, uncovered, before chilling, covered. Reheat shanks before proceeding.*

Reduce oven temperature to 325° F.

Transfer shanks with a slotted spoon to another roasting pan or deep ovenproof platter and keep warm, covered, in oven. Strain cooking liquid through a sieve into a 1-quart glass measuring cup and reserve solids, discarding zest. Let liquid stand until fat rises to top and skim and discard fat. (There should be about 1½ cups liquid. If necessary, in a saucepan boil liquid until it is reduced.) Add reserved solids to liquid and pour over shanks.

Serve shanks sprinkled with *gremolata* and garnished with caper berries. Serves 6.

PHOTO ON PAGE 21

Gremolata

¼ cup finely chopped fresh parsley leaves
1 tablespoon freshly grated lemon zest
1½ teaspoons minced garlic, or to taste

In a small bowl toss all ingredients together well.
Makes about ⅓ cup.

PHOTO ON PAGE 21

PORK

Rosemary Garlic Pork Rib Roast with
Roasted Carrots and Onions

3 bunches small thin carrots (not baby carrots,
    about 2 pounds)
¾ pound small white onions, halved lengthwise
3 bacon slices, chopped
an 8-rib pork rib roast (about 4½ pounds)
2 garlic cloves, sliced thin
about ¼ cup small leaf clusters from fresh
    rosemary sprigs
¼ cup water
1 tablespoon chopped fresh parsley leaves

Garnish: fresh rosemary and parsley sprigs

Preheat oven to 350° F.
In a large roasting pan combine carrots and onions
and sprinkle with bacon.
Trim fat on pork roast to ¼ inch thick. With a
paring knife make shallow slits in fat about 1 inch
apart and in each insert a garlic slice and a rosemary
leaf cluster. Season roast with salt and freshly ground
black pepper and arrange, fat side up, on vegetables.
Roast pork and vegetables 1 hour and 20 minutes, or
until pork registers 160° F. on a meat thermometer.
Transfer pork to a platter and let stand 15 minutes.
Pour off fat from pan. To pan with vegetables add
water and cook over high heat, stirring to loosen
brown bits, until most liquid is evaporated. Toss
vegetables with parsley.
Arrange vegetables on platter with pork and garnish with rosemary and parsley sprigs. Serves 6.

PHOTO ON PAGE 32

Roast Pork Loin with
Shiitake and Leek Compote

1 large leek (white and pale green
    parts only)
a 1-pound center-cut boneless pork loin
1 tablespoon plus 1 teaspoon chopped fresh
    parsley leaves
1 teaspoon unsalted butter or
    olive oil
½ pound fresh *shiitake* mushrooms,
    stems discarded and caps cut into
    ½-inch slices
½ teaspoon salt
½ cup dry red wine
½ cup beef broth

Garnish: fresh parsley sprigs

Cut leek crosswise into ½-inch slices and in a
bowl soak in water to cover, agitating occasionally
to dislodge any sand, 5 minutes. Lift leek out of
water and drain in a colander.
Trim any fat from pork. Season pork with salt and
pepper and pat with 1 tablespoon chopped parsley.
In a 10-inch oven-proof non-stick or cast-iron skillet
heat butter or oil over moderately high heat until hot
but not smoking and brown pork loin, turning it.
Transfer pork to a plate.
Preheat oven to 425° F.
In fat remaining in skillet cook mushrooms and
leek with salt over moderately high heat, stirring
occasionally, until liquid mushrooms give off is
evaporated, about 5 minutes. Add red wine and beef
broth and bring to a boil. Put pork on vegetables in
skillet and roast in middle of oven 40 minutes, or
until a thermometer inserted in center of pork
registers 160° F.
Transfer pork to a cutting board and let stand 10
minutes. If vegetable compote is too liquid, cook
over high heat, stirring occasionally, until almost all
liquid is evaporated. Stir remaining teaspoon chopped parsley into compote.
Slice pork thin and serve, garnished with parsley,
with compote. Serves 4.

Each serving: 216 calories,
8 grams fat (33% of calories from fat)

PHOTO ON PAGES 86 AND 87

Grilled Garlic Lime Pork Tenderloin

For marinade
6 large garlic cloves, chopped
2 tablespoons soy sauce
2 tablespoons grated fresh gingerroot
2 teaspoons Dijon mustard
⅓ cup fresh lime juice
½ cup olive oil
cayenne to taste

4 pork tenderloins (about ¾ pound each),
  trimmed

Accompaniment: jalapeño onion marmalade
  (recipe follows)

Make marinade:
In a blender or small food processor blend marinade ingredients with salt and pepper to taste.

In a large sealable plastic bag combine pork with marinade. Seal bag, pressing out excess air, and put in a shallow baking dish. *Marinate pork, chilled, turning occasionally, at least 1 day and up to 2 days.*
Prepare grill.

Let pork stand at room temperature about 30 minutes before grilling. Remove pork from marinade, letting excess drip off, and grill on an oiled rack set 5 to 6 inches over glowing coals, turning every 5 minutes, until a meat thermometer registers 160° F., 15 to 20 minutes.

Transfer meat to a cutting board and let stand 5 minutes before slicing.

Serve pork with onion marmalade. Serves 6.

PHOTO ON PAGE 65

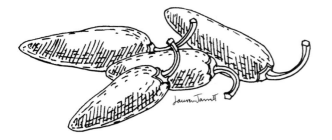

Jalapeño Onion Marmalade

1¼ pounds red or yellow onions, chopped fine
  (about 4 cups)
3 tablespoons olive oil
2 fresh *jalapeño* chilies, seeded and minced
  (wear rubber gloves)
2 tablespoons honey or sugar
3 to 4 tablespoons red-wine vinegar
¼ cup water

In a large heavy skillet cook onions in oil with salt and pepper to taste over moderate heat, stirring, until softened. Add *jalapeños* and cook, stirring, 1 minute. Add honey or sugar and cook, stirring, 1 minute. Add vinegar and simmer, stirring, until almost all liquid is evaporated. Add water and simmer, stirring, until mixture is slightly thickened and onions are very tender, about 10 minutes. Season marmalade with salt and pepper. *Marmalade may be made 2 days ahead and chilled, covered. Reheat marmalade before serving.* Makes about 2 cups.

Jalapeño Honey Mustard Pork Kebabs

2 tablespoons Dijon mustard
1 tablespoon honey
1 large garlic clove, minced and mashed
  to a paste with ¼ teaspoon salt
1 tablespoon fresh lemon juice
1 fresh or pickled *jalapeño* chili, seeded and
  minced (wear rubber gloves)
1 pork tenderloin (about ¾ pound), trimmed
  and cut crosswise into 1½-inch pieces

Accompaniment if desired: lemon, rosemary, and
  toasted walnut couscous (recipe follows)

Prepare grill.
In a bowl whisk together mustard, honey, garlic paste, lemon juice, *jalapeño,* and salt and pepper to taste and reserve 1 tablespoon of marinade in a small bowl for basting kebabs.

Add pork to marinade remaining in bowl. Toss pork pieces to coat well and marinate 15 minutes.

Thread pork onto two 10-inch metal skewers and grill on an oiled rack set 5 to 6 inches over glowing coals 5 minutes. Turn kebabs and baste with reserved marinade. Grill kebabs, turning and basting them, 10 to 15 minutes more, or until pork is cooked through and registers 160° F. on a meat thermometer. (Alternatively, pork kebabs may be grilled in a hot well-seasoned ridged grill pan over moderately high heat.)

Serve kebabs with couscous. Serves 2.

Lemon, Rosemary, and Toasted Walnut Couscous

⅓ cup finely chopped shallot or onion
1 tablespoon butter
1 cup water
⅔ cup couscous
1 teaspoon freshly grated lemon zest
1½ teaspoons minced fresh rosemary leaves or
    ½ teaspoon crumbled dried rosemary
¼ cup walnuts, toasted lightly and
    chopped fine
2 teaspoons fresh lemon juice, or to taste

In a small heavy saucepan cook shallot or onion in butter over moderately low heat, stirring, until softened. Add water and bring to a boil.

Stir in couscous, zest, and rosemary and cover pan. Remove pan from heat and let stand 5 minutes. Fluff couscous with a fork and stir in walnuts, lemon juice, and salt and pepper to taste. Serves 2.

Ham with Apple Mustard Glaze

a 12- to 14-pound shankless skinless
    smoke-cured ham*
whole cloves for studding ham
½ cup apple jelly
2 tablespoons Dijon mustard

Accompaniments
assorted relishes such as pickled watermelon
    rind** and pickled bell peppers**
brandied fruits**

*available at many butcher shops and by mail
    order from Citarella, 2135 Broadway,
    New York, NY 10023, tel. (212) 874-0383

**available by mail order from Maison Glass
    Delicacies, tel. (800) 822-5564 or, in
    New York City, (212) 755-3316

Preheat oven to 350° F.

Score top of ham into diamonds and stud center of each diamond with a clove. On a rack in a roasting pan bake ham in middle of oven 1½ hours.

In a small saucepan heat jelly over moderate heat, stirring, until melted and smooth. Remove saucepan from heat and stir in mustard. Spread glaze evenly on top of baked ham and bake 35 minutes more.

Transfer ham to a platter and let stand 15 minutes. Serve ham with relishes and brandied fruits. Serves 8 with leftovers.

PHOTO ON PAGE 85

LAMB

Lamb Chops with Olive Salsa

½ teaspoon dried oregano, crumbled
1 tablespoon plus 1 teaspoon fresh lemon juice
2 teaspoons olive oil
four 1-inch-thick rib lamb chops
    (about 1 pound total)
½ cup Kalamata or other brine-cured black olives,
    pitted and chopped coarse
1 plum tomato, seeded and diced
¼ cup diced red onion
1 tablespoon chopped fresh parsley leaves
½ teaspoon freshly grated lemon zest

Preheat broiler.

On a small plate stir together oregano, 1 tablespoon lemon juice, and 1 teaspoon olive oil. Dip both sides of lamb chops in mixture to coat and put on rack of a broiling pan, seasoning both sides of chops with salt and pepper.

In a bowl stir together olives, tomato, onion, parsley, zest, remaining teaspoon lemon juice, remaining teaspoon oil, and salt and pepper to taste.

Broil lamb chops 2 inches from heat 4 to 5 minutes on each side for medium-rare meat.

Spoon olive salsa over lamb chops. Serves 2.

Broiled Spiced Lamb with Gingered Mint Pesto

two 2-pound boneless top rounds of lamb
1 tablespoon ground cardamom
2 teaspoons salt
¾ cup gingered mint pesto (recipe follows)
4 teaspoons white-wine vinegar
6 tablespoons plain yogurt
2 to 3 tablespoons hot water

Let lamb stand at room temperature 30 minutes. In a small bowl stir together cardamom, salt, and pepper to taste.

Preheat broiler.

Pat lamb dry with paper towels and rub both sides with cardamom mixture. Broil lamb on rack of a broiler pan set 6 inches from heat 14 minutes on each side for medium-rare. Transfer lamb to a cutting board and let stand 10 minutes.

In a bowl whisk together pesto, vinegar, yogurt, and 2 tablespoons hot water, adding additional hot water if necessary to reach desired consistency.

Carve lamb across the grain into ½-inch-thick slices and serve with pesto. Serves 6 to 8.

Gingered Mint Pesto

2½ cups packed fresh mint leaves, washed well
    and spun dry
1½ tablespoons minced peeled fresh gingerroot
⅓ cup salted roasted cashews
½ cup olive oil
1 large garlic clove, minced
¼ teaspoon sugar

In a food processor blend together all ingredients with salt and pepper to taste until smooth. *Pesto keeps, surface covered with plastic wrap, chilled, 1 week.* Makes about 1 cup.

Spice-Rubbed Lamb Chops with Roasted Tomatoes

3 plum tomatoes, cut lengthwise into
    ¼-inch-thick slices
3 teaspoons olive oil
two ¾- to 1-inch-thick shoulder lamb chops
    (8 to 10 ounces each)

2 teaspoons ground cumin
½ teaspoon coarse salt
½ teaspoon freshly ground black pepper

Preheat oven to 450° F. and lightly oil a small baking pan.

Arrange tomatoes in one layer in prepared pan and brush with 1 teaspoon oil. Roast tomatoes in middle of oven 20 minutes, or until browned lightly, and keep warm.

Pat lamb chops dry. In a small dish stir together cumin, salt, and pepper and rub mixture on both sides of lamb chops.

In a 9-inch heavy non-stick skillet heat remaining 2 teaspoons oil over moderate heat until hot but not smoking and cook lamb chops 3 to 5 minutes on each side for medium-rare meat. Transfer lamb chops to 2 plates and serve with roasted tomatoes. Serves 2.

Osso Buco of Lamb Shanks with
Tomatoes and Garlic

2 tablespoons olive oil
4 lamb shanks (about 1 pound each), cut
    crosswise into 1½-inch-thick pieces by butcher
10 large garlic cloves, crushed
1½ pounds plum tomatoes, seeded and chopped
½ cup shredded fresh basil leaves
¼ cup water
1 teaspoon salt

Accompaniment: white bean purée
    (recipe follows)

In a 6- to 8-quart heavy kettle heat oil over moderately high heat until hot but not smoking and brown lamb shanks well, turning occasionally, about 10 minutes.

Scatter garlic cloves, tomatoes, and shredded basil over shanks and add water, salt, and freshly ground black pepper to taste.

Simmer (braise) *osso buco,* covered, over moderately low heat 1½ hours, or until very tender. *Osso buco may be made 2 days ahead. Cool completely before chilling, covered.*

Serve *osso buco* with bean purée. Serves 4 to 6.

White Bean Purée

1 pound dried *cannellini* or Great Northern beans,
  picked over
¼ cup olive oil
6 garlic cloves
1 tablespoon minced fresh tarragon leaves
5 cups water
2½ teaspoons salt

In a large bowl soak beans overnight in cold water
to cover by 2 inches and drain.

In a 6-quart heavy kettle cover beans with water
and bring to a boil. Drain beans in a colander.

In kettle combine beans, oil, garlic, tarragon, and
5 cups water and simmer, covered, 1 hour more, or
until beans are very tender.

Drain beans, reserving cooking liquid. In a food
processor purée beans in 2 batches, adding ¼ to ½
cup reserved cooking liquid and salt and pepper to
taste to each batch, until smooth. Serves 6.

Grilled Leg of Lamb with Hot Red Pepper Relish

a 7- to 8-pound leg of lamb, trimmed of excess
  fat, boned, and butterflied by butcher
  (4 to 4¾ pounds boneless)
2 onions, chopped
6 large garlic cloves,
  chopped
¾ cup red-wine vinegar
½ cup honey
⅓ cup Worcestershire sauce

Accompaniment: hot red pepper relish
  (recipe follows)

Cut lamb into 2 pieces where there is a natural
separation in meat and put each piece into a large
sealable plastic bag.

In a food processor purée all remaining ingredients (except relish) until smooth and divide marinade
evenly between plastic bags. Seal bags, pressing out
excess air, and put in a shallow baking pan. *Marinate lamb, chilled, turning bags once or twice, at
least 8 hours or overnight.*

Prepare grill.

Discard marinade and grill lamb on an oiled rack
set 5 to 6 inches over glowing coals 7 to 10 minutes
on each side for medium-rare. Transfer lamb to a
cutting board and let stand 10 minutes.

Serve lamb, thinly sliced across the grain, with
relish. Serves 8.

PHOTO ON PAGE 54

Hot Red Pepper Relish

2 pounds red bell peppers, chopped fine
  (about 4 cups)
2 onions, chopped (about 2 cups)
2 cups cider vinegar
¾ cup sugar
2 teaspoons mustard seeds
2 teaspoons salt
1 teaspoon crushed dried hot red
  pepper flakes

In a heavy saucepan stir together ingredients and
simmer, stirring occasionally, about 1 hour, or until
reduced to about 3 cups. *Relish may be made 1
month ahead and chilled, covered.*

Serve relish chilled or at room temperature.
Makes about 3 cups.

139

Rosemary-Roasted Buffalo Tenderloin
with Gorgonzola Butter

¼ pound Gorgonzola cheese, softened
½ stick (¼ cup) unsalted butter, softened
3 tablespoons olive oil
a 3½-pound buffalo tenderloin*, cut crosswise
    into eight to ten 1¼-inch-thick steaks
¼ cup Dijon mustard
¾ cup packed fresh rosemary leaves, chopped

*available at some butcher shops and by mail
    order from Denver Buffalo Company,
    tel. (800) 289-2833 or (303) 831-1299

Discard Gorgonzola rind and in a small bowl stir
together cheese and butter until smooth. On a sheet
of plastic wrap form Gorgonzola butter into a log
about 4 inches long. *Chill log, wrapped in plastic
wrap, until firm, at least 1 hour. Butter may be made
1 week ahead.*

Preheat oven to 450° F.

In a 12-inch heavy skillet (preferably cast-iron)
heat 1½ tablespoons oil over moderately high heat
until hot but not smoking and sear half of steaks
until browned, about 2 minutes on each side,
transferring to a shallow baking pan. Sear remaining
steaks in remaining 1½ tablespoons oil in same
manner.

When steaks are just cool enough to handle,
spread tops and sides with mustard and sprinkle with
rosemary and salt and freshly ground black pepper to
taste. Roast steaks in middle of oven 8 minutes for
medium-rare (coating should just begin to brown).
Transfer steaks to a cutting board and let stand about
3 minutes. Cut butter into about 20 thin slices.

Cut each steak in half horizontally. Tuck a butter
slice between steak halves and top steaks with
another butter slice. Serves 8 generously.

POULTRY

Spiced Poussins

2 tablespoons cuminseed
a 3-inch cinnamon stick, broken
    into pieces
10 whole cloves
¼ cup paprika
¾ teaspoon cayenne
twelve ¾-pound *poussins** (baby chickens) or
    three 3-pound chickens, quartered
3 garlic cloves, chopped and mashed to a paste
    with 1 teaspoon salt
1 tablespoon freshly grated lemon zest
2 tablespoons fresh lemon juice
2 tablespoons olive oil
½ stick (¼ cup) unsalted butter
2 tablespoons chopped fresh parsley leaves

Garnish: parsley sprigs

*available at some butcher shops

With a mortar and pestle or in an electric spice
grinder grind cuminseed, cinnamon, and cloves and
in a small bowl mix with paprika, cayenne, and salt
to taste. In a non-aluminum container large enough
to hold chickens stir together garlic paste, zest,
lemon juice, oil, and 2 tablespoons spice mixture
(reserving remainder) to make marinade.

Rinse chickens and pat dry with paper towels. Put
chickens in container and rub with marinade to coat.
Marinate chickens, covered and chilled, at least 2
hours or overnight.

Preheat oven to 450° F.

Put half of chickens in each of 2 large roasting
pans. Brush chickens with any marinade left in
container and season with salt. If using *poussins,*
truss and arrange breast sides up (they should fit
without touching). If using chicken quarters, arrange
skin sides up. Sprinkle chickens with reserved spice
mixture.

Roast chickens in upper and lower thirds of oven
20 minutes. In a small saucepan melt butter. Brush
chickens with butter and sprinkle with chopped parsley. Switch pans between upper and lower racks and
roast chickens 20 to 30 minutes more, or until a meat
thermometer inserted in fleshy part of a thigh
registers 175° F. and juices run clear when thigh is
pierced with a skewer.

Serve chickens warm or at room temperature and
garnish with parsley sprigs. Serves 12 as part of a
buffet.

PHOTO ON PAGE 38

Poached Chicken Breasts with Arugula Pesto Sauce

For arugula pesto sauce
3 cups packed arugula (about ¾ pound),
    washed well and spun dry
⅓ cup pine nuts, toasted golden and cooled
½ cup freshly grated Parmesan
½ teaspoon salt
1 large garlic clove, chopped
3 tablespoons olive oil
¼ cup hot water plus additional if desired

3 cups chicken broth
2 cups water
3 whole boneless skinless chicken breasts
    (about 1½ pounds), halved

Make arugula pesto sauce:
In a food processor pulse together all sauce ingredients except oil and water until arugula is chopped fine. With motor running add oil in a stream, blending mixture until smooth. *Sauce may be made up to this point 1 week ahead and chilled, its surface covered with plastic wrap. Bring sauce to room temperature to continue.* Stir in ¼ cup hot water plus additional for thinner consistency if desired.

In a 6-quart saucepan bring broth and water to a boil. Add chicken and simmer, covered, 9 minutes. Remove pan from heat and let chicken stand in cooking liquid, covered, until cooked through, about 20 minutes. *Chicken may be poached 1 day ahead, cooled completely, uncovered, in cooking liquid, and chilled, covered. Bring chicken to room temperature to continue.* Drain chicken and slice ¼ inch thick. Serve chicken with sauce. Serves 6.

Cold Poached Chicken with Chinese Garlic Sauce

For chicken
2 cups water
four ¼-inch-thick slices fresh gingerroot
¼ cup Scotch
1 whole boneless skinless chicken breast
    (about ½ pound)
For Chinese garlic sauce
1 tablespoon soy sauce
2 garlic cloves, minced

1½ teaspoons rice vinegar (not seasoned)
1¼ teaspoons sugar
1 teaspoon Asian chili oil, or 1 teaspoon Asian
    sesame oil plus Tabasco to taste

Garnish: 3 tablespoons chopped fresh coriander
    sprigs

Poach chicken:
In a 1½-quart saucepan bring water to a boil with gingerroot, Scotch, and salt to taste. Add chicken and simmer, covered, 12 minutes, or until just cooked through. Transfer chicken with tongs to a bowl and chill, covered, 20 minutes.
Make sauce while chicken is cooling:
In a bowl stir together sauce ingredients until sugar is dissolved.
Halve chicken and cut across grain into thin slices. Spoon sauce over chicken and sprinkle with coriander. Serves 2.

Grilled Chicken with Tomato and Bread Salad

For salad
½ pound crusty peasant-style bread, torn into
    bite-size pieces (about 6 cups)
3 large vine-ripened tomatoes (about 1½ pounds),
    cut into ¾-inch pieces
¾ cup finely chopped inner (very pale green)
    celery ribs and leaves
⅓ cup small brine-cured black olives such as
    Gaeta or Niçoise, halved and pitted
¼ cup finely chopped red onion
2 tablespoons drained capers
2 to 3 tablespoons red-wine vinegar
2 garlic cloves, minced and mashed to a paste
    with ½ teaspoon salt
⅓ cup extra-virgin olive oil
For chicken
3 whole boneless skinless chicken breasts
    (about 1½ pounds), halved
vegetable oil for brushing chicken

1 cup fresh basil leaves, torn into pieces

Garnish: whole celery leaves

Make salad:
Preheat broiler.
On a large baking sheet spread bread in one layer
and toast under broiler about 4 inches from heat until pale golden, about 3 minutes on each side. Cool
bread. *Bread may be toasted 2 days ahead and kept
in a sealable bag at room temperature.*
In a bowl toss together bread, tomatoes, chopped
celery, olives, onion, and capers. In a blender or
small food processor blend together vinegar, garlic
paste, olive oil, and salt and pepper to taste until
smooth and drizzle over salad. Toss salad well and
let stand at room temperature while grilling chicken.
Grill chicken:
Prepare grill.
Brush chicken with vegetable oil and season with
salt and pepper. Grill chicken on a rack set 5 to 6
inches over glowing coals 4 to 5 minutes on each
side, or until just cooked through. (Alternatively,
chicken may be grilled in 2 batches in a hot well-
seasoned ridged grill pan over moderately high
heat.) Transfer chicken to a cutting board and cool.

Stir basil into salad. Slice chicken on the diagonal
and serve with salad. Garnish each serving with
whole celery leaves. Serves 6.

PHOTO ON PAGE 58

Malaysian-Style Chicken Curry

6 shallots, chopped
4 large garlic cloves, chopped
a 1-inch piece fresh gingerroot, peeled and
    chopped
2 tablespoons water
3 whole boneless chicken breasts with skin
    (about 2¼ pounds), halved
2 tablespoons vegetable oil
2 tablespoons curry powder
a 14-ounce can unsweetened coconut milk*
1½ cups chicken broth
a 3-inch fresh *jalapeño* chili, slit in 4 places
1 cinnamon stick
1 whole clove
1 star anise
⅓ cup coarsely chopped fresh coriander

Accompaniment: cooked rice

*available at many Asian markets, specialty
    foods shops, and supermarkets

In a food processor chop fine shallots, garlic, and
gingerroot. Add water and purée to a paste.
Pat chicken dry with paper towels and season with
salt. In a large heavy casserole heat oil over moderately high heat until hot but not smoking and brown
chicken in 2 batches, transferring with tongs as
browned to a large plate. Reduce heat to moderately
low. Add shallot paste and cook, stirring, 1 minute.
Add curry powder and cook, stirring, 1 minute. Add
chicken with any juices accumulated on plate and
remaining ingredients except coriander and simmer,
covered and turning chicken once, until cooked
through, about 15 minutes.
Transfer chicken to plate with tongs and boil
sauce gently, stirring occasionally, until thickened,
about 5 minutes. Discard *jalapeño*, cinnamon stick,
clove, and star anise and season sauce with salt. Add
chicken and coriander and serve over rice. Serves 6.

Chicken and Mushroom Marsala

3 whole boneless chicken breasts with skin
    (about 2¼ pounds), halved
1½ tablespoons olive oil
3½ tablespoons unsalted butter
1 onion, sliced thin
¾ pound mushrooms, sliced thin
½ cup Marsala
1 cup chicken broth
2 tablespoons minced fresh parsley leaves

Pat chicken dry and season with salt and pepper. In a large heavy skillet heat oil and 1½ tablespoons butter over moderately high heat until hot but not smoking and brown chicken in 2 batches, transferring with tongs to a large plate as browned.

Discard all but 1 tablespoon fat from skillet and sauté onion and mushrooms, stirring occasionally, until liquid mushrooms give off is evaporated. Add Marsala and cook mixture, stirring, until Marsala is almost evaporated. Add broth and chicken with any juices that have accumulated on plate and simmer, turning chicken once, until cooked through, about 15 minutes. Transfer chicken with tongs to a platter.

Simmer mushroom sauce until liquid is reduced to about ½ cup. Remove skillet from heat and stir in remaining 2 tablespoons butter and salt and pepper to taste, stirring until butter is just incorporated. Spoon mushroom sauce around chicken and sprinkle with parsley. Serves 6.

Sautéed Worcestershire Chicken

1 whole boneless chicken breast with skin
    (about ¾ pound), halved
2 teaspoons olive oil
1 garlic clove, minced
2 tablespoons Worcestershire sauce
1 tablespoon balsamic vinegar
½ cup low-salt chicken broth
1½ teaspoons finely chopped fresh oregano, or
    ½ teaspoon dried, crumbled
¼ teaspoon fresh lemon juice

Pat chicken dry and place between 2 sheets of plastic wrap. With a meat pounder flatten chicken lightly to about ½-inch thickness and season with salt and pepper.

In a large non-stick skillet heat oil over moderate heat and cook chicken, skin sides down, 6 minutes on each side. Add garlic, Worcestershire sauce, vinegar, broth, and oregano and simmer until chicken is cooked through, about 4 minutes. Transfer chicken with tongs to a platter.

Simmer sauce until reduced to about ¼ cup. Add lemon juice and salt and pepper to taste and pour sauce over chicken. Serves 2.

Provençal Chicken Breasts with Rosemary Orzo

3 whole boneless chicken breasts with skin
    (about 2¼ pounds), halved
2 tablespoons olive oil
½ cup dry white wine
2 large garlic cloves, minced
white part of 4 leeks, halved lengthwise, sliced
    ¼ inch thick crosswise, washed well,
    and drained
2 cups chicken broth
a 28- to 32-ounce can whole tomatoes,
    drained and chopped
1 teaspoon freshly grated orange zest
1 cup drained Niçoise or Kalamata olives

Accompaniment: rosemary *orzo* (recipe follows)

Pat chicken dry with paper towels and season with salt and pepper. In a large heavy flameproof casserole heat oil over moderately high heat until hot but not smoking and brown chicken in 2 batches, transferring with tongs as browned to a large plate.

Add wine to casserole and boil, scraping up browned bits, until almost evaporated. Add garlic, leeks, broth, tomatoes, zest, and chicken with any juices accumulated on plate and simmer, covered, turning chicken once, until chicken is cooked through, about 15 minutes. Transfer chicken to a platter.

Add olives to tomato mixture and boil sauce until thickened slightly. Season sauce with salt and pepper. Serve chicken with sauce and rosemary *orzo*. Serves 6.

Rosemary Orzo

1 pound *orzo* (rice-shaped pasta)
3 tablespoons extra-virgin olive oil
1 tablespoon finely chopped fresh rosemary
    leaves

Bring a 6-quart saucepan of salted water to a boil and cook *orzo* until tender, about 10 minutes. Drain *orzo* well and in a large bowl toss with oil, rosemary, and salt and pepper to taste. Serves 6.

Grilled Tandoori-Spiced Chicken Breasts over Mesclun Salad

For marinade
1 small onion, chopped
3 garlic cloves, chopped
a 1-inch piece fresh gingerroot, peeled
    and chopped
2 tablespoons fresh lemon juice
1 tablespoon water
½ cup plain yogurt
2 teaspoons ground coriander
1 teaspoon ground cumin
1 teaspoon salt
½ teaspoon ground turmeric
¼ teaspoon cayenne
⅛ teaspoon each ground mace, cloves,
    cinnamon, and nutmeg

3 whole boneless skinless chicken breasts
    (about 1½ pounds), halved
1½ tablespoons white-wine vinegar

⅓ cup olive oil
10 cups packed mesclun (mixed baby greens,
    about ½ pound)

Make marinade:

In a blender or small food processor grind onion with garlic, gingerroot, lemon juice, and water to form a paste. In a bowl stir together onion paste and remaining marinade ingredients.

With a sharp paring knife make three ½-inch-deep diagonal cuts in each chicken breast half, being careful not to cut all the way through. Rub chicken with marinade, rubbing it into cuts. In a large resealable plastic bag marinate chicken, chilled, overnight.

Prepare grill.

Grill chicken on an oiled rack 5 to 6 inches over glowing coals until cooked through, about 7 minutes on each side, and transfer to a platter. Let chicken stand while preparing salad.

In a large bowl whisk together vinegar and salt and pepper to taste and add oil in a stream, whisking until emulsified. Add mesclun and toss lightly.

Slice chicken ¼ inch thick and serve over salad. Serves 6.

Orange Braised Chicken Thighs with Green Olives

4 chicken thighs with skin
2 teaspoons olive oil
3 large garlic cloves, minced
1 medium onion, sliced thin
½ teaspoon ground cumin
½ cup fresh orange juice
1 tablespoon fresh lemon juice
⅓ cup small pitted green olives

Rinse chicken and pat dry. Season chicken with salt and pepper. In a heavy skillet heat oil over moderately high heat until hot but not smoking and brown chicken, transferring as browned to a plate.

Pour off all but about 1 tablespoon fat from pan. Reduce heat to moderate and in skillet cook garlic, stirring, until it begins to turn golden. Add onion and cook, stirring, until pale golden. Stir in cumin, citrus juices, and salt and pepper to taste and add chicken and olives. Simmer chicken, covered, 25 minutes, or until tender. Serves 2.

Smoked Chicken and Sun-Dried Tomato Sandwiches with Basil Olive Pesto

3 ounces dried tomatoes (about ¾ cup),
    not packed in oil
a long loaf (about 20 inches) French or
    Italian bread
about ½ cup basil olive pesto (recipe follows)
6 to 8 ounces smoked chicken breast, sliced thin
½ bunch arugula, trimmed, washed well, and
    spun dry (about 1 cup)

In a heatproof bowl pour enough boiling water over tomatoes to cover and let stand 20 to 30 minutes, or until soft. Drain tomatoes and pat dry.

Cut loaf diagonally into 4 pieces and halve each piece horizontally. Spread pesto on cut sides of bread and make 4 sandwiches with chicken, tomatoes, and arugula. Makes 4 sandwiches.

PHOTO ON PAGE 51

Basil Olive Pesto

1 large garlic clove
1 cup packed fresh basil leaves, washed well
    and spun dry
1 cup packed fresh parsley leaves (preferably
    flat-leaf) washed well and spun dry
⅓ cup pine nuts
¼ cup olive oil
¼ cup Kalamata or other brine-cured black
    olives, pitted and chopped fine

To a food processor with motor running add garlic and blend until minced. Add basil, parsley, and nuts and blend well. Add oil and blend until smooth. Transfer to a bowl and stir in olives. *Pesto may be made 5 days ahead and chilled, its surface covered tightly with plastic wrap.*

Bring pesto to room temperature before using. Makes about ¾ cup.

Roasted Chicken Legs with Jalapeño and Tomato

1 tablespoon olive oil
2 teaspoons fresh lime juice
2 whole chicken legs (about 1 pound total)
2 small plum tomatoes, cut into ½-inch slices
2 *jalapeño* chilies, seeded, if desired, and cut into
    ¼-inch slices (wear rubber gloves)
1 small onion, cut into ¼-inch slices
1 garlic clove, sliced thin
½ cup low-salt chicken broth

Preheat oven to 450° F.

In a bowl stir together oil and lime juice. Add chicken legs and toss to coat. Arrange chicken legs, skin sides up, in a roasting pan and season with salt and pepper.

To oil mixture remaining in bowl add tomatoes, chilies, onion, garlic, and salt to taste and toss well. Spread vegetable mixture around chicken legs in one layer and roast in upper third of oven 30 minutes, or until chicken is cooked through.

Transfer chicken to a platter and keep warm, covered with foil. To vegetables in pan add broth and boil over moderately high heat, scraping up browned bits, until sauce thickens slightly, 2 to 3 minutes. Serve chicken with sauce and vegetables. Serves 2.

ASSORTED FOWL

Roasted Cornish Hens with Chili Butter

2 tablespoons unsalted butter, softened
2½ teaspoons chili powder
½ teaspoon fresh lemon juice
¼ teaspoon cayenne
¼ teaspoon salt
a pinch sugar
two 1½-pound Cornish hens, split lengthwise

Preheat oven to 450° F.

In a bowl stir together butter, chili powder, lemon juice, cayenne, salt, and sugar. Rinse and pat hens dry and arrange, skin sides up, on rack of a broiler pan. Loosen skin near breastbones and rub about 1 teaspoon chili butter under skin of each breast. Rub remaining chili butter on skin and roast hens in middle of oven until juices run clear when fleshy part of a thigh is pierced, about 25 minutes. Serves 2.

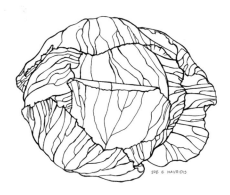

Braised Pheasant with Red Cabbage Wild Rice

For wild rice
½ cup wild rice
1 cup chicken broth
1 tablespoon olive oil
4 slices bacon
1 small onion, sliced thin
2 cups thinly sliced red cabbage (about ⅙ head)
2 teaspoons red-wine vinegar
For pheasant
a 2-pound pheasant*
1½ cups water
1 bay leaf
½ teaspoon salt
¼ teaspoon black pepper
¼ teaspoon ground allspice
1½ tablespoons olive oil
⅓ cup golden raisins
¼ cup minced shallots (about 3)
¼ cup gin
½ cup dry white wine
1 teaspoon tomato paste
a 3-inch fresh rosemary sprig plus ½ teaspoon
    minced leaves
½ cup halved red and/or green seedless grapes

*available at specialty butcher shops and by mail
    order from D'Artagnan, tel. (800) 327-8246
    or, in New Jersey, (201) 792-0748

Make wild rice:
Preheat oven to 350° F.
In a fine sieve rinse wild rice well and drain. In a
small saucepan bring broth to a simmer. In a small

flameproof casserole sauté rice in olive oil over
moderately high heat, stirring, 1 minute and stir in
hot broth and salt and pepper to taste. Bring mixture
to a boil and bake, covered, in middle of oven 1
hour, or until liquid is absorbed and rice is tender.

While rice is cooking, in a 10-inch skillet cook
bacon over moderate heat until crisp and transfer to
paper towels to drain. Transfer all but 1 tablespoon
drippings to a bowl and reserve. Heat drippings
remaining in skillet over moderately high heat until
hot but not smoking and sauté onion and cabbage,
stirring, until softened. Add vinegar and salt and
pepper to taste and sauté, stirring, 1 minute. Crumble
bacon. Just before serving, stir cabbage mixture and
bacon into wild rice.

Make pheasant while rice is cooking:
Rinse pheasant under cold water and pat dry
inside and out. Cut pheasant into 6 serving pieces,
transferring feet, back, neck, and wing tips to a small
saucepan. To saucepan add water and bay leaf and
simmer, uncovered, 15 to 20 minutes, or until reduced to about ¾ cup. Strain stock through a fine
sieve into a heatproof bowl.

In a small bowl stir together salt, pepper, and
allspice. Pat pheasant dry again and sprinkle evenly
with allspice mixture. In a 10-inch heavy ovenproof
skillet heat oil with 1 tablespoon reserved drippings
over moderately high heat until hot but not smoking
and sauté pheasant until golden, about 5 minutes on
each side. Transfer pheasant to a plate.

In fat remaining in skillet cook raisins and shallots
over moderate heat, stirring, until shallots are
softened. Stir in gin and boil until most is evaporated.
Stir in wine and boil until reduced by about half. Stir
in stock, tomato paste, rosemary sprig, and salt and
pepper to taste and bring sauce to a boil.

Add pheasant to sauce, skin sides down, and
braise, tightly covered, in middle of 350° F. oven
until breast meat is cooked through and tender, about
10 minutes. Transfer breasts to a clean plate and
keep warm, covered. Braise legs and thighs until
cooked through and tender, about 10 minutes more.
Transfer legs and thighs to plate and keep warm,
covered. Stir minced rosemary and grapes into sauce
and boil until slightly thickened, about 1 minute.

Divide pheasant between 2 dinner plates, spoon-
ing sauce over it, and serve with red cabbage wild
rice. Serves 2.

For the following recipe we've selected a 22½-inch kettle grill to cook the turkey for a burnished mahogany-colored bird with tender, moist meat. For a smoky flavor, add wood chips. The chips need to be soaked in water for thirty minutes, drained well, and placed directly on the charcoal briquettes after the coals are ready. Cooking time and results may vary according to the weather and type of grill. (Alternatively, the turkey can be roasted in the oven, following the cooking instructions given in the turkey recipe on page 150.) Do not stuff a turkey that is to be grilled because it is difficult to maintain the steady temperature necessary to adequately cook the stuffing. Lemon halves and herbs (discarded after cooking) enhance the bird's flavor and the pan juices. The three-onion stuffing can be baked separately in your oven.

Grilled Turkey with Cranberry Gravy

1 cup wood chips* (preferably apple, cherry, or
    hickory) if desired
a 12- to 14-pound turkey, neck and giblets
    (excluding liver) reserved for making gravy
2 to 3 lemons, halved
fresh herb sprigs such as sage, parsley,
    and thyme
1 stick (½ cup) unsalted butter, softened
1 cup water
For gravy
a 12-ounce bag fresh or unthawed frozen
    cranberries, picked over
¾ cup sugar
1 cup water
3 tablespoons all-purpose flour
4 cups turkey giblet stock (recipe follows) or
    chicken broth

Garnish: fresh lemon halves and/or slices and
    fresh thyme and flat-leafed parsley sprigs
Accompaniment: three-onion stuffing (page 149)

*available by mail order from Bridge
    Kitchenware Corp., tel. (800) 274-3435 or,
    in New York City, (212) 688-4220

Soak wood chips in water to cover 30 minutes and drain well.

Rinse turkey and pat dry inside and out. Season turkey inside and out with salt and pepper and pack neck cavity loosely with some lemon halves and herbs. Fold neck skin under body and fasten with a skewer. Fill body cavity loosely with remaining lemon halves and herbs and truss turkey.

Put an oiled rack inside a metal roasting pan that will fit inside grill. Spread turkey with butter and put on rack in pan. Add water to pan.

Prepare grill:

Open vents in lid and bottom of grill and put 25 briquettes on 2 opposite sides of bottom (50 briquettes total), leaving middle clear. Position rack with wider openings over briquettes and light briquettes. (They will be ready for cooking as soon as they turn grayish-white in color, 20 to 30 minutes.) Shake excess water off wood chips and put evenly on top of briquettes. When chips begin to smoke, in about 2 minutes, the grill is ready.

Grill turkey on rack in pan in grill, covered, over glowing coals 1 hour. (Do not remove lid during cooking.) Remove lid and add 10 more briquettes on each side. Grill turkey, covered, 1 hour more. Remove lid and add 10 more briquettes on each side. Grill turkey 1 hour more and insert a meat thermometer in fleshy part of a thigh. If thermometer registers 180° F. and juices run clear when thigh is pierced, turkey is done. If turkey is not done, add 10 more briquettes on each side and test for doneness in same manner every 15 minutes.

Transfer turkey to a heated platter, reserving juices in pan, and discard string. Keep turkey warm, covered loosely with foil.

Begin making gravy while grilling turkey:

In a saucepan cook cranberries and sugar over moderately low heat, stirring frequently, until sugar is melted and cranberries burst. In a blender in batches purée cranberry mixture until smooth, transferring to a bowl. *Cranberry mixture may be made 1 day ahead and chilled, covered. Bring mixture to room temperature before proceeding.*

Skim fat from pan juices, reserving 3 tablespoons fat, and deglaze pan with water over moderately high heat, scraping up brown bits. Simmer pan juices 3 minutes, stirring, and reserve off heat. In a saucepan whisk together reserved fat and flour and cook *roux* over moderately low heat, whisking, 3 minutes. Add pan juices and stock or broth in a stream and add cranberry mixture, whisking occasionally. Boil gravy, whisking occasionally, until reduced to about 5 cups, 15 to 20 minutes, and strain through a sieve into a saucepan. Season gravy with salt and pepper and keep warm.

Discard lemon halves and herbs from turkey cavities. Garnish turkey with lemon halves and/or slices and herbs and serve with three-onion stuffing. Serves 8.

PHOTO ON PAGE 79

Turkey Giblet Stock

neck and giblets (excluding liver) from a
   12- to 14-pound turkey
5 cups chicken broth
6 cups water
1 celery rib, chopped
1 carrot, chopped
1 onion, quartered
1 bay leaf
2 fresh flat-leafed parsley sprigs
½ teaspoon dried thyme, crumbled
1 teaspoon whole black peppercorns

In a large deep saucepan bring neck, giblets, broth, water, celery, carrot, and onion to a boil, skimming froth. Add remaining ingredients and cook, uncovered, at a bare simmer 2 hours, or until liquid is reduced to about 6 cups. Strain stock through a fine sieve into a bowl. *Stock may be made 2 days ahead. Cool stock completely, uncovered, and keep chilled or frozen in an airtight container.* Makes about 6 cups.

Three-Onion Stuffing

7 cups ½-inch pieces firm white sandwich bread
   (about 12 slices)
1¼ pounds leeks (about 8 small), halved
   lengthwise and cut crosswise into ½-inch-thick
   pieces (about 5¼ cups)
3 medium red onions, cut into 1-inch pieces
   (about 5½ cups)
12 large shallots (about ½ pound), cut lengthwise
   into sixths
3 large celery ribs, chopped (about 1¼ cups)
3 tablespoons minced garlic (about 10 small
   cloves)
2 tablespoons chopped fresh thyme leaves
1 tablespoon chopped fresh sage leaves
1 cup fresh flat-leafed parsley leaves, washed
   well, spun dry, and chopped
3 tablespoons unsalted butter
3 tablespoons olive oil
1 cup turkey giblet stock (recipe precedes) or
   chicken broth

Preheat oven to 350° F.

In a shallow baking pan spread bread in one layer and bake in middle of oven, stirring occasionally, until golden, 10 to 15 minutes. Transfer bread to a large bowl.

In a bowl of water wash leeks and drain by lifting leeks from water into a colander.

In a large heavy skillet cook leeks, red onions, shallots, celery, garlic, and herbs with salt and pepper to taste in butter and oil over moderate heat, stirring, until onion mixture is softened, about 10 minutes. Add onion mixture to bread with salt and pepper to taste and toss to combine well. Cool stuffing and transfer to a buttered 4-quart baking dish. *Stuffing may be made 1 day ahead and chilled, covered.*

During last 1½ hours of grilling turkey, drizzle stuffing with stock or broth and bake, covered, in middle of oven 1 hour. Bake stuffing, uncovered, 20 to 30 minutes more, or until golden brown. Makes about 14 cups.

*Roast Turkey with Sausage Fennel Stuffing
and Madeira Gravy*

a 12- to 14-pound turkey, neck and giblets
    (excluding liver) reserved for making gravy
sausage fennel stuffing (recipe follows)
1 stick (½ cup) unsalted butter, softened
2 cups turkey giblet stock (page 149) or
    chicken broth
For gravy
1¼ cups Sercial Madeira
½ cup all-purpose flour
4 cups turkey giblet stock or chicken broth

Garnish: fresh small fennel bulbs, quartered with
    fronds attached, fresh small white onions with
    greens attached, fresh thyme sprigs

Preheat oven to 325° F.

Rinse turkey and pat dry inside and out. Season
turkey inside and out with salt and pepper and pack
neck cavity loosely with some stuffing. Fold neck
skin under body and fasten with a skewer. Fill body
cavity loosely with some remaining stuffing and
truss turkey. Transfer remaining stuffing to a buttered 1½- to 2-quart shallow baking dish and reserve,
covered and chilled.

Spread turkey with butter and on a rack in a
roasting pan roast in oven until a meat thermometer
inserted in fleshy part of a thigh registers 180° F. and
juices run clear when thigh is pierced, 3¼ to 4 hours.

During last 1½ hours of roasting, drizzle reserved
stuffing with stock or broth and bake, covered, 1
hour. Bake stuffing, uncovered, 30 minutes more.
Transfer turkey to a heated platter, reserving juices
in roasting pan, and discard string. Keep turkey
warm, covered loosely with foil.

Make gravy:

Skim fat from pan juices, reserving ⅓ cup fat, and
deglaze pan with Madeira over moderately high
heat, scraping up brown bits. Bring Madeira to a boil
and remove pan from heat.

In a saucepan whisk together reserved fat and
flour and cook *roux* over moderately low heat,
whisking, 3 minutes. Add Madeira mixture and stock
or broth in a stream, whisking, and simmer, whisking occasionally, 5 minutes. Season gravy with salt
and pepper and transfer to a heated gravy boat.

Garnish turkey with fennel, onions, and thyme.
Serves 8.

PHOTO ON PAGES 76 AND 77

Sausage Fennel Stuffing

1 pound sweet Italian sausage, casing discarded
½ stick (¼ cup) unsalted butter
2 medium-large onions, chopped fine
1½ pounds fennel bulbs, stalks trimmed flush with
    bulbs and bulbs chopped fine (4½ cups)
2 teaspoons fennel seeds, chopped fine
¼ cup Pernod or other anise-flavored apéritif
2 teaspoons dried thyme, crumbled
2 teaspoons dried tarragon, crumbled
5 cups corn bread for stuffing (recipe follows) or
    packaged corn bread stuffing

In a 10- to 12-inch heavy skillet cook sausage
over moderately high heat, stirring and breaking up
lumps with a fork, until no longer pink. Transfer
sausage with a slotted spoon to a large bowl.

Add butter to fat remaining in skillet and cook
onions, chopped fennel, fennel seeds, and salt to
taste over moderate heat, stirring, until fennel is
softened, about 10 minutes. Add apéritif, thyme, and
tarragon and cook, stirring, until most liquid is
evaporated. Add mixture to sausage with corn bread
or packaged stuffing and toss to combine well.
Season stuffing with salt and pepper and cool completely. *Stuffing may be made 2 days ahead and
chilled, covered.* (To prevent bacterial growth do not
stuff turkey cavities ahead.) Makes about 10 cups,
enough to stuff a 12- to 14-pound turkey with extra
to bake on the side.

Corn Bread for Stuffing

1½ cups yellow cornmeal
1 cup all-purpose flour
1 tablespoon baking powder
1 teaspoon salt
1 cup milk
1 large egg
3 tablespoons unsalted butter,
    melted and cooled

Preheat oven to 425° F. and grease an 8-inch square baking pan.

In a bowl whisk together cornmeal, flour, baking powder, and salt. In a small bowl whisk together milk, egg, and butter and add to cornmeal mixture, stirring only until just combined.

Pour batter into pan and bake in middle of oven 20 to 25 minutes, or until pale golden and a tester comes out clean. Cool corn bread in pan on a rack 5 minutes. Invert corn bread onto rack and cool completely.

Crumble corn bread coarse into a large shallow baking pan. *Let corn bread stand at room temperature until stale, at least 3 hours or overnight.*

Preheat oven to 300° F.

Toast corn bread in middle of oven, stirring occasionally, until dried and golden, about 30 minutes. Makes about 5½ cups.

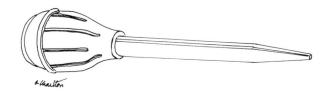

Turkey Breast Braciola

1 large head escarole (about 1½ pounds),
    washed well and drained
3 tablespoons olive oil
1 large onion, chopped
½ cup raisins
1½ cups low-salt chicken broth
⅓ cup freshly grated Parmesan
¼ cup pine nuts, toasted
1 slice homemade-type white bread, minced
    (about ½ cup coarse bread crumbs)
1 skinless boneless turkey breast half
    (2 to 2½ pounds)
¼ pound thinly sliced prosciutto
½ cup dry white wine
2 teaspoons fresh lemon juice

Coarsely chop enough escarole to measure about 7 cups loosely packed and reserve remaining escarole. In a 12-inch skillet heat 2 tablespoons oil over moderately high heat until hot but not smoking and sauté onion, stirring occasionally, until it begins to brown. To onion add chopped escarole and cook, stirring frequently, until wilted. Stir in raisins and ½ cup broth and cook over high heat until most liquid is evaporated. Remove skillet from heat and stir Parmesan, pine nuts, and bread into filling.

Put turkey on a long sheet of plastic wrap. Butterfly turkey breast: Beginning from a long side make a horizontal lengthwise cut almost but not all the way through turkey and spread turkey open to form a larger, thinner piece of meat. Top turkey with another sheet of plastic wrap and pound with a meat mallet or bottom of a heavy skillet until meat measures about 12 by 8 inches, being careful not to make any holes in it.

Discard top sheet of plastic wrap and arrange prosciutto, overlapping slightly, in one layer over turkey. Spread a ½-inch-thick layer of filling over prosciutto, leaving a ½-inch border all around and reserving any remaining filling. Beginning with a long side and using plastic wrap as a guide, roll up turkey and turn it seam side down (discard plastic wrap). Tie rolled turkey with kitchen string lengthwise and then crosswise at 1-inch intervals and season with salt and pepper.

In a 12-inch deep skillet heat remaining tablespoon oil over moderately high heat until hot but not smoking and brown turkey, turning it. Add wine, remaining cup broth, and any remaining filling and braise, covered, over moderately low heat, turning turkey halfway through cooking, 35 minutes. Transfer turkey to a cutting board and cool. Strain braising liquid through a sieve into a small saucepan. Boil liquid until reduced to about ½ cup and skim off foam. Stir in lemon juice and cool sauce completely. *Turkey and sauce may be made 2 days ahead and chilled separately, covered with plastic wrap.*

Discard string from rolled turkey and cut turkey crosswise into ½-inch-thick slices. Shred reserved escarole and in a bowl toss with half of sauce. Arrange escarole on a platter with turkey slices and drizzle turkey with remaining sauce. Serves 12 as part of a buffet.

PHOTO ON PAGES 36 AND 37

CHEESE DISHES

Blue Cheese and Walnut Soufflés and Mesclun with Red Pepper Vinaigrette

For soufflés
¼ cup finely chopped walnuts,
    toasted
4 tablespoons all-purpose flour
3 tablespoons unsalted butter
⅔ cup milk
5 ounces cold Saga blue cheese, rind
    discarded, chopped and softened
    (about 1 cup)
3 large egg yolks
5 large egg whites
For vinaigrette
2 tablespoons Sherry vinegar
¼ cup extra-virgin olive oil
¼ cup finely chopped red bell pepper
¼ cup finely chopped yellow bell pepper

6 cups *mesclun* (mixed baby greens, about
    ½ pound), rinsed and spun dry

Garnish: finely chopped red and yellow bell
    peppers and edible flower petals*

*available at specialty produce markets

Make soufflés:
Preheat oven to 350° F. and generously butter six
½-cup soufflé dishes or custard cups.

In a small bowl stir together walnuts and ½ tablespoon flour. Coat soufflé dishes or custard cups with
walnut mixture, knocking out excess.

In a small heavy saucepan melt butter over low
heat and whisk in remaining 3½ tablespoons flour.
Cook *roux*, whisking constantly, 3 minutes and add
milk in a stream, whisking. Bring mixture to a boil

over moderate heat, whisking, and cook until
thickened, about 30 seconds. Remove pan from heat
and transfer mixture to a bowl. Cool mixture
slightly. Whisk cheese, yolks, and salt and freshly
ground black pepper to taste into milk mixture until
cheese is melted.

In a bowl with an electric mixer beat whites until
they just hold stiff peaks. Stir one third of whites
into cheese mixture to lighten and fold in remaining
whites gently but thoroughly.

Divide soufflé mixture among prepared soufflé
dishes or cups and put in a large baking pan just
large enough to hold them. Add enough hot water to
pan to reach halfway up sides of soufflé dishes or
cups and bake soufflés in middle of oven until
puffed and golden brown, about 25 minutes. Remove
pan from oven and let soufflé dishes or cups stand in
pan 15 minutes. (Soufflés will fall.)

Lightly butter a baking sheet.

Remove soufflé dishes or cups from pan and run a
knife around edge of each dish or cup, carefully
lifting edge of each soufflé slightly to help release it
from bottom. Invert soufflé onto hand and carefully
put, top side up, onto prepared baking sheet. *Soufflés
may be prepared up to this point 2 days ahead and
chilled, covered.*

Increase oven temperature to 425° F.

Bake soufflés in middle of oven until puffed
slightly and heated through, about 5 minutes.

Make vinaigrette while soufflés are baking:

In a small bowl whisk together vinegar and salt
and pepper to taste. Add oil in a stream, whisking,
and whisk until emulsified. Stir in bell peppers. *Vinaigrette may be made 1 day ahead and chilled,
covered. Bring vinaigrette to room temperature and
whisk before proceeding with recipe.*

In a bowl toss *mesclun* with vinaigrette and divide
among 6 salad plates. Arrange soufflés along side of
mesclun and garnish with bell peppers and flowers.
Serves 6.

PHOTO ON PAGE 43

Chipotle Cheese Fondue

½ pound finely diced Gruyère cheese
    (about 2 cups)
½ pound finely diced Emmenthal cheese
    (about 2 cups)
1½ tablespoons cornstarch
2 large garlic cloves, halved
1⅓ cups dry white wine
1 tablespoon fresh lemon juice
2 to 3 tablespoons kirsch
freshly grated nutmeg to taste if desired
3 canned whole *chipotle* chilies in *adobo**, or to
    taste, minced (about 1½ tablespoons)
fried shallots (recipe follows), thinly sliced
scallion greens, and/or crumbled cooked bacon
    for stirring into fondue if desired

Accompaniments
assorted cooked vegetables such as broccoli,
    carrots, pearl onions, and potatoes
breadsticks
cubes of day-old French, Italian, or
    sourdough bread

*available at Hispanic markets, some specialty
    foods shops, and by mail order from
    Adriana's Caravan, tel. (800) 316-0820 or,
    in Brooklyn, NY, (718) 436-8565

In a bowl toss together cheeses and cornstarch.
Rub inside of a heavy 3- to 4-quart saucepan with
garlic halves, leaving garlic in pan, and add wine and
lemon juice. Bring liquid just to a boil and stir in
cheese mixture by handfuls. Bring mixture to a bare
simmer over moderate heat, stirring, and stir in
kirsch, nutmeg, chilies, and pepper to taste. Transfer
fondue to a fondue pot and set over a low flame.
Stir in fried shallots, scallion greens, and/or bacon
if using and serve fondue with accompaniments for
dipping. (Stir fondue often.) Serves 4.

PHOTO ON PAGES 12 AND 13

Fried Shallots

1½ cups thinly sliced shallots (about 8 large)
4 tablespoons vegetable oil

In a heavy 10- to 12-inch skillet cook shallots in
oil over moderately high heat, stirring, until golden
brown. Transfer shallots with a slotted spoon to
paper towels to drain and season with salt. Makes
about ⅔ cup.

CHEESE SANDWICHES

*Grilled Fontina, Salami, and
Roasted Pepper Sandwiches*

4 oval slices pumpernickel bread
4 teaspoons Dijon mustard
3 ounces thinly sliced Genoa salami
a 7-ounce jar roasted red peppers, drained and
    patted dry on paper towels
¼ pound Fontina cheese (preferably Italian),
    sliced thin

Preheat broiler.
On a baking sheet toast both sides of bread about
3 inches from heat until surface is crisp and spread
one side with mustard. Divide salami among toasts
and top with roasted peppers. Cover peppers with
Fontina and broil sandwiches until cheese is melted,
about 1 minute. Serves 4.

153

*Prosciutto and Brie Sandwiches
with Rosemary Fig Confit*

4 *ciabatta* rolls* (about 4 inches square)
   or a long loaf (about 20 inches) French
   or Italian bread
about ½ cup rosemary fig confit (recipe follows)
¼ pound thinly sliced prosciutto
¼ pound Brie cheese, cut into thin slices

*available at some specialty bakeries

With a serrated knife halve rolls horizontally or
cut loaf diagonally into 4 pieces, halving each piece
horizontally.
   Spread cut sides of bread with *confit* and make 4
sandwiches with prosciutto and Brie. Makes 4
sandwiches.

PHOTO ON PAGE 51

Rosemary Fig Confit

1 cup dried Calimyrna figs, chopped fine
½ cup dry white wine
½ cup water
3 tablespoons honey
1 teaspoon chopped fresh rosemary leaves

In a 1½-quart heavy saucepan stir together ingredients and simmer, covered, 20 minutes. Remove lid
and simmer mixture, stirring occasionally, until most
liquid is evaporated and mixture is thickened. In a
food processor coarsely purée fig mixture. *Confit
may be made 5 days ahead and chilled, covered.*
   Bring confit to room temperature before using.
Makes about 1¼ cups.

*Grilled Gorgonzola, Pear, and
Watercress Sandwiches*

4 ounces chilled Gorgonzola cheese (for strong
   flavor) or 6 ounces chilled Saga Blue cheese
   (for milder flavor)
1 firm-ripe pear such as Bartlett or Anjou
four ½-inch-thick slices whole-grain bread
1 cup watercress sprigs (about ½ bunch, coarse
   stems discarded)

Preheat broiler.
   Cut cheese into thin slices. Halve pear lengthwise
and core with a melon-ball cutter. Slice pear thin
crosswise.
   On a baking sheet toast both sides of bread about
3 inches from heat until golden. Divide watercress
among toasts and cover with overlapping pear slices.
Arrange cheese over pear slices and broil sandwiches
until cheese is melted, about 1 minute. Serves 4.

*Toasted Smoked-Mozzarella and
Radicchio Sandwiches*

2 teaspoons olive oil
½ pound *radicchio,* chopped (about 4 cups)
1 teaspoon balsamic or red-wine vinegar
2 tablespoons finely chopped fresh parsley leaves
six ½-inch-thick slices country or Italian bread,
   each about 3 to 4 inches long
1 garlic clove, halved crosswise
about 6 ounces smoked mozzarella cheese, cut
   into thin slices

In a heavy skillet heat oil over moderately high
heat until hot but not smoking and sauté *radicchio*
with vinegar, stirring, until wilted and tender, about
1 to 2 minutes. Season *radicchio* with salt and pepper and stir in parsley. Remove skillet from heat.
   Preheat broiler.
   On a baking sheet toast both sides of bread about
3 inches from heat until golden. Rub one side of
each toast with garlic and season with salt. Divide
radicchio among toasts, spreading evenly, and cover
radicchio with mozzarella. Broil toasts until cheese
is melted, 1 to 2 minutes. Serves 6 as a first course
or light lunch.

EGG DISHES

Scrambled Egg, Potato, and Bacon Tostadas

vegetable oil for frying tortillas
twelve 8-inch corn tortillas
12 slices bacon (about 1 pound)
4 russet (baking) potatoes
¼ cup water
½ stick (¼ cup) unsalted butter
12 large eggs
1 bunch scallions,
   sliced thin

Accompaniments
red and green tomato salsa (recipe follows)
corn and avocado relish (recipe follows)
sour cream
chopped fresh coriander sprigs

In a 10-inch heavy skillet heat ½ inch oil over moderate heat until hot but not smoking and fry corn tortillas, 1 at a time, turning with tongs, until pale golden and crisp, about 1½ minutes. Transfer tortillas as fried with tongs to paper towels to drain and cool completely. *Tortillas may be fried 1 week ahead and kept in an airtight container at room temperature.*

Preheat oven to 350° F.

In a shallow baking pan arrange bacon in one layer and cook in oven, turning occasionally, until crisp. Transfer bacon to paper towels to drain and crumble. *Bacon may be made 1¼ hours ahead and kept warm on baking sheet in turned-off oven.*

Peel potatoes and cut into ½-inch cubes. In a 12-inch non-stick skillet heat water and 2 tablespoons butter over moderate heat until butter is melted. Add potatoes and cook, covered, over moderately low heat 6 minutes. Remove skillet lid and cook potatoes over moderately high heat, stirring occasionally, until golden and tender. *Potatoes may be made 1 hour ahead and kept warm on baking sheet in turned-off oven.*

In a bowl whisk together eggs, scallions, and salt and pepper to taste. In skillet heat remaining 2 tablespoons butter over moderate heat until melted. Add eggs and cook, stirring and breaking up into bite-size pieces, until just cooked through. *Eggs may be made 45 minutes ahead and kept covered.*

Spoon potatoes, bacon, and eggs onto tortillas and serve with accompaniments. Serves 6.

PHOTO ON PAGE 67

Red and Green Tomato Salsa

½ pound green tomatoes or fresh tomatillos
1 pound vine-ripened tomatoes, chopped fine
   (about 2½ cups)
½ cup finely chopped red onion
1 tablespoon fresh lime juice
2 teaspoons salt

If using tomatillos, discard outer husks and rinse tomatillos under warm water.

Chop tomatoes or tomatillos fine (there should be about 1½ cups) and in a bowl stir together with remaining ingredients. Let salsa stand at room temperature 30 minutes. *Salsa may be made 4 hours ahead and chilled, covered.* Makes about 3½ cups.

Corn and Avocado Relish

2 cups fresh corn (cut from about 3 ears)
¾ cup finely chopped onion
¾ cup cider vinegar
2 tablespoons sugar
1½ teaspoons salt
1½ teaspoons dry mustard
2 firm-ripe avocados (preferably California)

In a heavy 2-quart saucepan combine all ingredients except avocados. Boil corn mixture, stirring occasionally, 5 minutes and cool completely. *Corn mixture may be made 1 week ahead and chilled, covered.*

Strain corn mixture through a sieve into a bowl, reserving cooking liquid. Halve, pit, and peel avocados. In a bowl mash 1 avocado half. Finely chop remaining avocado and add to mashed avocado with corn mixture and 2 tablespoons reserved cooking liquid, tossing to combine well. *Relish may be made 1 hour ahead and chilled, its surface covered with plastic wrap.* Makes about 3 cups.

Herbed Ham and Cheddar Frittata

2 scallions, minced
1 garlic clove, minced
1 tablespoon olive oil
4 large eggs
1 teaspoon fresh thyme leaves, minced, or
　¼ teaspoon dried, crumbled
1 teaspoon fresh rosemary leaves, minced, or
　¼ teaspoon dried, crumbled
¼ pound ham steak, chopped, rinsed, and patted
　dry (about ¾ cup)
⅓ cup grated extra-sharp Cheddar
　(about 2 ounces)
1 tablespoon minced fresh parsley leaves

In an 8- or 9-inch flameproof heavy skillet cook scallions and garlic in oil over moderately low heat, stirring, until softened. In a bowl whisk together eggs, thyme, rosemary, and pepper to taste. Add egg mixture to scallion mixture and cook, without stirring, 2 minutes. Add chopped ham and cook, without stirring, 8 minutes, or until edges are set but center is still soft.

While *frittata* is cooking, preheat broiler.

Sprinkle Cheddar on *frittata* and broil about 4 inches from heat until cheese is bubbling, about 1 minute. Sprinkle with parsley and cut into wedges. Serves 2.

ZOE MAVRIDIS

Zucchini and Spinach Frittata

6 teaspoons olive oil
1 zucchini (about ½ pound), cut into ¼-inch dice
1 large bunch spinach, washed well, spun dry,
　and chopped coarse
10 large eggs
1 tablespoon chopped fresh tarragon leaves

In a large non-stick skillet heat 2 teaspoons oil over moderately high heat until hot but not smoking and sauté zucchini until it begins to brown. Add spinach and cook, stirring occasionally, until just wilted. Season mixture with salt and pepper. Remove skillet from heat and cool vegetables slightly.

Preheat oven to 225° F. and grease a large baking sheet.

In a large bowl beat eggs lightly and stir in vegetables, tarragon, and salt and pepper to taste. In a 9-inch heavy omelet pan heat 1 teaspoon oil over moderately low heat until hot but not smoking and add 1 cup egg mixture, tilting pan to distribute evenly. Cook egg mixture until set underneath but still slightly wet in center, 3 to 4 minutes. Slide *frittata* halfway out of pan onto prepared baking sheet and fold second half over to make a half circle. (Eggs will continue to cook from residual heat.) Keep *frittata* warm in oven. Make 3 more *frittate* with remaining oil and egg mixture in same manner. *Keep frittate warm, covered with foil, up to 1 hour.*

Cut each *frittata* into 8 wedges. Makes 32 wedges.

PHOTO ON PAGE 37

Egg Salad and Green Bean Sandwiches

16 green beans, trimmed
6 hard-cooked large eggs, chilled
¼ cup chopped celery
¼ cup chopped sweet onion such as Vidalia,
　Walla Walla, or Maui
¼ cup mayonnaise
1 tablespoon honey Dijon mustard
eight ½-inch-thick slices multigrain bread
　(each about 4 by 2½ inches)

In a small saucepan of boiling salted water cook beans until just tender, about 3 minutes. Drain beans and plunge into a bowl of ice and cold water to stop cooking. Remove beans from water and pat dry with paper towels.

Chop eggs and in a bowl stir together with celery, onion, mayonnaise, mustard, and salt and pepper to taste. Spread egg salad on 4 bread slices and top each sandwich with 4 beans and remaining bread slices. Makes 4 sandwiches.

BREAKFAST DISHES

Plum Streusel Coffeecake

For streusel
1 cup all-purpose flour
½ cup firmly packed light brown sugar
½ cup walnuts
¾ stick (6 tablespoons) unsalted butter, cut
    into pieces and softened
1 teaspoon cinnamon
¼ teaspoon freshly grated nutmeg
For cake batter
1 stick (½ cup) unsalted butter,
    softened
¾ cup granulated sugar
2 large eggs
1 teaspoon vanilla
1¼ cups all-purpose flour

1 teaspoon baking powder
½ teaspoon salt

¾ pound plums (4 to 5 medium), sliced
confectioners' sugar for sifting over cake

Preheat oven to 350° F. and butter and flour a 9-inch round or square baking pan at least 2 inches deep, knocking out excess flour.
Make streusel:
In a food processor pulse together streusel ingredients until combined well and crumbly.
Make cake batter:
In a bowl with an electric mixer beat butter with sugar until light and fluffy and add eggs, 1 at a time, beating well after each addition. Beat in vanilla. Sift in flour with baking powder and salt and beat until just combined.

Spread batter in pan, smoothing top, and arrange plum slices over it in slightly overlapping concentric circles. Sprinkle streusel over plum slices and bake cake in middle of oven 1 hour, or until a tester comes out clean. *Coffeecake may be made 1 week ahead: Cool cake completely in pan on a rack and freeze, wrapped well in plastic wrap and foil. Reheat cake, unwrapped but not thawed, in a preheated 350° F. oven until heated through, 35 to 40 minutes. Cool cake slightly on a rack and sift confectioners' sugar over it. Serve coffeecake warm or at room temperature.*

PHOTO ON PAGE 66

PASTA AND GRAINS

Angel's Hair Pasta with Lemon and Pine Nuts

¾ teaspoon minced garlic
2 tablespoons olive oil
2 tablespoons pine nuts, toasted golden
2 tablespoons fresh lemon juice
1½ teaspoons freshly grated lemon zest
¼ cup minced flat-leafed parsley leaves
¼ pound angel's hair pasta or *cappellini*

Bring a large saucepan of salted water to a boil for pasta.

In a small saucepan cook garlic in oil over moderately low heat, stirring, until softened and transfer mixture to a large bowl. Add pine nuts, crushing them lightly with back of a fork, lemon juice, zest, parsley, and salt and pepper to taste.

Cook pasta in boiling water until *al dente*. Reserve 2 tablespoons cooking water and drain pasta well. Add pasta with reserved cooking water to bowl and toss with lemon mixture until it is absorbed. Serve pasta warm or at room temperature. Serves 2 as a side dish.

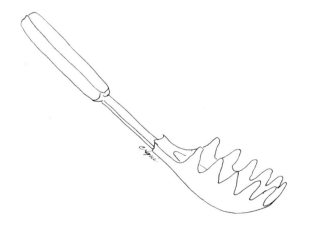

Curried Couscous

2 teaspoons olive oil
½ cup finely chopped onion
1 garlic clove, minced and mashed to a paste
  with a pinch of salt
½ teaspoon curry powder
¾ cup chicken broth
3 tablespoons raisins
½ cup couscous
¼ cup finely chopped fresh mint leaves

In a non-stick skillet heat oil over moderately high heat until hot but not smoking and cook onion with salt to taste, stirring, until lightly browned. Reduce heat to moderate. Add garlic paste and curry powder and cook, stirring, until garlic is pale golden. Remove skillet from heat and keep mixture warm.

In a small saucepan bring broth to a boil. Stir in raisins and couscous and let stand, covered, off heat 5 minutes. Fluff couscous with a fork and transfer to a bowl. Stir in onion mixture, mint, and salt and pepper to taste. Serves 2.

Red, White, and Green Lasagne

2 tablespoons extra-virgin olive oil
3 large red bell peppers, chopped
15 ounces ricotta (about 2 cups)
1½ pounds broccoli, flowerets cut into ¾-inch
  pieces and stems cut into ½-inch dice
2 cups rich winter tomato sauce (recipe follows)
twelve 7- by 3½-inch sheets dry no-boil lasagne
  pasta
10 ounces mozzarella cheese, grated
  (about 2½ cups)
1¼ cups freshly grated Parmesan
  (about 5 ounces)

In a large non-stick skillet heat oil over moderately high heat until hot but not smoking and sauté bell peppers, stirring, until crisp-tender. In a bowl stir together bell peppers and ricotta, stirring until combined well. In a vegetable steamer set over simmering water steam broccoli, covered, until crisp-tender, 3 to 5 minutes, and stir into ricotta mixture with salt and black pepper to taste.

Preheat oven to 375° F.

Pour 1 cup tomato sauce into a baking dish, 13 by 9 by 2 inches (tomato sauce will not cover bottom completely), and cover with 3 lasagne sheets, making sure they do not touch each other. Drop about 1½ cups ricotta mixture by spoonfuls onto pasta and gently spread with back of a spoon. Sprinkle ¾ cup mozzarella and ⅓ cup Parmesan over ricotta mixture and make 2 more layers in same manner, beginning and ending with pasta. Spread remaining cup tomato sauce over pasta, making sure pasta is completely covered, and sprinkle with remaining mozzarella and Parmesan.

Cover dish tightly with foil, tenting slightly to prevent foil from touching top layer, and bake in middle of oven 30 minutes. Remove foil and bake lasagne 10 minutes more, or until top is bubbling. Let lasagne stand 5 minutes before serving. Serves 8 as a main course.

Rich Winter Tomato Sauce

1½ ounces (½ cup packed) dried tomatoes
   (not packed in oil)
1 cup boiling hot water
1 large onion, chopped
   (about 2 cups)
3 garlic cloves, minced
2 tablespoons unsalted butter
a 28- to 32-ounce can whole tomatoes with juice

In a small bowl soak dried tomatoes in boiling water 30 minutes and drain in a sieve. Chop soaked tomatoes coarse.

While dried tomatoes are soaking, in a saucepan cook onion and garlic in butter over moderately low heat, stirring, until softened. Add canned tomatoes with juice, stirring to break up tomatoes, chopped soaked tomatoes, and salt and freshly ground black pepper to taste and simmer sauce, uncovered, stirring occasionally, 30 minutes.

Purée sauce through the fine disk of a food mill or force it through a coarse sieve set over a bowl. *Sauce may be made 1 week ahead and chilled, covered.* Makes about 3½ cups.

Linguine with Zucchini, Carrots, and Mixed Herb Pesto

4 medium carrots
3 medium zucchini
1 pound dried *linguine*
¾ cup mixed herb pesto
   (recipe follows)

In a 6-quart kettle bring 5 quarts salted water to a boil for pasta.

Using a mandoline cut carrots and zucchini into ⅛-inch-thick julienne strips. (Alternatively, using a sharp knife, halve carrots and zucchini crosswise and cut lengthwise into ⅛-inch-wide pieces.)

Cook *linguine* in boiling water 8 minutes, or until barely tender. Add carrots and cook 1 minute. Add zucchini and cook 1 minute. Reserve ⅔ cup cooking water and drain pasta and vegetables.

In a large bowl stir together pesto and reserved hot cooking water. Add pasta and vegetables and toss well. Serves 6.

Mixed Herb Pesto

1 cup packed fresh flat-leafed parsley leaves,
   washed well and spun dry
½ cup packed fresh basil leaves, washed well
   and spun dry
1 tablespoon fresh thyme leaves
1 tablespoon fresh rosemary leaves
1 tablespoon fresh tarragon leaves
½ cup freshly grated Parmesan (about 1½ ounces)
⅓ cup olive oil
¼ cup walnuts, toasted golden brown
   and cooled
1 tablespoon balsamic vinegar

In a food processor blend together all ingredients with salt and pepper to taste until smooth. *Pesto keeps, its surface covered with plastic wrap, chilled, 1 week.* Makes about ¾ cup.

Saffron Linguine with Spicy Shrimp and Vegetables

¾ pound medium shrimp (about 24), shelled,
    leaving tails intact, and deveined if desired
1½ teaspoons olive oil
¼ teaspoon dried hot red pepper flakes,
    or to taste
¼ cup dry white wine or vermouth
1 medium onion, chopped fine (about ¾ cup)
1 tablespoon minced garlic, or to taste
1½ tablespoons tomato paste
½ cup chicken broth
1 medium fennel bulb (about 1 pound),
    trimmed and chopped coarse
1 medium yellow bell pepper, cut into
    thin strips
1 tablespoon very hot water
¼ teaspoon crumbled saffron threads
½ pound *linguine*
a 14- to 16-ounce can whole tomatoes, drained
    and chopped, or 2 cups cherry tomatoes,
    quartered
1 cup fish stock or bottled clam juice
½ pound fresh spinach, coarse stems discarded,
    washed well, spun dry, and chopped coarse
⅓ cup finely chopped fresh parsley leaves

Bring a kettle of salted water to a boil for pasta.

In a bowl toss shrimp with 1 teaspoon oil, ⅛ teaspoon red pepper flakes, and salt and pepper to taste. Heat a 12-inch non-stick skillet over moderately high heat until hot enough to make drops of water scatter and sauté shrimp in 2 batches until golden and cooked through, 1 to 2 minutes on each side, transferring as cooked to a plate.

To skillet add wine or vermouth and boil until most is evaporated. Add remaining ½ teaspoon oil, onion, garlic, remaining ⅛ teaspoon red pepper flakes, and salt and pepper to taste and cook over moderate heat, stirring, until onion is softened. In a bowl whisk together tomato paste and chicken broth and add to skillet with fennel and bell pepper. Simmer mixture, covered, until fennel is tender, about 10 minutes.

In a very small bowl or ramekin combine hot water and saffron.

While fennel mixture is simmering, add *linguine* to boiling water and cook until *al dente*. Drain *linguine* well in a colander and return to kettle. Toss *linguine* with saffron mixture until evenly coated and keep warm.

To simmering fennel mixture add tomatoes and fish stock and simmer 2 minutes. Add shrimp and spinach and cook, covered, until just heated through and spinach is slightly wilted, 1 to 2 minutes. To pasta add vegetable mixture, parsley, and salt and pepper to taste and toss well. Serves 4.

Each serving: 387 calories,
4.9 grams fat (11% of calories from fat)

PHOTO ON PAGES 88 AND 89

Black Linguine with Orange and Red Peppers

4 large garlic cloves, minced
a scant ¼ teaspoon dried hot red pepper flakes
2 tablespoons olive oil
2 orange bell peppers, cut into
    thin strips
1 red bell pepper, cut into thin strips
¾ cup dry white wine
½ cup chicken broth or water
½ pound black *linguine,* fettuccine, or spaghetti
    (squid or cuttlefish ink pasta)*
⅓ cup finely chopped fresh parsley leaves

Garnish: fresh flat-leafed parsley sprigs

*available at specialty foods shops and by mail
    order from Balducci's, tel. (800) 572-7041

In a 5-quart kettle bring 4 quarts salted water to a boil for pasta.

In a 12-inch heavy skillet cook garlic with pepper flakes in oil over moderate heat, stirring, until garlic begins to turn golden. Add bell peppers with salt to taste and cook, stirring, until softened. Add wine and boil, stirring occasionally, until almost all liquid is evaporated. Add broth or water and simmer, covered, until bell peppers are tender, about 5 minutes. *Pepper mixture may be made 1 day ahead and chilled, covered. Reheat mixture in skillet before proceeding.*

In boiling water cook pasta until *al dente* and drain in a colander. Add pasta to pepper mixture with parsley and toss with salt and pepper to taste over moderate heat until combined well and heated through.

Divide pasta mixture among 6 small plates and garnish with parsley. Serves 6 to 8 as a first course.

PHOTO ON PAGE 71

Asparagus Lemon Pasta

1½ pounds asparagus, trimmed and cut diagonally
   into ½-inch-thick pieces
3 tablespoons unsalted butter
¾ cup heavy cream
2 tablespoons freshly grated lemon zest
   (from about 3 lemons)
¼ cup fresh lemon juice
¾ teaspoon salt
1 pound bow-tie pasta
⅓ cup finely chopped fresh parsley leaves

Accompaniment: freshly grated Parmesan

In a steamer set over boiling water steam asparagus, covered, until crisp-tender, about 3 minutes. Transfer asparagus to a colander and rinse under cold water to stop cooking. Drain asparagus well.

In a 6-quart kettle bring 5 quarts salted water to a boil for pasta.

In a deep 12-inch skillet heat butter and cream over moderately low heat until butter is melted and stir in zest, lemon juice, and salt. Remove skillet from heat and keep sauce warm, covered.

Cook pasta in boiling water, stirring occasionally, until *al dente*. Ladle ¼ cup pasta water into sauce and drain pasta in colander.

Immediately add pasta and asparagus to sauce and cook over moderate heat, tossing, 1 minute, or until heated through. Add parsley and salt and pepper to taste and toss well.

Sprinkle pasta with a little Parmesan and serve more on the side. Serves 4 as a main course.

Cashew Sesame Noodles

For sauce
2 large garlic cloves, chopped
3 tablespoons soy sauce
1½ tablespoons rice vinegar
¼ cup Asian sesame oil
¾ teaspoon dried hot red pepper flakes,
   or to taste
1 teaspoon sugar
½ cup salted roasted cashews
⅓ cup water

1 pound thin spaghetti
1½ cups loosely packed fresh coriander sprigs,
   washed well, spun dry, and chopped fine

Garnish: chopped salted roasted cashews and
   fresh coriander sprigs

Make sauce:
In a blender blend sauce ingredients with salt and pepper to taste until smooth. *Sauce may be made 3 days ahead and chilled, covered. Bring sauce to room temperature and stir before using.*

Just before serving, in a 6-quart kettle bring 5 quarts salted water to a boil and cook spaghetti until *al dente*. In a colander drain spaghetti and rinse well under cold water. Drain spaghetti well and in a bowl toss with sauce and chopped coriander.

Garnish noodles with cashews and coriander sprigs. Serves 6 to 8 as a side dish.

PHOTO ON PAGE 65

Roasted Garlic Orzo

3 large garlic cloves, unpeeled
1 teaspoon poppy seeds if desired
1 tablespoon unsalted butter
2 tablespoons chopped fresh parsley leaves
½ cup *orzo* (rice-shaped pasta)

Preheat oven to 450° F.

Tightly wrap garlic in foil and roast in middle of oven about 25 minutes, or until tender.

Bring a small saucepan of salted water to a boil for *orzo*.

While garlic is roasting, in a small skillet dry-roast poppy seeds over moderate heat, shaking skillet, until fragrant, being careful not to burn them.

Carefully unwrap garlic packet and cool slightly. Squeeze garlic cloves from skins into a small bowl and mash to a paste with butter. Stir in parsley and poppy seeds.

Cook *orzo* in boiling water until tender and reserve about ¼ cup cooking water. Drain *orzo* well and add to garlic mixture with enough reserved cooking water to melt butter and prevent *orzo* from sticking together. Season *orzo* with salt and pepper. Serves 2 as a side dish.

Sesame Orzo with Charred Scallions

1 tablespoon sesame seeds
¾ cup *orzo* (rice-shaped pasta)
2 teaspoons Asian sesame oil
1 bunch scallions (about 6), cut diagonally
    into 1-inch pieces

In a small heavy skillet dry-roast sesame seeds over moderate heat, stirring, until golden, about 4 minutes, and transfer to a bowl.

In a 3-quart saucepan bring 2 quarts salted water to a boil. Add *orzo* and cook, stirring occasionally, until *al dente*. In a colander drain *orzo* and rinse under cold water. Drain *orzo* well and add to dry-roasted sesame seeds.

In an 8-inch non-stick skillet heat oil over high heat until hot but not smoking and sauté scallions, stirring occasionally, until lightly charred and tender, about 3 minutes. Stir scallion mixture into *orzo* and season with salt and pepper. Serves 2 as a side dish.

Corn-Bread Stuffing Pudding

1 small onion, chopped fine
½ cup finely chopped green bell pepper
1 large garlic clove, minced
1 tablespoon unsalted butter
2 large eggs
1½ cups milk
2 cups packaged corn-bread stuffing mix

Preheat oven to 375° F. and butter a 9-inch round cake pan.

In a small heavy skillet cook onion, bell pepper, and garlic in butter over moderate heat, stirring occasionally, until onion is golden. In a bowl whisk together eggs and milk and stir in onion mixture, stuffing, and salt and pepper to taste. Turn mixture into cake pan and bake in middle of oven until top is golden, about 25 minutes. Cut pudding into wedges. Serves 2 with leftovers.

Broiled Polenta with Winter Tomato Sauce

1 recipe basic polenta (recipe follows), kept warm
¼ pound Fontina cheese, preferably Italian,
    grated (about 1 cup)
2 tablespoons olive oil plus additional for
    brushing polenta
1 large onion
1 garlic clove, chopped
a 28- to 32-ounce can whole tomatoes
    including juice
1 tablespoon chopped fresh parsley leaves

Accompaniment: freshly grated Parmesan

In a bowl stir together warm polenta and Fontina until smooth. Pour polenta into a lightly oiled shallow 1½-quart bowl and cool. *Polenta may be made 2 days ahead and chilled, covered.*

In a large skillet heat 2 tablespoons oil over moderately high heat until hot but not smoking and sauté onion with salt to taste, stirring, until golden and tender, about 10 minutes. Add garlic and sauté, stirring, 1 minute. Add tomatoes with juice, stirring to break up tomatoes, and simmer, covered, 30 minutes. Stir in parsley. Keep sauce warm.

Preheat broiler.

Unmold polenta onto a cutting board and cut into ¾-inch-thick slices. Arrange slices in one layer in a lightly oiled shallow baking pan and brush slices with additional oil.

Broil polenta about 3 inches from heat until edges are golden, about 5 minutes. Turn polenta over and broil until edges are golden, about 3 minutes more.

Arrange polenta on a platter and spoon sauce over it. Serve polenta with Parmesan. Serves 4 as a main course.

Cornmeal may be either fine- or coarse-grained. Both work well in the following recipe: We used a fine-grained variety found in most supermarkets.

Basic Polenta

4 cups water
1 teaspoon salt
1 cup cornmeal or instant polenta

In a heavy saucepan bring water and salt to a boil and gradually whisk in cornmeal in a thin stream. Cook polenta over moderately low heat (it should be barely boiling), stirring constantly, until very thick and pulls away from side of pan, about 40 minutes for cornmeal and about 15 minutes for instant polenta. Remove pan from heat and cover to keep warm. Stir polenta just before using. *Polenta will keep warm, covered, 20 minutes.* Makes about 3 cups.

Parmesan Sage Polenta Sticks

4 cups water
1¼ teaspoons salt
1 tablespoon minced fresh sage leaves
1⅓ cups yellow cornmeal
½ stick (¼ cup) unsalted butter
1 cup freshly grated Parmesan (about ¼ pound)

Butter a 13- by 9-inch glass baking dish.
In a large heavy saucepan bring water to a boil

and add salt. Add sage and ⅓ cup cornmeal, a little at a time, stirring constantly. Reduce heat to low and add remaining cup cornmeal in a stream, stirring constantly. Cook mixture over low heat, whisking, 1 minute and remove pan from heat.

Add 2 tablespoons butter and ⅓ cup Parmesan and stir polenta until butter is incorporated. Working quickly, spread polenta evenly in baking dish and chill until firm, about 20 minutes. *Polenta may be prepared up to this point 1 day ahead and chilled, covered.*

Preheat broiler and line a baking sheet with foil.

In a small saucepan melt remaining 2 tablespoons butter over low heat. Invert polenta onto a work surface. Halve polenta lengthwise and cut each half crosswise into 14 sticks. Arrange polenta sticks on baking sheet and brush with melted butter. Broil sticks about 4 inches from heat until golden, about 4 to 6 minutes. Turn sticks over and sprinkle with remaining ⅔ cup Parmesan. Broil sticks until cheese is golden, about 2 to 3 minutes more. Makes 28 polenta sticks.

PHOTO ON PAGE 21

Fried Rice with Tomatoes

For sauce
1½ tablespoons light soy sauce*
1½ tablespoons Chinese rice wine* or
   medium-dry Sherry
2 teaspoons sugar
1¾ teaspoons salt
⅛ teaspoon white pepper

3½ tablespoons scallion oil (recipe follows)
1 tablespoon minced peeled fresh gingerroot
2 teaspoons minced garlic
about 4 shallots, cut into ¼-inch dice (¾ cup)
about 8 fresh water chestnuts* or about 6 ounces
   jícama, peeled and cut into ⅓-inch dice (⅔ cup)
about 4 broccoli stems, peeled and cut into ⅓-inch
   dice (¾ cup)
1¼ pounds plum tomatoes (about 10), peeled,
   seeded, and cut into ½-inch cubes
6 cups cooked rice (recipe follows)
1 cup thinly sliced scallion

*available at Asian markets and some
   supermarkets

Make sauce:
In a bowl stir together sauce ingredients until sugar is dissolved.

Heat a wok over high heat 30 seconds. Add oil and with a Chinese spatula or large metal slotted spoon coat wok. Heat oil until a wisp of white smoke appears. Add gingerroot and garlic and stir-fry 10 seconds. Add shallots and stir-fry 2 minutes. Add water chestnuts or *jícama* and broccoli and stir-fry 2 minutes. Add tomatoes and stir-fry until combined well. Add sauce and stir-fry until sauce begins to thicken. Add rice and stir-fry until mixture is combined well and rice is hot, about 3 minutes. Add scallion and toss until combined well. Serves 3 generously as a main course.

Scallion Oil

2 cups peanut oil
3 cups 3-inch pieces scallions (about 3 bunches),
   white parts smashed lightly

Heat a wok over moderate heat until hot. Add oil and scallions and fry scallions until white parts are golden, about 8 minutes. Transfer scallions with a slotted spoon to paper towels to drain and reserve for another use or discard.

Strain hot oil carefully through a fine sieve into a heatproof bowl and cool completely. *Oil keeps in a glass jar with a tight-fitting lid in a cool place up to 6 months.* Do not refrigerate oil. Makes 2 cups.

Cooked Rice

2 cups extra long-grain white rice (such as
   Carolina rice)
15 ounces cold water

In a 3-quart heavy saucepan wash rice in cold water to cover by 2 inches, rubbing it lightly between your hands. Pour off water and wash rice 2 more times in same manner. Drain rice well in a large sieve.

In pan combine rice with cold water. Bring water, uncovered, to a boil over high heat and stir with chopsticks. Boil rice until water is partially evaporated and grains on top appear dry, about 2 minutes. Reduce heat to very low and cook rice, covered, stirring occasionally, until tender, about 6 minutes.

Fluff rice with chopsticks and keep covered until ready to serve. Makes about 6 cups.

Yellow Rice with Sofrito

For sofrito
1 tablespoon minced onion
1 tablespoon minced red or green bell pepper
1 tablespoon chopped fresh coriander sprigs
1 small garlic clove, minced
2 teaspoons olive oil

¼ teaspoon turmeric
¾ cup long-grain rice
1½ cups water
½ teaspoon salt

Make sofrito:
In a 1½-quart heavy saucepan cook onion, bell

pepper, coriander, and garlic in oil over moderately low heat, stirring, until vegetables are soft, about 5 minutes.

Add turmeric and cook, stirring, 30 seconds. Stir in long-grain rice, water, and salt and bring to a boil, uncovered. Boil rice, uncovered, without stirring, until surface of rice is covered with steam holes and grains on top appear dry, 5 to 8 minutes. Reduce heat to as low as possible and cook rice, tightly covered, 15 minutes more. Remove pan from heat and let rice stand, covered, 5 minutes. Serves 2.

Butternut Squash Risotto

1 small butternut squash (about 1½ pounds)
1¾ cups chicken broth
½ cup water
1 small onion, chopped (about ½ cup)
1 large garlic clove, sliced thin
1¼ teaspoons minced peeled fresh gingerroot
3 tablespoons unsalted butter
½ cup Arborio or long-grain rice
¼ cup dry white wine
2 tablespoons chopped fresh chives

Garnish: chopped fresh chives and Parmesan
   curls shaved with a vegetable peeler from a
   ¼-pound piece Parmesan at room temperature

Preheat oven to 450° F.

Halve squash lengthwise and discard seeds. Peel one half and cut into ¼-inch dice. Put remaining half, cut side down, in an oiled shallow baking pan with diced squash and season with salt and pepper. Bake squash in middle of oven, stirring diced squash occasionally, until tender and browned lightly, 15 to 20 minutes. Holding halved squash in a kitchen towel, scoop out flesh and chop coarse.

In a saucepan bring broth and water to a simmer and keep at a bare simmer.

In another saucepan cook onion, garlic, and gingerroot in butter over moderately low heat, stirring, until softened. Stir in rice and cook over moderate heat, stirring constantly, about 1 minute. Add wine and cook, stirring, until absorbed. Stir in ¼ cup broth and cook, stirring constantly and keeping at a simmer throughout, until absorbed. Continue simmering and adding broth, about ¼ cup at a time, stirring constantly and letting each addition be absorbed before adding next, until about half of broth has been added. Stir in diced and chopped squash and continue simmering and adding broth in same manner until rice is tender and creamy-looking but still *al dente*, about 18 minutes. Stir in chives and salt and pepper to taste.

Spoon risotto into 2 shallow serving bowls and garnish with chives and Parmesan curls. Serves 2.

165

Rice and Green Chili Pilaf

1 small onion, chopped fine
1 tablespoon vegetable oil
1 large garlic clove, minced
a 4-ounce can mild green chilies, drained
   and chopped
½ cup long-grain white rice
¾ cup low-salt chicken broth
1 scallion green, sliced thin, if desired

In a small heavy saucepan cook onion in oil over moderately low heat, stirring, until softened. Stir in garlic, chilies, and rice and cook, stirring occasionally, until rice is translucent, about 1 minute. Add chicken broth and salt and pepper to taste and bring to a boil. Reduce heat to low and cook pilaf, covered, until liquid is evaporated and rice is tender, about 20 minutes. Fluff pilaf and stir in scallion green. Serves 2.

Wild Rice with Fennel and Porcini

½ ounce dried *porcini* mushrooms* (about ½ cup)
¾ cup boiling-hot water plus 1 cup cold water
¼ teaspoon salt
½ cup wild rice
1 cup diced fennel bulb (sometimes called anise,
   about 1 medium)
½ cup chopped red onion
2 tablespoons unsalted butter

*available at specialty foods shops and some
  supermarkets

In a bowl soak *porcini* in boiling-hot water 20 to 30 minutes, or until softened. Slowly strain soaking liquid through a fine sieve lined with a coffee filter or a double thickness of rinsed and squeezed cheesecloth into a small saucepan, being careful to leave last tablespoon containing sediment in bowl. Boil soaking liquid until reduced to about ⅓ cup. Wash *porcini* under cold water to remove any grit and pat dry. Chop *porcini* coarse.

Bring reduced *porcini* liquid to a boil with cold water, salt, and rice and simmer, covered, 45 to 50 minutes, or until rice is tender and liquid is absorbed. (If rice is tender before liquid is absorbed, drain in a colander.) Transfer rice to a serving bowl and keep warm, covered.

In a heavy skillet cook fennel, onion, and *porcini* in butter over moderate heat, stirring, until fennel is tender, about 10 minutes. Add fennel mixture to rice and toss to combine. *Rice may be made 3 hours ahead and kept, covered, at room temperature. Reheat rice in skillet, adding water to prevent it from sticking to skillet.* Serves 2 generously.

PHOTO ON PAGE 23

VEGETABLES

Steamed Asparagus with Ginger Garlic Sauce

2 pounds asparagus, trimmed and cut diagonally
    into ½-inch-thick slices
2 teaspoons cornstarch
½ cup water
2 tablespoons soy sauce
1 tablespoon medium-dry Sherry or Scotch
1 teaspoon sugar
½ teaspoon salt
1 teaspoon Asian sesame oil
1 tablespoon vegetable oil
2 tablespoons minced peeled fresh gingerroot
1½ tablespoons minced garlic
2 tablespoons sesame seeds, toasted lightly

In a steamer set over boiling water steam asparagus, covered, until just crisp-tender, about 1 minute.
Transfer asparagus to a colander and rinse under
cold water to stop cooking. Drain asparagus well.

In a 1-cup measure stir together cornstarch and
water until dissolved and stir in soy sauce, Sherry or
Scotch, sugar, salt, and sesame oil.

Heat a wok or large heavy skillet over high heat
until hot and add vegetable oil. Heat vegetable oil
until hot but not smoking and stir-fry gingerroot and
garlic 30 seconds. Add asparagus and stir-fry 30 seconds. Stir cornstarch mixture and add to asparagus.
Bring liquid to a boil, stirring, and stir-fry mixture
until asparagus is well coated. Sprinkle asparagus
with sesame seeds and toss. Serves 6.

Asparagus with Hazelnut Vinaigrette

For vinaigrette
1 large shallot, minced
2 tablespoons Sherry vinegar or
    red-wine vinegar
1 tablespoon Dijon mustard
½ teaspoon sugar
⅓ cup extra-virgin olive oil
¼ cup hazelnuts, toasted and skinned
    (procedure on page 233) and
    chopped

1 hard-cooked large egg
2 pounds asparagus, trimmed and lower 2 inches
    of stalks peeled

Make vinaigrette:

In a bowl whisk together shallot, vinegar, mustard, sugar, and salt and pepper to taste. Add oil in a
stream, whisking until emulsified and whisk in
hazelnuts.

Finely chop egg. In a deep 10- to 12-inch skillet
bring 1½ inches salted water to a boil and cook
asparagus over high heat until crisp-tender, about 2
to 4 minutes. Transfer asparagus with tongs to a
colander and drain.

Transfer asparagus to a serving dish. Spoon
vinaigrette over asparagus and sprinkle with egg.
Serve asparagus warm or at room temperature.
Serves 6.

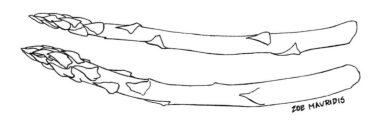

ZOE MAVRIDIS

Asparagus, Leek, Shiitake, and Potato Ragout

2 large leeks (white and pale green parts only)
1 pound small red potatoes
3 tablespoons olive oil
1 pound asparagus, trimmed and cut diagonally
    into 1-inch pieces
½ pound fresh *shiitake* mushrooms, stems
    discarded and caps quartered
1½ cups chicken broth
½ lemon
¼ cup chopped fresh mint leaves
3 tablespoons finely chopped fresh parsley leaves

Cut leeks crosswise into ½-inch slices and in a bowl soak in water, agitating occasionally to dislodge any sand, 5 minutes. Lift leeks out of water and drain in a colander.

Quarter potatoes. In a 12- to 14-inch non-stick skillet heat 1 tablespoon oil over moderately high heat until hot but not smoking and sauté potatoes with salt to taste, stirring occasionally, until golden, about 5 minutes. Transfer potatoes to a bowl.

In skillet heat 1 tablespoon oil until hot but not smoking and sauté leeks, stirring occasionally and shaking skillet, until lightly browned, about 3 to 4 minutes. Transfer leeks to bowl with potatoes.

In skillet heat remaining tablespoon oil until hot but not smoking and sauté asparagus, stirring occasionally, 2 minutes. Add mushrooms and sauté, stirring occasionally, until mushrooms are softened, about 3 minutes.

Add broth and bring to a boil. Add potatoes and leeks and simmer, covered, until vegetables are tender, about 5 minutes.

Squeeze a little lemon juice over vegetables and stir in mint, parsley, and salt and pepper to taste. Serves 4 as a main course or 6 as a side dish.

Green and Wax Beans with Walnut Gremolata

¾ pound green and/or wax beans, trimmed
1 tablespoon unsalted butter
1½ teaspoons olive oil
2 tablespoons chopped walnuts
1 garlic clove, minced
1 tablespoon chopped fresh parsley leaves

2 teaspoons fresh lemon juice
¼ teaspoon freshly grated lemon zest

Bring a large saucepan two-thirds full of salted water to a boil over high heat. Add beans and simmer 5 minutes, or until crisp-tender. Drain beans.

In a large skillet heat butter and oil over moderate heat until foam subsides and cook walnuts, stirring occasionally, until golden. Add garlic and cook, stirring, 1 minute. Stir in beans, parsley, lemon juice, zest, and salt to taste and heat through. Serves 2 generously.

Green Beans with Hazelnuts and Lemon

1½ pounds green beans, trimmed
1 to 2 tablespoons olive oil
1½ teaspoons freshly grated lemon zest,
    or to taste
⅓ cup hazelnuts, toasted until golden and
    chopped fine

In a kettle of boiling salted water cook beans until just tender, 3 to 8 minutes. Drain beans in a colander and in a large bowl toss while still hot with oil, zest, nuts, and salt and pepper to taste. *Beans may be made 1 day ahead and chilled, covered. Reheat beans, preferably in a microwave.* Serves 8.

PHOTO ON PAGES 76 AND 77

Lemon Tarragon Green Beans

2 pounds green beans, trimmed
2 tablespoons extra-virgin olive oil
3 tablespoons fresh lemon juice, or to taste
2 tablespoons finely chopped fresh tarragon
    leaves, or to taste

Garnish: fresh tarragon sprigs

In a large kettle of boiling salted water blanch beans in 2 batches 2 to 3 minutes, or until just tender. With a slotted spoon transfer beans as blanched to a large bowl filled with ice and cold water. Drain beans well and pat dry. *Beans may be prepared up to this point 1 day ahead and chilled, covered.*

Just before serving, in a large bowl toss together beans, oil, lemon juice, tarragon, and salt and pepper to taste. Serve beans garnished with tarragon sprigs. Serves 8.

PHOTO ON PAGE 54

Green Beans and Crisp Onion Rings

2 tablespoons all-purpose flour
1 tablespoon sugar
1 teaspoon salt
1 small red onion, cut into ¼-inch-thick slices
vegetable oil for frying
½ pound green beans, trimmed and cut into
   3-inch pieces
½ tablespoon unsalted butter
1 teaspoon Worcestershire sauce

In a small bowl whisk together flour, sugar, and salt. Separate onion slices into rings and toss in flour mixture to coat.

In a 9-inch skillet heat ½ inch oil to 380° F. on a deep-fat thermometer. Shake off excess flour from half of onion rings and fry them, turning, until golden, 1 to 2 minutes. Transfer onion rings with tongs to paper towels to drain and fry remaining onion rings in same manner.

In a vegetable steamer set over boiling water steam beans, covered, about 6 minutes, or until tender. In a large bowl toss beans with onion rings, butter, Worcestershire sauce, and salt and pepper to taste. Serves 2.

Balsamic-Glazed Beets

3½ pounds beets (4 pounds with greens attached, reserving greens for another use), scrubbed and trimmed, leaving about 1 inch of stems attached
3 tablespoons balsamic vinegar
2 tablespoons pure maple syrup or honey
1 tablespoon olive oil
1½ teaspoons minced fresh thyme leaves

In a large saucepan cover beets with salted water by 1 inch. Simmer beets, covered, 35 to 45 minutes, or until tender, and drain in a colander. Cool beets until they can be handled and slip off skins and stems. Cut beets lengthwise into wedges. *Beets may be prepared up to this point 2 days ahead and chilled, covered. Bring beets to room temperature before proceeding.*

In a large skillet stir together vinegar, syrup or honey, and oil and add beets. Cook beet mixture with salt and pepper to taste over moderate heat, stirring, until heated through and coated well. Sprinkle half of thyme over beets and toss gently.

Serve beets sprinkled with remaining thyme. Serves 8.

PHOTO ON PAGE 76

Ginger and Garlic Broccoli

1 small bunch broccoli (about 1¼ pounds)
2 tablespoons vegetable oil
3 tablespoons very thin matchsticks of peeled
  fresh gingerroot
1 garlic clove, sliced thin
2 tablespoons water
1½ tablespoons soy sauce
1 tablespoon seasoned rice vinegar if desired

Cut broccoli into 1-inch flowerets. Trim and peel stems and cut into ¼-inch slices.

In a 10-inch heavy skillet heat oil over moderately high heat until hot but not smoking and cook gingerroot and garlic, swirling skillet occasionally, until just golden. With a slotted spoon transfer gingerroot and garlic to paper towels to drain.

Add broccoli to skillet and cook, stirring frequently, until browned well, about 5 minutes. In a small bowl stir together water, soy sauce, and vinegar. Add mixture to skillet and cook until most liquid is evaporated, about 1 minute. Serve broccoli sprinkled with gingerroot and garlic. Serves 2.

Stir-Fried Broccoli with Pickled Red Onions

¼ pound small red onions (about 5, each about
  1½ inches in diameter), sliced thin
¼ cup red-wine vinegar
¾ teaspoon salt
3 bunches broccoli (about 3 pounds), lower
  3 inches of stems discarded
¼ cup vegetable oil

In a small saucepan bring onions, vinegar, and salt to a boil, covered, and remove pan from heat. Cool onion mixture, uncovered, and drain.

Bring a kettle of salted water to a boil for broccoli. Cut broccoli into 2½-inch flowerets and cut remaining stems into ¼-inch-thick slices. Blanch flowerets 3 minutes and drain well in a colander.

In a large skillet heat 2 tablespoons oil over moderately high heat until hot but not smoking and sauté half of flowerets and stems with salt to taste, stirring occasionally, until crisp-tender, 3 to 5 minutes, transferring to a bowl. Sauté remaining

flowerets and stems in remaining 2 tablespoons oil in same manner. Sprinkle broccoli with pickled red onions. Serves 8.

Steamed Broccoli Rabe with Garlic

½ cup water
1 tablespoon soy sauce
1 large garlic clove, sliced thin
1 bunch broccoli rabe, hollow or
  coarse stems discarded

In a 12-inch skillet bring water and soy sauce with garlic to a boil. Add broccoli rabe and cook, covered, over moderately high heat 2 minutes. Remove cover and cook until water is evaporated and broccoli rabe is tender. Season broccoli rabe with salt. Serves 4.

Each serving: 26 calories,
0.3 gram fat (8% of calories from fat)

PHOTO ON PAGE 86

Sautéed Cabbage with Bacon Bread Crumbs

3 slices bacon, chopped
3 cups thinly sliced cabbage
  (about ½ small head)
2 tablespoons water
1 slice firm white sandwich bread, ground
  coarse in a food processor or blender
¼ teaspoon caraway seeds

In a heavy skillet cook bacon over moderate heat, stirring, until crisp and transfer with a slotted spatula to paper towels to drain. Transfer 1 teaspoon drippings to a small bowl and reserve. In drippings remaining in skillet cook cabbage with salt and pepper to taste, stirring occasionally, until golden and add water. Cook cabbage until crisp-tender and transfer to a serving dish.

In skillet heat reserved drippings over moderately high heat until hot but not smoking and sauté bread crumbs and caraway seeds with salt and pepper to taste, stirring, until bread crumbs are golden. Stir in bacon and sprinkle over cabbage. Serves 2.

Napa Cabbage with Peas and Prosciutto

2 tablespoons olive oil
1 cup frozen peas (about 6 ounces), thawed
1 small Napa cabbage, trimmed and sliced thin
  crosswise (about 4 cups)
1 ounce prosciutto, chopped fine
  (about ¼ cup)
1 teaspoon freshly grated lemon zest
½ teaspoon fresh lemon juice, or to taste
2 tablespoons freshly grated Parmesan

In a large heavy skillet heat oil over moderate heat until hot but not smoking and cook peas, cabbage, prosciutto, and zest, stirring, 4 to 5 minutes, or until cabbage is wilted and tender. Remove skillet from heat and stir in lemon juice, Parmesan, and salt and pepper to taste. Serves 2.

Honey Ginger-Glazed Carrots

3 pounds carrots, cut into 3- by ½-inch sticks
3 tablespoons honey
2 tablespoons unsalted butter
1 tablespoon finely chopped peeled fresh
  gingerroot

In a kettle cover carrot sticks with salted water by 2 inches and boil, uncovered, until tender, about 10 minutes.

While carrots are cooking, warm honey, butter, and gingerroot over moderate heat, stirring, until butter is melted.

Drain carrots well and in a bowl toss with honey glaze and salt and pepper to taste. Serves 8.

PHOTO ON PAGES 84 AND 85

Collard Greens with Red Onions and Bacon

½ pound sliced bacon, cut crosswise into fourths
3 medium red onions, chopped coarse
1¼ cups chicken broth
¼ cup cider vinegar
2 tablespoons firmly packed dark brown sugar,
  or to taste
½ teaspoon dried hot red pepper flakes,
  or to taste
4 pounds collard greens (preferably small leaves),
  coarse stems and ribs discarded and leaves
  and thin stems washed well, drained, and
  chopped coarse

In a deep heavy kettle cook bacon in 2 batches over moderate heat until crisp and transfer to paper towels to drain. Pour off all but about 3 tablespoons drippings and in drippings remaining in kettle cook onions, stirring occasionally, until browned slightly and softened. Transfer onions with a slotted spoon to a bowl.

To kettle add chicken broth, vinegar, brown sugar, red pepper flakes, and about half of bacon, stirring until sugar is dissolved. Add about half of collards, tossing until wilted slightly, and add remaining collards, tossing until combined. Simmer collards, covered, 30 minutes. Stir in onions and simmer, covered, 30 minutes more, or until collards are very tender.

Serve collards topped with remaining bacon. Serves 8.

PHOTO ON PAGE 84

Corn Chive Pudding

two 10-ounce packages frozen corn kernels,
 thawed
¼ cup sugar
1¼ teaspoons salt
2 cups milk
4 large eggs
½ vanilla bean, split lengthwise and seeds
 scraped, reserving pod for another use
½ stick (¼ cup) unsalted butter, melted
 and cooled
3 tablespoons all-purpose flour
¼ cup chopped fresh chives
a pinch freshly grated nutmeg

Garnish: 3 tablespoons chopped fresh chives

Preheat oven to 350° F. and butter a 1½-quart
quiche dish or pie plate.

In a food processor pulse half of corn until
chopped coarse. In a bowl stir together chopped corn
and remaining corn kernels and sprinkle with sugar
and salt, stirring until combined well.

In another bowl whisk together milk, eggs, vanilla
seeds, butter, flour, and chives and stir into corn
until combined well. Pour pudding into quiche dish
or pie plate and sprinkle with nutmeg. Bake pudding
in middle of oven until center is just set, about 45
minutes. Garnish pudding with chives. Serves 8.

PHOTO ON PAGE 84

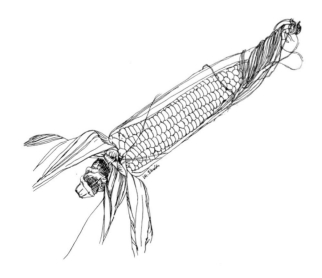

Grilled Corn on the Cob

8 ears corn in husks, outer layer of husks
 discarded or torn into strips for tying corn

Prepare grill.

Peel back corn husks carefully, without breaking
off, and discard silks. Fold husks back into place and
tie ends together with strips of outer husk or kitchen
string. In large bowls cover corn with cold water and
soak 10 minutes. Drain corn and grill on a rack set 5
to 6 inches over glowing coals, turning occasionally,
15 minutes. Serves 4.

PHOTO ON PAGES 60 AND 61

Grilled Eggplant Sandwiches with Lemon Aïoli, Feta, and Mint

1 medium eggplant (about 1 pound), cut
 crosswise into ¼-inch-thick slices
3 tablespoons olive oil
2 tablespoons mayonnaise
¼ teaspoon minced garlic, or to taste
1 teaspoon fresh lemon juice
1 loaf French bread (about 16 by 3 inches)
3 ounces chilled feta, crumbled (about ¾ cup)
¼ cup fresh mint leaves, washed and spun dry

Preheat grill.

Brush eggplant with oil and season with salt and
pepper. Grill eggplant in batches on a rack set 5 to 6
inches over glowing coals, turning once, until tender,
about 3 minutes, transferring with tongs to a baking
sheet to cool. (Alternatively, eggplant may be
broiled about same amount of time.)

In a small bowl whisk together mayonnaise,
garlic, and lemon juice to make *aïoli.*

Cut bread into four 4-inch-long pieces and halve
each piece horizontally. Spread 4 halves with *aïoli.*
Make sandwiches on bread with eggplant, feta, and
mint. Makes 4 sandwiches.

Sautéed Fennel, Radicchio, and Pine Nuts

1 tablespoon olive oil
1 tablespoon pine nuts
1 large garlic clove, sliced

½ fennel bulb (sometimes called anise), stalks
    trimmed flush with bulb and bulb cut
    lengthwise into ¼-inch slices
1 teaspoon fresh lemon juice
½ head *radicchio,* cut into 1-inch pieces

In a 10-inch non-stick skillet heat oil over moderately high heat until hot but not smoking and sauté pine nuts, stirring, until golden. With a slotted spoon transfer pine nuts to paper towels to drain.

In skillet cook garlic over moderate heat, stirring, until golden and with slotted spoon discard. Add fennel to skillet and cook, stirring, until golden, about 2 minutes. Add lemon juice and salt and pepper to taste and cook until fennel is crisp-tender. Stir in *radicchio* and sauté over moderately high heat, tossing with 2 wooden spoons, just until *radicchio* is wilted and tender. Add pine nuts and season with salt and pepper. Serves 2.

Grilled Fennel

2 small fennel bulbs (sometimes called anise,
    about 1 pound), stalks trimmed flush with bulb
olive oil for brushing fennel
½ lemon

Prepare grill.

Quarter fennel bulbs lengthwise into wedges. In a steamer set over boiling water steam fennel, covered, until just tender, 8 to 10 minutes.

Brush fennel quarters with oil and grill on an oiled rack set 5 to 6 inches over glowing coals 2 to 3 minutes on each side, or until golden. (Alternatively, fennel may be grilled in a hot well-seasoned ridged grill pan over moderately high heat.) Transfer grilled fennel with tongs to a serving dish. Squeeze lemon to taste over fennel and season with salt and pepper. Serves 2.

Braised Leeks with Lemon

4 small or 3 medium leeks, tough outer leaves
    discarded and leeks trimmed to about 7 inches
    long and cut lengthwise into quarters or eighths
2 tablespoons unsalted butter

¼ cup chicken broth
1 teaspoon freshly grated lemon zest

In a shallow dish soak leeks in cold water to cover 15 minutes, rubbing occasionally to remove any grit. In a heavy skillet melt butter over moderate heat. Lift leeks out of water and with water still clinging to them add to skillet. Cook leeks, stirring occasionally, 5 minutes and add broth and zest. Braise leeks, covered, 5 minutes, or until very tender, and season with salt and pepper. Serves 2.

PHOTO ON PAGE 23

Leeks with Shallot Caper Vinaigrette

4 small to medium leeks (about 1 pound
    untrimmed)
1½ teaspoons Sherry vinegar*
    or white-wine vinegar,
    or to taste
1 tablespoon minced shallot
½ teaspoon Dijon mustard
2 tablespoons extra-virgin olive oil
1 teaspoon drained capers,
    chopped fine
1 tablespoon minced fresh parsley leaves

*available at specialty foods shops and many
    supermarkets

Trim leeks to about 5 inches and trim root ends, leaving them intact. Cut each leek in half lengthwise and wash well, discarding any tough outer leaves.

In a skillet just large enough to hold them in one layer arrange leek halves, cut sides down, and add enough water to reach halfway up sides of leeks. Simmer leeks, covered, until tender, 5 to 10 minutes, drain, and immediately plunge into a bowl of ice and cold water.

In a small bowl whisk together vinegar, shallot, mustard, and salt and pepper to taste and add oil in a stream, whisking until emulsified. Whisk in capers and parsley.

Transfer leeks to paper towels. Pat and gently squeeze leeks until dry and divide between 2 plates. Spoon vinaigrette over each serving. Serves 2 as a first course.

Green Onion Casserole

8 medium bunches scallions, cut crosswise
    into 1-inch pieces (about 16 cups)
2 garlic cloves, minced
3 tablespoons unsalted butter
¼ cup heavy cream
½ cup freshly grated Parmesan
1 tablespoon olive oil
2 cups fresh bread crumbs

Preheat oven to 350° F. and butter a 1½-quart shallow baking dish.

In a kettle cook scallions and garlic in butter over moderate heat until scallions are softened, about 20 minutes. Stir in cream and ¼ cup Parmesan and transfer to baking dish.

In a skillet heat oil over moderately high heat until hot but not smoking and sauté bread crumbs, stirring, until golden brown, about 3 minutes. Transfer bread crumbs to a bowl and cool. Add remaining ¼ cup Parmesan and season with salt and pepper. Top casserole with bread crumb mixture. *Casserole may be prepared up to this point 1 day ahead and chilled, covered. Bring casserole to room temperature before proceeding.* Bake casserole, uncovered, in middle of oven until hot, 15 to 20 minutes. Serves 8.

PHOTO ON PAGE 84

Roast "Chrysanthemum" Onions

16 small yellow onions (each about 2 inches
    in diameter)
1 teaspoon sugar
¼ cup chicken broth
3 tablespoons unsalted butter

Preheat oven to 450° F.

Peel onions and with a sharp knife trim root end of each onion flat so that it is still intact but will stand on end. Standing each onion on its root end, cut parallel vertical slices at ¼-inch intervals into but not through onion, stopping about ¾ inch above root end. Rotate each onion 90 degrees and cut parallel vertical slices in same manner to form a crosshatch pattern, keeping onions intact.

In a lightly buttered shallow baking dish large enough to let onions open put onions, root ends down, and sprinkle with sugar and salt to taste.

In a small saucepan heat broth and butter over moderately high heat until butter is melted and pour over onions. Cover onions with foil and roast in middle of oven 45 minutes, or until tender. Remove foil and roast onions, basting occasionally, 30 to 45 minutes more, or until golden. *Onions may be made 1 day ahead and chilled, covered. Reheat onions before serving.* Serves 8.

PHOTO ON PAGE 77

Parsnip Fennel Purée

2 large parsnips (about ½ pound), peeled and cut
    into ½-inch-thick slices
1 small fennel bulb (sometimes called anise),
    stalks trimmed flush with bulb and bulb
    chopped (about 1 cup)
½ tablespoon unsalted butter

In a saucepan cover parsnips and fennel with salted water and boil, covered, 15 to 20 minutes, or until very tender. Drain vegetables well in a large sieve. In a food processor purée hot vegetables with butter and season with salt and freshly ground black pepper to taste. Serves 2.

Yellow Bell Pepper Squares with Garlic Bread Crumbs

2 tablespoons olive oil
3 yellow or red bell peppers, cut into 1-inch
    squares
1 garlic clove, minced
1 cup fresh bread crumbs

In a large heavy non-stick skillet heat oil over moderately high heat until hot but not smoking and sauté bell peppers with salt and pepper to taste, stirring occasionally, until just tender, about 5 minutes. Stir in garlic and bread crumbs and cook, stirring, 5 minutes, until bread crumbs are browned and bell peppers are very tender.

Serve warm or at room temperature. Serves 2 as a side dish.

174

Roasted Peppers and Potatoes with Bagna Cauda

5 large yellow bell peppers
5 large red bell peppers
1½ pounds russet (baking) potatoes
2 tablespoons olive oil
For bagna cauda
¼ cup olive oil
2 large garlic cloves, chopped and mashed
    to a paste with ½ teaspoon salt
5 anchovy fillets,
    mashed to a paste
1 tablespoon chopped fresh parsley leaves

Preheat broiler.

In a large shallow roasting pan broil peppers about 2 inches from heat, turning every 5 minutes, until skins are blistered and charred, 15 to 25 minutes. Transfer peppers to a bowl and let steam, covered, until cool. Starting at blossom end peel peppers lengthwise and discard stems. Cut peppers into thirds and discard seeds and ribs. *Peppers may be made 3 days ahead and chilled, covered. Drain peppers before using.*

Preheat oven to 450° F.

Peel potatoes and cut crosswise into ¼-inch-thick slices. In a shallow baking pan toss potatoes with oil and salt and pepper to taste and spread in one layer in pan. Roast potatoes until golden, about 20 minutes.

Potatoes may be roasted 8 hours ahead and kept covered at room temperature.
    Make bagna cauda:

In a saucepan heat oil, garlic paste, and anchovy paste over moderate heat, stirring, until warm and stir in parsley.

On a platter toss peppers and potatoes with warm *bagna cauda* to coat and season with salt and pepper. Serves 12 as part of a buffet.

PHOTO ON PAGE 36

New Potatoes in Chive Butter

3 tablespoons unsalted butter, softened
½ cup ½-inch pieces fresh chives
3 pounds small new potatoes (about 1 to 1½
    inches in diameter), scrubbed

In a large bowl combine butter, chives, and salt and freshly ground black pepper to taste.

If desired cut two intersecting strips with a channel knife around middle of each potato.

In a large saucepan cover potatoes with salted water by 1 inch and simmer until just tender, 15 to 20 minutes. Drain potatoes in a colander and add to butter mixture, tossing to combine. Serve potatoes warm. Serves 6.

PHOTO ON PAGE 42

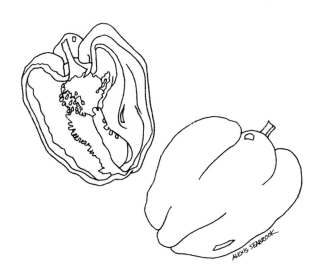

Duchesse Potato Ghosts

4 pounds large red potatoes
¾ stick (6 tablespoons) unsalted butter,
    cut into pieces
1¼ cups milk
3 large egg yolks

Garnish: small dark seeds such as *nigella** (black
    onion seeds), cumin seeds, or caraway seeds
    for ghosts' "eyes"

*available at Middle Eastern and East Indian
    markets

Peel and quarter potatoes and in a large saucepan
cover with salted cold water by 2 inches. Bring
water to a boil and simmer potatoes until tender,
about 15 minutes.

While potatoes are simmering, in a small saucepan heat butter with milk over moderately low heat
until melted and keep warm.

Drain potatoes in a colander and force through a
ricer or food mill into a large bowl. With an electric
mixer beat in milk mixture, yolks, and salt and pepper to taste.

Preheat oven to 400° F.

Spread about one third potatoes in a buttered 1-
quart gratin dish and transfer remaining potatoes to
a pastry bag fitted with a ¾-inch plain tip. Onto potatoes in dish pipe potatoes close together into pointed
mounds to form "ghosts" and garnish each mound
with 2 seeds for "eyes." *Potatoes may be prepared up
to this point 1 day ahead and chilled, covered loosely.*

Bake potatoes until heated through and tops of
"ghosts" are golden, 15 to 20 minutes. Serves 6 to 8.

PHOTO ON PAGE 72

Potato and Kipper Gratin

1 large russet (baking) potato
    (about ¾ pound)
a 3¼-ounce can kippers, drained, patted dry,
    and broken into bite-size pieces
1 small onion, chopped fine
1½ tablespoons drained capers
1 cup heavy cream

Preheat oven to 350° F. and butter an 8-inch-
square glass baking dish.

Peel potato and slice very thin, about ¹⁄₁₆ inch
thick. In baking dish layer half of potatoes and all of
kippers, onion, and capers and top with remaining
potatoes and salt and pepper to taste. Pour cream
over mixture and bake in middle of oven until potatoes are tender and top is golden, about 20 minutes.
Serves 2.

Aligot Gratin
(Potato and Cheese Purée)

1¾ pounds russet (baking) potatoes
3 tablespoons unsalted butter, softened
4 garlic cloves, minced
¾ cup milk
1 pound fresh mozzarella cheese,
    chopped fine
⅔ cup well-chilled heavy cream
2 tablespoons drained bottled horseradish

In a large saucepan cover potatoes with salted
water by 2 inches and simmer until very tender,
about 50 minutes. Drain potatoes. Return potatoes to
pan and heat over low heat, shaking pan, until dry.
Cool potatoes until they can be handled.

Peel potatoes and force through a ricer or medium
disk of a food mill into pan. Add butter, garlic, and
milk and cook mixture over moderately low heat,
beating constantly with a wooden spoon, until fluffy
and heated through, about 2 minutes.

Add mozzarella and salt and pepper to taste and
cook, beating, until cheese is melted and mixture
forms long elastic strands when lifted with spoon.

Divide *aligot* among 6 buttered 1-cup shallow
gratin dishes or one 6-cup buttered gratin dish. *Aligot
may be prepared up to this point 1 day ahead and
chilled, covered. Bring aligot to room temperature
before proceeding.*

Preheat broiler.

In a bowl with an electric mixer beat cream until
it holds soft peaks and beat in horseradish and salt to
taste. Spread horseradish cream over *aligot* and broil
about 4 inches from heat until golden, about 1 minute. Serves 6.

PHOTO ON PAGE 28

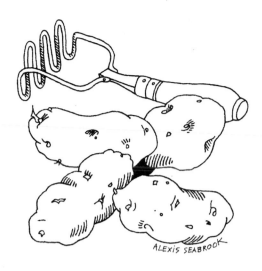

ALEXIS SEABROOK

Parsley Leaf Potatoes

¾ stick (6 tablespoons) unsalted butter, melted
12 small russet (baking) potatoes
  (about 4 pounds)
24 fresh flat-leafed parsley leaves, washed and
  spun dry

Preheat oven to 450° F.

Pour butter into 1 large or 2 small shallow baking pans and tilt to coat. Put potatoes, 1 at a time, on a work surface and halve horizontally. Put a parsley leaf on cut side of each potato half and season potatoes with salt. Put potatoes, cut sides down, in melted butter. Sprinkle potatoes with salt to taste and roast, cut sides down, 35 minutes, or until golden. (Potatoes may be kept warm, covered with foil, about 15 minutes.) Serves 8 generously.

Roasted Potatoes and Onions with Wilted Greens

1 pound small red potatoes (each about 1 inch
  in diameter)
1 medium red onion, halved lengthwise and cut
  lengthwise into ½-inch-thick slices
1 tablespoon olive oil
¼ pound spinach or arugula, coarse stems
  discarded, leaves washed well and spun dry
  (about 3 cups)
2 teaspoons cider vinegar, or to taste

Preheat oven to 450° F.

Cut potatoes in half (quarter any larger potatoes). In a shallow baking pan toss potatoes and onion slices with oil and season with salt and pepper. Roast potatoes and onions in middle of oven, stirring occasionally, until lightly browned and tender, about 25 minutes.

Transfer hot potatoes and onions to a bowl. Add spinach or arugula, vinegar, and salt and pepper to taste, tossing until greens are wilted.

Serve dish warm or at room temperature. Serves 2 as a side dish.

Scalloped Potatoes and Parsnips

1 large red onion
2 tablespoons water
2 parsnips
  (about ½ pound)
2 small russet (baking) potatoes
  (about ¾ pound total)
1¼ cups low-fat (1%) milk
¾ cup chicken broth
1½ tablespoons all-purpose flour
a pinch freshly grated nutmeg

Halve onion lengthwise and cut crosswise into ¼-inch-thick slices. In a large saucepan cook onion in water, covered, over moderate heat, stirring occasionally, 5 minutes, or until softened. Remove cover and cook onion until any liquid in saucepan is evaporated.

Preheat oven to 425° F.

Peel parsnips and potatoes. Grate parsnips coarse and cut potatoes crosswise into ⅛-inch-thick slices. In a bowl whisk together milk, broth, and flour until combined well. Add milk mixture to onion with parsnips, potatoes, nutmeg, and salt to taste and simmer, stirring frequently, 1 minute.

Pour vegetable mixture carefully into a shallow 1½-quart baking dish and bake in lower third of oven 45 minutes, or until top is golden brown and scalloped potatoes are tender when pierced with a knife. Serves 4.

Each serving: 187 calories,
1.3 grams fat (6% of calories from fat)

PHOTO ON PAGE 87

Steamed Acorn Squash with Lime and Scallion

1 small acorn squash
2 teaspoons fresh lime juice
1 tablespoon extra-virgin olive oil
1 scallion, chopped fine

Halve squash lengthwise and discard seeds and strings. Using outer ridges as a guide, cut squash lengthwise into sections. Arrange squash on a steamer rack in a saucepan and steam over boiling water, covered, until tender, about 15 minutes.

While squash is steaming, in a bowl whisk together lime juice, oil, and salt and pepper to taste.

On a platter drizzle squash with dressing and sprinkle with scallion. Serves 2.

Roasted Golden Nugget Squash

3 golden nugget* or golden acorn squash
  (3 to 3½ pounds total)
1 tablespoon olive oil

*available at specialty produce markets, many
  supermarkets, and some Asian markets

Preheat oven to 400° F.

Cut each squash into 6 wedges and scoop out and discard seeds and strings. In a large shallow baking pan drizzle squash with oil, rubbing to coat flesh. Season squash with salt and pepper and arrange, cut edges down, in pan.

Bake squash, turning it over halfway through baking, until tender, about 40 minutes. Serves 6 to 8.

PHOTO ON PAGE 72

Scallion Griddlecakes

¼ cup all-purpose flour
¼ teaspoon baking soda
½ teaspoon salt
2 tablespoons milk
2 tablespoons sour cream
1 large egg, beaten lightly
1 cup chopped scallion greens
  (about 6)
2 tablespoons vegetable oil

In a bowl whisk together flour, baking soda, and salt. In a blender or food processor blend milk, sour cream, egg, and ½ cup scallion until smooth. Add milk mixture to flour mixture and stir in remaining ½ cup scallion until combined well.

In a large non-stick skillet heat oil over moderately high heat until hot but not smoking and working in 2 batches drop batter by tablespoons into skillet. Spread batter into cakes 2 inches in diameter and cook 2 to 3 minutes on each side, or until golden. Transfer griddlecakes with a metal spatula to a heatproof plate and keep warm. Makes about 8 griddlecakes, serving 2 as a side dish.

Shredded Sweet Potato with Cumin and Scallion

1 pound sweet potatoes (about 2 medium)
1½ tablespoons vegetable oil
½ teaspoon ground cumin
¼ cup minced scallion
1 teaspoon fresh lemon juice, or to taste

Peel sweet potatoes and quarter lengthwise. In a food processor shred sweet potatoes.

In a 12-inch non-stick skillet heat oil over moderately high heat until hot but not smoking and sauté sweet potatoes with cumin and salt and pepper to taste, stirring, until just tender, about 3 minutes. Stir in scallion and lemon juice. Serves 2.

Whipped Chipotle Sweet Potatoes

5½ pounds sweet potatoes (about 8 large),
   scrubbed
1½ to 2 canned *chipotle* chilies in *adobo* sauce*,
   minced and mashed to a paste (about
   1 tablespoon)
3 tablespoons unsalted butter, cut into pieces
   and softened

*available at some supermarkets and specialty
   foods shops and by mail order from Mo
   Hotta-Mo Betta, tel. (800) 462-3220

Preheat oven to 450° F. and line a baking sheet
with foil.

Prick potatoes and bake in middle of oven 1 to 1½
hours, or until very soft. Cool potatoes until they can
be handled and scoop flesh into a bowl. With an
electric mixer beat potatoes with chili paste, butter,
and salt and pepper to taste just until smooth and
spread in a buttered 2-quart shallow baking dish.
*Potatoes may be prepared up to this point 1 day
ahead and chilled, covered. Bring potatoes to room
temperature before proceeding.*

Reduce oven temperature to 350° F. Bake potatoes in middle of oven until hot, 20 to 25 minutes.
Serves 8.

Savory Tomato Bread Puddings

a 14½-ounce can stewed tomatoes
   including juice
1½ tablespoons firmly packed dark brown sugar
1 teaspoon Worcestershire sauce
a pinch cayenne
2 tablespoons unsalted butter,
   melted
4 slices (each about ⅜ inch thick) firm white
   sandwich bread, crusts discarded, cut into
   ¾-inch squares

Preheat oven to 400° F.

In a small saucepan simmer tomatoes, brown
sugar, Worcestershire sauce, and cayenne, stirring,
5 minutes.

In a bowl drizzle butter over bread squares and
toss to coat. Divide bread squares between two 1-cup

soufflé dishes or custard cups and top each serving
with half of tomato mixture.

Bake tomato puddings in middle of oven 20 minutes. Serves 2.

Tomato and Onion Tart

2 large onions (about 1½ pounds), sliced thin
2 tablespoons olive oil
butter pastry dough for a single-crust 12-inch tart
   (page 180)
½ pound dry jack* or Gruyère cheese, shredded
   (about 2 cups)
½ pound plum tomatoes, cut into ½-inch wedges
½ pound medium yellow tomatoes** (about 2) or
   plum tomatoes, cut into ½-inch wedges
¼ cup Niçoise olives, pitted

*available at cheese shops and by mail order
   from Dean & DeLuca, tel. (800) 221-7714
   or in New York City, (212) 431-1691
**available at specialty produce markets and
   some specialty foods shops

In a heavy skillet cook onions with salt to taste in
oil, covered, over moderate heat, stirring occasionally, until softened, about 20 minutes. Remove lid
and cook onions, stirring occasionally, until golden
and any liquid is evaporated. Remove skillet from
heat and cool onions slightly.

Preheat oven to 375° F.

On a lightly floured surface with a floured rolling
pin roll out dough into a 14-inch round (about ⅛ inch
thick). Fold round in half and transfer to a 12-inch
tart pan with a removable fluted rim or a 12-inch
quiche dish. Unfold dough, easing to fit, and trim
overhang to ¾ inch. Fold overhang toward center
and press against side of pan or dish. Spread onion
mixture over dough and top with cheese. Arrange
tomato wedges and olives in concentric circles over
cheese and season with salt and pepper.

Bake tart in middle of oven 1 hour, or until pastry
is golden, and cool on a rack. Remove rim of pan if
necessary.

Serve tart warm or at room temperature. Serves
12 to 16 as part of a buffet.

PHOTO ON PAGE 39

Butter Pastry Dough

2 cups all-purpose flour
1½ teaspoons salt
1½ sticks (¾ cup) cold unsalted butter,
    cut into bits
6 to 7 tablespoons ice water

In a large bowl whisk together flour and salt and with a pastry blender or fingertips blend in butter until mixture resembles coarse meal. Add ice water, 1 tablespoon at a time, tossing with a fork to incorporate, until mixture begins to form a dough. On a work surface smear dough in 3 or 4 forward motions with heel of hand to slightly develop gluten in flour and make dough easier to work with. Form dough into a ball and flatten to form a disk. *Chill dough, wrapped in plastic wrap, at least 1 hour and up to 1 week.* Makes enough pastry dough for a single-crust 12-inch tart.

Sesame Zucchini

2 medium zucchini
1 tablespoon Asian sesame oil
1½ teaspoons sesame seeds, toasted lightly
1 teaspoon soy sauce, or to taste
1 tablespoon fresh lemon juice

Halve zucchini lengthwise and cut crosswise into ½-inch pieces. In a steamer set over simmering water steam zucchini, covered, until just tender, about 5 minutes.

In a small bowl toss zucchini with sesame oil and seeds, soy sauce, and salt to taste until coated well and sprinkle with lemon juice. Serve warm or at room temperature. Serves 2.

Root Vegetable Purée

2 pounds rutabagas, peeled and cut into ¾-inch
    pieces (about 6 cups)
¾ pound carrots, peeled and cut into 1-inch
    pieces (about 1 cup)
3 pounds large red potatoes
½ stick (¼ cup) unsalted butter,
    cut into pieces

In a large saucepan cover rutabagas and carrots with salted water. Bring water to a boil and simmer, covered, until vegetables are very tender, 40 to 50 minutes.

While rutabagas and carrots are simmering, peel potatoes and cut into ¼-inch pieces. In another large saucepan cover potatoes with salted water. Bring water to a boil and simmer potatoes, covered, until tender, 15 to 20 minutes.

Drain rutabagas and carrots well in a large sieve and in a food processor purée until smooth. Drain potatoes well in sieve and force through a ricer or food mill fitted with medium disk into a large bowl. Stir in rutabaga-carrot purée, butter, and salt and pepper to taste and combine well. *Purée may be made 3 days ahead and chilled, covered. Reheat purée before serving.* Serves 8.

PHOTO ON PAGE 77

Fennel-Marinated Vegetables in Lettuce Cones

2 teaspoons fennel seeds
3 tablespoons white-wine vinegar
½ cup extra-virgin olive oil
12 scallions (white and pale green parts only),
    quartered lengthwise
2 orange or red bell peppers, cut into
    ¼-inch-wide strips
2 yellow bell peppers, cut into ¼-inch-wide strips
3 celery ribs, cut into ¼-inch-wide strips about
    4 inches long
1 medium *jícama* (about ¾ pound), peeled
    and cut into ¼-inch-wide strips about
    4 inches long
12 large soft-leafed lettuce leaves, washed,
    drained well, and thick rib cut out to
    facilitate rolling

In a small dry heavy skillet toast fennel seeds over moderate heat, shaking skillet occasionally, until fragrant, about 3 minutes.

In a blender blend seeds, vinegar, oil, and salt and pepper to taste until emulsified.

In a glass baking dish combine fennel marinade and all vegetables except lettuce leaves. *Marinate vegetables, covered and chilled, overnight.*

Divide vegetables among lettuce leaves, letting excess marinade drip off, and roll up leaves to enclose vegetables. (Use toothpicks to secure lettuce cones if necessary.) Serves 6.

PHOTO ON PAGE 25

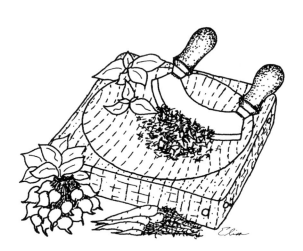

Southwestern Ratatouille

1 small onion, chopped fine
1 tablespoon olive oil
1 garlic clove, minced
1 medium zucchini, quartered lengthwise and
    cut crosswise into ½-inch pieces
½ cup fresh corn (cut from about 1 ear)
⅓ cup chopped red bell pepper
1 to 2 teaspoons minced fresh *jalapeño* chili
    including seeds (wear rubber gloves)
¼ teaspoon ground cumin
1 medium vine-ripened tomato, chopped
2 tablespoons chopped fresh coriander sprigs

In a 10-inch skillet cook onion in olive oil over moderate heat, stirring, until golden. Add garlic and cook, stirring, 1 minute. Add zucchini, corn, and bell pepper and cook, stirring, 1 minute. Cook vegetables, covered, stirring occasionally, 2 minutes, or until softened.

Add *jalapeño,* cumin, tomato, and salt and pepper to taste and cook, uncovered, stirring occasionally, until zucchini is just tender, 2 to 3 minutes. Stir in coriander. Serves 2.

Spring Vegetables with Shallots and Lemon

2 tablespoons olive oil
1 tablespoon unsalted butter
4 shallots, cut crosswise into
    thin slices
1 pound sugar snap peas,
    trimmed
1 pound asparagus, trimmed and cut
    diagonally into ½-inch slices
3 pounds fresh fava beans, shelled,
    blanched in boiling water 1 minute, and
    outer skins removed, or 1 pound frozen
    Fordhook lima beans, blanched and if desired
    skinned in same manner
two 3-inch strips lemon zest removed
    with a vegetable peeler and cut
    crosswise into julienne strips
2 teaspoons fresh lemon juice

In a skillet heat 1 tablespoon oil and ½ tablespoon butter over moderately high heat until foam subsides and sauté shallots, stirring, until tender, about 2 minutes. With a slotted spoon transfer shallots to a bowl. In fat remaining in skillet sauté snap peas with salt to taste, stirring occasionally, until crisp-tender and add to shallots.

In skillet heat remaining tablespoon oil and remaining ½ tablespoon butter over moderately high heat until foam subsides and sauté asparagus with salt to taste, stirring occasionally, until crisp-tender. Add fava or lima beans and sauté, stirring occasionally, 2 minutes. Add zest, lemon juice, snap peas and shallots, and salt and pepper to taste and sauté, stirring, until just heated through. Serves 6.

PHOTO ON PAGE 32

Steamed Vegetables with Basil Pecan Pesto

6 medium carrots, cut diagonally into
 ⅛-inch-thick slices
2 fennel bulbs (sometimes called anise), stalks
 trimmed flush with bulb and bulb cut
 lengthwise into ⅛-inch-thick slices
1½ pounds small red potatoes, cut into
 ¼-inch-thick slices
1½ pounds green beans,
 trimmed
1¼ cups basil pecan pesto (recipe follows)
3 to 4 tablespoons hot water

On a large steamer rack in a kettle layer carrots, then fennel, and then potatoes and steam over boiling water, covered, until potatoes are tender, about 10 minutes. Transfer steamed vegetables to a platter. Steam beans, covered, until just tender, about 10 minutes, and transfer to platter. In a food processor blend pesto with 3 tablespoons hot water, adding additional hot water if necessary to reach desired consistency.

Serve vegetables warm or at room temperature with pesto. Serves 6 as a main course.

Basil Pecan Pesto

2 cups packed fresh basil leaves, washed well
 and spun dry
⅔ cup olive oil
½ cup pecans, toasted until golden brown
 and cooled
⅓ cup freshly grated Parmesan
2 large garlic cloves, chopped and mashed to a
 paste with ½ teaspoon salt

In a food processor blend together ingredients with salt and pepper to taste until smooth. *Pesto keeps, its surface covered with plastic wrap, chilled, 1 week.* Makes about 1¼ cups.

OTHER SIDE DISHES

Fried Plantains

4 firm-ripe plantains*
vegetable oil for deep-frying

*available at Hispanic markets and some specialty
 produce markets and supermarkets

With a small sharp knife cut ends from each plantain and halve plantains crosswise. Cut a lengthwise slit through skin along inside curve. Beginning in center of slit pry skin from plantain and with rippled blade of a *mandoline* or decorating knife cut flesh crosswise into ⅛-inch-thick slices.

In a deep fryer or large deep skillet heat 1½ inches oil to 375° F. on a deep-fat thermometer and fry 12 to 15 plantain slices at a time, turning them, 2 to 3 minutes, or until golden, transferring with a skimmer or slotted spoon to paper towels to drain. (Plantain slices should be slightly crisp on outside but soft on inside.) Season plantain slices with salt. *Plantain slices are best served immediately but may be made 1 day ahead, cooled completely, and kept in an airtight container. Reheat plantain slices on a rack in a shallow baking pan in a preheated 350° F. oven 5 minutes, or until heated through.* Serves 8.

PHOTO ON PAGE 16

SALADS

ENTRÉE SALADS

Sprouted-Bean and Chicken Salad

3 cups chicken broth
2 cups water
3 whole boneless skinless chicken breasts
    (about 1½ pounds), halved
2½ tablespoons white-wine vinegar
2 tablespoons fresh lemon juice
½ teaspoon sugar
⅓ cup olive oil
2 tablespoons mayonnaise
1 tablespoon finely chopped fresh tarragon leaves
2½ cups assorted sprouted beans*
    (about 6 ounces)
1 cup chopped celery
3 scallions, sliced thin

*available at natural foods stores and most
    supermarkets

In a 6-quart kettle bring broth and water to a boil. Add chicken and simmer, covered, 9 minutes. Remove kettle from heat and let chicken stand in cooking liquid, covered, until cooked through, about 20 minutes. *Chicken may be poached 1 day ahead, cooled completely, uncovered, in cooking liquid, and chilled, covered. Bring chicken to room temperature to continue.* Cut chicken into ½-inch pieces.

In a bowl whisk together vinegar, lemon juice, sugar, and salt and pepper to taste until sugar is dissolved. Whisk in oil and mayonnaise in a stream, whisking until emulsified. Add chicken and remaining ingredients and toss until combined. Serves 6.

Black-Eyed Pea and Ham Salad

½ cup dried black-eyed peas, picked over
¼ teaspoon salt
1 tablespoon balsamic vinegar
½ cup finely chopped red bell pepper
⅓ cup finely chopped celery
¼ cup finely chopped red onion
1 teaspoon minced fresh *jalapeño* chili including
    seeds (wear rubber gloves)
1½ tablespoons olive oil
¼ pound cooked ham steak, coarsely chopped
1 teaspoon honey

In a saucepan combine peas with salt and water to cover by 2 inches and simmer, uncovered, until just tender, 25 to 30 minutes (do not overcook). Drain peas and in a bowl toss with vinegar, vegetables, *jalapeño,* and 1 tablespoon oil.

In a small skillet heat remaining ½ tablespoon oil over moderately high heat until hot but not smoking and sauté ham, stirring, 1 minute. Add honey and sauté, stirring, 1 minute. Add ham to salad and toss well. Serves 2.

Grilled Lemongrass Beef and Noodle Salad

For marinade
2 stalks fresh lemongrass*, outer leaves
    discarded and root ends trimmed
6 garlic cloves, minced
2 tablespoons Asian fish sauce*
    (preferably nuoc mam)
1 tablespoon soy sauce
4 teaspoons sugar
2 tablespoons vegetable oil
½ teaspoon Asian sesame oil

a 1- to 1¼-pound skirt steak or flank steak
½ pound dried rice-stick noodles*
    (rice vermicelli)
½ cup fresh basil leaves (preferably Thai
    basil*), washed well and spun dry
½ cup fresh mint leaves, washed well and
    spun dry
½ cup fresh coriander leaves, washed well
    and spun dry
about 1 cup nuoc cham (Vietnamese lime
    sauce, recipe follows)
a 1-pound seedless (European) cucumber,
    halved lengthwise and cut diagonally
    into ¼-inch-thick slices
about 2 tablespoons toasted rice powder
    (page 185)
2 to 4 small thin fresh red or green Asian
    chilies* (1 to 2 inches long) or serrano
    chilies, seeded and sliced very thin
    (wear rubber gloves)

Garnish: Thai basil*, mint, or coriander sprigs

*available at Asian markets or by mail order from
    Adriana's Caravan, tel. (800) 316-0820, or
    Uwajimaya, tel. (800) 889-1928

Make marinade:
Thinly slice lower 6 inches of lemongrass stalks, discarding remainder of stalks. In a food processor or blender finely grind together sliced lemongrass and garlic. Add remaining marinade ingredients and blend well.

In a large resealable plastic bag combine marinade and steak and seal bag, pressing out excess air.

Marinate steak, chilled, turning bag once or twice, at least 4 hours or overnight.

In a large bowl soak noodles in hot water to cover 15 minutes, or until softened and pliable.

Prepare grill (or preheat broiler). Bring a kettle of salted water to a boil for noodles.

Discard marinade and grill steak on an oiled rack set 5 to 6 inches over glowing coals 3 to 5 minutes on each side for medium-rare. (Alternatively, steak may be broiled on rack of a broiler pan 3 inches from heat for same amount of time.) Transfer steak to a board and let stand 5 minutes.

While steak is cooking, drain noodles in a colander and cook in boiling water 30 seconds to 1 minute, or until just tender. Drain noodles again and rinse under cold water to stop cooking. Drain noodles well.

In a large bowl toss noodles with herbs and half of nuoc cham.

Divide cucumber among 4 bowls or plates and top with noodles. Sprinkle each serving with 1 to 1½ teaspoons rice powder. Thinly slice steak on the diagonal and divide among noodles, mounding it. Sprinkle chilies over each serving and garnish with herb sprigs. Serve remaining nuoc cham on the side. Serves 4.

PHOTO ON PAGE 48

Nuoc Cham
(Vietnamese Lime Sauce)

6 tablespoons fresh lime juice
3 tablespoons Asian fish sauce* (preferably
    nuoc mam)
¼ cup sugar
½ cup warm water
1 garlic clove, forced through a garlic press
2 small thin fresh red or green Asian chilies*
    (1 to 2 inches long) or serrano chilies, seeded
    and chopped fine (wear rubber gloves)

*available at Asian markets or by mail order from
    Adriana's Caravan, tel. (800) 316-0820, or
    Uwajimaya, tel. (800) 889-1928

In a small bowl stir together all ingredients until sugar is dissolved. Makes about 1 cup.

Toasted Rice Powder

2 tablespoons raw white rice

In a dry small heavy skillet (not non-stick) toast rice over moderate heat, stirring, until deep golden, about 5 to 8 minutes, and transfer to a bowl to cool. In an electric coffee or spice grinder or in a blender grind rice to a powder. Sift powder through a fine sieve into a bowl. *Powder keeps in a tightly sealed jar 1 month.* Makes about 2 tablespoons.

Squid Salad with Tamarind Sauce

For sauce
2 tablespoons tamarind* (from a pliable block)
¼ cup warm water
2 tablespoons fresh lime juice
1½ tablespoons Asian fish sauce* (preferably *nuoc mam*)
2 garlic cloves, minced

2 teaspoons sugar
Tabasco to taste if not drizzling *sriracha* sauce on salad

1 pound cleaned large squid
⅓ cup fresh basil leaves (preferably Thai basil*), washed well and spun dry
⅓ cup fresh mint leaves, washed well and spun dry
1 cup thinly sliced red onion
sriracha sauce* (Asian chili sauce) to taste if desired

*available at Asian markets or by mail order from Adriana's Caravan, tel. (800) 316-0820, or Uwajimaya, tel. (800) 889-1928

Make sauce:
In a bowl stir together tamarind and warm water, mashing tamarind gently, about 4 minutes and strain through a fine sieve into a bowl, pressing hard on solids. Add remaining sauce ingredients, stirring until sugar is dissolved.

Flower-cut squid (procedure follows) or cut squid sacs crosswise into ½-inch rings and halve flaps crosswise. Halve large tentacles. In a large saucepan of boiling salted water cook squid 45 seconds, or just until opaque, and drain in a colander. Rinse squid under cold water to stop cooking and drain well. Add squid to sauce, tossing well. *Salad may be prepared up to this point 1 day ahead and chilled, covered. Bring salad to room temperature before proceeding with recipe.*

Add herbs and onion to salad and toss well. Serve salad drizzled with *sriracha* sauce. Serves 4.

PHOTO ON PAGES 46 AND 47

To Flower Cut Squid

Remove flaps from body sacs and reserve. Cut each body sac lengthwise along seam to form a flat piece and rinse squid well.

Spread squid inner side up on a work surface. Holding a sharp knife at a 45-degree angle to work surface, score squid diagonally every ⅛ to ¼ inch in a crosshatch pattern. Score flaps in same manner. Cut squid into 1-inch pieces.

Octopus, Cannellini, and Arugula Salad

a 3½-pound frozen octopus, thawed
2 carrots, sliced
1 large onion, sliced
3 large fresh parsley sprigs
1 teaspoon whole black peppercorns
8 whole cloves
1 bay leaf
2 celery ribs, 1 rib halved and the other cut into
    ¼-inch-thick slices
½ cup dried *cannellini* or Great Northern beans
1 bunch arugula, washed well and spun dry
3 tablespoons lemon juice
2 tablespoons extra-virgin olive oil
¼ teaspoon dried hot red pepper flakes

Cut tentacles from octopus and discard head. In a kettle combine octopus, carrots, onion, parsley, peppercorns, cloves, bay leaf, and halved celery rib with water to cover. Bring water to a boil and simmer, covered, 40 minutes, or until octopus is tender. Remove kettle from heat and cool 30 minutes.

While octopus is cooking and cooling, in a saucepan simmer beans in 4 cups water, covered, about 45 minutes, or until tender, and remove pan from heat. Cool beans in cooking liquid and drain.

Transfer octopus with tongs to a colander and rinse gently under cold water to remove as much of purple outer coating as possible without removing suction cups. Drain octopus and cut into 1½-inch-long pieces. In a bowl combine octopus and beans. *Salad may be prepared up to this point 1 day ahead and chilled, covered.*

Chop enough arugula to measure about ½ cup. In a bowl toss together octopus and beans, chopped and whole arugula, celery slices, juice, oil, red pepper flakes, and salt and pepper to taste. Serves 12.

PHOTO ON PAGE 34

Warm Teriyaki Beef Salad

3 tablespoons soy sauce
2 tablespoons seasoned rice vinegar
1½ tablespoons medium-dry Sherry
¾ pound flank steak, cut across grain into
    ¼-inch-thick slices
1 large garlic clove,
    minced
2 teaspoons grated peeled fresh gingerroot
½ pound mushrooms
3 scallions
1 small cucumber
2 tablespoons vegetable oil
1 cup fresh bean sprouts
2 tablespoons water
2 cups packed spinach leaves, washed
    well and spun dry

In a measuring cup stir together soy sauce, vinegar, and Sherry. In a bowl toss steak with garlic, gingerroot, and 2 tablespoons soy sauce mixture and marinate while preparing vegetables.

Discard stems from mushrooms and cut mushrooms and scallions into thin strips, keeping them separate. Peel cucumber and cut in half lengthwise. With a spoon scrape seeds from cucumber halves, discarding seeds, and cut each half crosswise into ¼-inch-thick slices.

In a large non-stick skillet heat 1 tablespoon oil over high heat until very hot but not smoking and brown steak, stirring frequently, until any liquid is evaporated, about 3 minutes. Transfer steak to a clean bowl.

In skillet heat remaining tablespoon oil over moderately high heat until hot but not smoking and sauté mushrooms, stirring occasionally, until liquid they give off is evaporated. Add scallions and sprouts and cook 1 minute. Remove skillet from heat and add steak, remaining soy sauce mixture, and water.

In a large bowl toss together spinach, cucumber, and warm steak mixture. Serves 2.

Green Papaya Salad with Shrimp

¼ pound small shrimp (about 9),
    shelled
For dressing
1 large garlic clove, forced through a
    garlic press
3 tablespoons fresh lime juice
1½ tablespoons Asian fish sauce*
    (preferably *nuoc mam*)
1 tablespoon sugar

1 small thin fresh red or green Asian chili* (1 to 2 inches long) or *serrano* chili, or to taste, seeded and chopped fine (wear rubber gloves)

¾ pound green papaya*, peeled, seeded, and coarsely shredded, preferably in a food processor (about 3 cups)
1 carrot, shredded fine
⅓ cup fresh coriander leaves, washed well and spun dry

Garnish: 2 tablespoons roasted peanuts, crushed

*available at Asian markets or by mail order from Adriana's Caravan, tel. (800) 316-0820, or Uwajimaya, tel. (800) 889-1928

In a small saucepan of boiling salted water cook shrimp 45 seconds to 1 minute, or until cooked through. In a colander drain shrimp and rinse under cold water to stop cooking. Halve shrimp horizontally and devein.
Make dressing:
In a large bowl whisk together dressing ingredients until sugar is dissolved.
Add shrimp, papaya, carrot, and coriander to dressing, tossing well. *Salad may be made 2 hours ahead and chilled, covered. Bring salad to room temperature before serving.*
Serve salad sprinkled with peanuts. Serves 4.

PHOTO ON PAGE 48

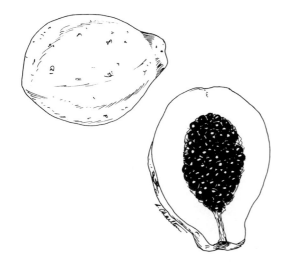

Salmon, Wild Rice, and Watercress Salad

4 cups water
½ teaspoon salt
¾ cup wild rice (¼ pound)
½ cup converted white rice
For salmon cooking liquid
1 cup water
½ cup dry white wine
2 tablespoons firmly packed light brown sugar
½ lemon, sliced very thin
1 medium onion, sliced thin
3 tablespoons raisins
1 tablespoon pickling spices tied in a cheesecloth bag

a ¾-pound piece salmon fillet with skin
1 bunch watercress, washed and spun dry, coarse stems discarded, and sprigs chopped coarse

In a saucepan bring water and salt to a boil and stir in wild rice. Simmer wild rice, covered, 20 minutes and stir in white rice. Simmer rice, covered, 20 minutes, or until tender. Drain rice in a sieve and rinse under cold water to cool. Drain rice well.
Make salmon cooking liquid:
In a medium saucepan bring cooking liquid ingredients to a boil and simmer, covered, 5 minutes to blend flavors.
Season salmon with salt and add to cooking liquid. (Liquid will not cover fish.) Steam salmon, covered, 7 minutes and remove pan from heat. In pan cool salmon to room temperature. Transfer salmon and cooking liquid to a bowl and chill, covered. *Salmon may be prepared up to this point 1 day ahead and chilled, covered.*
Remove salmon from cooking liquid and discard skin, breaking salmon into large flakes. Remove lemon, onion, and raisins from cooking liquid with a slotted spoon and reserve. In a bowl combine rice and ¼ cup cooking liquid and discard remaining liquid and pickling spices. Chop 4 reserved lemon slices and discard remaining lemon. To rice mixture add chopped lemon, reserved onion and raisins, salmon, watercress, and salt and pepper to taste and toss mixture. Serves 4.

Each serving: 384 calories, 9.8 grams fat (23% of calories from fat)

Southwestern Chicory Salad

1½ tablespoons extra-virgin olive oil
1 tablespoon white-wine vinegar
½ teaspoon Dijon mustard
¼ teaspoon chili powder
1 navel orange
3 cups packed chicory (curly endive) or escarole,
    washed well, spun dry, and chopped
1 large vine-ripened tomato, cut into ½-inch
    pieces
1 avocado (preferably California), pitted, peeled,
    and cut into ½-inch pieces
½ small red onion, sliced thin

In a salad bowl stir together oil, vinegar, mustard, and chili powder. Cut a slice from top and bottom of orange with a sharp knife to expose flesh and arrange orange with a cut side down on a cutting board. Cutting from top to bottom, remove peel and pith. Cut sections free from membranes. Add orange sections and remaining ingredients to dressing and toss to coat. Serves 2.

Caesar-Style Salad

½ cup plain nonfat yogurt
½ teaspoon anchovy paste
1 teaspoon fresh lemon juice
1 teaspoon balsamic vinegar
1 teaspoon Dijon mustard
½ teaspoon Worcestershire sauce
1 garlic clove, minced and mashed to a paste
    with ¼ teaspoon salt
¼ cup freshly grated Parmesan
    (about 1 ounce)
1 head romaine, rinsed, spun dry, and cut into
    wide strips (about 7 cups)
¼ cup finely chopped red onion

In a small food processor blend together yogurt, anchovy paste, lemon juice, vinegar, Dijon mustard, Worcestershire sauce, garlic paste, 2 tablespoons Parmesan, and salt and pepper to taste and transfer to a bowl or jar. *Chill dressing, covered, at least 1 hour and up to 2 days.*

Divide romaine strips among 4 bowls and drizzle dressing over salads. Sprinkle each salad with 1 tablespoon onion and ½ tablespoon remaining Parmesan. Serves 4.

Each serving: 63 calories,
2.2 grams fat (31% of calories from fat)

PHOTO ON PAGES 88 AND 89

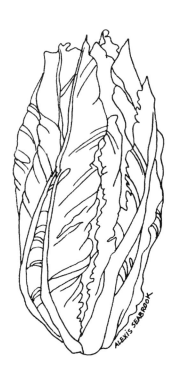

Watercress and Romaine Salad with Ginger Vinaigrette

5 teaspoons white-wine vinegar
2 teaspoons minced peeled fresh gingerroot
⅓ cup olive oil
2 bunches watercress, coarse stems discarded,
    washed well and spun dry (about 6 cups)
2 small heads romaine, leaves washed, spun dry,
    and torn into pieces (about 8 cups)

In a large bowl whisk together vinegar, gingerroot, and salt and pepper to taste and whisk in oil until emulsified. Add greens and toss to coat with vinaigrette. Serves 6.

PHOTO ON PAGE 67

Watercress, Celery, and Parsley Salad

2 teaspoons white-wine vinegar
1 tablespoon Dijon mustard
2 tablespoons olive oil
1 bunch watercress, coarse stems discarded,
    washed well and spun dry (about 3 cups)
1 celery rib, sliced thin crosswise
¼ cup fresh flat-leafed parsley leaves, washed
    well and spun dry

In a bowl whisk together vinegar, mustard, and salt and pepper to taste and whisk in olive oil until dressing is emulsified. Add watercress, celery, and parsley and toss to combine well. Serves 2.

Watercress, Celery, and Red Onion Salad

4 small celery ribs, sliced thin diagonally
three ¼-inch slices red onion
1 bunch watercress, coarse stems discarded,
    washed well and spun dry (about 2 cups)
1 tablespoon white-wine vinegar
1 teaspoon Dijon mustard
3 tablespoons extra-virgin olive oil
8 Kalamata olives, pitted and chopped
    (about ¼ cup)
1 tablespoon drained capers, chopped

In a bowl soak celery and onion in ice and cold water 15 minutes and drain. Pat celery and onion dry and in a salad bowl toss with watercress.

In a small bowl whisk together vinegar and mustard and add oil in a slow stream, whisking until emulsified. Stir in olives and capers and season with salt and pepper.

Pour vinaigrette over salad and toss well. Serves 2 as a first course.

Watercress Salad with Green Goddess Dressing

2 tablespoons mayonnaise
1 tablespoon plain yogurt
1 teaspoon anchovy paste, or to taste
1½ teaspoons white-wine vinegar, or to taste
1 small scallion, minced

2 teaspoons minced fresh tarragon leaves
1 tablespoon minced fresh chives
1 tablespoon minced fresh parsley leaves
1 bunch watercress, coarse stems discarded,
    washed well and spun dry (about 3 cups)
½ cucumber, peeled, seeded, and chopped
1 cup vine-ripened cherry tomatoes, halved
    if large

In a bowl whisk together mayonnaise, yogurt, anchovy paste, vinegar, scallion, herbs, and salt and pepper to taste.

Divide watercress, cucumber, and cherry tomatoes between 2 plates and spoon dressing over salads. Serves 2.

Date, Goat Cheese, and Mesclun Salad

For vinaigrette
2 tablespoons red-wine vinegar
1 tablespoon soy sauce
½ cup extra-virgin olive oil

8 cups *mesclun* (mixed baby greens, about
    ¾ pound), rinsed and spun dry
8 dried dates (preferably Medjool), pitted and cut
    lengthwise into thin strips (about 1 cup)
6 ounces Laura Chenel's Chabis* or other soft
    goat cheese, cut into pieces, at room
    temperature

*available at some specialty foods shops or by
    mail order from Laura Chenel Chèvre, 4310
    Fremont Drive, Sonoma, CA 95476,
    tel. (707) 996-4477

Make vinaigrette:
In a small bowl whisk together vinegar, soy sauce, and salt and freshly ground black pepper to taste and add oil in a stream, whisking until emulsified. *Vinaigrette may be made 1 day ahead and chilled, covered. Bring vinaigrette to room temperature and whisk before proceeding.*

In a bowl toss *mesclun* with vinaigrette and divide among 8 salad plates. Top salads with dates and goat cheese. Serves 8.

PHOTO ON PAGE 78

*Mixed Bitter Greens with
Sautéed Mushrooms*

1½ teaspoons minced garlic (about 1 large clove)
½ teaspoon dried rosemary, crumbled
¼ cup extra-virgin olive oil
½ pound *cremini* or white mushrooms, trimmed
　　and quartered (about 3 cups)
2 tablespoons red-wine vinegar plus additional
　　to taste if desired
1 medium head chicory, rinsed and spun dry
　　(about 6 cups)
1 large Belgian endive, cut lengthwise into strips
　　(about 1½ cups)
1 head *radicchio,* shredded (about 2 cups)

In a heavy skillet cook garlic and rosemary in 2
tablespoons oil over moderate heat, stirring, 30
seconds. Add mushrooms with salt and pepper to
taste and cook, stirring, until tender, about 5 minutes. Stir in 1 tablespoon vinegar and remove skillet
from heat.

In a large bowl toss chicory, endive, and *radicchio* with warm mushroom mixture. To skillet add 1
tablespoon vinegar, remaining 2 tablespoons oil, and
salt and pepper to taste and heat through, stirring.
Add hot dressing to salad and toss well. Add additional vinegar if using. Serves 4.

PHOTO ON PAGE 12

*Avocado, Hearts of Palm, and Red Onion Salad
with Coriander Vinaigrette*

For vinaigrette
1 small garlic clove
¼ cup fresh coriander, washed and spun dry
3 tablespoons fresh lemon juice
½ teaspoon sugar
¼ teaspoon salt
½ cup olive oil
For salad
a 14-ounce can hearts of palm, drained
4 firm-ripe California avocados
1 small red onion, sliced thin
Boston lettuce leaves (from about 2 heads)

Make vinaigrette:
In a blender purée garlic and coriander with lemon
juice, sugar, and salt. With motor running add oil in a
stream, blending until dressing is emulsified.
Make salad:
Cut hearts of palm and avocado into ¾-inch cubes
and in a large bowl with a rubber spatula gently toss
with onion and vinaigrette until combined well.
Line 8 salad plates with lettuce leaves and mound
avocado mixture on top. Serves 8.

PHOTO ON PAGE 16

*Asparagus and Mushroom Salad
with Shaved Parmesan*

1 pound medium to thick asparagus,
　　trimmed
½ pound mushrooms, stems trimmed even
　　with caps
4 medium radishes, halved lengthwise and
　　sliced thin crosswise
2 tablespoons fresh lemon juice
2 teaspoons Dijon mustard
½ teaspoon salt, or to taste
⅓ cup extra-virgin olive oil
1 bunch watercress, coarse stems discarded,
　　washed well and spun dry (about 3 cups)
a ¼-pound piece Parmesan at room temperature

With a sharp knife cut asparagus diagonally into very thin slices and transfer to a large bowl. Halve large mushrooms. Slice mushrooms very thin and add with radishes to asparagus. Toss salad gently.

In a bowl whisk together lemon juice, mustard, and salt. Add oil in a stream, whisking, and whisk until emulsified. Drizzle dressing over salad and toss gently. Grind pepper to taste over salad.

Spread watercress on a small platter and top with asparagus salad. With a vegetable peeler shave about half of Parmesan into curls over salad, reserving remaining Parmesan for another use. Serves 6.

Black Bean, Corn, and Tomato Salad

3 tablespoons fresh lemon juice
2 tablespoons olive oil
a 15-ounce can black beans, rinsed and drained
1 cup cooked fresh corn (from about 2 ears)
1 plum tomato, seeded and chopped
1 scallion, minced
2 tablespoons minced fresh parsley leaves
a pinch cayenne
4 large Boston lettuce leaves, rinsed and spun dry

In a bowl whisk together lemon juice, oil, and salt to taste. Stir in remaining ingredients, except lettuce leaves, with salt and black pepper to taste and let salad stand, stirring once or twice, about 15 minutes for flavors to develop. Line 2 plates with lettuce and divide salad between them. Serves 2.

Green Bean and Fingerling Potato Salad

2 pounds purple and/or white fingerling
    potatoes*, scrubbed
1 pound green beans, trimmed
¼ cup chopped mixed fresh herbs such as chives
    and garlic chives (with blossoms if desired)
    and thyme, summer savory, parsley, and
    mint leaves
2 tablespoons extra-virgin olive oil
½ teaspoon freshly grated lemon zest

*available at specialty produce markets and
    some specialty foods shops

In a large kettle simmer potatoes in salted water to cover until tender when pierced with a fork, about 10 minutes, and drain in a large colander.

In a large saucepan cook beans in 3 inches salted boiling water over high heat until crisp-tender, about 3 to 5 minutes. With tongs or a slotted spoon transfer beans to colander with potatoes and drain well.

In a bowl toss together warm potatoes, beans, herbs, oil, zest, and salt and pepper to taste. *Salad may be made 1 day ahead and chilled, covered.*

Serve salad warm or at room temperature. Serves 12 as part of a buffet.

PHOTO ON PAGE 38

White Bean and Red Onion Salad

1½ cups dried Great Northern or other
    white beans, picked over
1½ teaspoons salt
2 bay leaves
1 tablespoon coriander seeds, crushed coarse
For dressing
2 garlic cloves if desired
2 to 3 tablespoons fresh lemon juice
½ cup extra-virgin olive oil, or to taste

1 cup thinly sliced red onion
½ cup chopped fresh coriander sprigs or
    parsley leaves

In a large saucepan combine beans with water to cover by 2 inches and add salt, bay leaves, and coriander seeds. Simmer beans, uncovered, stirring occasionally and adding more hot water if necessary to keep beans covered, 1 to 1¼ hours, or until beans are just tender but not mushy.

Make dressing while beans are cooking:
Mince garlic fine and in a large bowl stir together well with lemon juice and oil.

In a colander drain beans, discarding bay leaves, and add to dressing. Toss salad and season with salt and pepper. Cool salad and stir in onion and herbs. *Salad may be made 1 day ahead and chilled covered.*

Serve salad at room temperature, thinning if necessary with 1 to 2 tablespoons water. Makes 5 cups.

PHOTO ON PAGE 51

Two-Bean Salad with Vegetables

¼ cup olive oil
2 tablespoons fresh lemon juice
1 cup canned black beans, rinsed and drained well
3 large plum tomatoes, seeded and cut into
     ¼-inch-thick dice
3 celery ribs, cut into ¼-inch-thick slices
6 large radishes, quartered lengthwise and cut
     into ¼-inch-thick slices
¾ pound green beans

In a bowl whisk together oil, lemon juice, and salt and coarsely ground black pepper to taste. Add black beans, tomatoes, celery, and radishes and toss to combine. *Salad may be prepared up to this point 2 days ahead and chilled, covered.*

In a 3-quart saucepan of boiling salted water cook green beans until just tender, about 5 minutes, and drain in a colander. Cut beans into 1½-inch pieces and stir into salad. Serve salad at room temperature. Serves 4.

PHOTO ON PAGE 61

Salade Chaude aux Lentilles avec Vinaigrette à la Moutarde
(Warm Lentil Salad with Mustard Vinaigrette)

1 cup *lentilles du Puy* (French green lentils)*,
     picked over and rinsed
6 cups water
1 onion, chopped fine
3 bacon slices, chopped
1 garlic clove, halved
¼ teaspoon dried thyme
2 fresh flat-leafed parsley sprigs plus ½ cup
     leaves, chopped fine
2 carrots, diced fine (about ¾ cup)
For vinaigrette
2 teaspoons white-wine vinegar
1½ tablespoons Dijon mustard, or to taste
¼ cup olive oil

1 bunch arugula, coarse stems discarded and
     leaves washed well and spun dry

*available at specialty foods shops and some
     natural foods stores

In a heavy saucepan combine lentils, water, onion, bacon, garlic, thyme, and parsley sprigs and simmer, covered, 20 minutes. Stir in diced carrots and simmer mixture, covered, until lentils are tender, about 10 minutes. *Lentils may be made 2 days ahead and kept in cooking liquid, covered and chilled. Reheat lentils before proceeding with recipe.*

Make vinaigrette:

Transfer 2 tablespoons lentil-cooking liquid to a medium bowl and whisk in vinegar, mustard, and salt and pepper to taste. Add oil in a stream, whisking, and whisk dressing until emulsified.

Drain lentils well in a sieve and discard parsley sprigs and garlic. Toss lentils with chopped parsley and vinaigrette and season with salt and pepper.

Just before serving, arrange arugula decoratively around salad. Serves 6.

PHOTO ON PAGES 26 AND 27

Beet and Asian Pear Salad with Baby Greens

4 trimmed beets (about 1 pound), scrubbed
1 Asian pear or firm-ripe pear such as Bartlett
     or Anjou
1 tablespoon apple jelly
2 teaspoons fresh lemon juice
½ teaspoon Dijon mustard
¼ pound mixed baby greens (about 4 cups)

Garnish: chopped fresh chives

In a saucepan simmer beets in water to cover by 1 inch, covered, 40 minutes, or until tender. Drain beets and cool. *Beets may be prepared up to this point 1 day ahead and chilled, covered.*

Peel beets and cut into ¾-inch wedges. Peel and core pear and cut into ½-inch wedges. In a small saucepan heat jelly, lemon juice, and mustard over low heat, stirring, until blended and jelly is melted. In a bowl combine beets and pear with warm dressing, tossing to coat.

Divide greens among 4 salad plates and spoon beet mixture over them. Sprinkle salads with chives. Serves 4.

Each serving: 71 calories,
0.4 gram fat (4% of calories from fat)

PHOTO ON PAGE 87

Parsley Cabbage Salad with Sherry Vinaigrette

¼ medium head cabbage, chopped fine
　(about 2 cups)
1 cup packed fresh flat-leafed parsley leaves,
　washed well, spun dry, and chopped coarse
3 tablespoons medium-dry Sherry
2 teaspoons extra-virgin olive oil
1 teaspoon red-wine vinegar

In a bowl toss together cabbage and parsley. In a small saucepan simmer Sherry until reduced to about 1 tablespoon and cool. Drizzle salad with Sherry, oil, vinegar, and salt and pepper to taste and toss well. Serves 2.

Eggplant Salad

½ cup olive oil
3 tablespoons fresh lemon juice
1 tablespoon Dijon mustard
1 garlic clove, chopped and mashed to a paste
　with 1 teaspoon salt
½ cup packed fresh basil leaves, washed well
　and spun dry
2 large eggplants (about 1½ pounds each), cut
　crosswise into ½-inch-thick slices
¼ cup pine nuts, toasted

Preheat broiler.
In a blender blend oil, lemon juice, mustard, garlic paste, and half of basil until smooth. In a measuring cup reserve ¼ cup dressing and in a large bowl toss remaining dressing with eggplant slices.

Arrange half of eggplant slices in one layer on a large baking sheet and broil 4 inches from heat until golden, 8 to 10 minutes. Turn slices and broil until golden, 5 to 7 minutes more. Transfer slices to a plate to cool and broil remaining slices in same manner.

Arrange eggplant and remaining basil on a platter. Drizzle salad with reserved dressing and sprinkle with pine nuts. Serves 12 as part of a buffet.

PHOTO ON PAGE 39

Potato Salad with Yogurt and Cucumber

1 pound boiling potatoes (about 3), peeled
　and cut into 1-inch pieces
¼ cup plain yogurt
1 small garlic clove, minced and mashed to a
　paste with ¼ teaspoon salt
1 tablespoon chopped fresh mint leaves or
　1 teaspoon dried, crumbled
1 small cucumber, halved lengthwise, seeded,
　and cut into ¼-inch-thick slices

In a saucepan combine potatoes with salted water to cover by 1 inch and simmer until just tender, 8 to 10 minutes. In a colander rinse potatoes under cold water to stop cooking and drain well.

In a bowl stir together yogurt, garlic paste, and mint. Add cucumbers and potatoes to yogurt mixture with salt and pepper to taste and toss well. Serves 2.

Potato and Toasted Corn Salad
with Buttermilk Dressing

3 pounds small red potatoes
1 tablespoon olive oil
1½ cups fresh corn (cut from about
   3 ears) or thawed frozen
½ cup buttermilk
2 tablespoons mayonnaise
1 tablespoon white-wine vinegar
3 large scallions, chopped

Cut potatoes into ¾-inch wedges. In a large saucepan of boiling salted water cook potatoes until just tender, 8 to 10 minutes, and drain well.

In a large skillet heat oil until hot but not smoking and cook corn, covered, over moderately high heat, shaking skillet occasionally, until browned, about 3 minutes. Cool corn slightly and combine with potatoes in a large bowl. *Potatoes and corn may be cooked 1 day ahead and chilled, covered.*

In a bowl stir together buttermilk, mayonnaise, and vinegar. To potatoes and corn add buttermilk mixture, scallions, and salt and pepper to taste, tossing to coat. Serves 8.

PHOTO ON PAGE 45

Smoky Potato Salad

1½ pounds small red potatoes
1 tablespoon salt
6 slices bacon
4 tablespoons vegetable oil
5 scallions
2 tablespoons cider vinegar

In a 3-quart saucepan combine potatoes with cold water to cover by 2 inches and bring to a boil. Add salt and simmer, covered, until potatoes are just tender, 10 to 15 minutes. In a colander drain potatoes and cool. *Potatoes may be boiled 2 days ahead and chilled, covered.*

Prepare grill.

In a skillet cook bacon over moderate heat until crisp. Transfer bacon to paper towels to drain and reserve 1 tablespoon drippings. Break bacon into large bits.

Halve potatoes and toss gently with 1 tablespoon oil to coat well. Arrange potatoes, cut sides down, on an oiled rack set 5 to 6 inches over glowing coals and grill until golden, 4 to 5 minutes. (Alternatively, potatoes may be grilled in a hot well-seasoned large ridged grill pan over moderately high heat.)

Cut scallions crosswise into 1½-inch pieces and quarter pieces lengthwise.

In a large bowl toss potatoes with reserved drippings, bacon, remaining 3 tablespoons oil, vinegar, scallions, and salt and coarsely ground black pepper to taste. Serve potato salad at room temperature. Serves 4.

PHOTO ON PAGE 61

Herb Salad Spring Rolls with Spicy Peanut Sauce

a 1.8- to 2-ounce package bean-thread
   (cellophane) noodles*
1½ tablespoons rice vinegar
2 large Boston lettuce leaves, washed well and
   spun dry
eight 8-inch rounds rice paper* plus additional
   in case some tear
2 tablespoons roasted peanuts, crushed
1 scallion, cut into 2-inch julienne strips
¼ cup finely shredded carrot
⅓ cup thinly sliced cabbage
¼ cup fresh basil leaves (preferably Thai basil*),
   washed well and spun dry
¼ cup fresh mint leaves, washed well and
   spun dry
¼ cup fresh coriander leaves, washed well and
   spun dry

Accompaniment: spicy peanut sauce
   (recipe follows)

*available at Asian markets or by mail order from
   Adriana's Caravan, tel. (800) 316-0820, or
   Uwajimaya, tel. (800) 889-1928

In a bowl soak noodles in very hot water to cover 15 minutes and drain well in a colander. Reserve half of noodles for another use. With scissors cut remaining noodles into 3- to 4-inch lengths and in a small bowl toss with vinegar and salt to taste.

Cut out and discard ribs from lettuce leaves, halving each leaf.

In a shallow baking pan or cake pan soak 2 rounds rice paper in hot water to cover until very pliable, 45 seconds to 1 minute.

Carefully spread 1 soaked round on a paper towel, leaving remaining round in water, and blot with paper towels. Arrange 1 piece of lettuce leaf on bottom half of sheet, leaving a 1-inch border along edge. Top lettuce with about one fourth peanuts and about one fourth noodles, arranging them in a line across lettuce. Top noodles with one fourth each of scallion, carrot, cabbage, and herbs. Roll up filling tightly in rice paper, folding in sides after first roll to completely enclose filling, and continue rolling.

Spread remaining soaked rice paper round on paper towel and blot with another paper towel. Wrap rice paper around spring roll in same manner. (Double wrapping covers any tears and makes roll more stable and easier to eat.) Wrap spring roll in rinsed and squeezed paper towel and put in a resealable plastic bag. Make 3 more rolls with remaining ingredients in same manner. *Rolls may be made 1 day ahead and chilled, wrapped in wet paper towels in sealed plastic bag. Before serving, bring rolls to room temperature.*

Discard paper towels. Halve rolls diagonally and serve with peanut sauce. Serves 4 as a first course.

PHOTO ON PAGES 46 AND 47

Spicy Peanut Sauce

3 garlic cloves, minced
¼ teaspoon dried hot red pepper flakes, or to taste
1 tablespoon vegetable oil
1 tablespoon tomato paste
3 tablespoons creamy peanut butter
3 tablespoons hoisin sauce*
½ teaspoon sugar
¾ cup water

*available at Asian markets or by mail order from Adriana's Caravan, tel. (800) 316-0820, or Uwajimaya, tel. (800) 889-1928

In a small saucepan cook garlic and red pepper flakes in oil over moderate heat, stirring, until garlic is golden. Whisk in remaining ingredients and bring to a boil, whisking. Simmer sauce, whisking, until thickened, about 1 minute. *Sauce may be made 3 days ahead and chilled, covered.*

Serve sauce warm or at room temperature. Makes about 1 cup.

Snow Pea and Napa Cabbage Slaw

½ pound snow peas, trimmed and strings discarded
1½ pounds Napa cabbage, cut into thin shreds (about 9 cups)
2 medium carrots, shredded
1 medium yellow bell pepper, cut into thin strips
3 scallions, chopped fine
1 tablespoon fresh lemon juice
1 tablespoon rice vinegar
3 tablespoons olive oil

In a large saucepan of boiling water blanch snow peas 15 seconds and transfer with a slotted spoon to a bowl of ice and cold water to stop cooking. Drain snow peas well and slice thin diagonally. In a large bowl toss snow peas with remaining ingredients and salt and pepper to taste. Serves 6.

PHOTO ON PAGE 65

Warm Cherry Tomato Salad

2 tablespoons balsamic vinegar
2 tablespoons extra-virgin olive oil
1¼ teaspoons minced garlic
6 cups assorted vine-ripened cherry tomatoes*,
    some halved
⅓ cup finely shredded fresh basil leaves

Garnish: basil sprigs

*available at some specialty produce markets
    and by mail order from Chefs' Produce
    Team, 1400 East Olympic Blvd., Suite C,
    Los Angeles, CA 90021, tel. (213) 624-8909

In a large non-stick skillet heat vinegar, oil, and
garlic over moderate heat until just simmering. Add
tomatoes and salt and freshly ground black pepper to
taste and cook, tossing, until slightly tender and
heated through, 1 to 2 minutes.

Toss tomatoes with shredded basil and garnish
with basil sprigs. Serves 6.

PHOTO ON PAGE 42

SALADS WITH FRUIT

Fig, Ham, and Nectarine Salad in Wine Syrup

½ cup dry white wine
½ cup water
¼ cup sugar
2 pints fresh green and/or purple figs, stemmed
2 large firm-ripe nectarines
a ¼-pound piece Smithfield ham or prosciutto,
    cut into ¼-inch-thick julienne strips

Garnish: mint sprigs and/or fresh grape leaves

In a saucepan boil wine and water with sugar until
sugar dissolves, about 3 minutes, and remove pan
from heat. Cool wine syrup and chill. *Syrup may be
made 1 week ahead and chilled, covered.*

Halve figs and cut nectarines into thin wedges. In
a bowl gently toss fruit with ham or prosciutto and
half of wine syrup.

Arrange salad on a platter and pour remaining
wine syrup over it. Garnish salad with mint and/or
grape leaves. Serves 12 as part of a buffet.

PHOTO ON PAGE 10

Melon with Feta, Red Onion, and Pine Nuts

1 tablespoon vegetable oil
2 red onions, sliced ¼ inch thick
2 cantaloupes
1 honeydew melon
¼ cup chopped fresh mint leaves
1 tablespoon fresh lime juice
½ cup crumbled feta cheese
    (about 4 ounces)
¼ cup pine nuts, toasted

In a large skillet heat oil over moderate heat until
hot but not smoking and cook onions, stirring occasionally, until just softened. Remove skillet from
heat and cool onions.

With a sharp knife cut a slice from top and bottom
of each melon to expose flesh and arrange cut side
down on a board. Cutting from top to bottom, remove rind. Halve melons, discarding seeds, and cut
1 cantaloupe half and 1 honeydew half into wedges,
1-inch-thick. Arrange wedges on a platter. Cut remaining melon into ¾-inch chunks and in a bowl
toss with mint, lime juice, and pepper to taste.

Spoon melon mixture over melon wedges on platter and top with onions, feta, and pine nuts. Just
before serving, toss mixture to combine. Serves 8.

PHOTO ON PAGE 45

Minted Orange, Fennel, and Red Onion Salad

For dressing
1 teaspoon coriander seeds
2 tablespoons fresh orange juice
2 tablespoons Sherry vinegar or
    red-wine vinegar
¾ teaspoon salt
3 tablespoons olive oil

1 medium-large red onion
1 large fennel bulb (about 1 pound)

3 large navel oranges

¼ cup loosely packed fresh mint leaves

Make dressing:

Heat a dry small heavy skillet over moderate heat until hot and toast coriander seeds, stirring, until fragrant and a little darker, about 2 minutes. With a mortar and pestle or in a spice grinder or cleaned electric coffee grinder grind coriander to a coarse powder. In a bowl whisk together coriander and remaining dressing ingredients. *Dressing may be made 1 day ahead and chilled, covered.*

With a Japanese rotary slicer or other thin-slicing device slice onion crosswise into thin spirals or rings. In a bowl of ice and cold water soak onion (separate rings if necessary) 15 minutes.

Trim stalks from fennel and with slicing device thinly slice fennel bulb crosswise.

With a sharp knife cut a slice from top and bottom of each orange to expose flesh and arrange cut side down on a cutting board. Cutting from top to bottom, remove peel and pith. Cut oranges crosswise into ¼-inch-thick slices.

Drain red onion well and pat dry between paper towels.

Arrange fennel, onion, and orange decoratively on a platter and scatter with mint. Whisk dressing and drizzle over salad. Serves 6.

PHOTO ON PAGE 20

Farfalle Salad with Grilled Shrimp and Broccoli

1 pound large shrimp (about 24), shelled and deveined

1 pound broccoli, cut into 1-inch flowerettes and stems cut into ¼-inch slices

½ pound *farfalle*
  (bow-tie pasta)

a 28-ounce can peeled whole tomatoes, seeded, drained, reserving ¼ cup juice, and chopped

¼ cup red-wine vinegar

1 garlic clove, minced and mashed to a paste with ½ teaspoon salt

1 teaspoon sugar

1 tablespoon chopped fresh thyme leaves

1 tablespoon chopped fresh parsley leaves

1 tablespoon extra-virgin olive oil

Prepare grill.

In a bowl toss shrimp with salt to taste. Thread shrimp on metal skewers and grill on an oiled rack set 5 to 6 inches over glowing coals until cooked through, about 3 minutes on each side. (Alternatively, shrimp may be cooked without skewers in a hot well-seasoned ridged grill pan over high heat for about same time.)

In a 6-quart kettle bring 5 quarts salted water to a boil and cook broccoli until crisp-tender, about 5 minutes. Transfer broccoli with a slotted spoon to a colander and rinse under cold water to stop cooking. Drain broccoli well and transfer to a bowl.

In same kettle of salted boiling water cook *farfalle* until just tender and drain in colander, rinsing under cold water to stop cooking.

In a bowl stir together tomatoes with reserved juice, vinegar, garlic paste, sugar, thyme, and parsley. Add *farfalle,* broccoli, shrimp, and salt and freshly ground black pepper to taste and toss to coat. Just before serving add oil to salad and toss to coat. *Salad may be made 2 hours ahead and chilled, covered.* Serves 4.

Each serving: 370 calories,
5 grams fat (12% of calories from fat)

Mediterranean Couscous and Lentil Salad

1 cup lentilles du Puy* (French green lentils)
   or brown lentils
3 tablespoons white-wine vinegar
1¼ cups water
1 cup couscous
½ teaspoon salt
¼ cup olive oil (preferably extra-virgin)
1 large garlic clove, minced and mashed to
   a paste with ¼ teaspoon salt
½ cup finely chopped fresh mint leaves
1 bunch arugula, coarse stems discarded and
   leaves washed well, spun dry, and chopped
2 cups vine-ripened cherry tomatoes, halved
¼ pound feta cheese, crumbled (about 1 cup)

*available at specialty foods shops and some
   natural foods stores

In a small saucepan simmer lentils in water to cover by 2 inches until tender but not falling apart, 15 to 20 minutes, and drain well. Transfer hot lentils to a bowl and stir in 1 tablespoon vinegar and salt and pepper to taste. Cool lentils completely, stirring occasionally.

In a saucepan bring water to a boil and add couscous and salt. Remove pan from heat and let stand, covered, 5 minutes. Fluff couscous with a fork and transfer to a large bowl. Stir in 1 tablespoon oil and cool completely, stirring occasionally.

In a small bowl whisk together garlic paste, remaining 2 tablespoons wine vinegar, remaining 3 tablespoons oil, and salt and pepper to taste. Stir lentils and dressing into couscous. *Chill salad, covered, at least 3 hours and up to 24.*

Just before serving, stir in remaining ingredients and season with salt and pepper. Serves 6.

PHOTO ON PAGE 66

Warm Pasta Salad with Mushrooms and Radicchio

⅓ pound *orecchiette* (ear-shaped pasta) or
   farfalle (bow-tie pasta)
2 tablespoons olive oil
½ pound fresh *shiitake* mushrooms, stems
   discarded and caps sliced

½ pound fresh white mushrooms, sliced
1 large garlic clove, minced
3 tablespoons red-wine vinegar
½ cup low-salt chicken broth
¾ cup frozen baby peas, thawed
½ teaspoon Dijon mustard
¼ pound *radicchio,* shredded (about 2 cups)
⅓ cup freshly grated Parmesan

In a kettle of boiling salted water cook pasta until *al dente.*

While pasta is cooking, in a large non-stick skillet heat 1 tablespoon oil over moderately high heat until hot but not smoking and sauté all mushrooms with salt and pepper to taste, stirring occasionally, until golden brown. Add garlic and 1 tablespoon vinegar and cook, stirring, 1 minute. Add broth and peas and simmer 3 minutes.

Drain pasta in a colander and stir into mushroom mixture. Toss mixture and remove skillet from heat. In a large bowl whisk together mustard, remaining tablespoon oil, and remaining 2 tablespoons vinegar until blended. Add *radicchio* and toss to coat with dressing. Add pasta mixture and Parmesan and toss well. Serves 2.

Toasted Bulgur Salad with Corn and Tomatoes

1½ cups coarse bulgur*
2¾ cups water
1 teaspoon salt
1 tablespoon extra-virgin olive oil
2 cups fresh corn (cut from 4 to 6 ears)

1 pint vine-ripened cherry tomatoes, halved
¾ cup chopped scallions
3 tablespoons red-wine vinegar,
    or to taste

*available at natural food stores and many
    supermarkets

In a large heavy dry skillet toast bulgur over moderately high heat, stirring occasionally, 5 to 10 minutes, or until it makes popping sounds and is browned lightly. Transfer bulgur to a bowl and cool.

In a saucepan bring water with salt to a boil and stir in toasted bulgur. Reduce heat and simmer bulgur, covered, about 20 minutes, or until water is absorbed. Remove pan from heat and let bulgur stand, covered, 10 minutes. Transfer bulgur to bowl and cool.

While bulgur is cooking, in skillet heat oil over moderate heat until hot but not smoking and cook corn, stirring, 2 to 3 minutes or until just tender. Cool corn and add to bulgur with cherry tomatoes, scallions, vinegar, and salt and pepper to taste, tossing to combine. *Salad may be made 6 hours ahead and chilled, covered.*

Serve salad at room temperature. Serves 8.

PHOTO ON PAGE 54

Lebanese-Style Tabbouleh
(Parsley and Bulgur Salad)

⅔ cup bulgur
2 cups water
⅔ cup minced red onion
1 teaspoon salt
½ teaspoon ground allspice
1 tablespoon dried mint leaves, crumbled, or
    ½ cup finely chopped fresh
2½ cups finely chopped fresh parsley leaves
    (preferably flat-leafed)
½ cup finely chopped scallion
¼ cup fresh lemon juice
¼ cup extra-virgin olive oil
1½ cups finely diced seeded seedless cucumber

Put bulgur in a heatproof bowl. Bring water to a boil and pour over bulgur. Let bulgur stand 1 hour.

While bulgur is soaking, in a large bowl stir together onion, salt, allspice, and dried mint, if using (do not add fresh mint at this time), and let stand for 30 minutes. Drain bulgur in a sieve, pressing hard to extract as much water as possible, and add to onion mixture with remaining ingredients, including fresh mint, if using.

Toss salad well and season with salt and pepper. Serves 4 to 6.

Wheat Berry Waldorf Salad

4 cups water
¾ teaspoon salt
1 cup wheat berries (whole-grain wheat,
    sometimes called hard wheat)*
1 Gala or McIntosh apple
1 Granny Smith apple
2 tablespoons walnuts, toasted and chopped
1 celery rib, sliced thin
⅔ cup packed fresh mint leaves, washed well,
    spun dry, and chopped
½ cup dried sour cherries**
¼ cup golden raisins
2 scallions, chopped
3 tablespoons seasoned rice vinegar
3 tablespoons fresh orange juice
¾ teaspoon freshly grated orange zest
8 Boston lettuce leaves

*available at natural foods stores and some
    specialty foods shops
**available at specialty foods shops and many
    supermarkets

In a saucepan bring water and salt to a boil and add wheat berries. Simmer wheat berries, covered, 1½ hours, or until tender. Drain wheat berries in a colander and cool to room temperature.

Cut apples into ½-inch chunks and in a large bowl toss with wheat berries and all remaining ingredients except lettuce. Season salad with salt and pepper and serve over lettuce. Serves 4.

Each serving: 369 calories,
3.8 grams fat (9% of calories from fat)

SAUCES

Bourbon Barbecue Sauce

¼ cup bourbon
¼ cup soy sauce
¼ cup Dijon mustard
¼ cup ketchup
¼ cup firmly packed brown sugar
3 scallions, chopped fine
1 tablespoon minced fresh rosemary leaves

In a bowl stir together all ingredients. Makes about 1¼ cups.

Mango and Red Pepper Barbecue Sauce

2 tablespoons olive oil
1 medium onion, chopped
1 medium red bell pepper,
  chopped
1 teaspoon salt
⅓ cup red-wine vinegar
3 tablespoons molasses
2 tablespoons Worcestershire sauce
¼ teaspoon ground allspice
1 medium mango (about 1 pound),
  peeled and cut into chunks
2 to 3 fresh *jalapeño* chilies, or to taste,
  seeded (wear rubber gloves)

In a skillet heat oil over moderate heat until hot but not smoking and cook onion and bell pepper with salt until softened and edges begin to brown. Stir in vinegar, molasses, Worcestershire sauce, and allspice and bring to a boil. Simmer mixture 1 minute to blend flavors and cool slightly.

Spoon mixture into a blender. Add mango and *jalapeños* and blend until smooth. Makes 1½ cups.

Gingered Plum Barbecue Sauce

4 black plums (about ¾ pound), cut into
  1-inch chunks
1 tablespoon finely grated peeled fresh gingerroot
1 garlic clove, chopped
3 tablespoons hoisin sauce*
2 tablespoons firmly packed brown sugar
2 tablespoons water
1 tablespoon soy sauce
1 star anise or ¼ teaspoon anise seeds
1 tablespoon cider vinegar
2 scallions, chopped

*available at specialty foods shops, Asian
  markets, and most supermarkets

In a saucepan simmer all ingredients except vinegar and scallions, covered, stirring occasionally, until plums are falling apart, about 20 minutes. Add vinegar and simmer, uncovered, stirring frequently, until sauce is consistency of ketchup, about 10 minutes. Discard star anise or anise seeds and stir in scallions. Makes about 1 cup.

Spicy Southern Barbecue Sauce

1 tablespoon olive oil
1 small green bell pepper,
  chopped fine
1 small onion, chopped fine
⅔ cup bottled cayenne pepper sauce, such as
  Durkee RedHot
⅔ cup fresh orange juice
¼ cup honey

In a small saucepan heat oil over moderate heat until hot but not smoking and cook bell pepper and onion, stirring occasionally, until softened and golden. Add remaining ingredients and simmer 5 minutes, or until slightly thickened. Makes 1⅓ cups.

Tandoori-Style Barbecue Sauce

1 tablespoon vegetable oil
2 teaspoons paprika
½ teaspoon ground cumin
¼ teaspoon ground cardamom
¼ teaspoon ground ginger
⅛ teaspoon cayenne
¼ cup plain yogurt
2 tablespoons fresh lemon juice
1 large garlic clove, chopped and mashed
    with ½ teaspoon salt

In a small saucepan cook oil, paprika, cumin, cardamom, ginger, and cayenne over moderate heat until mixture begins to sizzle and cook, stirring, 1 minute more. In a bowl stir together remaining ingredients and salt to taste and stir in spice mixture until combined. Makes about ½ cup.

Curried Tomato Barbecue Sauce

3 tablespoons curry powder
2 tablespoons vegetable oil
1 medium vine-ripened tomato (about ½ pound),
    cut into 1-inch chunks
2 tablespoons fresh lemon juice
1 teaspoon sugar

In a small saucepan cook curry powder and oil over moderate heat until mixture begins to sizzle. Cook mixture, stirring, 1 minute, and stir in remaining ingredients. Cook sauce, stirring, until smooth, about 10 minutes. Makes about 1 cup.

Pink Applesauce with Horseradish

5 red apples such as McIntosh (about 1½ pounds)
2 garlic cloves
½ cup sugar
⅔ cup water
1 tablespoon drained beet horseradish

Cut apples into ½-inch chunks (do not peel) and in a heavy saucepan cook with garlic, sugar, and water, covered, over moderate heat, stirring occasionally, 20 minutes, or until apple chunks are translucent and tender. Remove lid and cook mixture, stirring occasionally, about 10 minutes more, or until almost all liquid is evaporated.

Force apple mixture through a coarse sieve or food mill fitted with fine disk into a bowl, discarding solids, and stir in horseradish. *Applesauce may be made 4 days ahead and chilled, covered.*

Serve applesauce chilled or at room temperature with poultry or pork. Makes about 1¾ cups.

Balsamic Rhubarb Compote

3 tablespoons balsamic vinegar
⅔ cup sugar
¾ teaspoon grated peeled fresh gingerroot
2 fresh rhubarb stalks, leaves discarded, ends
    trimmed, and stalks cut crosswise into
    ¼-inch-thick slices, or 2 cups frozen sliced
    rhubarb, thawed, reserving liquid

In a saucepan simmer vinegar with sugar and gingerroot, stirring, until sugar is dissolved and stir in rhubarb (with reserved liquid if using frozen). If using fresh rhubarb, simmer until crisp-tender, about 1 minute, and transfer with a slotted spoon to a bowl. If using frozen, as soon as mixture returns to a simmer transfer rhubarb with slotted spoon to bowl. Simmer liquid until thickened slightly, about 5 minutes, and remove pan from heat. Stir in rhubarb.

Serve compote warm or at room temperature. Makes about 2 cups.

PHOTO ON PAGE 32

Cranberry, Shallot, and Dried-Cherry Compote

½ pound shallots (about 16, each about 1 inch
    in diameter)
1 tablespoon unsalted butter
¾ cup sugar
½ cup white-wine vinegar
1 cup dry white wine
½ teaspoon salt
1 cup dried unsweetened sour cherries*
    (about 8 ounces)
2 cups fresh or unthawed frozen cranberries,
    picked over
½ cup water

*available at specialty foods shops, many
    supermarkets, and by mail order from
    Chukar Cherries, tel. (800) 624-9544

In a saucepan of boiling water blanch shallots 1
minute and drain. Peel shallots and separate into
cloves where possible.

In a heavy saucepan cook shallots in butter over
moderate heat, stirring, until coated well. Add sugar
and 1 tablespoon vinegar and cook, stirring, until
sugar mixture turns a golden caramel. Add remaining vinegar, wine, and salt and boil 1 minute.
Add cherries and simmer, covered, 45 minutes, or
until shallots are tender.

Add cranberries and water and boil gently, uncovered, stirring occasionally, 10 minutes, or until
cranberries burst. Transfer compote to a bowl and
cool. *Compote may be made 5 days ahead and
chilled, covered.*

Serve compote at room temperature. Makes about
3 cups.

PHOTO ON PAGE 77

Pear Apple Chutney

2 firm-ripe red Bartlett pears
2 Granny Smith apples
1 cup golden raisins
½ cup rice vinegar (not seasoned)
¼ cup sugar
1 tablespoon finely chopped peeled fresh
    gingerroot
1 teaspoon mustard seeds
½ teaspoon cinnamon

Halve and core pears and apples. Cut 2 pear
halves and 2 apple halves into ¼-inch-thick slices
and chop remaining pears and apples.

In a saucepan combine sliced and chopped pears
and apples with remaining ingredients and bring to a
simmer, stirring gently. Simmer chutney, covered,
stirring occasionally, until fruit is just tender, 10 to
15 minutes, and cool. *Chutney may be made 1 day
ahead and chilled, covered.* Serve chutney chilled or
at room temperature. Makes about 4 cups.

PHOTO ON PAGES 84 AND 85

Kumquat, Seville Orange, and Apricot Marmalade

1 cup Ma Made prepared Seville oranges,*
   thin- or thick-cut
1 cup thinly sliced kumquats (about 5 ounces)
1 cup thinly sliced dried apricots (about ¼ pound)
2¼ cups sugar
½ cup water

*available at some specialty foods shops and
   by mail order from Williams-Sonoma,
   tel. (800) 541-2233

In a saucepan bring all ingredients to a boil, stirring, and simmer, stirring occasionally, 15 minutes, or until slightly thickened. Let marmalade cool in a heatproof bowl and chill, covered, until cold, about 2 hours. *Marmalade keeps, covered and chilled, 2 weeks.* Makes about 3 cups.

Herbed Mayonnaise

½ cup fresh parsley leaves, washed well, spun
   dry, and minced
¼ cup minced fresh chives
1 tablespoon minced fresh tarragon leaves or
   1 teaspoon dried, crumbled
1 teaspoon Dijon mustard
1 cup mayonnaise

In a bowl stir ingredients together until combined well and chill, covered, 30 minutes. *Sauce may be made 1 week ahead and chilled, covered.*
   Serve sauce with fish or chicken. Makes 1½ cups.

Spicy Saffron Mayonnaise

7 garlic cloves
¼ teaspoon saffron threads
½ teaspoon salt
1 cup mayonnaise
1 tablespoon fresh lemon juice, or to taste
¼ teaspoon cayenne

In a small saucepan of boiling water simmer garlic 5 minutes. While garlic is simmering, set a rack over pan and put saffron in a heatproof saucer on rack. Heat saffron 3 or 4 minutes, or until brittle. Remove saucer and rack and crumble saffron into a bowl. Drain garlic and mash to a paste with salt. Add garlic paste, mayonnaise, lemon juice, and cayenne to saffron and whisk sauce until smooth.

Chill sauce, its surface covered with plastic wrap, at least 1 hour for flavors to develop. (Color of sauce will deepen as saffron softens and dissolves.) *Sauce may be made 1 week ahead and chilled, covered.* Stir sauce before serving.

Serve sauce with steamed lobster or stirred into fish soups. Makes about 1¼ cups.

Pickled Carrot, Fennel, and Red Pepper Relish

1 pound carrots (about 7 medium)
1 red bell pepper
1 medium fennel bulb (sometimes called
   anise, about ¾ pound)
1 small onion
¾ cup cider vinegar
⅓ cup sugar
2 tablespoons vegetable oil
2 tablespoons ketchup
1 tablespoon mustard seeds
1½ teaspoons salt
1 garlic clove, crushed

With a *mandoline,* another hand-held slicer, or a sharp knife cut carrots into short ⅛-inch-thick julienne strips. With a sharp knife cut bell pepper into short ⅛-inch-thick julienne strips. In a steamer set over simmering water steam carrots, covered, 5 to 6 minutes, or until crisp-tender, and transfer to a bowl. Steam bell pepper 1 to 2 minutes, or until crisp-tender, and add to carrots.

Halve fennel bulb lengthwise and core. Cut fennel into short ⅛-inch-thick julienne strips. Halve onion lengthwise and cut into short ⅛-inch-thick julienne strips. Add fennel and onion to carrot mixture.

In a saucepan bring remaining ingredients to a boil, stirring to dissolve sugar, and pour over vegetables. *Marinate vegetables, covered and chilled, at least 1 hour and up to 1 week.*

Serve relish chilled or at room temperature with poultry, veal, pork, or lamb. Makes about 4 cups.

Spicy Butternut Squash and Orange Relish

six 4- by 1-inch strips orange zest removed
    with a vegetable peeler
a 1½-pound butternut squash
1 cup water
1 cup sugar
¼ teaspoon dried hot red pepper flakes
3 navel oranges
1 tablespoon balsamic vinegar
1 scallion, minced

Chop zest fine and in a small saucepan blanch in boiling water 1 minute. Drain zest in a fine sieve.

Halve squash lengthwise and discard seeds. Peel squash and cut into ½-inch dice.

In a saucepan bring water and sugar to a boil with red pepper flakes, stirring to dissolve sugar. Add squash and zest and simmer, covered, 5 minutes, or until squash is tender. Transfer mixture to a bowl and cool.

With a serrated knife cut peel and pith from oranges and working over bowl of squash cut orange sections free from membranes, letting sections drop into squash mixture and squeezing excess juice from membranes into mixture. Stir vinegar into relish. *Relish may be prepared up to this point 1 week ahead and chilled, covered.*

With a slotted spoon transfer relish to a serving bowl and stir in scallion. Serve relish chilled or at room temperature with poultry or lamb. Makes about 4 cups.

Spiced Pear and Shallot Relish

½ cup dry red wine
½ cup water
⅓ cup sugar
¼ cup fresh lemon juice
1 cinnamon stick
¼ teaspoon whole cloves
¼ teaspoon whole allspice
3 firm-ripe Bosc pears
2 shallots, minced

In a saucepan bring wine, water, sugar, and lemon juice to a boil, stirring to dissolve sugar. Tie spices in a cheesecloth bag and add to wine syrup. Simmer syrup 5 minutes.

Peel and core pears and cut into ¼-inch dice. Poach pears in syrup at a bare simmer, uncovered, stirring once or twice, 5 minutes and discard spice bag. Remove pan from heat and stir in shallots. *Relish may be made 1 week ahead and chilled, covered.*

Serve relish chilled or at room temperature with poultry or pork. Makes about 2¾ cups.

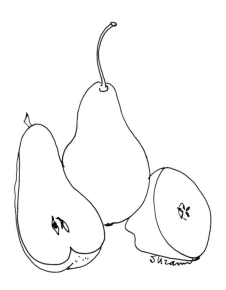

Cranberry and Pickled Beet Relish

½ cup red-wine vinegar
½ cup water
⅔ cup sugar
a 12-ounce bag fresh or frozen cranberries,
    picked over
a 16-ounce jar sliced pickled beets, drained
    and quartered

In a saucepan bring vinegar, water, and sugar to a boil, stirring to dissolve sugar. Add cranberries and simmer, stirring occasionally, about 20 minutes, or until thick. Stir in beets and cool. *Relish may be made 4 days ahead and chilled, covered.*

Serve relish chilled or at room temperature with poultry, beef, or game. Makes about 3 cups.

DESSERT SAUCES

Butterscotch Sauce

1 cup firmly packed light brown sugar
¼ cup light corn syrup
½ stick (¼ cup) unsalted butter
½ cup heavy cream
1½ teaspoons vanilla
¼ teaspoon fresh lemon juice

In a small heavy saucepan combine brown sugar, corn syrup, butter, and a pinch salt and cook over moderate heat, stirring, until sugar is dissolved. Boil syrup, without stirring, until it registers 280° F. on a candy thermometer, about 5 minutes. Remove pan from heat and stir in cream, vanilla, and lemon juice until smooth. (Sauce will thicken as it cools.) *Sauce keeps, covered and chilled, 3 weeks.* Serve sauce warm or at room temperature over ice cream. Makes about 1⅓ cups.

Dark Hot Fudge Sauce

⅔ cup heavy cream
¾ cup firmly packed dark brown sugar
2 ounces unsweetened chocolate, chopped fine
2 tablespoons unsalted butter
2 tablespoons light corn syrup
1½ teaspoons vanilla
⅛ teaspoon salt

In a small heavy saucepan heat cream and brown sugar over moderate heat, stirring, until sugar is dissolved. Add chocolate, butter, and corn syrup and cook, stirring, just until smooth. Bring mixture to a boil over moderate heat and boil 8 minutes. Remove pan from heat and stir in vanilla and salt. *Sauce keeps, covered and chilled, 3 weeks. Cool sauce completely before covering (any condensation will make it grainy). Reheat sauce, uncovered, over simmering water in a double boiler.* Serve sauce hot over ice cream. Makes about 1 cup.

Maple Praline Ice-Cream Sauce

½ cup Grade B maple syrup (or Grade A maple syrup flavored with 3 drops maple extract)
¼ cup firmly packed light brown sugar
⅛ teaspoon salt
½ cup heavy cream
1 tablespoon unsalted butter
½ cup pecans, chopped coarse and toasted lightly

In a 2-quart heavy saucepan combine maple syrup, brown sugar, salt, and cream and cook mixture over moderately low heat, stirring and washing down any sugar crystals clinging to side with a brush dipped in cold water, until sugar is dissolved. Boil mixture over moderate heat, undisturbed, until thickened and a candy thermometer registers 220° F. Stir in butter and pecans, stirring until butter is melted, and cool sauce until warm. *Sauce keeps, covered and chilled, 1 week.* Serve sauce warm over ice cream. Makes about 1 cup.

DESSERTS

Apple Walnut Upside-Down Cake with Calvados Caramel Sauce

For topping
3 to 3½ Golden Delicious apples (about 1½ pounds)
1½ sticks (¾ cup) unsalted butter
⅔ cup sugar
½ cup coarsely chopped walnuts

For cake batter
½ Golden Delicious apple
1½ cups all-purpose flour
1½ teaspoons baking powder
¾ teaspoon salt
½ teaspoon cinnamon
1 stick (½ cup) unsalted butter, softened
⅔ cup sugar
1 teaspoon vanilla
2 tablespoons minced peeled fresh gingerroot
2 large eggs
½ cup sour cream

Accompaniments
Calvados caramel sauce (recipe follows)
whipped cream

Make topping:
Peel, core, and quarter apples.

In a well-seasoned 10¼- by 2-inch cast-iron skillet melt butter over moderately low heat just until melted (butter should not separate). Stir in sugar until combined well. Arrange apple quarters decoratively, rounded sides down, in skillet and sprinkle walnuts evenly in between apples. Cook mixture, undisturbed, 25 to 35 minutes, or until apples are tender in centers and sugar is a golden caramel.

Preheat oven to 375° F.

Make cake batter while topping is cooking:
Peel apple and chop fine.

In a bowl whisk together flour, baking powder, salt, and cinnamon.

In another large bowl with an electric mixer beat softened butter and sugar until light and fluffy. Beat in vanilla and minced gingerroot and add eggs, 1 at a time, beating well after each addition. Beat in sour cream and with mixer on low speed beat in flour mixture gradually until just combined. Fold chopped apple into batter.

Remove skillet from heat and spoon batter over topping. Leaving a ¼-inch border of cooked apples uncovered, with a metal spatula spread batter evenly, being careful not to disturb topping. Put skillet in a shallow baking pan and bake cake in middle of oven 25 to 35 minutes, or until a tester comes out with crumbs adhering and cake is golden brown. Cool cake in skillet on a rack 10 minutes. Run a thin knife around edge of skillet and carefully invert cake onto a plate.

Serve cake warm or at room temperature with caramel sauce and whipped cream.

Calvados Caramel Sauce

1½ cups sugar
½ cup water
3 tablespoons Calvados or other apple brandy
2 tablespoons unsalted butter

In a dry heavy saucepan (about 2 quarts) cook sugar over moderate heat, stirring with a fork, until melted and cook without stirring, swirling pan, until it becomes a golden caramel. Remove pan from heat and carefully add water and Calvados or other apple brandy down side of pan (caramel will bubble and steam). Return pan to heat and simmer, stirring, until caramel is dissolved. Stir in butter. *Sauce may be made 3 days ahead and chilled, covered. Reheat sauce to warm before serving.* Makes about 1¼ cups.

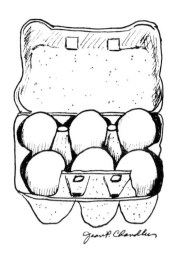

Jean P. Chandler

*Almond and Chocolate Dacquoise with
Cranberry Sauce*

For meringue layers
6 large egg whites
¾ teaspoon cream of tartar
¼ teaspoon salt
1½ cups sugar
1 teaspoon vanilla
1 cup whole almonds, toasted, cooled completely,
    and ground fine
For cranberry sauce
1 cup fresh or unthawed frozen cranberries,
    each berry halved
½ cup raspberry preserves
⅓ cup sugar
⅓ cup water
2 tablespoons fresh lemon juice

4½ ounces fine-quality bittersweet chocolate
    (not unsweetened), chopped
2 cups heavy cream
2 tablespoons sugar
½ teaspoon vanilla

Garnish: chocolate holly leaves (page 208)
    and cranberries coated lightly in honey and
    rolled in sugar

Preheat oven to 325° F. Line 2 baking sheets with
parchment paper and, using an 8-inch round cake
pan as a guide, trace 3 circles on parchment (2 on
one sheet and 1 on other). Turn parchment paper
over (circles will show through paper).

Make meringue layers:

In a large bowl with an electric mixer beat whites
with cream of tartar and salt until they hold soft
peaks. Add sugar all at once and vanilla and beat
until meringue holds stiff glossy peaks. Fold in
almonds gently but thoroughly and divide meringue
evenly among parchment paper circles, spreading to
fill in circles.

Bake meringue layers in upper and lower thirds of
oven, switching position of sheets halfway through
baking, 1 hour, or until firm and pale golden.
Remove parchment paper from sheets and cool
meringue layers on it on racks. Carefully peel off
parchment paper and put meringues, smooth sides
up, on a work surface. *Meringue layers may be made
1 day ahead and kept, wrapped well in plastic wrap,
in a cool dry place.*

Make cranberry sauce:

In a heavy saucepan combine cranberries,
preserves, sugar, water, and lemon juice and simmer
until thickened slightly, 10 to 15 minutes. *Sauce may
be made 2 days ahead and chilled, covered.*

In a double boiler or a metal bowl set over a
saucepan of barely simmering water melt chocolate,
stirring until smooth. Remove top of double boiler or
bowl from heat and transfer chocolate to a sealable
plastic bag. Seal bag, pressing out excess air.
Squeeze chocolate to one corner and snip off corner
as close to edge as possible to make a ⅛-inch hole.
Drizzle chocolate over smooth sides of meringues
(do not spread to coat) and chill, uncovered, until
chocolate is set, about 30 minutes.

In a bowl beat cream with sugar and vanilla until
cream holds stiff peaks.

Assemble dacquoise:

Put 1 meringue layer, chocolate side down, on a
cake plate and spread evenly with about half of
whipped cream. Repeat layering in same manner
with another meringue, remaining whipped cream,
and remaining meringue and chill *dacquoise* in a
cake keeper at least 8 hours. *Dacquoise may be
assembled and kept chilled up to 2 days.*

Garnish *dacquoise* with chocolate leaves and
sugared cranberries. Slice *dacquoise* with a serrated
knife and serve chilled with cranberry sauce.

PHOTO ON PAGE 80

If you choose to use holly leaves in the following recipe please note that although the leaves are non-toxic, holly berries are poisonous and should be kept away from food.

Chocolate Holly Leaves

4 ounces fine-quality bittersweet chocolate
(not unsweetened), chopped
15 fresh holly leaves (without berries) or small
lemon leaves, washed well and patted dry

In a double boiler or a metal bowl set over a saucepan of barely simmering water melt chocolate, stirring until smooth, and remove double boiler or pan from heat. With a ½-inch pastry brush coat underside of each leaf about ⅛ inch thick with chocolate. Chill leaves, chocolate sides up, until chocolate is set, about 30 minutes, and carefully peel off holly or lemon leaves. *Chocolate leaves may be made 1 week ahead and kept frozen, in layers separated by wax paper in an airtight container lined with wax paper.* Makes 15 chocolate leaves.

Banana Walnut Upside-Down Cakes

3 tablespoons unsalted butter, softened
2 tablespoons firmly packed brown sugar
2 tablespoons lightly toasted chopped walnuts
1 banana
¼ cup all-purpose flour
¼ teaspoon baking powder
⅛ teaspoon ground cardamom
3 tablespoons granulated sugar
1 large egg
¼ teaspoon vanilla

Preheat oven to 350° F.

In a small saucepan melt 2 tablespoons butter and divide between two 1-cup ramekins. Sprinkle brown sugar and chopped walnuts over butter. Cut banana into ¼-inch-thick slices and arrange over walnuts, overlapping and pressing lightly to fit.

In a small bowl whisk together flour, baking powder, cardamom, and a pinch salt. In a bowl with an electric mixer beat together remaining tablespoon butter and granulated sugar until combined well. Beat in egg and vanilla until combined and beat in flour mixture until batter is just combined. Divide batter between ramekins and bake on a baking sheet in middle of oven until a tester comes out clean, about 25 minutes. Run a sharp knife around edges of ramekins and invert cakes onto plates. Serves 2.

Carrot Cupcakes with Molasses Cream Cheese Icing

For cupcakes
1½ cups all-purpose flour
1 teaspoon baking soda
¼ teaspoon salt
1½ teaspoons cinnamon
½ teaspoon freshly grated nutmeg
¾ cup vegetable oil
1 cup firmly packed light brown sugar
2 large eggs
½ teaspoon vanilla
1¾ cups finely shredded carrots (about 4)
⅓ cup walnuts, chopped fine, toasted lightly,
and cooled
½ cup sweetened flaked coconut, toasted
lightly and cooled
For icing
½ cup (about 4 ounces) cream cheese,
softened
½ stick (¼ cup) unsalted butter,
softened
1 tablespoon unsulfured molasses
2 tablespoons confectioners' sugar

Make cupcakes:
Preheat oven to 350° F. and line twelve ½-cup muffin tins with paper liners.

In a bowl whisk together flour, baking soda, salt, and spices. In another bowl whisk together oil, brown sugar, eggs, and vanilla and with a wooden spoon beat in flour mixture until combined well. Add carrots, walnuts, and coconut, stirring until just combined. Fill muffin tins two thirds full with batter (there will be enough batter remaining to make 4 more cupcakes) and bake in middle of oven until a tester comes out clean, about 18 minutes. Turn cupcakes out onto a rack and cool completely. Muffin tins may be used again immediately to bake second cupcake batch. *Cupcakes may be made 2 days ahead and kept in airtight containers.*

Make icing:

In a bowl beat together icing ingredients until fluffy. *Icing may be made 2 days ahead and chilled in an airtight container. Soften icing at room temperature to spreading consistency.*

Spread icing on cupcakes. Makes 16 cupcakes.

PHOTO ON PAGE 24

Pecan Caramel Cheesecake

For crust
seven 5- by 2½-inch graham crackers
½ cup coarsely chopped pecans, toasted and
    cooled
6 tablespoons unsalted butter, melted and cooled
For filling
2 pounds cream cheese, softened
1½ cups firmly packed light brown sugar
¼ cup all-purpose flour
4 large eggs
½ cup sour cream
2 teaspoons vanilla
½ teaspoon salt
For topping
1 cup granulated sugar
1 cup heavy cream
1 tablespoon unsalted butter
1 teaspoon vanilla

1 cup pecan halves, toasted lightly and cooled

Make crust:

In a food processor grind graham crackers and pecans fine and in a bowl stir together with butter. Press mixture into bottom of a 9- by 2½-inch springform pan. Chill crust 30 minutes.

Preheat oven to 325° F.

Make filling:

In a large bowl with an electric mixer beat cream cheese until light and fluffy. Add brown sugar gradually, beating until combined well. Beat in flour and add eggs, 1 at a time, beating well after each addition. Add sour cream, vanilla, and salt, beating until combined well.

Pour filling into crust and bake in middle of oven 1 hour, or until edges are just set but middle trembles slightly (cheesecake will continue to set as it cools). Turn off oven and cool cheesecake in oven with oven door propped open about 6 inches until cooled completely, about 2 hours.

Make topping:

In a dry heavy saucepan cook ½ cup sugar over moderately low heat until melted. Cook sugar, swirling pan, until a deep caramel. Carefully add remaining ½ cup sugar and cream and simmer, stirring occasionally, until caramel is dissolved. Simmer mixture, without stirring, until it registers 225° F. on a candy thermometer and remove pan from heat. Stir in butter and vanilla and cool to room temperature.

Pour caramel topping over cooled cheesecake, spreading evenly. Arrange toasted pecan halves decoratively on top of caramel and chill cheesecake, covered, overnight. Remove side of pan before serving.

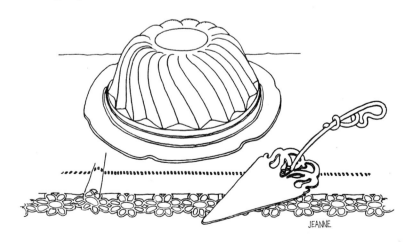

JEANNE

Devil's Food Cake with Chocolate Spider Web

For cake layers
1 cup boiling water
¾ cup unsweetened cocoa powder
   (not Dutch process)
½ cup milk
1 teaspoon vanilla
2 sticks (1 cup) unsalted butter, softened
1¼ cups firmly packed dark brown sugar
¾ cup granulated sugar
4 large eggs
2 cups all-purpose flour
1¼ teaspoons baking soda
½ teaspoon salt
For chocolate web and spider
½ cup semisweet chocolate chips
For coffee meringue frosting
2 large egg whites
1 cup granulated sugar
¼ cup water
1 tablespoon instant espresso powder

Make cake layers:
Preheat oven to 350° F. Grease three 9-inch round cake pans and line each bottom with a round of wax paper. Grease paper and dust pans with flour, knocking out excess flour.

In a bowl whisk boiling water into cocoa until smooth and whisk in milk and vanilla.

In a bowl with an electric mixer beat together butter and sugars until light and fluffy and beat in eggs, 1 at a time, beating well after each addition.

Into another bowl sift together flour, baking soda, and salt and add to egg mixture in batches alternately with cocoa mixture, beginning and ending with flour mixture and beating well after each addition.

Divide batter among pans, smoothing tops, and bake in upper and lower thirds of oven, switching position of pans halfway through baking, 20 to 25 minutes, or until a tester comes out clean and layers begin to pull away from sides of pans.

Cool layers in pans on racks 10 minutes and turn out onto racks to cool completely. *Cake layers may be made ahead and kept, wrapped in plastic wrap, at room temperature 2 days or frozen 1 week.*

Make chocolate web and spider:
On a sheet of parchment paper draw an 11-inch circle with a pen or pencil and draw a spider web on it, extending some of ends beyond circle (see drawing A). Tear off a large corner of the paper and on it draw a spider (see drawing B). Turn drawings over onto a large baking sheet.

In a metal bowl set over a saucepan of simmering water melt chocolate chips, stirring until smooth.

a.

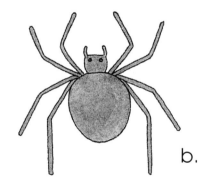

b.

Transfer melted chocolate to a pastry bag fitted with a #3 plain tip (slightly smaller than ⅛ inch). (Or, for a makeshift pastry bag: Transfer chocolate to a small sealable plastic bag and seal bag, pressing out excess air. Squeeze chocolate to one corner of bag and snip off about 1⁄16 inch from corner, making a small hole.)

Pipe chocolate on web, beginning with spokes, and on spider. *Freeze web and spider on baking sheet until very firm, at least 1 hour and up to 1 day.*

Make coffee meringue frosting:
In a metal bowl set over a saucepan of simmering water beat frosting ingredients with a hand-held electric mixer on low speed until mixture is warm

and sugar is dissolved. Beat frosting on high speed 7 minutes, or until thick and fluffy. Remove bowl from heat and beat frosting until slightly cooled.

Assemble cake:

Put a cake layer on a plate and spread top with some frosting. Top with another layer and spread top with more frosting. Top with remaining layer and frost top and side of cake with remaining frosting.

Working quickly, invert paper with frozen web onto another sheet of parchment or wax paper and peel off paper quickly but carefully. Invert spider web carefully onto cake and let soften at room temperature until overhanging edges begin to droop. Press overhang gently against side of cake. *Cake may be assembled and decorated 4 hours ahead and kept in a cake keeper, chilled. Let cake stand at room temperature 30 minutes before serving.*

Just before serving, peel chocolate spider from paper and put on cake.

PHOTO ON PAGE 73

Miniature Double-Chocolate Cakes

3 ounces fine-quality bittersweet chocolate
   (not unsweetened), chopped
¾ stick (6 tablespoons) unsalted butter, cut
   into pieces
⅔ cup granulated sugar
½ teaspoon vanilla
⅓ cup all-purpose flour
¼ teaspoon salt
3 large eggs
½ cup miniature semisweet chocolate chips
   (about 3 ounces)
confectioners' sugar for sifting over cakes

Preheat oven to 375° F. and generously butter twenty-four ⅛-cup muffin tins (about 1½ inches across top and ¾ inch deep).

In a metal bowl set over a saucepan of barely simmering water melt chocolate and butter, whisking until smooth. Remove bowl from heat and whisk in granulated sugar and vanilla. Add flour and salt, whisking until just combined, and whisk in eggs, 1 at a time, whisking well after each addition.

Fill each tin about three fourths full with batter and sprinkle about 1 teaspoon chips over each cake.

Bake cakes in middle of oven 12 to 15 minutes, or until a tester comes out with crumbs adhering. Turn cakes out onto a rack and cool. *Cakes may be made 4 days ahead and kept in an airtight container at room temperature.* Sift confectioners' sugar over cakes. Makes 24 miniature cakes.

Grape Milliard
(Grape Custard Cake)

1 pound seedless red grapes (about 3 cups),
   rinsed well and drained
½ stick (¼ cup) unsalted butter, softened
⅓ cup granulated sugar
1 whole large egg
1 large egg yolk
½ cup all-purpose flour
¼ teaspoon salt
½ cup milk
1 tablespoon Armagnac, or to taste
confectioners' sugar for dusting *milliard*

Accompaniment: lightly sweetened whipped
   cream

Preheat oven to 300° F.

In a shallow glass baking dish arrange grapes in one layer and bake in middle of oven 30 minutes. Cool grapes completely. Reserve 1 cup grapes and transfer remaining grapes to a 6- to 8-cup shallow baking dish.

Increase temperature to 375° F.

In a bowl with an electric mixer cream together butter and granulated sugar until light and fluffy and beat in whole egg and yolk until combined well. Add flour and salt and beat on low speed until just combined. Add milk and Armagnac, beating until batter is just combined, and pour over grapes in baking dish, spreading evenly. Arrange reserved grapes decoratively on top of batter.

Bake *milliard* in middle of oven until a tester comes out clean, about 30 minutes, and cool slightly on a rack.

Dust *milliard* with confectioners' sugar and serve warm or at room temperature with whipped cream. Serves 6.

PHOTO ON PAGE 29

Coconut Cake with Lime Curd

For cake layers

3 cups White Lily flour* or cake flour
  (not self-rising)

1 tablespoon baking powder

1 teaspoon salt

1 cup whole milk

½ cup fresh coconut liquid (from about
  3 coconuts, procedure follows)
  or water

1½ teaspoons vanilla

2½ sticks (1¼ cups) unsalted butter,
  softened

1¾ cups sugar

5 large eggs

For lime curd

6 large egg yolks

¾ cup sugar

½ cup fresh lime juice

3 tablespoons heavy cream

¾ stick (6 tablespoons) cold unsalted butter,
  cut into pieces

2 teaspoons freshly grated lime zest

1 cup shredded fresh coconut (procedure follows)
  or sweetened flaked coconut

For frosting

2 large egg whites

1½ cups sugar

½ cup water

1 tablespoon light corn syrup

1 teaspoon freshly grated lime zest

1 teaspoon fresh lime juice

4 cups shaved fresh coconut (procedure follows)
  or 2½ cups sweetened flaked coconut

*available by mail order from The White Lily
  Foods Company, P.O. Box 871, Knoxville, TN
  37901, tel. (423) 546-5511

Preheat oven to 350° F. Line bottoms of three
buttered 9- by 2-inch round cake pans with rounds of
wax paper or parchment paper and butter paper. Dust
pans with flour, knocking out excess.

Make cake layers:

In a bowl whisk together flour, baking powder,
and salt. In a glass measure stir together milk,
coconut liquid or water, and vanilla. In a large bowl
with an electric mixer beat butter on medium speed 1
minute and add sugar in a slow stream, beating. Beat
mixture, scraping bowl occasionally, until light and
fluffy, about 2 minutes. Beat in eggs, 1 at a time,
beating well after each addition. Reduce speed to
low and beat in flour mixture in 4 batches alternately
with milk mixture, beginning and ending with flour
mixture and scraping bowl occasionally, until batter
is just combined (do not overbeat).

Divide batter among pans, smoothing tops and
tapping pans on counter to allow any air bubbles to
escape. Bake cake layers in middle and lower thirds
of oven (arrange pans so they overlap only slightly)
until a tester inserted in center comes out clean,
about 30 minutes. Run a thin knife around edges of
pans and invert cake layers onto racks. Remove wax
paper carefully and cool cake layers completely.
*Cake layers may be made 1 day ahead and kept,
wrapped in plastic wrap, in an airtight container in
a cool dry place. (Alternatively, cake layers may be
made 5 days ahead and frozen, wrapped in plastic
wrap and foil. Thaw cake layers in refrigerator 1
day before proceeding.)*

Make lime curd:

In a heavy saucepan whisk together yolks, sugar,
lime juice, cream, and butter and cook over moderately low heat, whisking constantly, 5 minutes, or
until mixture just reaches a boil (do not let boil).
Strain curd through a fine sieve into a bowl and stir
in zest. *Cool curd, its surface covered with plastic
wrap, and chill at least 4 hours and up to 2 days.*

Assemble cake layers and lime curd:

Put 1 cake layer on a cake plate and spread evenly
with about half of lime curd. Sprinkle with ½ cup
shredded fresh or sweetened flaked coconut and chill
15 minutes. Repeat layering in same manner with
another cake layer, remaining lime curd, and
remaining ½ cup coconut and top with remaining
cake layer. Chill cake 15 minutes.

Make frosting:

In top of a double boiler off heat or in a large
metal bowl with a hand-held electric mixer beat
together frosting ingredients until combined. In
double boiler or in bowl set over a saucepan of
boiling water beat mixture on high speed until it
holds stiff glossy peaks, about 7 minutes.
(Depending on mixer and weather, this may take

longer.) Remove top of double boiler or bowl from heat and beat frosting until cool and spreadable.

Frost top and side of cake and coat with shaved fresh or sweetened flaked coconut.

To Extract Coconut Liquid

3 heavy coconuts without any cracks and
  containing liquid

Pierce softest eye of each coconut with a metal skewer or small screwdriver and working over a bowl shake coconut, draining liquid and reserving coconuts for shredding or shaving (both procedures follow). Makes about a scant ¾ cup liquid.

Because coconuts can be difficult to crack, we offer an easy method that involves baking the coconut briefly. If the coconut doesn't crack while in the oven, it will once force is applied.

To Shred or Shave Fresh Coconut

drained coconuts (reserved from preceding recipe)

Preheat oven to 400° F.
Bake drained coconuts in oven 15 minutes.
With a hammer or back of a heavy cleaver, break shells and remove meat, levering it out carefully

with point of a strong knife or small screwdriver. Remove brown membrane with a sharp paring knife or vegetable peeler.

To shred coconut:

In a food processor fitted with fine shredding blade shred coconut meat from about 1 coconut in batches or shred by hand on fine shredding side (small tear-shaped holes) of a 4-sided grater until you have about 1 cup, reserving remaining coconut meat for another use.

To shave coconut:

With a vegetable peeler shave edges of coconut meat pieces until you have about 3½ cups, reserving remaining coconut meat for another use. *Coconuts may be shredded or shaved 1 day ahead and chilled in a sealable plastic bag.*

Lemon Poppyseed Cake with Fruit Compote

1¼ cups all-purpose flour
⅔ cup sugar
½ cup cornstarch
1 tablespoon poppyseeds
2¼ teaspoons baking powder
1 teaspoon salt
2 tablespoons butter
1 cup skim milk
2 teaspoons freshly grated lemon zest
1½ teaspoons vanilla
1 large egg
fruit compote (page 214)

Preheat oven to 350° F. and grease and flour an 8- by 2-inch cake pan, knocking out excess flour.

In a bowl whisk together flour, sugar, cornstarch, poppyseeds, baking powder, and salt and with fingers blend in butter until incorporated. In a large measuring cup lightly beat together milk, zest, vanilla, and egg.

Stir milk mixture into flour mixture until just blended and pour batter into pan. Bake cake 35 minutes, or until a tester comes out clean. Remove cake from pan and cool on a rack.

Serve wedges of cake topped with fruit compote. Serves 8.

Each serving: 300 calories,
4.4 grams fat (13% of calories from fat)

Fruit Compote

½ cup water
½ cup sugar
2 tablespoons fresh lemon juice
1 tablespoon fresh thyme leaves
1 teaspoon vanilla
4 cups seasonal fruit (such as 1 cup quartered
   strawberries, 1 cup blackberries, and 1 plum
   and 1 nectarine, each cut into wedges)

In a small saucepan bring water with sugar, lemon juice, and thyme to a boil, stirring occasionally, and boil until sugar is dissolved. Cool syrup to room temperature and stir in vanilla. In a bowl combine fruit and syrup and chill until cold. *Compote may be made 4 hours ahead and chilled, covered.* Makes about 4 cups.

Cornmeal Cake with Sweet Rosemary Syrup and Blackberries

For cake
1 stick (½ cup) unsalted butter,
   softened
1 cup sugar
1 cup yellow cornmeal
¾ cup all-purpose flour
1 teaspoon baking powder
¾ teaspoon salt
2 whole large eggs
1 large egg yolk
⅔ cup milk
For rosemary syrup
¾ cup sugar
¾ cup water
⅓ cup fresh rosemary leaves, chopped
1 tablespoon fresh lemon juice
½ teaspoon vanilla

Accompaniments
lightly sweetened whipped cream
2 half-pints blackberries

Make cake:
Preheat oven to 350° F. and butter and flour an 8- by 2-inch cake pan, knocking out excess flour.

In a bowl with an electric mixer beat together butter and sugar until light and fluffy. Add remaining cake ingredients and beat on low speed until combined. Beat batter on high speed until pale yellow, about 3 minutes.

Pour batter into pan and bake in middle of oven 40 minutes, or until a tester comes out with a few crumbs adhering.

Make rosemary syrup while cake is baking:
In a small saucepan heat all syrup ingredients except vanilla, stirring until sugar dissolves, and simmer 10 minutes. Remove pan from heat and stir in vanilla. Cool syrup 30 minutes and strain through a sieve into a 2-cup measure.

Cool cake in pan on a rack 10 minutes. Invert cake onto hand and return, right side up, to rack. While cake is still warm, gradually brush ⅓ cup syrup over it, allowing syrup to soak in before adding more. Chill remaining syrup in a small pitcher, covered. *Syrup-soaked cake may be made 1 day ahead and kept wrapped in plastic wrap at room temperature.*

Serve cake, cut into wedges, with whipped cream, blackberries, and remaining rosemary syrup.

Ginger Crunch Cake with Strawberry Sauce

For crunch topping
1 cup pecans, toasted and chopped fine
½ cup gingersnap cookie crumbs (from about
   eight 2-inch gingersnaps)
½ cup firmly packed light brown sugar
½ stick (¼ cup) unsalted butter, melted
For ginger cake
1¾ cups all-purpose flour
¾ teaspoon baking soda
¾ teaspoon ground ginger
¾ teaspoon cinnamon
¾ teaspoon salt
¾ cup unsulfured molasses
⅔ cup buttermilk
⅓ cup granulated sugar
¾ stick (6 tablespoons) unsalted butter, softened
1 large egg, beaten lightly

3 cups well-chilled heavy cream
1 teaspoon vanilla
4 tablespoons granulated sugar

1 pint strawberries
1 tablespoon fresh lemon juice

Garnish: strawberries, with leaves and blossoms
if desired (leaves and blossoms not
recommended for eating)

Preheat oven to 350° F. Grease three 8- by 2-inch
round cake pans.
Make crunch topping:
In a bowl combine crunch topping ingredients,
stirring until combined. Divide topping among pans
and press evenly onto bottom of each.
Make ginger cake:
In a large bowl whisk together flour, baking soda,
ginger, cinnamon, and salt. Add remaining ginger
cake ingredients and with an electric mixer beat on
high speed 2 minutes. Carefully spread batter over
topping in pans and bake in upper and lower thirds
of oven, switching position of pans in oven halfway
through baking, 20 minutes in all, or until a tester
inserted in center of each layer comes out clean.

Immediately invert cake layers onto racks lined
with wax paper and cool completely. *Cake layers
may be made 2 weeks ahead and frozen, wrapped
separately in plastic wrap. Thaw layers in refrigerator before proceeding.*

In a chilled bowl with chilled beaters of an
electric mixer beat 2 cups cream with vanilla and
2 tablespoons sugar until it just holds stiff peaks.
Assemble cake:
Arrange 1 cake layer, crunch side up, on a cake
plate and spread with a heaping cup whipped cream.
Repeat with another cake layer and another heaping
cup whipped cream and top with third cake layer,
crunch side up. Leaving top plain, spread remaining
whipped cream on side of cake to coat (a final coating will be added later). *Chill cake, covered loosely
with plastic wrap, at least 4 hours (to facilitate
slicing) and up to 24.*

Hull strawberries and slice half of them. In a bowl
with a potato masher mash sliced berries with lemon
juice and remaining 2 tablespoons sugar. In a food
processor purée remaining berries and strain through
a fine sieve into bowl with mashed berry mixture.
*Sauce may be made 1 day ahead and chilled,
covered.*

In a chilled bowl with chilled beaters of electric
mixer beat remaining cup cream until it just holds
stiff peaks and spread decoratively on side of cake.
Arrange some whole strawberries on top of cake and
garnish plate with additional whole strawberries.

Serve cake with strawberry sauce.

PHOTO ON PAGE 33

Maple Leaf Butter Cookies

2 sticks (1 cup) unsalted butter, softened
1 cup sugar
½ cup Grade B maple syrup (or Grade A maple
   syrup flavored with 3 drops maple extract,
   or to taste)
1 large egg yolk
3 cups all-purpose flour
1 teaspoon salt

In a standing electric mixer beat together butter and sugar until light and fluffy and beat in maple syrup and yolk until mixture is combined well. Sift flour and salt over mixture and fold in thoroughly. *Chill dough, wrapped in plastic wrap, at least until firm, about 2 hours, and up to 4 days.*
Preheat oven to 350° F.
Divide dough in half. Keeping one half chilled, lightly flour other half and on a lightly floured surface gently pound with a rolling pin to soften. Roll out dough ⅛ inch thick and with a 3-inch floured maple-leaf cookie cutter cut out cookies, chilling scraps. Arrange cookies on buttered baking sheets and if desired mark cookies decoratively with back of a knife. Make more cookies in same manner with remaining dough and with all scraps pressed together.
Bake cookies in batches in middle of oven until edges are golden, about 12 minutes, and transfer to racks to cool. *Cookies keep in airtight containers 1 week.* Makes about 40 cookies.

Chocolate Chip Apricot Bars

For apricot filling
6 ounces dried apricots (about 1 cup firmly
   packed), chopped fine
¼ cup granulated sugar
¾ cup water
1 teaspoon vanilla
For chocolate chip mixture
1⅓ cups pecans (about 4 ounces)
1 cup all-purpose flour
⅔ cup firmly packed light brown sugar
½ teaspoon salt
⅔ cup semisweet chocolate chips
1 stick (½ cup) cold unsalted butter,
   cut into bits

confectioners' sugar for sprinkling bars

Make apricot filling:
In a 1½-quart heavy saucepan combine apricots, sugar, and water and simmer, covered, 15 minutes. Remove lid and simmer mixture, stirring and mashing apricots, until excess liquid is evaporated and filling is thickened. Stir in vanilla.
Preheat oven to 350° F. and grease and flour an 8-inch square baking pan, knocking out excess flour.
Make chocolate chip mixture:
In a shallow baking pan toast pecans in middle of oven until golden brown, 8 to 10 minutes, and cool. In a food processor pulse pecans, flour, brown sugar, and salt until nuts are coarsely chopped. Add chocolate chips and butter and pulse until pecan mixture resembles coarse crumbs.
Press about half of chocolate chip mixture onto bottom of baking pan and spread evenly with apricot filling. Crumble remaining chocolate chip mixture evenly over apricot filling, pressing it down slightly, and bake confection in middle of oven 1 hour, or until golden. Cool confection completely in pan on a rack. Sprinkle confection with confectioners' sugar and cut into 16 bars. Makes 16 bars.

Raspberry Brownie Thins à la Mode

1 ounce unsweetened chocolate, chopped
½ stick (¼ cup) unsalted butter, cut into 4 pieces
¼ cup sugar
¼ cup seedless raspberry jam
1 large egg
¼ cup all-purpose flour
⅛ teaspoon salt

Accompaniments
vanilla ice cream
raspberry brandy

Preheat oven to 350° F. Grease and flour an 8-inch square baking pan, knocking out excess flour.

In a metal bowl or top of a double boiler set over barely simmering water melt chocolate and butter, stirring until smooth, and remove from heat. Whisk in sugar and raspberry jam until smooth. Add egg and whisk until smooth. Add flour and salt and whisk until smooth.

Spread batter evenly in pan and bake in middle of oven 12 to 15 minutes, or until just set and a tester comes out with crumbs adhering. Cool brownies in pan on a rack 5 minutes and cut into 9 squares.

Arrange 2 or 3 warm brownies on each of 2 dessert plates, reserving remaining brownies for later consumption. Top brownies with scoops of vanilla ice cream and drizzle with brandy. Serves 2, with leftovers.

S'mores
(Bittersweet Chocolate and
Marshmallow Cookie Sandwiches)

24 Carr's wheatmeal biscuits*
1¼ three-ounce bars Lindt or other fine-quality
    bittersweet chocolate (not unsweetened),
    broken into 36 pieces
12 marshmallows

*available at specialty foods shops and many
    supermarkets

Prepare grill.

Arrange 12 biscuits on twelve 8-inch square sheets of foil and arrange 3 pieces chocolate in a flat triangle on each. Toast marshmallows over flames until golden and put 1 marshmallow on top of each chocolate triangle. Top marshmallows with remaining biscuits to make sandwiches and wrap in foil.

On a rack set 5 to 6 inches over glowing coals heat s'mores 1 minute on each side, or until chocolate is melted. Makes 12 s'mores, serving 4 to 6.

Coconut Macadamia Shortbread

½ cup salted macadamia nuts
2 tablespoons granulated sugar
¾ stick (6 tablespoons) unsalted butter, softened
¼ cup confectioners' sugar
1 cup cake flour (not self-rising)

½ teaspoon baking powder
¼ teaspoon salt
½ cup plus 1 tablespoon sweetened shredded
    coconut

Preheat oven to 325° F. and generously butter a 9-inch round cake pan.

In a food processor pulse nuts and granulated sugar just until ground fine (do not grind to a paste).

In a bowl with an electric mixer beat butter and confectioners' sugar until light and fluffy. In another bowl whisk together flour, baking powder, salt, nut mixture, and ¼ cup coconut. Beat flour mixture into butter mixture until just combined.

On a lightly floured surface knead dough 5 to 8 times, or until it just comes together. With floured hands (dough will be sticky) press dough evenly into prepared baking pan and sprinkle with remaining 5 tablespoons coconut, pressing lightly to make it adhere. Bake shortbread in middle of oven 30 minutes, or until pale golden.

While shortbread is still warm, loosen edges from pan with a thin knife and cut into 8 wedges. Let shortbread cool in pan on a rack (shortbread will be fragile). Makes 8 cookies.

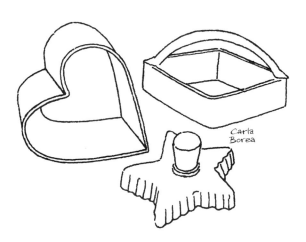

Carla Borea

Coconut Lime Squares

For crust
¾ cup plus 2 tablespoons all-purpose flour
¾ stick (6 tablespoons) cold unsalted butter,
  cut into bits
⅓ cup sweetened flaked coconut, toasted
  and cooled
¼ cup confectioners' sugar
¼ teaspoon salt
For custard
4 large eggs
1 cup granulated sugar
⅓ cup all-purpose flour
½ cup plus 2 tablespoons fresh lime juice
  (from about 5 limes)
1 tablespoon freshly grated lime zest
  (from about 2 limes)

⅓ cup sweetened flaked coconut, toasted
  and cooled

Make crust:
Preheat oven to 325° F. and butter and flour an 8-inch square baking pan, knocking out excess flour.

In a bowl blend together with fingertips flour, butter, coconut, confectioners' sugar, and salt until mixture resembles coarse meal. Pat mixture into pan and bake in middle of oven 25 to 30 minutes, or until golden brown.

Make custard:
Reduce oven temperature to 300° F.

In a bowl whisk together eggs and sugar until combined well and stir in flour, lime juice, and zest. Pour mixture over crust and and bake in middle of oven 20 minutes.

Top custard with coconut and bake 5 to 10 minutes more, or just until set. Cool confection in pan on a rack and chill 1 hour. Cut confection into 16 squares. Makes sixteen 2-inch squares.

Lemon Meringue Pie

For shell
1 recipe pastry dough for a single-crust 9- to
  10-inch pie (recipe follows)
raw rice or pie weights for weighting shell
For filling
1 cup sugar
5 tablespoons cornstarch
¼ teaspoon salt
1 cup water
½ cup milk
4 large egg yolks
1 tablespoon unsalted butter
½ cup fresh lemon juice
2 teaspoons freshly grated lemon zest
For meringue
4 large egg whites
¼ teaspoon cream of tartar
½ cup sugar

Make shell:
On a lightly floured surface with a floured rolling pin roll out dough into a 13-inch round (about ⅛ inch thick) and fit into a 9-inch (1-quart) pie plate. Trim edge of dough, leaving a ½-inch overhang, and crimp edge decoratively. Prick shell in several places with a fork and chill, covered, 30 minutes.

Preheat oven to 400° F.

Line shell with wax paper and fill with rice or pie weights. Bake shell in middle of oven 10 minutes. Remove paper and rice carefully and bake shell until golden, about 12 minutes more. Cool shell in pie plate on a rack.

Reduce oven temperature to 350° F.
Make filling:
In a heavy saucepan whisk together sugar, cornstarch, and salt and gradually whisk in water and milk, whisking until cornstarch is dissolved. In a bowl whisk together yolks. Cook milk mixture over moderate heat, whisking, until it comes to a boil. Gradually whisk about 1 cup milk mixture into yolks and whisk yolk mixture into milk mixture. Simmer mixture, whisking, 3 minutes. Remove pan from heat and whisk in butter, lemon juice, and zest until

butter is melted. Cover surface of filling with plastic wrap to prevent a skin from forming.

Make meringue:

In a bowl with an electric mixer beat whites with cream of tartar and a pinch salt until they hold soft peaks. Beat in sugar in a slow stream, beating until meringue just holds stiff peaks.

Pour warm filling into shell and spread meringue on top, covering filling completely, sealing it to pastry. Draw meringue up into peaks and bake in oven until meringue is golden, about 15 minutes.

Pastry Dough

1¼ cups all-purpose flour
6 tablespoons cold unsalted butter, cut into bits
2 tablespoons cold vegetable shortening
¼ teaspoon salt
2 to 4 tablespoons ice water

In a small bowl with a pastry blender or in a food processor blend or pulse together flour, butter, shortening, and salt until mixture resembles coarse meal. Add 2 tablespoons ice water and toss or pulse until water is incorporated. Add enough remaining ice water, 1 tablespoon at a time, tossing with a fork or pulsing to incorporate, until mixture begins to form a dough. On a work surface smear dough in 3 or 4 forward motions with heel of hand to slightly develop gluten in flour and make dough easier to work with. Form dough into a ball and flatten to form a disk. Wrap dough in plastic wrap and chill 1 hour. Makes enough dough for a single-crust 9- to 10-inch pie.

It is best to top this pie with meringue and brown just before serving, or the meringue may weep.

Sweet Potato Meringue Pie

For filling
2 pounds sweet potatoes (about 4 medium)
1⅔ cups half-and-half
½ cup sugar
2 whole large eggs
1¼ teaspoons cinnamon
¼ teaspoon ground allspice
¼ teaspoon freshly grated nutmeg
½ teaspoon salt

1 recipe pastry dough for a single-crust 9- to 10-inch pie (recipe precedes)
For meringue
3 large egg whites
¾ cup sugar

confectioners' sugar for dusting

Make filling:

Preheat oven to 400° F. and line a baking sheet with foil.

Prick potatoes and bake on baking sheet 1 to 1¼ hours, or until very soft. Cool potatoes until they can be handled and scoop out enough flesh to measure 2 cups, reserving any remaining flesh for another use.

In a blender or food processor purée potatoes with remaining filling ingredients until smooth. *Filling may be made 1 day ahead and chilled, covered. Bring filling to room temperature before proceeding.*

On a lightly floured surface roll out pastry dough into a 14-inch round (about ⅛ inch thick) and fit into a 9- to 10-inch (1-quart) glass pie plate, crimping edge decoratively. Chill shell 30 minutes.

Preheat oven to 375° F. with a baking sheet on middle rack.

Pour filling into shell and bake on heated sheet in oven 1 hour, or until filling is set but center still shakes slightly. (Filling will set as pie cools.) Cool pie on a rack. *Pie may be prepared up to this point 1 day ahead and chilled, covered loosely. Bring pie to room temperature before proceeding.*

Preheat oven to 450° F.

Make meringue:

In a metal bowl set over a saucepan of simmering water stir together whites and sugar until sugar is dissolved. Remove bowl from pan and with an electric mixer beat meringue on high speed until it holds stiff, glossy peaks.

Transfer meringue to a pastry bag fitted with a large star tip and pipe tall pointed mounds close together, covering pie.

Bake pie until meringue is golden, 4 to 5 minutes.

Just before serving, dust pie lightly with confectioners' sugar. Serve warm or at room temperature.

Mascarpone Cheesecake Tart with Nectarines

For crust
six 5- by 2½-inch graham crackers
1¼ cups coarsely crushed *amaretti** (Italian almond macaroons, about 3 ounces)
3 tablespoons sugar
3 tablespoons unsalted butter, melted
For filling
1½ cups *mascarpone* cheese* (about ¾ pound) at room temperature
½ cup sugar
2 large eggs
1 tablespoon fresh lemon juice
2 teaspoons freshly grated lemon zest
1 teaspoon vanilla extract
¼ teaspoon almond extract
3 tablespoons all-purpose flour
¼ teaspoon salt
For topping
2 pounds nectarines (about 8)
2 tablespoons sugar, or to taste

*available at specialty foods shops and some supermarkets

Preheat oven to 350° F. and lightly butter a 9-inch springform pan.

Make crust:

In a food processor finely grind graham crackers and *amaretti* with sugar. Add butter and blend until combined well. Press mixture onto bottom and about ¾ inch up side of pan. Bake crust in middle of oven 10 to 15 minutes, or until crisp and golden, and cool completely in pan on a rack.

Make filling:

In a bowl with an electric mixer beat *mascarpone* with sugar until smooth and add eggs, 1 at a time, beating well after each addition. Beat in lemon juice, zest, and extracts. Beat in flour and salt until combined well.

Pour filling into crust. Bake tart in middle of oven 30 minutes, or until pale golden and set, and cool completely in pan on rack. Remove side of pan and transfer tart to a plate. *Chill tart, covered, at least 4 hours and up to 24.*

Make topping just before serving:

Slice nectarines and in a bowl toss with sugar. Let nectarines stand, tossing occasionally, until sugar is dissolved and juices are released, about 5 minutes.

Mound topping on tart and serve immediately.

PHOTO ON PAGE 62

Chocolate Pecan Banana Tarts

½ sheet frozen puff pastry (about ¼ pound), thawed
1 firm-ripe large banana
1 ounce fine-quality bittersweet chocolate (not unsweetened), chopped fine
¼ cup pecan halves, toasted lightly, cooled, and chopped
2 teaspoons sugar
1 tablespoon unsalted butter, cut into bits

Preheat oven to 425° F.

On a lightly floured surface with a floured rolling pin roll out pastry into a 10- by 5-inch rectangle and cut in half to form two squares. On a baking sheet arrange squares about 2 inches apart.

Cut banana diagonally into ¼-inch-thick slices. Sprinkle pastry squares evenly with chocolate, leaving a ½-inch border on all sides, and arrange banana slices decoratively over chocolate. Top banana slices with pecans, sugar, and butter and chill 10 minutes, or until pastry is firm.

Bake tarts in middle of oven 10 to 15 minutes, or until pastry is golden brown and cooked through, and cool slightly on a rack. Serves 2.

Candied Quince Tart

For pastry shell
1½ cups all-purpose flour
6 tablespoons confectioners' sugar
1 stick (½ cup) cold unsalted butter, cut into bits
¼ teaspoon salt
3 tablespoons sour cream
1 large egg yolk
¼ teaspoon vanilla
an egg wash made by beating 1 large egg with 1 tablespoon water
For candied quince

1 large quince (about ¾ pound)
1½ cups water
1 cup sugar
1 cinnamon stick
4 whole cloves
2 teaspoons fresh lemon juice, or to taste

Make pastry shell:

In a food processor or in a bowl with a pastry blender pulse or blend together flour, confectioners' sugar, butter, and salt until mixture resembles coarse meal. In a small bowl stir together sour cream, yolk, and vanilla until combined well and add to flour mixture. Pulse or blend mixture just until dough forms a ball. Form three fourths dough into a large, thick disk and form remaining one fourth dough into a small, thick disk. *Chill disks, wrapped in plastic wrap, at least 30 minutes and up to 2 days.*

Put large dough disk in middle of a sheet of parchment paper and cover with plastic wrap. Roll out dough into an 11-inch round (about ⅜ inch thick) and cut out a 10-inch circle. Reserve trimmings and slide parchment onto a large baking sheet.

On a lightly floured surface roll out small dough disk in same manner and with a 1½-inch fluted tear-shaped cutter cut out leaves. Brush 1 side of each leaf with egg wash and arrange leaves, egg-wash side down, on edge of pastry round, overlapping slightly and alternating angle of leaves to form a shallow border. Gather trimmings (including reserved) and reroll. Make and arrange more leaves in same manner. (You will need a total of about 36 leaves.)

Brush leaves with egg wash and with back of a small knife score leaves decoratively. Lightly prick inside (not leaves) of shell all over with a fork and chill 30 minutes.

Preheat oven to 375° F. while shell is chilling.

Bake shell in middle of oven, checking after 10 minutes and lightly pricking again if center rises, until pale golden, 15 to 17 minutes. Cool shell completely on baking sheet on a rack. *Shell may be made 1 day ahead and kept in an airtight container at room temperature.*

Make filling:

Peel quince and cut lengthwise into 8 wedges, coring it. Cut each wedge crosswise into thin slices and in a 1½-quart heavy saucepan combine with water, sugar, cinnamon stick, and cloves. Bring mixture to a boil, stirring until sugar is dissolved, and simmer 1½ to 2 hours, or until quince is tender and has turned a deep pink (near end of cooking), and syrup is reduced and thickened. Discard cinnamon stick and cloves and stir in lemon juice.

Cool filling 5 minutes and spread evenly in shell. *Tart may be made 1 day ahead and kept in an airtight container at room temperature.*

FROZEN DESSERTS

Grapefruit and Campari Granita

1⅓ cups sugar
1 cup water
3 cups fresh pink grapefruit juice (from about 4 pink grapefruits) with some pulp
¼ cup Campari

Garnish: 3-inch-long pieces grapefruit zest, removed with a vegetable peeler

In a saucepan bring sugar and water to a boil, stirring until sugar is dissolved. Cool syrup. Stir in grapefruit juice and Campari and freeze in a shallow metal pan, stirring and crushing lumps with a fork every 30 minutes, 3 to 4 hours, or until mixture is firm but not frozen. Scrape *granita* with a fork to lighten texture. Serve *granita* in chilled goblets and garnish with zest. Makes about 7 cups.

Spiced Strawberry Sorbet

⅔ cup sugar
⅔ cup water
3 tablespoons black peppercorns, crushed coarse
1 quart strawberries (preferably local), hulled
2 tablespoons balsamic vinegar, or to taste

Accompaniments
toasted almond *phyllo* crisps (recipe follows)
whole and/or halved strawberries

In a saucepan combine sugar and water and bring to a boil, stirring until sugar is dissolved. Stir in peppercorns and remove pan from heat. Cover pan and let syrup stand 1 hour.

Strain syrup through a fine sieve into a food processor or blender and discard peppercorns. Purée hulled strawberries with syrup until very smooth and force through sieve into a bowl, discarding seeds and other solids. Stir in vinegar and chill, covered, until cold. Freeze mixture in an ice-cream maker.

Serve sorbet with crisps and strawberries. Makes about 1 quart.

PHOTO ON PAGE 59

Toasted Almond Phyllo Crisps

½ cup whole blanched almonds, toasted lightly
    and cooled
½ cup granulated sugar
six 17- by 12-inch *phyllo* sheets, thawed if frozen,
    stacked between 2 sheets wax paper, and
    covered with a dampened kitchen towel
¾ stick (6 tablespoons) unsalted butter, melted
confectioners' sugar for sprinkling crisps

Preheat oven to 350° F.

In a food processor grind almonds fine with granulated sugar. *Almond sugar may be made 2 days ahead and kept in an airtight container at room temperature.*

On a work surface arrange 1 *phyllo* sheet and brush with some butter. Sprinkle sheet evenly with about 2 tablespoons almond sugar. Top sheet with remaining 5 *phyllo* sheets, brushing and sprinkling each with butter and almond sugar in same manner.

Trim edges of stacked *phyllo* if uneven and cut into 24 rectangles, each about 4 by 2 inches. (Cut stacked *phyllo* lengthwise into 3 strips and cut each crosswise into eighths.) Cut each rectangle diagonally to form 2 triangles for a total of 48 cookies.

Arrange triangles, sugared sides up, in one layer on 2 heavy baking sheets and bake in batches in middle of oven until golden brown, 10 to 15 minutes. Transfer crisps to racks and cool.

Sprinkle crisps with confectioners' sugar. *Crisps keep in an airtight container at room temperature 4 days.* Makes 48 crisps.

Jasmine Tea Sorbet

3 cups water
2½ tablespoons fine-quality jasmine tea leaves*
¾ cup plus 2 tablespoons sugar

*available at Asian markets and by mail order
    from Adriana's Caravan, tel. (800) 316-0820,
    or Uwajimaya, tel. (800) 889-1928

In a small saucepan bring water to a boil. Add tea leaves and remove pan from heat. Cover pan and steep tea 5 minutes. Add sugar, stirring until dissolved, and strain tea through a fine sieve into a bowl. Chill tea, covered, until cold and freeze in an ice-cream maker. *Sorbet may be made 1 week ahead.* Makes about 3 cups.

PHOTO ON PAGE 49

Minted Lemongrass Sorbet

3 stalks fresh lemongrass*, outer leaves
  discarded and root ends trimmed
3 cups water
¾ cup fresh mint leaves, washed well and
  spun dry
¾ cup sugar

*available at Asian markets and by mail order
  from Adriana's Caravan, tel. (800) 316-0820,
  or Uwajimaya, tel. (800) 889-1928

Thinly slice as much of lemongrass stalks as possible, discarding dried upper portion. In a saucepan simmer water with sliced lemongrass, covered, 5 minutes. Add mint leaves and simmer, uncovered, 1 minute. Remove pan from heat and add sugar, stirring until dissolved.

In a blender purée mixture and strain through a fine sieve into a bowl, pressing hard on solids. Chill syrup, covered, until cold and freeze in an ice-cream maker. *Sorbet may be made 1 week ahead.* Makes about 3 cups.

PHOTO ON PAGE 49

Raspberry Frozen Yogurt Cake with Raspberry Amaretto Sauce

For cake layer
2 whole large eggs
1 large egg yolk
1 cup plus 2 tablespoons cake flour
  (not self-rising)
1¼ teaspoons baking powder
¼ teaspoon salt
⅓ cup milk
¼ cup Amaretto (almond-flavored liqueur)
1 stick (½ cup) unsalted butter,
  softened
¾ cup sugar
For raspberry frozen yogurt
1 pint raspberries (about 2½ cups)
⅓ cup sugar
2 tablespoons water
2 pints vanilla frozen yogurt,
  softened

Garnish: ½ pint raspberries (about 1 cup) and
  ½ cup sliced almonds, toasted until golden
  and cooled
Accompaniment: raspberry Amaretto sauce
  (page 224)

Preheat oven to 350° F. Line bottom of a buttered 9- by 2-inch springform pan with a round of wax paper or parchment and butter paper. Dust pan with flour, knocking out excess.

Make cake layer:

In a bowl whisk together whole eggs and yolk. Into another bowl sift together flour, baking powder, and salt. In a small bowl stir together milk and Amaretto. In a bowl with an electric mixer on medium speed beat butter 1 minute and beat in sugar in a stream, scraping bowl occasionally, until light and fluffy, about 4 minutes. Beat in egg, a little at a time, beating well after each addition, until pale and fluffy. Stir in flour mixture in 3 batches alternately with milk mixture, beginning and ending with flour mixture and stirring until smooth after each addition.

Turn batter into pan, smoothing top, and bake in middle of oven 25 minutes, or until a tester comes out clean. Cool cake layer in pan on a rack 10 minutes. Run a thin knife around edge of pan and remove side of pan. Invert cake layer onto rack. Remove paper carefully and cool cake completely. With a long serrated knife halve cake horizontally. Clean springform pan and line with 2 sheets plastic wrap, leaving at least a 1-inch overhang. Put bottom half of cake, cut side up, in pan.

Make raspberry frozen yogurt:

In a food processor purée raspberries with sugar and water and force through a fine sieve into a large bowl. Add frozen yogurt and stir until purée is well incorporated.

Working quickly, spoon about half of frozen yogurt over cake in pan, spreading evenly. Top with other half of cake layer, cut side down, and spoon remaining frozen yogurt on top, spreading evenly.

Arrange raspberries on top of cake, pushing slightly into frozen yogurt, and sprinkle almonds over top of cake. *Freeze cake, covered, at least until frozen hard, about 6 hours, and up to 1 week.*

Let cake soften in refrigerator at least 30 minutes and up to 45 minutes before serving. Remove cake from pan. Serve cake with sauce.

Raspberry Amaretto Sauce

2 pints raspberries (about 3¾ cups)
¾ cup sugar
2 tablespoons Amaretto (almond-flavored liqueur)

In a food processor purée raspberries with sugar and Amaretto and force through a fine sieve into a bowl. *Sauce may be made 3 days ahead and chilled, covered.* Makes about 1½ cups.

Frozen Peanut Butter Pie

40 thin chocolate wafers, ground fine in a blender
    or food processor (about 2¼ cups crumbs)
1 stick (½ cup) unsalted butter, melted
½ cup sugar
1 cup milk
1 cup creamy peanut butter
½ teaspoon vanilla
1¼ cups well-chilled heavy cream
⅓ cup salted roasted peanuts, chopped fine

Garnish: lightly sweetened whipped cream and
    salted roasted peanuts

Reserve ¼ cup cookie crumbs. In a bowl combine remaining cookie crumbs and butter and press onto bottom and side of a 10-inch (1½-quart) pie plate. Chill shell.

In a heavy saucepan dissolve sugar in milk over moderate heat, stirring, and remove pan from heat. Whisk in peanut butter and vanilla until combined well and cool in a bowl set in a larger bowl of ice water, stirring occasionally.

In another bowl beat cream until it just holds stiff peaks and fold into peanut-butter mixture with chopped peanuts. Turn mixture into pie shell, smoothing top. Sprinkle reserved chocolate cookie crumbs around edge of pie.

Pipe rosettes of whipped cream decoratively onto crumbs and top rosettes with peanuts. *Freeze pie, uncovered, at least until frozen hard, about 5 hours, and up to 2 days, covered with plastic wrap and foil after 5 hours.*

Let pie stand in refrigerator 30 minutes before serving.

Midwestern Butterscotch Fudge Marshmallow Sundaes

½ cup miniature marshmallows
2 pints super-premium vanilla ice cream
1 cup dark hot fudge sauce (page 205)
1 cup butterscotch sauce (page 205)

Oil blades of kitchen scissors with flavorless vegetable oil and cut miniature marshmallows into quarters. Scoop ice cream into 8 sundae dishes and spoon heated hot fudge sauce over it. Spoon heated butterscotch sauce over each sundae and top with marshmallows. Serves 8.

California Gingered Fruit Salsa Sundaes

½ cup raspberries
2 tablespoons sugar
3 to 4 tablespoons minced crystallized ginger,
    or to taste
1 small firm-ripe mango, diced fine (about ⅔ cup)
6 large strawberries, diced fine
½ cup finely diced fresh pineapple
½ teaspoon balsamic vinegar
1 pint super-premium vanilla frozen yogurt

In a bowl crush raspberries coarse with sugar and let stand 5 minutes. Stir in ginger, mango, strawberries, pineapple, and balsamic vinegar. Scoop frozen yogurt into 4 sundae dishes and spoon salsa over it. Serves 4.

Southern Peanut Butterscotch Sundaes

½ cup salted roasted peanuts, chopped coarse
3 tablespoons Southern Comfort
1 cup butterscotch sauce (page 205)
1 pint super-premium chocolate ice cream

Reserve 3 tablespoons peanuts for sprinkling. In a saucepan stir remaining peanuts and Southern Comfort into butterscotch sauce and cook over moderately low heat, stirring, until heated through. Scoop ice cream into 4 sundae dishes and spoon sauce over it. Sprinkle sundaes with reserved peanuts. Serves 4.

Pacific Northwest Bing Cherry Hazelnut Sundaes

1 cup sugar
1 cup heavy cream
1 tablespoon kirsch, or to taste
¼ teaspoon salt
½ cup hazelnuts, toasted, loose skins rubbed off,
   and chopped
1 pint super-premium vanilla or cherry ice cream
16 to 20 Bing cherries, pitted and chopped coarse

In a dry heavy saucepan (about 1-quart capacity) cook sugar over moderate heat, without stirring, until it begins to melt. Continue cooking sugar, stirring with a fork, until melted and swirl pan until sugar is a deep golden caramel. Remove pan from heat and stir in cream, kirsch, and salt, stirring until smooth (mixture will bubble up). Stir in hazelnuts and cool sauce. Scoop ice cream into 4 sundae dishes and spoon sauce over it. Sprinkle sundaes with cherries. Serves 4.

New England Cranberry Maple Walnut Sundaes

1½ cups pure maple syrup
½ cup dried cranberries, chopped
⅓ cup walnuts, toasted lightly and chopped
1 pint super-premium vanilla or coffee ice cream

In a saucepan simmer maple syrup 5 minutes and stir in cranberries and walnuts. Remove pan from heat and cool sauce. Scoop ice cream into 4 sundae dishes and spoon sauce over it. Serves 4.

FRUIT FINALES

Maple-Glazed Apple Slices

4 Golden Delicious apples
   (about 1½ pounds)
2 tablespoons unsalted butter
3 tablespoons Grade B maple syrup (or Grade A
   maple syrup flavored with 1 drop maple
   extract, or to taste)
1 tablespoon water
1 teaspoon fresh lemon juice
¼ teaspoon cinnamon

Peel and core apples and cut into ¼-inch-thick slices. In a 12-inch heavy skillet heat butter over moderately high heat until foam subsides and sauté apples, turning them, until golden and tender. Stir in maple syrup, water, lemon juice, cinnamon, and a pinch salt and cook, stirring, until apples are glazed. Serves 6.

Individual Berry Cobblers with Lemon Buttermilk Ice Cream

For pastry stars
2 sheets frozen puff pastry (about 1 pound),
    thawed
an egg wash made by whisking 1 large egg yolk
    with 1 tablespoon water
For berry mixture
⅓ cup water
3 tablespoons fresh lemon juice
3½ tablespoons cornstarch
5 cups fresh blackberries
5 cups fresh raspberries
2½ to 2¾ cups sugar, or to taste

Accompaniment: lemon buttermilk ice cream
    (recipe follows)

Preheat oven to 400° F.
Make pastry stars:
On a lightly floured surface with a lightly floured rolling pin roll out each puff pastry sheet into a 14- by 13-inch rectangle. With 1 or more star-shaped cutters cut out 24 pastry stars. Divide pastry stars between 2 baking sheets, arranging in one layer, and freeze 5 minutes.

Brush top of each pastry star lightly with some egg wash (be careful not to drip down edges of pastry) and bake in middle and lower thirds of oven, switching position of sheets in oven after 5 minutes, 10 to 15 minutes, or until pastry stars are puffed and golden brown. Transfer pastry stars to a rack and cool completely. *Pastry stars may be made 2 days ahead and kept in a sealable plastic bag at room temperature.*

Make berry mixture:
In a large bowl whisk together water, lemon juice, and cornstarch until combined well. Add berries and sugar, tossing gently to combine well. Divide berry mixture among eight 1½-cup shallow ramekins or baking dishes and put in 2 shallow baking pans. Bake berries in middle and lower third of oven 25 minutes and cool slightly.

To assemble cobbler:
Top each serving with 3 pastry stars and a scoop of ice cream. Serve cobblers hot or warm. Serves 8.

PHOTO ON PAGE 55

Lemon Buttermilk Ice Cream

6 large egg yolks
⅓ cup fresh lemon juice
¾ cup sugar
2 cups buttermilk
zest of 1 large lemon

In a small heavy saucepan whisk together yolks, lemon juice, and sugar and cook over moderate heat, whisking constantly, about 15 minutes, or until a candy thermometer registers 175° F. (do not boil). Strain mixture through a sieve into a bowl and cool, its surface covered with plastic wrap.

Whisk buttermilk and zest into lemon curd until combined well and freeze in an ice-cream maker. Makes about 1 quart.

Melon and Pineapple with Lemon Mint Syrup

1½ cups water
½ cup sugar
1 cup packed fresh mint leaves
1 tablespoon plus 1 teaspoon fresh lemon juice
1 small watermelon, cut into wedges
1 cantaloupe, seeded and cut into wedges

½ honeydew melon, seeded and cut into wedges
½ pineapple, cut lengthwise into ½-inch wedges

Garnish: fresh mint sprigs

In a saucepan bring water and sugar to a boil, stirring until sugar is dissolved. In a heatproof bowl pour syrup over mint and steep 5 minutes. Strain mixture through a fine sieve into a pitcher, discarding mint, and stir in lemon juice. *Chill syrup, covered, at least until cold and up to 1 week.*

Arrange fruit on a large platter and garnish with mint sprigs. Serve syrup on the side. Serves 6.

Baked Pears on Sugared Puff Pastry with Caramel Sauce

For pastry bases
¼ cup granulated sugar
1 sheet frozen puff pastry (about ½ pound), thawed
For pears and sauce
2 large firm-ripe Bartlett pears (about 1 pound)
2 tablespoons unsalted butter, cut into bits
½ cup granulated sugar
1 tablespoon fresh lemon juice
½ cup heavy cream
1 tablespoon *poire William* (French pear brandy), or to taste

confectioners' sugar for sprinkling pastry

Make pastry bases:
Preheat oven to 375° F. and lightly butter a heavy baking sheet.

Sprinkle a work surface with granulated sugar and roll out pastry about ⅛ inch thick, turning once to coat both sides with sugar. Cut out 4 rectangles, each about 4½ by 3½ inches, and transfer to baking sheet, reserving scraps for another use. Prick pastry all over with a fork and chill on baking sheet in freezer until well chilled, about 15 minutes.

Lightly butter bottom of another heavy baking sheet and put directly on top of pastry rectangles to weight them while baking. Bake pastry (between 2 baking sheets) in middle of oven 25 to 35 minutes, or until golden brown, and transfer to a rack to cool.

Pastry bases may be made 1 day ahead and kept in an airtight container at room temperature.

Make pears and sauce:
Lightly butter a baking dish just large enough to hold 4 pear halves in one layer.

Peel, halve, and core pears. Arrange pear halves, cut sides up, in baking dish. Divide butter among pear cavities and sprinkle ¼ cup sugar over pears. Sprinkle lemon juice over pears and bake in middle of 375° F. oven 15 minutes. Remove baking dish from oven and turn pears over. Baste pears with cooking juices and return to oven. Bake pears until tender, about 15 minutes more. Transfer pears to a plate and keep warm.

Transfer cooking juices to a small heavy saucepan. Add remaining ¼ cup granulated sugar and boil, swirling pan, until mixture turns a deep golden caramel. Slowly add heavy cream (caramel will bubble up) and simmer sauce, whisking, until slightly thickened, about 5 minutes. Stir *poire William* into caramel sauce.

Sprinkle each pastry base with confectioners' sugar and top with a pear half. Serve baked pears with caramel sauce. Serves 4.

Blood Orange, Grapefruit, and Pomegranate Compote

1½ cups dry white wine
¼ cup dry Sherry
¼ cup honey
½ cup firmly packed light brown sugar
6 pink grapefruits
3 blood oranges or 1½ navel oranges
1 pomegranate

In a saucepan bring white wine, Sherry, honey, and brown sugar to a boil, stirring until sugar is dissolved. Transfer syrup to a heatproof bowl and chill until cold.

Cut peel and pith from grapefruits and oranges and cut fruit sections free from membranes. Halve pomegranate and squeeze gently to yield seeds with juice. Divide citrus sections, pomegranate seeds and juice, and wine syrup among 6 dessert bowls. *Chill, covered, at least 15 minutes and up to 1 hour.* Stir compote before serving. Serves 6.

Baked Pear and Orange Crisp

a 16-ounce can sliced pears, drained
¼ cup quick-cooking rolled oats
2 tablespoons unsalted butter
2 tablespoons all-purpose flour
2 tablespoons firmly packed light brown sugar
1 navel orange
1 tablespoon orange-flavored liqueur
1 tablespoon dried currants

Preheat oven to 450° F.
Arrange sliced pears in one layer on paper towels to drain.

In a small bowl blend oats, butter, flour, brown sugar, and a pinch salt until mixture resembles coarse meal.

Cut peel and pith from orange and cut orange sections free from membranes. In a buttered 2-cup shallow baking dish toss together orange sections, pears, liqueur, and currants. Sprinkle oat mixture over fruit and bake in middle of oven 15 minutes, or until top is crisp and golden. Serves 2.

Plum and Almond Cobbler

½ cup firmly packed light brown sugar
2 tablespoons cornstarch
½ teaspoon cinnamon
2½ pounds prune plums or other plums, pitted and quartered
2 tablespoons fresh lemon juice
2 tablepoons unsalted butter, cut into bits
1 cup granulated sugar
¾ cup all-purpose flour
1 teaspoon baking powder
½ teaspoon salt
¾ cup sliced almonds
1 large egg, beaten lightly

In a large bowl whisk together brown sugar, cornstarch, and cinnamon and add plums, lemon juice, and butter. Toss mixture well and spoon into a shallow 3-quart baking dish.

Preheat oven to 375° F.

In a food processor pulse together granulated sugar, flour, baking powder, salt, and ½ cup almonds until almonds are ground fine. Add egg and pulse until blended. Spoon flour mixture over plum mixture, pulling some plum wedges up for presentation. Sprinkle remaining ¼ cup almonds over cobbler.

Bake cobbler in middle of oven 45 minutes, or until golden and bubbling, and cool on a rack.

Serve cobbler warm or at room temperature. Serves 12.

Strawberry Rhubarb Napoleons and Lemon Cream

For filling
1 pound rhubarb, cut into ¼-inch-thick slices (about 3 cups)
½ cup firmly packed light brown sugar
¼ teaspoon cinnamon
1½ teaspoons fresh lemon juice
1 pint strawberries

1 sheet frozen puff pastry (about ½ pound), thawed

Garnish: confectioners' sugar
Accompaniment: lemon cream (recipe follows)

Make filling:
In a heavy saucepan combine all filling ingredients except strawberries and simmer over low heat, stirring occasionally, 10 minutes, or until rhubarb is soft and falling apart. Transfer mixture to a bowl and cool completely. Hull strawberries and cut into ¼-inch-thick slices (there will be about 2 cups). Add strawberries to rhubarb mixture, tossing to combine well. *Filling may be made 1 day ahead and chilled, covered. Bring filling to room temperature before assembling napoleons.*

Preheat oven to 375° F.

On a lightly floured surface roll pastry into a 14-by 10-inch rectangle, about ⅛ inch thick. Cut pastry into 4 strips, each 14 by 2½ inches. Working with 1 pastry strip at a time, with long side facing you, cut three 4-inch-long parallelograms from each strip, discarding end scraps, for a total of 12 parallelograms. Invert 2 baking sheets and arrange 6 parallelograms in one layer on each. Freeze pastry 15 minutes, or until firm.

Remove 1 baking sheet from freezer and invert a

metal rack directly onto pastry to cover completely. (Rack will weight down pastry to form a decorative pattern.) Bake pastry with rack in middle of oven until golden brown and cooked through, 10 to 15 minutes. Carefully remove rack from pastry and transfer pastry to another rack to cool completely. *Pastries may be baked 4 days ahead and kept in an airtight container at room temperature.*

Assemble napoleons:

Arrange 6 parallelograms, design sides up, on dessert plates and top each with about ½ cup filling. Put remaining 6 parallelograms, design sides up, on top of filling and sprinkle with confectioners' sugar.

Serve napoleons with lemon cream. Serves 6.

PHOTO ON PAGE 43

Lemon Cream

½ cup well-chilled heavy cream
2 tablespoons confectioners' sugar
3 tablespoons sour cream
2 teaspoons freshly grated lemon zest

Garnish: fresh lemon zest removed with a
   vegetable peeler and cut into julienne strips

In a bowl with an electric mixer beat heavy cream with sugar until it holds soft peaks. Fold in sour cream and zest. *Lemon cream may be made 1 hour ahead and chilled, covered. Whisk cream lightly before serving.*

Serve lemon cream garnished with zest. Makes about 1⅓ cups.

PHOTO ON PAGE 43

Dried Fruits and Nuts

1 cup dried apricots
½ cup dried dates (preferably Medjool)
½ cup walnut halves
½ cup natural pistachios
¼ cup dark raisins
¼ cup golden raisins

In a bowl toss ingredients to combine well. Makes 3 cups.

CONFECTIONS

Gold-Dusted Bourbon Pecan Balls

2 tablespoons unsweetened cocoa powder
¾ cup plus 1 tablespoon confectioners' sugar
¼ teaspoon edible gold powder* if desired
2 cups vanilla-wafer crumbs (from about
   55 cookies)
½ cup pecans, toasted, cooled, and chopped fine
⅓ cup bourbon
3 tablespoons honey

*available by mail order from the New York
   Cake & Baking Center, tel. (800) 942-2539 or,
   in New York City, (212) 675-CAKE

In a small bowl sift together cocoa powder and 1 tablespoon confectioners' sugar and whisk in gold powder until combined well.

In a bowl stir together wafer crumbs and pecans. In a small bowl whisk together bourbon, remaining ¾ cup confectioners' sugar, and honey and pour into crumb mixture, stirring with a fork until combined well. Form teaspoons of mixture into balls and roll, 4 at a time, in cocoa mixture. *Bourbon balls may be kept, in layers separated by wax paper in an airtight container lined with wax paper, in a cool dry place 1 week.* Makes about 4½ dozen bourbon balls.

Chocolate Orange Fudge

2 cups superfine sugar
2 ounces unsweetened chocolate, chopped
⅔ cup heavy cream
¼ teaspoon salt
1 tablespoon unsalted butter
⅓ cup finely chopped candied orange peel*

Garnish: candied orange peel, cut into small
 thin slices

*available in specialty foods shops and by
 mail order from Maison Glass Delicacies,
 tel. (800) 822-5564 or, in New York City,
 (212) 755-3316

Butter an 8-inch square glass baking dish.

In a heavy 2-quart saucepan combine sugar, chocolate, cream, and salt and cook over moderate heat, stirring constantly, until sugar is dissolved and chocolate is melted. Cook mixture, without stirring, until a candy thermometer registers 238° F. Remove pan from heat and add butter and orange peel, swirling pan without stirring. Cool fudge 5 minutes and beat with a wooden spoon until it just begins to lose its gloss (do not overbeat or fudge will seize). Pour fudge immediately into baking dish and cool 15 minutes, or until it begins to harden. Cut fudge into 1-inch squares and cool completely. *Fudge may be kept, in layers separated by wax paper in an airtight container lined with wax paper, in a cool dry place 2 weeks.*

Garnish fudge with candied orange peel slices. Makes about 1 pound.

PUDDINGS AND OTHER DESSERTS

Fried Custard Squares with Rum Sauce

For custard squares
2½ cups milk
1 cinnamon stick
¼ cup star anise*
5 large eggs
6 tablespoons cornstarch
⅔ cup plus ¼ cup sugar
½ teaspoon salt
1 cup fine dry bread crumbs
1½ teaspoons ground cinnamon
1 cup all-purpose flour
For sauce
1½ cups water
1 cup firmly packed light brown sugar
½ cup plus 1 tablespoon dark rum
¼ cup star anise*
fresh lime juice to taste

vegetable oil for deep-frying

Garnish: 2 star fruit (also known as
 carambola)**, sliced thin, and 8 star anise*

*available at some supermarkets and by mail
 order from Adriana's Caravan,
 tel. (800) 316-0820 or, in Brooklyn, NY,
 (718) 436-8565
**available seasonally at specialty produce
 markets and some supermarkets

Make custard squares:
Butter an 8-inch square baking pan.

In a heavy saucepan bring milk just to a boil with cinnamon stick and star anise and keep at a bare simmer 15 minutes. Pour hot milk through a sieve into a large glass measuring cup or heatproof pitcher.

In a bowl with an electric mixer beat together 3 eggs, cornstarch, ⅔ cup sugar, and salt and add hot milk in a stream, beating until smooth. Return custard to saucepan and bring to a boil, whisking constantly. (Custard may look curdled as it begins to thicken but will become smooth as it is boiled and whisked.) Boil custard, whisking vigorously, 1 minute and remove saucepan from heat. (Custard will be very thick and smooth.)

Immediately pour custard into baking pan, smoothing top, and chill, its surface covered with plastic wrap, until firm, about 1½ hours. Cut custard into 2-inch squares.

In a small bowl whisk together bread crumbs, remaining ¼ cup sugar, and ground cinnamon. In another small bowl lightly whisk remaining 2 eggs.

Have ready flour in a bowl and a tray lined with wax paper. Working with 1 custard square at a time, coat square with flour, shaking off excess, and then with egg, letting excess drip off. Coat square with bread crumb mixture, transferring to tray. Chill squares, uncovered, 30 minutes.

Make sauce:

In a saucepan combine water, brown sugar, ½ cup rum, and star anise and simmer, uncovered, 15 minutes. Stir in remaining tablespoon rum and lime juice and pour mixture through a sieve into a glass measuring cup or heatproof pitcher.

Preheat oven to 325° F. and set a rack in a shallow baking pan.

In a heavy 12- to 14-inch skillet heat 1½ inches oil over moderately high heat until it registers 375° F. on a deep-fat thermometer and fry squares in 3 batches until golden, about 15 seconds on each side. Carefully transfer squares as fried with a slotted spatula to rack to drain and keep warm in oven.

Onto each of 8 dessert plates pour 2 tablespoons sauce. Halve 12 custard squares diagonally and arrange 3 triangles on each plate. Garnish desserts with star fruit and star anise. Serves 8.

PHOTO ON PAGE 17

Chocolate Orange Crème Brûlée

4 ounces fine-quality bittersweet chocolate
  (not unsweetened), chopped
1¾ cups heavy cream
6 large egg yolks
1 large whole egg
½ cup granulated sugar
1¾ cups milk
2 tablespoons Grand Marnier
1 teaspoon freshly grated orange zest
¼ cup firmly packed light brown sugar or
  raw sugar

Preheat oven to 325° F.

Put chocolate in a small metal bowl. In a heavy saucepan heat ½ cup cream over moderately high heat until it just comes to a boil and pour over chocolate. Let chocolate stand until softened and whisk mixture until smooth.

In a bowl whisk together yolks, whole egg, and granulated sugar and whisk in chocolate mixture. In pan heat remaining 1¼ cups cream and milk until

mixture just comes to a boil. Add milk mixture to egg mixture in a stream, whisking, and whisk in Grand Marnier and zest. Skim off any froth.

Divide custard among eight ½-cup flameproof ramekins set in a roasting pan and add enough hot water to pan to reach halfway up sides of ramekins. Bake custards in middle of oven until they are just set but still tremble slightly, about 40 minutes. Remove ramekins from pan and cool custards. *Chill custards, covered loosely with plastic wrap, at least 4 hours or overnight.*

Set broiler rack so that custards will be 2 to 3 inches from heat and preheat broiler.

Sift brown sugar evenly over custards and broil custards on a baking sheet until sugar is melted and caramelized, about 2 minutes. (Alternatively, raw sugar may be sprinkled over custards and caramelized with a blowtorch.) Chill custards 20 minutes. Serves 8.

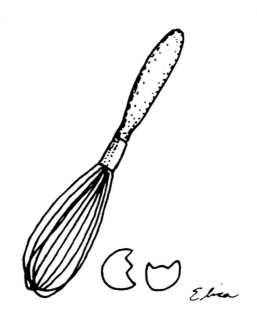

ramekins set in a roasting pan and add enough hot water to pan to reach halfway up sides of ramekins. Bake custards in middle of oven until they are just set but still tremble slightly, about 40 minutes. Remove ramekins from pan and cool custards. *Chill custards, covered loosely with plastic wrap, at least 4 hours or overnight.*

Set broiler rack so that custards will be 2 to 3 inches from heat and preheat broiler.

Sift brown sugar evenly over custards and broil custards on a baking sheet until sugar is melted and caramelized, about 2 minutes. (Alternatively, raw sugar may be sprinkled over custards and caramelized with a blowtorch.) Chill custards 20 minutes. Serves 8.

Panettone Bread and Butter Pudding

⅔ cup pitted prunes, chopped
4 tablespoons grappa (Italian brandy)
½ pound panettone*, brioche, or challah, cut lengthwise into ⅓-inch-thick slices
about 3 tablespoons unsalted butter, softened
3 cups milk
1 vanilla bean, split lengthwise
¾ cup granulated sugar
3 large whole eggs
3 large egg yolks

Garnish: confectioners' sugar

*available at some Italian markets and specialty foods shops and by mail order from Grace's Marketplace, tel. (800) 325-6126

In a small saucepan macerate prunes in grappa 30 minutes. Simmer mixture until most liquid is evaporated and spread prunes in a 2-quart gratin dish (about 14 inches long) or other shallow baking dish.

Preheat broiler.

Lightly butter one side of panettone slices and trim crusts if desired. Cut into 3- to 4-inch squares and halve squares diagonally to form triangles. Arrange triangles, buttered sides up, in one layer on a large baking sheet and broil about 4 inches from heat until golden, about 30 seconds to 1 minute. Cool triangles and arrange slices, toasted sides up and

Coffee Crème Brûlée

6 large egg yolks
1 large whole egg
⅔ cup granulated sugar
1¾ cups heavy cream
1¾ cups milk
1½ tablespoons instant espresso powder
2 tablespoons Kahlúa
¼ cup firmly packed light brown sugar or raw sugar

Preheat oven to 325° F.

In a bowl whisk together yolks, whole egg, and granulated sugar. In a heavy saucepan heat cream and milk over moderately high heat until mixture just comes to a boil and stir in espresso powder and Kahlúa, stirring until powder is dissolved. Add milk mixture to egg mixture in a stream, whisking, and skim off any froth.

Divide custard among eight ½-cup flameproof

overlapping slightly, over prunes in baking dish. *Pudding may be prepared up to this point 6 hours ahead and kept covered at room temperature.*

Preheat oven to 400° F.

In a heavy saucepan bring milk to a bare simmer over moderate heat with vanilla bean and sugar and remove pan from heat. Scrape seeds from vanilla bean with a knife into milk (discard pod) and whisk to break up seeds. In a large heatproof bowl whisk together whole eggs and yolks and add hot milk in a slow stream, whisking.

Ladle custard evenly over toasts and set dish in a larger baking pan. Add enough hot water to pan to reach halfway up side of dish and bake pudding in middle of oven 25 minutes, or until puffed and set.

Remove dish from water bath and cool pudding to warm or room temperature. Just before serving dust pudding with confectioners' sugar. Serves 6.

PHOTO ON PAGE 18

Panna Cotta with Praline Caramel Sauce

1 envelope plus 1 teaspoon unflavored gelatin
   (about 1 tablespoon plus ¼ teaspoon)
¼ cup milk
1 cup confectioners' sugar
2 vanilla beans, split lengthwise
½ teaspoon salt
3 cups heavy cream
For praline
¼ cup granulated sugar
1 tablespoon light corn syrup
1 tablespoon water
¼ cup hazelnuts, toasted and skinned
   (procedure follows) and chopped
½ teaspoon baking soda
For caramel sauce
1 cup granulated sugar
¾ cup water

1½ cups sour cream

In a cup sprinkle gelatin over milk and let soften. In a large saucepan whisk together confectioners' sugar, vanilla beans, salt, and 2 cups heavy cream and bring just to a boil over moderately low heat, stirring occasionally. Remove pan from heat and scrape seeds from vanilla beans with a knife into liquid (discard pods). Add gelatin mixture, stirring until dissolved. Pour mixture into a large metal bowl and chill, stirring occasionally, to room temperature, about 1 hour.

Make praline while cream mixture is cooling:

In a small saucepan cook sugar, corn syrup, and water over moderate heat until a light caramel. Stir in hazelnuts and baking soda (mixture will foam up) and immediately spoon onto a sheet of foil. Cool praline and break into chunks. *Praline may be made 1 week ahead and frozen, wrapped in foil.*

Make caramel sauce:

In a dry heavy saucepan cook sugar over moderate heat, without stirring, until it begins to melt. Continue cooking sugar, stirring with a fork until melted and then swirling pan, until a deep golden caramel and remove pan from heat. Add water (mixture will bubble up) and simmer, stirring, until caramel is dissolved. Cool sauce and chill until cold. *Caramel sauce may be made 1 week ahead and chilled, covered. Before serving, thin sauce with water if necessary.*

In a small bowl whisk sour cream until smooth. In a chilled bowl with chilled beaters of an electric mixer beat remaining cup heavy cream until it just holds stiff peaks. Gently fold sour cream into whipped cream. Gently fold sour cream mixture into cooled gelatin mixture until smooth and pour into a 6½-cup mold or bowl. *Chill panna cotta, covered, at least until firm, about 4 hours and up to 2 days.*

To unmold *panna cotta* loosen edge and dip mold or bowl into a slightly larger bowl filled halfway with hot water. Invert mold or bowl onto a platter with a raised edge and unmold. Stir praline into caramel sauce and pour over *panna cotta.*

Cut *panna cotta* into wedges and spoon sauce over each serving. Serves 12.

To Toast and Skin Hazelnuts

Preheat oven to 350° F.

In a baking pan toast hazelnuts in one layer in oven 10 minutes, or until lightly colored and skins blister. Wrap nuts in a kitchen towel and let steam 1 minute. Rub nuts in towel to remove as much of skins as possible and cool.

Farina Pudding with Fresh Fruit

For pudding
1 cup milk
2 tablespoons uncooked farina
2 tablespoons honey
1 large egg
¼ teaspoon vanilla
For fruit
1 kiwi
½ mango
6 large strawberries
2 teaspoons fresh lime juice
2 teaspoons sugar

Make pudding:

In a small saucepan over moderate heat simmer milk, farina, honey, and a pinch salt, stirring constantly, 3 minutes. In a bowl beat egg lightly and stir in about one fourth farina mixture. Stir egg mixture into farina mixture and cook, stirring, until pudding just begins to boil.

Put pan in a bowl of ice and water and stir pudding until cool, about 5 minutes. Stir in vanilla and divide between 2 small dessert bowls. Cover surface of pudding with plastic wrap to prevent a skin from forming and chill 20 minutes, or until ready to serve.

Prepare fruit while pudding is chilling:

Peel and dice kiwi and mango. Hull and dice strawberries. In a small bowl stir together fruit, lime juice, and sugar and chill until ready to serve. Spoon fruit over pudding. Serves 2.

Rice Pudding with Cranberry Walnut Sauce

1⅓ cups milk
½ cup converted rice
3 tablespoons sugar
¼ teaspoon salt
¾ cup half-and-half
¼ cup red currant jelly
¼ cup water
2 tablespoons dried cranberries or raisins
1 tablespoon fresh lemon juice
1 large egg
½ teaspoon vanilla
1 tablespoon chopped toasted walnuts

In a heavy saucepan simmer milk, rice, sugar, salt, and ½ cup half-and-half, covered, until rice is tender and most liquid is absorbed, about 30 minutes.

While rice is cooking, in a small saucepan simmer jelly, water, cranberries or raisins, and lemon juice, covered, stirring occasionally, until jelly melts and sauce thickens slightly. Keep sauce warm.

In a measuring cup beat together egg, vanilla, and remaining ¼ cup half-and-half with a fork.

Remove rice from heat and stir in egg mixture. Cook rice pudding over low heat, stirring constantly, until thick and creamy, about 5 minutes.

Stir walnuts into sauce and serve rice pudding with sauce. Serves 2.

Bittersweet Chocolate Mousse in Phyllo with Raspberry Sauce

2 *phyllo* sheets, thawed if frozen
For sauce
a 10-ounce package frozen raspberries in
    light syrup
2 tablespoons granulated sugar
1 tablespoon *eau-de-vie de framboise* or
    raspberry liqueur
For mousse
2 tablespoons granulated sugar
1 tablespoon cornstarch
½ cup water
1 large egg
3 ounces fine-quality bittersweet chocolate
    (not unsweetened), chopped

1 tablespoon *eau-de-vie-de framboise* or
   raspberry liqueur
¼ cup well-chilled heavy cream

For serving
3 tablespoons well-chilled heavy cream,
confectioners' sugar,
unsweetened cocoa powder,
chocolate curls (procedure follows)

Preheat oven to 350° F.

On a work surface stack *phyllo* sheets and cut out three 6-inch squares (6 total), discarding scraps. Stack *phyllo* squares between 2 sheets of wax paper and cover with a kitchen towel. Line each of two ½-cup muffin tins with 1 *phyllo* square, pressing gently into bottom, with edges overhanging top of tin. Repeat with remaining squares in same 2 tins, overlapping corners in different directions, but do not reposition *phyllo* once in tin (it may tear).

Bake *phyllo* shells in middle of oven until edges are golden brown, 5 to 10 minutes. Carefully transfer *phyllo* shells to a rack and cool completely. *Phyllo shells may be made 1 day ahead and kept in an air-tight container at room temperature.*

Make sauce:

In a saucepan simmer raspberries and sugar, stirring occasionally, 10 minutes and stir in *eau-de-vie* or liqueur. In a blender purée mixture until smooth and strain through a sieve into a heatproof bowl. *Chill sauce, covered, at least 30 minutes and up to 2 days.*

Make mousse:

In a small saucepan whisk together sugar and cornstarch and add water and egg, whisking until smooth. Bring mixture to a boil over moderate heat, whisking, and simmer, whisking vigorously, 1 minute. Remove pan from heat and add chocolate and *eau-de-vie* or liqueur, stirring until chocolate is melted. Transfer mixture to a metal bowl set in a bowl of ice and cold water and beat until cold and lightened in color. In a bowl beat cream until it just holds stiff peaks and fold into chocolate mixture gently but thoroughly. *Chill mousse, covered, at least 30 minutes and up to 2 days.*

To serve:

In a bowl whisk cream until it just begins to thicken. Pour some raspberry sauce onto 2 dessert plates and dot with thickened cream. Pull point of a skewer or toothpick through cream to form hearts. With a sieve dust *phyllo* shells with confectioners' sugar and cocoa powder. Arrange shells on top of sauce and spoon ⅓ cup mousse into each shell (do not overfill). Top mousse with chocolate curls. Serves 2.

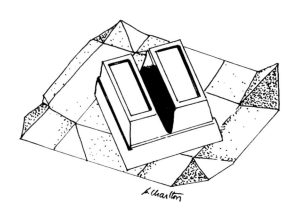

To Make Chocolate Curls

fine-quality bittersweet chocolate (not
   unsweetened), chopped

In a small metal bowl set over a saucepan of barely simmering water melt chocolate and on a baking sheet (not non-stick) spread it with a metal spatula as thinly and evenly as possible. Cool chocolate until firm to the touch but not hard. (Alternatively, chill chocolate on sheet in refrigerator; if it becomes too hard let it soften slightly at room temperature.) With a pastry scraper or metal spatula held at an angle scrape chocolate slowly from sheet, letting it curl. Transfer curls carefully as formed to another baking sheet lined with wax paper. *Chocolate curls may be made 1 day ahead and chilled, covered loosely.* An ounce of chocolate yields enough chocolate curls to garnish 2 to 4 servings.

Bittersweet Chocolate Soufflé

⅓ cup granulated sugar plus additional for
    coating soufflé dish
3 tablespoons all-purpose flour
3 large egg yolks
1½ cups milk
2 teaspoons vanilla
6 ounces fine-quality bittersweet
    chocolate (not unsweetened),
    chopped fine
6 large egg whites
¼ teaspoon salt

Garnish: confectioners' sugar
Accompaniment: lightly sweetened
    whipped cream

Preheat oven to 375° F. Butter a 6-cup soufflé dish and coat with additional granulated sugar, knocking out excess sugar. Butter and sugar a 6-inch-wide doubled piece of foil or wax paper long enough to fit around dish. Fit soufflé dish with collar extending 2 inches above rim.

In a large bowl whisk together flour and 1 tablespoon sugar. In a small bowl whisk together yolks and ¼ cup milk and add to flour mixture, whisking until smooth.

In a heavy saucepan heat remaining 1¼ cups milk over high heat until it just comes to a boil and whisk into yolk mixture in a slow stream. Transfer mixture to pan and cook over moderate heat, whisking, until it just comes to a boil. Cook mixture at a bare simmer, whisking constantly, until very thick, about 2 minutes. Remove pan from heat and whisk in vanilla and chocolate until custard is smooth. Transfer custard to a large bowl.

In another bowl with an electric mixer beat whites with salt until they just hold soft peaks. Beat in remaining sugar in a slow stream, beating until meringue just holds stiff peaks. Stir one fourth meringue into custard to lighten and fold in remaining meringue gently but thoroughly. Spoon mixture into soufflé dish. *Soufflé may be prepared up to this point 1 hour ahead and chilled, covered with a paper towel and plastic wrap (do not let paper towel touch surface of soufflé). Put cold soufflé in preheated oven.* Bake soufflé in middle of oven 30 minutes, or until firm and set in center.

Carefully remove collar from soufflé dish and sift confectioners' sugar over soufflé. Serve soufflé immediately with whipped cream. Serves 6 to 8.

BEVERAGES

ALCOHOLIC

Raspberry Lime Rickeys

a 10-ounce package frozen raspberries
    in light syrup, thawed
1¼ cups fresh lime juice
1 cup water
½ cup vodka
¼ cup Pernod
¾ cup superfine sugar
1 cup chilled club soda or seltzer

Garnish: fresh raspberries and lime slices

In a sieve set over a small bowl drain raspberries, pressing gently on berries with back of a spoon if necessary to yield ½ cup liquid, and reserve raspberries for another use. In a 2-quart pitcher stir together raspberry liquid, lime juice, water, vodka, Pernod, and sugar until sugar is dissolved and chill until cold. *Rickeys may be prepared up to this point 1 day ahead and chilled, covered.*

Just before serving, add club soda or seltzer, enough ice to fill pitcher, and some fresh raspberries and lime slices. Serve rickeys over ice in glasses and garnish with more fresh raspberries and lime slices. Makes about 6 cups.

PHOTO ON PAGE 44

Watermelon Vodka Coolers

For simple syrup
¼ cup water
¼ cup sugar

2 cups seeded watermelon chunks
2 ounces vodka, or to taste
¼ cup fresh lime juice, or to taste

Garnish: two 5- to 6-inch-long thin slices
    watermelon rind with some flesh attached

Make simple syrup:
In a saucepan boil water and sugar, stirring, until sugar is dissolved. Cool syrup and chill, covered, until cold.

In a blender purée watermelon until smooth and stir in ¼ cup syrup, vodka, and lime juice.

Serve coolers over ice in 2 tall glasses and garnish with watermelon rind. Serves 2.

Sangrita Bloody Marys

2 cans tomato juice, each 1 quart 14 ounces
    (about 12 cups total), chilled
2⅔ cups fresh orange juice (from about 8 oranges)
⅔ cup fresh lemon juice
2½ teaspoons red or green Tabasco
2 teaspoons Worcestershire sauce
2 cups aquavit such as Aalborg or Linie
    if desired

Garnish: celery stalks

In a large pitcher stir together all ingredients except aquavit. *Juice mixture may be made 3 hours ahead and chilled, covered.*

Stir in aquavit and serve over ice in glasses. Garnish drinks with celery. Makes about 17 cups.

PHOTO ON PAGE 67

Ice blocks for punch can take any form you wish. To accompany our Haunted House Dinner we rinsed out surgical gloves and filled them with water, tying them closed. After freezing the "water balloons" on a baking sheet, the gloves peeled off easily and we were left with icy hands to chill our punch.

Witches' Brew

For spice syrup
2 cinnamon sticks
5 whole cloves
3 tablespoons finely chopped peeled
   fresh gingerroot
⅓ cup water
⅓ cup sugar

a chilled 25.4-ounce bottle sparkling cider
   (about 3¼ cups)
a chilled 1-quart bottle cranberry juice cocktail
a chilled 1-liter bottle club soda or seltzer
1 cup dark rum if desired

For serving: ice blocks in any shape

Make spice syrup:
In a small saucepan bring syrup ingredients to a boil, stirring until sugar is dissolved, and simmer, covered, 5 minutes. Cool syrup. *Syrup may be made 1 week ahead and chilled, covered.*

In a punch bowl combine remaining ingredients and strain syrup through a fine sieve into punch. Stir punch and add ice blocks. Makes about 13 cups.

PHOTO ON PAGE 70

NON-ALCOHOLIC

Peach Basil Iced Tea

3 orange pekoe tea bags
1 cup loosely packed fresh basil leaves
4 cups water
five 5½-ounce cans peach nectar
   (about 3⅓ cups), chilled
¼ cup chilled simple syrup (recipe follows),
   or to taste

Garnish: peach slices and fresh basil sprigs

Put tea bags and basil in a quart-size glass measure or heatproof bowl.

In a saucepan bring water just to a boil and pour over tea bags. Steep tea 5 minutes and strain through a sieve into a heatproof pitcher. Cool tea and chill, covered, until cold, about 1 hour.

Stir in nectar and syrup. Serve tea over ice in tall glasses and garnish with peach slices and basil sprigs. Makes about 7 cups.

Simple Syrup

1⅓ cups sugar
1¼ cups water

In a saucepan bring sugar and water to a boil, stirring, and boil until sugar is completely dissolved. Cool syrup and chill, covered. *Syrup may be made 2 weeks ahead and chilled, covered.* Makes 2 cups.

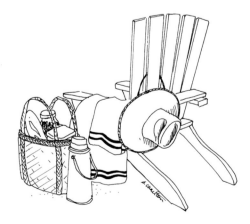

Apricot Iced Tea

3 orange pekoe tea bags
4 cups water
five 5½-ounce cans apricot nectar
     (about 3⅓ cups), chilled
½ cup chilled simple syrup (page 238),
     or to taste

Put tea bags in a heatproof pitcher.

In a saucepan bring water just to a boil and pour over tea bags. Steep tea 5 minutes and remove tea bags. Cool tea and chill, covered, until cold, 1 hour.

Stir in nectar and syrup. Serve tea over ice in tall glasses. Makes about 8 cups.

Iced Citrus Sun Tea

2½ cups orange juice
4 Celestial Seasonings Red Zinger
     tea bags
4 cups water
1 lemon
1 lime
¼ cup chilled simple syrup (page 238),
     or to taste
1 navel orange, sliced

Fill an ice-cube tray with orange juice and freeze, uncovered, until solid, about 4 hours. *Orange ice cubes may be made 1 week ahead and kept frozen in a plastic bag.*

In a pitcher combine tea bags and water and let tea stand at room temperature 4 hours.

Remove tea bags and chill tea, covered, until cold, about 30 minutes.

Cut half of lemon and lime into slices and squeeze remaining halves into tea. Stir syrup and all fruit slices into tea. Serve tea over orange juice ice cubes in tall glasses. Makes about 4 cups.

Ginger Iced Tea

4 China oolong tea bags
4 cups water
¼ cup sliced peeled fresh gingerroot
     (about a 2½- by 1½-inch piece)
½ cup plus 1 tablespoon chilled simple syrup
     (page 238), or to taste

Put tea bags in a quart-size glass measure or heatproof bowl.

In a saucepan bring water with gingerroot just to a boil and pour over tea bags. Steep tea 5 minutes and remove tea bags. Steep gingerroot 1½ hours more and strain tea through a fine sieve into a pitcher. Chill tea, covered, until cold, about 30 minutes.

Stir in syrup and serve tea over ice in tall glasses. Makes about 4 cups.

Black Currant Iced Tea

4 black currant tea bags
4 cups water
½ cup plus 1 tablespoon chilled simple syrup
     (page 238), or to taste
2 teaspoons raspberry vinegar
1 lime, cut into 4 wedges

Put tea bags in a heatproof pitcher.

In a saucepan bring water just to a boil and pour over tea bags. Steep tea 5 minutes and remove tea bags. Cool tea and chill, covered, until cold, 1 hour.

Stir in syrup and vinegar. Squeeze lime wedges into tea and add wedges. Serve tea over ice in tall glasses. Makes about 4 cups.

THE FLAVORS OF
ENGLAND, IRELAND, AND SCOTLAND

One visits England, Ireland, and Scotland to enjoy pastoral landscapes of rolling greenery dotted with sheep and cattle, quiet villages of thatched cottages and cobblestone streets, stately manor houses and ancient castles, rustic churches and soaring cathedrals. Even the cities — with their bustling museums and whirl of black cabs and doubledecker buses — are clean, manageable, and welcoming. After all, these are the lands of proper yet friendly people who are proud of their history and eager to share it with visitors. As in the past, a bountiful breakfast, hearty pub snack, or fanciful afternoon tea of indigenous fare can always be enjoyed, but for an exceptional luncheon or dinner one no longer needs to rely on European, Indian, or Asian restaurants. Recently, an awakening of food production and preparation has taken place, and today many inns and restaurants staffed with and often owned by innovative chefs are serving truly exciting fare.

Although situated in the northern Atlantic, these island countries are blessed by the presence of the Gulf Stream, which brings moderate temperatures and dependable light rains. Pastures are spacious and lush, and the livestock that feed on them produce some of the world's best meats and cheeses and other dairy products. Tender vegetables, succulent fruits, and aromatic fresh herbs are grown in the rich soil (most families have a garden, however small), and wild game is still abundant. In addition, surrounding seas as well as lakes and rivers are bountiful — oysters, crabs, mussels, lobsters, scallops, herring, kippers, turbot, plaice, periwinkles, mackerel, haddock, bass, cod, sole, eels, trout, and brill are all available. Irish and Scottish salmon are highly praised by gastronomes throughout the world.

Generally speaking, the traditional cuisines found throughout England, Ireland, and Scotland celebrate the natural flavors of domestic foods without complicated cooking methods or exotic ingredients. History tells us that the local people are of hearty stock, and they still seem to yearn for substantial down-home goodness. Comfort foods, such as warming soups, shepherd's pie, and stews, are ideal in this damp climate. Tea, cheese, and condiments all play major roles in daily life and are enjoyed by everyone — worker or royal. On the following pages, we offer a primer on each of these three essentials, share a bit of their history, and offer

Burnsall Village in Wharfdale, Yorkshire

suggestions for their use. Then, in three new menus from Gourmet's kitchens, we feature these staples as well as some other specialties held dear by each country.

As all visitors to England know, taking tea at 4 o'clock is not to be missed, so we've created an afternoon tea of our own. Here you will learn how to brew a proper pot of tea as well as make traditional tea sandwiches and a host of sweets including scones with raspberry jam, two beautiful cakes, lacy gingered cookies, and memorable lemon curd cream tartlets.

We turn to Ireland for a hearty country supper that showcases such local favorites as fish, lamb, potatoes, mushrooms, and berries. Our meal begins with a delicious and particularly pretty scrod dish topped with flavored bread crumbs and fresh tomatoes before it is baked in apple cider and vinegar. This is followed by an updated version of Dingle pie (originally, individual mutton pies that the farmers and fishermen of Dingle would snack on, warmed or cold). Our large pie is filled with boneless lamb shoulder, turnips, and parsnips slowly simmered in lamb stock for full flavor. The side dishes are all traditional specialties with new touches: Irish soda bread, the indispensable buttermilk quick bread also called "soda cake" due to its round shape (ours is studded with dried currants and caraway seeds); champ, a mashed potato and scallion dish (we've substituted leeks); mushrooms sautéed in a rich cream sauce (the Irish love their large field mushrooms and have a cultivated mushroom industry as well); and a salad of watercress, sorrel, beets, and hard-cooked eggs with a mustard vinaigrette. And, because berries are an Irish passion, we developed a luscious blackberry fool for dessert. Raspberries can be substituted in our recipe, if desired.

Finally, we conclude with an elegant four-course Scottish dinner which, like our Irish supper, begins with a taste of the sea — mussel soup, flavored with chopped dulse, the dried red seaweed found on Scotland's coast. Then, in keeping with the Scots' affinity for wild game, roasted pheasant is served with bread sauce, a milk and cream-based embellishment that has been popular since medieval times. Other accompaniments include apples baked in red currant jelly; clapshot, a classic mashed potato and rutabaga combination; and buttered carrots with lemon thyme. The evening continues with a cheese course (see pages 249-250 for suggestions) and ends with a spectacular typsy laird, a trifle that is *almost* too pretty to eat.

Let The Flavors of England, Ireland, and Scotland take you across the Atlantic for a spot of tea or a pint of ale and much, much more. It will soon become evident that these are the lands of tradition-minded people who excel at many things, including the perpetuation of cuisines refined to perfection.

TEA

It is impossible to imagine life in misty England, Scotland, or Ireland without tea. In fact, today the United Kingdom imports more than 352 million pounds of it per year. The British sip over 180 million cups a day, while their Irish neighbors drink, on average, even more cups per person. Breakfast, lunch, at least two tea breaks (one mid-morning and another mid-afternoon for workers), afternoon tea (for many others), and evening dinner are pre-ordained times to relax with this warming beverage. And then, of course, there are celebrations, moments of sorrow, or a hint of illness, when only tea will do.

Tea is the most ancient beverage in the world, and, while Chinese, Indian, and Japanese legends all offer charming stories of its discovery, the origins of tea are unclear. Although the Dutch had brought Chinese green tea (ch'a) to Europe some 50 years

earlier, it was not until 1658 that tea was served as a medicinal elixir and sold publicly at Thomas Garway's coffeehouse in London. Shortly thereafter, Queen Catherine, consort to Charles II, arrived from Portugal with dowry trunks packed with the precious brewing leaves. The aristocracy immediately embraced tea, and the beverage caught on quickly throughout the country. In 1680 Mary, the Duchess of York, brought tea to Scotland. The British East India Company soon began to import black as well as various green teas, and by the mid-eighteenth century black teas became the more popular.

As the British love affair with Chinese tea continued to grow, so did the obsession with procuring new sources for it. After discovering tea plants growing wild in India, English planters tried to grow the Chinese tea plant there, but were unsuccessful. (Britain eventually took control of China's tea markets in the 1840s.) The venturers instead concentrated on refining and propagating Indian tea using Chinese growing methods in Assam and Darjeeling (in India) and Java (in Indonesia).

In 1840 Anna, Duchess of Bedford, decided that late-afternoon tea served with cakes and pastries would be a good way to stave off hunger pangs until dinner, which was then served late in the evening. The idea caught on among the well-to-do, and by the 1880s they were dressing for the occasion and traveling to their neighbors' drawing rooms. Only the finest tea services were used, and during this period Josiah Spode's bone china creations were a source of English pride. Tea gardens at Marylebone, Ranelagh, and Vauxhall also became popular, fostering a less formal way to socialize. By the turn of the century, shops opened for tea and cakes, and fancy tea shops within department stores appeared. Also, posh hotels held 5 o'clock tea dances for young ladies and

gentlemen; unfortunately, these ended in 1939, when the young men went off to war.

During the late 1800s, while afternoon tea was being enjoyed by the upper classes, "high tea," generally taken around 6 o'clock, became the supper of the working folk of England. Unable to afford more than one solid meal a day (at lunchtime), they returned home from work to a pot of tea, leftovers from lunch, bread and cheese, cold meats, and perhaps sausages. As times improved, eggs, fish, roasted meats or poultry, mashed potatoes, and desserts became additional possibilities. Today, such high tea feasts are still enjoyed in the country in northern England and in Scotland.

Throughout Britain the art of making a proper pot of tea is taken quite seriously, and, although no two sources offer precisely the same instructions, we offer a list of basic steps at the beginning of our English Afternoon Tea menu (page 258). Generally speaking, the Irish prefer a much stronger brew that is, by most standards, quite bitter tasting. This is accomplished by putting many more tea leaves in the pot and brewing the tea over a low flame for a minimum of 10 minutes and up to several hours. Then, to offset the bitter result, many spoonfuls of sugar and whole milk are often added.

All tea comes from the same plant, a member of the Camelia family. Once the leaves are picked they are handled in various ways to procure a particular type of beverage. There are three main types of tea available:

Green teas are pale in color with a somewhat bitter taste. They are made from leaves that have been steamed to curtail fermentation, rolled on mats to release aromatic juices, and then heated to stop fermentation.

Black teas are stronger than green teas with a rich flavor due to fermentation. The leaves are withered on racks for 12 to 24 hours, rolled to encourage further oxidation, and then dried in a drying machine until the leaves become a dark brown with a reddish tinge.

Oolong teas from China are a partly fermented blend of green and black leaves, making them a moderate combination of the two.

Of course, the type of tea that you choose is a personal matter; just be aware that the taste of a particular tea will vary from region to region according to the flavor of the water. For traditional afternoon tea a good Indian black tea — such as the full-bodied Assam or flowery Darjeeling or refreshing Ceylon — served with milk is always appropriate. China's black teas are also popular, among them the bracing, woodsmoke-flavored Lapsang Souchong and Keemun, another strong-tasting choice with a rich, flowery aroma. Suggested oolongs include Formosa Oolong, a partially fermented amber-colored tea with a delicious ripe peach flavor, and Black Dragon, a delicate, pale alternative with a fruity flavor.

Many teas are blended to create new flavors, and several combinations are ideal for afternoon tea. Classics include hearty and fragrant Earl Grey, made from large-leafed China tea, Darjeeling, and oil of bergamot (a Mediterranean citrus fruit), and Lady Londonderry, a medium-strength aromatic brew made from Ceylon, Indian, and Formosa teas. Enthusiasts can experiment by making their own blends. Various black China teas can be combined, and, some say, a pinch of Gunpowder, a green tea from China, will improve the flavor. Half a teaspoon of an Oolong added to a pot of Ceylon or Darjeeling also gives a nice result.

Serious tea drinkers believe that this beverage must be made with tea leaves, but we would be remiss not to mention herbal teas brewed with the roots, stems, seeds, berries, and flowers (both fresh and dried) of various herb plants. These offer a delicate, naturally sweet or bitter, caffeine-free alternative. Flavored teas are also available, but you should be aware that some contain artificial additives. In many cases, you would be better off adding your own spices, fruits, or citrus rinds.

Although most of us (including the British) have resorted to the ease of using tea bags, an American invention, they contain broken leaves that infuse almost immediately. (Never try to make a second cup of tea from a tea bag as it will have little flavor.) Whole loose tea leaves, on the other hand, continue to hold flavor after they come in contact with boiling water, allowing one to "top up" the tea pot with more water for a second round of tea. Store fresh loose tea leaves in a clean, dry, air-tight container, and buy small amounts so that you can replenish your supply frequently. If stored properly, black teas should remain flavorful for up to 2 years. Green teas should be used within 6 months of picking, so you should buy only from a reliable merchant with quick-moving stock. Once a packet of tea bags has been opened, the tea will deteriorate very quickly. Also, be sure to store different types of tea in separate containers; otherwise, flavors will combine.

The peoples of Scotland, Ireland, and England each have their own idea about what should be served with tea. The Scottish and Irish are known for their bountiful farmhouse spreads with outstanding displays of hearty home-baked goods. Scottish favorites include oatcakes (mild, nutty-flavored crackers that are often served with cheese), short-breads, and drop scones ("pancakes"). The Irish tea table holds Guinness fruitcakes, cream cakes, barm brack (a tea bread full of dried fruits and spices), and, naturally, Irish Soda bread (page 270) with jam.

The English serve different foods for each type of tea they have created. To name a few there are nursery teas for children, with bite-size squares of cakes, crispy cinnamon toast, or finger sandwiches; club man's teas with hearty sandwiches and potted shrimp; birthday teas featuring everything from sausage rolls and sandwiches to special sweets, such as fairy cakes (little cupcakes with sprinkles); and summer garden teas, where strawberries and cream are a must. But it is afternoon tea that is the passion of England, served daily throughout the country at 4 o'clock. In many fine homes and hotels, the ritual may be reminiscent of Duchess Anna's gatherings back in the 1840s. Our English Afternoon Tea (page 255), in all its finery, offers some quintessential dishes and a few surprises, and many items may be made ahead of time.

We begin, as the English do, with a variety of dainty tea sandwiches, filled with cucumber, smoked salmon, or egg and cress. Then we turn to scones served with raspberry jam and clotted cream (a departure from the strawberry or black currant jam and clotted cream combination that travelers to England know so well), and stemmed strawberries perfect for dipping in yet more clotted cream. This luscious, dense cream, made in Devon and Cornwall, is a heavenly accompaniment that must be tried. Unfortunately, due to a very short shelf life, clotted cream is not available in stateside food shops. However, a pasteurized version occasionally can be found in specialty food shops and is available by mail order from Dean & DeLuca in New York City, tel. (800) 221-7714.

Every tea table must have at least one cake — ours has two! The gingerbread bundt cake with lemon glaze is a spectacular variation of a traditional sweet. In the early days, gingerbread was rolled out with a patterned rolling pin or cut into the shapes of saints and princes and gilded for religious feasts. Nowadays the British make gingerbread "husbands" with currant buttons and iced eyebrows or bake the cake in sheet pans. (Our recipe may be made in this latter form.) Our other offering is a "fancy sandwich cake" that is in keeping with the British love of sponge cake filled with jams and preserves. Toasted almonds and candied violets decorate this "fancy" cake that is quite easy to prepare.

Every afternoon tea *must* have a variety of remarkable sweets, and we happily oblige. Our raspberry and lemon cream tartlets are filled with Britain's famous lemon curd and topped with fresh raspberries, another British passion. We've also included a moist date walnut loaf, sliced and served with sweet butter, and brandy snaps, crisp curled cookies (once sold at medieval fairs) that offer sweetness with a touch of ginger.

Naturally, one *could* enjoy a cup of tea without accompaniments, but a bit of indulgence is very sweet indeed.

CHEESE

You do not have to be a cheese expert to be familiar with English cheeses. In fact, it is likely that the first variety you ever tasted was a Cheddar, England's pride and joy, which has reached international fame and is now produced all over the world. But this is just one of the many exceptional cheeses that England, Ireland, and Scotland have given us — and new ones are cropping up every year.

Blessed with a temperate, maritime climate, the British Isles provide rich grazing lands for livestock and therefore ideal conditions for making cheese. In Wiltshire, England, an archaeological dig unearthed some of the first terracotta cheese drainers, dating back to 2,500 B.C., and confirm the fact that cheesemaking has been ongoing here for thousands of years.

What was first a survival mainstay would develop centuries later into an honored farmhouse tradition. It is said that the English are as proud of their mellow blue cheese as they are of Shakespeare. In fact, until the advent of twentieth-century technology, the method for making Stilton had not changed for some two hundred years. And, in eighteenth-century Scotland, cheese was such an essential part of daily life that it was used as payment for university fees!

Today, England alone produces 199,000 tons of cheese a year in creameries and farmhouse dairies, but only three percent of the total manufactured is exported. Cheese is universally enjoyed throughout England, Ireland, and Scotland, often simply toasted on bread or as the centerpiece of a ploughman's lunch, accompanied by a robust beer or ale.

In the early days of English history, the need

247

for food that could be consumed during long winters when the fields lay dormant spurred the development of many long-lasting semi-hard cheeses that have become traditional specialties. Early documents tell us that when the Roman legions inhabited England in the first century A.D. they introduced methods for manufacturing hard cheeses. Their salty, crumbly cow's milk cheese, similar to Cheddar, was both portable and long-lasting, making it an ideal food for soldiers.

Sixth-century Benedictine monks, appreciating the simplicity, frugality, and energy value of cheese, further encouraged its production. And, in medieval times, the easily transported semi-hard cheeses continued to be popular with pilgrims, who travelled vast distances on foot to visit holy relics. Cheddar also became an important cheap, basic food for the poor of the seventeenth and eighteenth centuries, who often ate bread and cheese every day for dinner; and sometimes twice a day — for lunch *and* dinner.

Although England's semi-hard Cheddar became internationally famous (dominating cheesemaking in the New World, for example), the soft cheeses of England, Ireland, and Scotland remained within their regional provinces and forged reputations in local inns and taverns. The renowned Stilton became popular this way. First known as Quenby cheese, Stilton was originally created from a recipe that belonged to a local family and is thought to have been made commercially for the first time by their housekeeper, a Mrs. Orton. Around 1730, Cowper Thornhill, innkeeper of the Bell Inn in the village of Stilton, began to buy the cheese in large quantities — and the rest is history.

Before 1914, most farms in England were involved in making cheese and dozens of hard and soft varieties with individual, distinctive flavors were developed. Unfortunately, after the outbreak of World War 1, most of this production stopped and many local specialty cheeses disappeared forever. The limited amount that continued to be made was manufactured in large creameries, and the unique tastes of farmhouse varieties were lost to these bland, factory-made "block" cheeses. To further the problem, farmers were commissioned during World War ll to make the most of national resources: All milk available for cheese was to be used only for the less perishable harder cheeses such as Cheddar, Cheshire, Dunlop, and Leicester.

Happily, however, in recent years there has been a resurgence of traditional (farmhouse) cheesemaking. Now, organically farmed permanent grassland is grazed by traditional dairy breeds and any milk given by cows under antibiotics is excluded. This method has proven to be better for the animals, for the soil, and also for the consumer who enjoys a superior cheese. Today, ten percent of cheese made in the United Kingdom warrants this description. By the end of the 1980s there were over 200 farmers making cheeses such as Cheddar, Double Gloucester, Cheshire, Caerphilly, Lancashire, and Cotherstone, and there are now 250 varieties of farmhouse cheese. We should note, however, that at the end of 1994, Britain's Milk Marketing Board (a state-run price regulatory agency) was disbanded, and the price of milk sold to dairies has soared. This, many fear, will limit the number of farmhouse dairies that can continue to operate, and, consequently,

obtaining these outstanding cheeses will become more difficult.

As in England's pastoral northern areas, the traditionally Gaelic regions of Scotland and Celtic regions of Ireland prefer little matured, softer farmhouse cheeses, many of which are not available in the United States due to their highly perishable nature. Such favorites as the ancient Scottish Caboc (dating back to the fifteenth century), a full-cream cheese that is covered with toasted oatmeal, and Orkney, a soft cheese with a natural rind, become pungent after a few weeks. Ireland's Cooleeney, a very soft cheese with a distinctive flavor, and Milleens, a popular mild, washed-rind cheese from County Cork, also are rarely exported.

Below is a list of some English, Irish, and Scottish cheeses that we suggest for the cheese course in our traditional Scottish Dinner menu (page 273). As any cheese course should, the selections here complement the flavors of the menu and were chosen to offer a variety of cheese types, including soft and hard cheeses, mild and strong varieties, and goat's and cow's milk cheeses. They are listed by flavor, from very mild to strong, and should be tasted in that order. When choosing cheese varieties, remember that, like produce, they are seasonal, and at times availability is limited. Also, the less widely produced and distributed Irish and Scottish cheeses are made in very small quantities, so you may have to substitute. Always try to taste a cheese before purchasing it to see if the flavors will meld with the meal. And, since soft cheese does not keep very long, buy only as much as you will consume in a few days. If you have trouble finding these cheeses at your local cheeseshop, they can be obtained at various times of the year by mail order from Dean & DeLuca in New York City, tel. (800) 221-7714.

Croghan: A semi-soft goat's milk cheese made in County Wexford, Ireland, Croghan has a washed rind that is pink in color and a velvety smooth interior. Somewhat like Gouda, it has a generally light, clean, pleasant, buttery taste, but the goat's

milk gives this cheese a distinctive flavor. Production of this mild cheese is limited; it is mainly available from spring through Christmas.

Gubbeen: This semi-soft cow's milk cheese is a pleasant farmhouse variety made in County Cork, Ireland. It has a soft, washed rind with a cream-colored interior. Its flavor is slightly tangy.

Dunlop: The most famous of the Scottish cheeses, Dunlop was created in the Ayrshire parish of Dunlop (in Scotland's southwestern lowlands). It is thought that in the late seventeenth century an Irish refugee made the cheese here from an Irish recipe. This hard cow's milk cheese is manufactured with full-cream from Dunlop cows. Packaged in 3- to 4-inch balls or in 38-pound wheels that are covered with black wax, the cheese has an off-white color and firm texture. Its sweet, mild flavor is similar to a young, buttery Cheddar, but it is more moist, even when well-matured. Eaten quite young (4 months old), the cheese is often enjoyed with buttered oatcakes and Scottish ale.

Lancashire: An uncooked, semi-hard English cheese with a cream-colored interior and crumbly consistency, this cheese has a mild flavor that sharpens with age. Lancashire is made from raw cow's milk redolent of the salty taste of the region's seaside grazing fields. Although it is now almost exclusively produced in factories, it was once made by Lancashire county small landholders. It is a splendid accompaniment to biscuits and ideal for toasting. When heated, this cheese has the consistency of custard, so it is often used for the popular savory, Welsh rarebit.

Cheddar: Named for the small village of Cheddar in Somerset, this has been the most widely consumed and popular cheese in England since the Elizabethan period and has been copied throughout the world. This pressed, uncooked, semi-hard cheese has a dry rind and is traditionally made from whole cow's milk that has been mixed with the skimmed cream from the previous evening's milking. In the nineteenth century the production of Cheddar changed from handmade to machine-made, but traditional farmhouse Cheddar is still produced in Somerset, Devon, and Dorset, and also — between April and November — on the Isle of Arran in Scotland. "Farmhouse Cheddar" has a creamy, yellow color and a firm, elastic consistency. Its slightly nutty flavor is neither too sweet nor too sour and it is more moist than factory Cheddar. The cheese travels well and remains in excellent condition for a long time.

Stilton: England's most internationally respected and only "protected" cheese must, in order to be labeled "Stilton," be blue or white and made from the richest full-cream cow's milk with no applied pressure, forming its own crust or coat. The milk must come from English dairy herds in the district of Melton Mowbray and surrounding areas within the counties of Leicestershire, Derbyshire, and Nottinghamshire. It is formed in tall, cylindrical shapes, and, when ripe, has a crinkled rind with browned edges. The interior is off-white with green-blue veins that should be evenly distributed throughout. Once formed, Stilton softens as it matures. The flavor is smooth, mellow, and much milder than other blue cheeses. It is available all year, but best between November and April.

SAUCES AND CONDIMENTS

Breakfast, afternoon tea, dinner — whatever the meal, there is always a sauce or condiment to be found on an English, Irish, or Scottish table. What, after all, would toast be without orange marmalade? Scones without strawberry or raspberry jam? Or leg of lamb without mint sauce? Finding just the right accompaniment makes all the difference, and the fine tuning of such perfect pairings has long been a passion throughout the British Isles.

This great interest in condiments began in the seventeenth century, when the British East India Company transformed London into one of the greatest spice markets of the world. Originally spices imported from the Far East, Genoa, and Venice were used simply to perk up the blandness of salted meats and boiled fish, but soon they were combined with mustard, vinegar, herbs, and wine to create popular sauces for meat, fish, and poultry. The English took readily to Indian chutneys and pickles, and inventive home cooks began to imitate these exotic products at home. They soon learned to pickle cucumbers and melons, preserve elder shoots in spiced vinegar, and make Indian pickling brine for such vegetables as cabbage and onions. Mixed vegetable and tomato-based chutneys and pickles have become favorite accompaniments to pork pies, cold roasted meats, and even cheeses.

Curries, relishes, and ketchup sauces were developed during the eighteenth and nineteenth centuries to help foodstuffs withstand the long sea voyages of the spice merchants and to enliven the meals served to both passengers and crew. Many of the bottled sauces found in stores today are based on the vinegar-and-horseradish or soy-and-garlic combinations that were first used to transport walnuts, oysters, cockles, mushrooms, lemons, anchovies, and onions. These pickling agents became known as "catsups" (derived from caveach, a spiced vinegar pickle in which cooked fish was preserved). Some sauces were named for the individual who originated a particular blend and by the mid-nineteenth century, hundreds of British families had formulas for their own sauces for fish, meat or poultry, roast game, or general use. Some family sauces that were commercially produced at that time are still available: Harvey's, a good all-around sauce combining anchovies, walnut pickle, soy, shallots, cayenne, garlic, and vinegar; Worcestershire sauce, another all-purpose favorite, its main ingredients including vinegar, molasses, anchovies, onions, tamarind, garlic, cloves, and chilies; and Quinn's sauce, based on salt anchovies, for fish. Today's popular tomato sauces and ketchups (derived from "catsup" and now interchangeable with this word) were not universally known until about 1900, when canned, affordable tomatoes were imported in bulk from America. (Tomato ketchup is now the third most popular condiment in England, after vinegar and mustard.)

Technically, a preserve is a vegetable or fruit that is "preserved" for future use by special preparation such as pickling or canning. The word "preserves", however, is often associated with fruit canned or made into jams and jellies. Just as vegetables needed to be "put up" for long winters and long sea voyages, so too did perishable berries and currants. It was discovered that whole fruits or large pieces of fruits could be "preserved" in their original form by simply cooking them in sugar. Jams, jellies, and marmalades were offshoots of these original preserves, and eventually they became essentials — jams and marmalades as elements of breakfast and tea time, and jellies as accompaniments to both hot and cold roasted meats. Jam is made by boiling fruit with sugar to a thick consistency; jelly is the result of boiling fruit juice with sugar. A marmalade is a jam made with citrus.

Below is a list of some of the most popular sauces and condiments that the English, Irish, and Scottish enjoy as accompaniments to particular foods or as important ingredients in recipes for relishes and dressings. Although many easily can be made from scratch, most can be purchased ready-made. Many of these products are available by mail order from Bewley's Irish Imports, 1130 Greenhill Road, West Chester, PA 19380, tel. (610) 696-2682 and Penny Ha'Penny, Wilton, CT 06897, tel. (800) 762-7775.

Mustard: Although the mustard plant grew wild in ancient Britain, the spicy condiment made with its seeds did not become popular there until the arrival of the Romans, who are credited with making the first mustard paste by combining fermented grape juice (must) and mustard seed. (*Mustard* comes from the Latin *mustum ardens* meaning "burning must.") The hot, spicy prepared mustard was originally used to mask the pungent flavors of meat and smoked fish, and during the thirteenth century it began to be produced in large quantities for public sale. Both powdered and prepared English mustards are now used to flavor dressings, soups, and hearty meat stews. Prepared mustards are also enjoyed with smoked sausages and strong cheeses.

Cider Vinegar: As the name implies, the amber-colored vinegar — used in vegetable and salad dressings and as an essential chutney ingredient — is made from apples.

Malt Vinegar: The most popular vinegar in England, malt vinegar — once made from beer but now produced from a sugar infusion of cereal starches — is frequently sprinkled over fish and chips and also used in ketchups and chutneys and for pickling.

Worcestershire Sauce: This extremely popular rich, brown condiment is used on its own as a meat sauce and as a flavoring agent in fish, beef, and poultry sauces, soups, and salad dressings.

Fresh Mint Sauce: A refreshing condiment for lamb, fresh mint sauce is made simply by combining fresh mint, sugar, boiling water, and malt or white wine vinegar. The mixture should stand a few hours before serving and keeps, covered and chilled, up to one week.

Mint jelly: A classic of English cookery, mint jelly was first created by the Romans to complement the flavor of roast lamb. Made with fresh mint, apples, vinegar, and sugar, the resulting conserve (a preserve made from a mixture) is much sweeter than the fresh mint sauce described above.

Red Currant Jelly: A translucent, shiny preserve with a delicate flavor and red color, red currant jelly goes particularly well with the rich flavor of game birds and roasted meats.

Strawberry or Black Currant Jam: A must for afternoon teas, jam adds sweet flavor to scones. It is also a breakfast favorite on toast.

Orange Marmalade: Originating in Portugal, where it was made from quince *(marmelo),* this conserve was imported to England in the fourteenth century. Later, marmalades were made from different fruits — oranges being the most popular. In the eighteenth century strips of orange rind were added to the orange preserves and the idea took off commercially. Marmalade is a tangy staple of the English, Irish, and Scottish breakfast.

Lemon Curd: A thick, smooth combination of lemons, eggs, butter, and sugar, lemon curd is one of England's most irresistible dessert sauces, whether dolloped on pound cake, used as a tartlet filling, or served with scones. Jarred lemon curd is quite perishable and should be stored in the refrigerator.

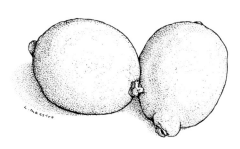

Fancy Sandwich Cake

ENGLISH AFTERNOON TEA

Tea and Minted Lemonade

•

Cucumber Tea Sandwiches

Smoked Salmon Tea Sandwiches

Egg and Cress Tea Sandwiches

Scones with Raspberry Jam and Clotted Cream

Stemmed Strawberries

Fancy Sandwich Cake

Gingerbread Bundt Cake with Lemon Glaze

Date Walnut Loaf

Brandy Snaps

Raspberry and Lemon Cream Tartlets

•

Serves 12 to 16

Cottage off Steep Hill,
Lincoln, England

Suggestions for our afternoon tea are offered in our tea primer (pages 243-246). Depending on the size of your tea party, you may want to brew more than one pot. Offering two or even three choices is a lovely idea, even if it means borrowing a friend's teapot. Throughout Britain the art of making a proper pot of tea is a serious matter. Although we were unable to find two sources that agree completely, we venture to offer the following instructions:

TO MAKE A PROPER POT OF TEA

•First, fill a kettle with fresh, cold water from the tap.

•Heat the kettle of water, and, when the water gets close to the boil, pour some of it into a teapot (preferably earthenware or porcelain) and swirl it around to warm the teapot. Throw the water in the teapot away and bring the water in the kettle to a rolling boil.

•Measure loose tea leaves (generally 1 heaping teaspoon for each cup plus one "for the pot") and add them to the heated teapot.

•Take the pot to the kettle so that the water will still be boiling as it hits the leaves. Don't boil the water for too long or the tea will taste flat. Pour the boiling water directly onto the tea leaves, stir well, and put a tea cozy over the pot.

•Wait for the tea to brew: 3 minutes for small leaves such as English and Irish Breakfast blends and Assam teas; 4 to 5 minutes for medium leaves such as Ceylon Breakfast; 5 to 6 minutes for large leaves such as Oolongs and Earl Grey.

•If you would like to use milk in your tea, pour a bit of cold whole milk (never skim or boiled milk or cream) into a bone china cup (not a mug) and *then* pour the tea into the cup, or *vice versa*. (This is a very controversial issue. The British Standards Institute proclaims that milk should be added first so that the hot tea can scald the milk, bringing out the tea's flavor. Many disagree.)

•Adding sugar to the teacup is optional, and some prefer to take their tea "straight" (without milk or sugar). Lemon goes well with some teas such as green or scented teas.

•Add more hot water to the pot as necessary, and when you've finished pouring, add more hot water for the second round.

Minted Lemonade

3 cups water
¾ cup sugar
zest of 4 lemons removed with a vegetable
    peeler
¾ cup fresh lemon juice
½ cup packed fresh mint leaves
4 cups ice cubes

Garnish: fresh mint sprigs and lemon slices

In a large saucepan boil water and sugar, stirring, until sugar is dissolved. Stir in zest, lemon juice, and mint and cool to room temperature.

Strain lemonade through a sieve into a 2-quart pitcher. Add ice and refrigerate until cold.

Serve lemonade garnished with mint sprigs and lemon slices. Makes about 2 quarts.

Cucumber Tea Sandwiches

1 European cucumber, peeled and sliced
    paper-thin
2 tablespoons malt vinegar* or
    cider vinegar
1 teaspoon coarse salt or ½ teaspoon
    table salt
¾ stick (6 tablespoons) unsalted butter,
    softened
12 very thin slices firm white sandwich bread

*available at specialty foods shops, some
    supermarkets, and by mail order from
    Balducci's, tel. (800) 225-3822

In a bowl combine cucumber, vinegar, and salt and chill, covered, 30 minutes. Drain cucumbers and pat dry with paper towels.

Spread butter on one side of each bread slice to cover completely and arrange 2 layers of cucumber on buttered side of 6 bread slices. Season cucumber layer with salt and freshly ground black pepper if desired and top with remaining bread slices, pressing gently. Trim crusts. *Sandwiches may be made 2 hours ahead and chilled, wrapped in plastic wrap.* Cut each sandwich diagonally into quarters. Makes 24 tea sandwiches.

Smoked Salmon Tea Sandwiches

¼ pound smoked salmon, minced
¼ cup heavy cream
¼ teaspoon Tabasco, or to taste
¾ stick (6 tablespoons) unsalted butter, softened
12 very thin slices firm whole-wheat sandwich
    bread
1 tablespoon chopped fresh chives

In a bowl with a fork stir together smoked salmon, cream, and Tabasco until mixture is blended well and creamy.

Spread butter on one side of each bread slice to cover completely and spread 1½ tablespoons salmon mixture evenly on buttered side of 6 bread slices. Sprinkle salmon mixture with chives and top with remaining bread, pressing gently. Trim crusts. *Sandwiches may be made 4 hours ahead and chilled, wrapped in plastic wrap.* Cut each sandwich into 3 strips. Makes 18 tea sandwiches.

Egg and Cress Tea Sandwiches

3 large hard-cooked eggs, chilled
3 tablespoons mayonnaise
¼ teaspoon curry powder, or to taste
¾ stick (6 tablespoons) unsalted butter,
    softened
6 very thin slices firm white sandwich bread
6 very thin slices firm whole-wheat sandwich
    bread
¼ cup mustard cress* or small watercress leaves

*available at some natural foods stores and
    specialty produce markets

Shred eggs on small teardrop-shaped holes of a grater. In a bowl stir together eggs, mayonnaise, curry powder, and salt to taste until smooth.

Spread butter on one side of each bread slice to cover completely and spread each white bread slice with 1½ tablespoons egg mixture. Arrange mustard cress or watercress leaves over egg mixture and top with whole-wheat bread slices, pressing gently. Trim crusts. *Sandwiches may be made 4 hours ahead and chilled, wrapped in plastic wrap.* Cut each sandwich into quarters. Makes 24 tea sandwiches.

Scones with Raspberry Jam and Clotted Cream

1½ cups all-purpose flour
2 tablespoons sugar

2 teaspoons cream of tartar
1 teaspoon baking soda
½ teaspoon salt
½ stick (¼ cup) cold unsalted butter,
    cut into bits
¼ cup milk
1 large egg

Accompaniments
raspberry jam
clotted cream*

*available at specialty foods shops and some
    supermarkets

Preheat oven to 425° F. and grease a large baking sheet.

In a bowl whisk together flour, sugar, cream of tartar, baking soda, and salt and blend in butter with fingertips until mixture resembles coarse meal. In a small bowl with a fork beat together milk and egg and stir into flour mixture until it just forms a soft dough.

On a floured surface with well-floured hands pat out dough into a ½-inch-thick round. With a floured 1¾-inch cutter cut out rounds and with a spatula carefully transfer to baking sheet. Gather and pat out scraps and cut out more rounds in same manner. Bake scones until just golden, about 7 to 10 minutes, and transfer to a rack to cool.

Serve scones warm or at room temperature with jam and clotted cream. Makes about 20 scones.

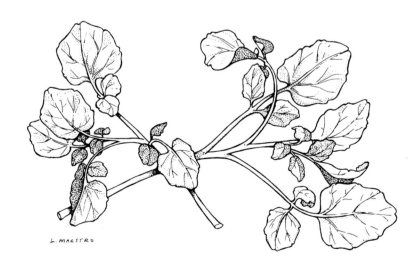

L. MAESTRO

Fancy Sandwich Cake

For cake
4 large eggs
⅔ cup granulated sugar
1 teaspoon vanilla
¼ cup clarified butter (procedure follows),
    melted and cooled to lukewarm
⅔ cup all-purpose flour, sifted onto a piece
    of wax paper
½ teaspoon salt

1 cup apricot preserves
1 cup confectioners' sugar
1 tablespoon unsalted butter, softened
2 tablespoons warm water
⅓ cup blanched whole almonds, toasted and
    chopped

Garnish: candied violets* if desired

*available at some specialty foods shops
    and by mail order from Dean & DeLuca,
    tel. (800) 221-7714

Make cake:
Preheat oven to 350° F. Line bottom of a buttered
8½-inch springform pan with a round of wax paper.
Butter paper and dust pan with flour, knocking out
excess flour.

In a metal bowl whisk together eggs and sugar. Set
bowl over a pan of simmering water and whisk
mixture until warm and sugar is dissolved. Remove
bowl from pan and beat mixture with a hand-held
electric mixer on medium speed 10 to 15 minutes, or
until tripled in volume and cooled. In a bowl combine
vanilla and butter. Sift flour and salt in batches
into egg mixture, gently folding after each addition
until just combined. Stir one fourth of batter into
butter mixture and fold butter mixture quickly into
remaining batter.

Pour batter into pan, smoothing top, and bake in
middle of oven about 30 to 35 minutes, or until top is
golden and a tester comes out clean. Cool cake in pan
on a rack 5 minutes. Remove side of pan and invert
cake onto rack. Remove paper carefully and cool cake
completely. *Cake may be made 1 day ahead and kept,
wrapped in plastic wrap, at room temperature.*

In a food processor or blender purée preserves. In
a small saucepan simmer ½ cup apricot purée over
moderately low heat, stirring occasionally, until
reduced to about ⅓ cup, about 5 minutes, and cool
slightly.

Cut cake in half horizontally and spread ½ cup
uncooked apricot purée between layers. Brush top and
side of cake with warm apricot purée and let stand
until coating dries slightly, about 30 minutes.

Transfer cake to a serving plate and slide 3-inch-
wide strips of wax paper under edge to catch drips of
icing. In a small bowl stir together confectioners'
sugar, butter, and warm water until smooth and
spread icing over top and side of cake. Let cake stand
until icing is slightly set, about 5 minutes, and gently
press almonds onto side of cake.

Remove wax paper strips and garnish top of cake
with candied violets. Let cake stand at room
temperature until icing is completely set, about 30
minutes. *Cake may be made 1 day ahead and kept,
covered loosely, in a cool, dry place.*

L maesTRo

To Clarify Butter

unsalted butter, cut into 1-inch pieces

In a heavy saucepan melt butter over low heat.
Remove pan from heat and let butter stand 3 minutes.
Skim froth and strain butter through a sieve lined with
a double thickness of rinsed and squeezed cheesecloth
into a bowl, discarding milky solids in bottom of pan.
Pour clarified butter into a jar or crock and chill,
covered. *Clarified butter keeps, covered and chilled,
indefinitely.* When clarified, butter loses about one
fourth its original volume.

Gingerbread Bundt Cake with Lemon Glaze

For cake
1½ cups firmly packed light brown sugar
2½ cups all-purpose flour
2½ tablespoons ground ginger
1 tablespoon cinnamon
¾ teaspoon baking soda
½ teaspoon salt
2½ sticks (1¼ cups) unsalted butter, softened
½ cup plain yogurt
3 large eggs
1 cup unsulphured molasses
For glaze
¾ cup confectioners' sugar
½ stick (¼ cup) unsalted butter
2 tablespoons fresh lemon juice

Make cake:
Preheat oven to 350° F. Grease a 3-quart bundt pan or 13- by 9-inch baking pan and dust with flour, knocking out excess flour.

Sift brown sugar into a bowl and whisk in flour, ginger, cinnamon, baking soda, and salt. Add butter and yogurt and with an electric mixer beat on low speed until dry ingredients are moistened. Beat mixture on high speed 3 minutes.

In another bowl whisk together eggs and molasses until combined. Add egg mixture to flour mixture in 3 batches, beating on high speed 30 seconds after each addition.

Pour batter into pan and bake about 1 hour and 15 minutes, or until a tester comes out clean. If using a bundt pan, cool cake in pan on a rack 10 minutes and turn out onto rack to cool completely. If using 13- by 9-inch pan, cool cake completely in pan on a rack.

Make glaze when cake is cool:
In a small saucepan simmer glaze ingredients, stirring occasionally, until reduced to about ½ cup.
Cool glaze to warm and brush over cooled cake.

Date Walnut Loaf

2½ cups all-purpose flour
2½ teaspoons baking powder
1 teaspoon salt
½ teaspoon ground allspice

2 cups dates (about 10 ounces), chopped
1 cup walnuts, toasted and chopped
½ stick (¼ cup) unsalted butter, softened
¾ cup firmly packed light brown sugar
1 large egg
¾ cup milk

Accompaniment: softened unsalted butter

Preheat oven to 350° F. Grease a loaf pan, 8½ by 4½ by 3 inches, and dust with flour, knocking out excess flour.

In a large bowl whisk together flour, baking powder, salt, and allspice and stir in dates and walnuts. In another bowl whisk together butter, brown sugar, and egg until combined well and whisk in milk. Stir milk mixture into flour mixture until just combined. Pour batter into pan and bake in middle of oven 1 hour, or until a tester comes out clean. Cool loaf in pan on a rack 10 minutes and turn out onto rack to cool completely. *Loaf keeps, wrapped well, chilled 3 days or frozen 3 weeks. Bring loaf to room temperature before serving.*

Serve loaf, sliced, with butter.

Brandy Snaps

3 tablespoons unsalted butter, melted
3 tablespoons firmly packed light brown sugar
3 tablespoons light corn syrup
2 teaspoons ground ginger

⅓ cup all-purpose flour
1 teaspoon fresh lemon juice plus additional if
   necessary

Preheat oven to 425° F. and line a large baking
sheet with parchment paper.

In a small saucepan cook butter, brown sugar, corn
syrup, and ginger over moderately low heat, stirring,
until smooth. Remove pan from heat and stir in flour
and 1 teaspoon lemon juice.

Make cookies in batches of 5. Drop batter by
teaspoons, evenly spaced, onto parchment paper and
bake in middle of oven 5 minutes, or until cookies are
bubbly and lacy. Cool on baking sheet until cookies
hold together when lifted from parchment paper but
are still soft, 1 to 2 minutes. Immediately transfer
cookies with a metal spatula to handle of a wooden
spoon and cool in curved shapes. Transfer cookies to
a rack to cool completely. Make more cookies with
remaining batter in same manner on same sheet of
parchment paper. If batter becomes too thick, stir in
additional lemon juice, ½ teaspoon at a time. *Brandy
snaps may be made 1 day ahead and kept in an
airtight container at room temperature.* Makes about
24 cookies.

Raspberry and Lemon Cream Tartlets

½ sheet (about 5 by 9 inches) frozen puff pastry,
   thawed
¼ cup well-chilled heavy cream
¼ cup lemon curd*
1 cup small raspberries,
   picked over

*available at some specialty foods shops and by
   mail order from Zabar's, 2245 Broadway,
   New York, NY 10024, tel. (212) 787-2000

Preheat oven to 375° F.

On a floured surface with a floured rolling pin roll
out pastry into a 10- by 8-inch rectangle. Cut pastry
lengthwise in half and crosswise into 2-inch-wide
strips to make 10 rectangles, each about 4 by 2
inches. Press rectangles into ten 3½- by 1½-inch
barquette molds and transfer molds to a shallow
baking pan. Bake shells in middle of oven 15 minutes
or until puffed and golden and cool in pan on a rack.

Remove shells from molds and cut each in half
horizontally to make 2 boat-shaped tartlet shells.
Gently press center of each shell to make room for
filling. *Tartlet shells may be made 2 days ahead and
kept in an airtight container at room temperature.*

In a small bowl beat cream until it just holds stiff
peaks. In a bowl stir lemon curd until smooth. Stir
about one fourth of whipped cream into lemon curd
to lighten and fold in remaining whipped cream
gently but thoroughly.

Spoon about 1 heaping teaspoon lemon cream into
each shell and top with 2 or 3 raspberries. Chill
tartlets, covered, if not serving immediately. *Tartlets
may be made 4 hours ahead and chilled, covered.*
Makes 20 tartlets.

Irish Soda Bread

AN IRISH COUNTRY SUPPER

Baked Scrod in Cider

Chalone Vineyard Pinot Blanc 1993

•

Dingle Pie
(Lamb, Turnip, and Parsnip Pie)

Irish Soda Bread

Creamed Mushrooms with Chives

Champ
(Mashed Potatoes with Leeks)

Sorrel, Watercress, and Beet Salad

Eberle Paso Robles Sauret Vineyard Zinfandel 1993

•

Blackberry Fool

•

Serves 6

Longueville's cattle in the morning mist,
County Cork, Ireland

Dingle Pie; Creamed
Mushrooms with
Chives; Champ;
Irish Soda Bread;
Sorrel, Watercress,
and Beet Salad

Baked Scrod in Cider

Blackberry Fool

266

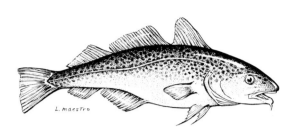

L. maestro

Baked Scrod in Cider

1 medium onion, sliced thin
6 scrod or cod fillets, skin removed
  (about ¼ pound each)
1 tablespoon Dijon mustard
4 slices bacon (preferably Irish back)
2 tablespoons vegetable oil if desired
1 cup fresh bread crumbs
2 tablespoons chopped fresh parsley leaves
2 plum tomatoes, seeded and diced
¾ cup unfiltered apple cider
¼ cup white-wine vinegar

Preheat oven to 350° F. and butter a 2-quart gratin dish or other shallow baking dish.

Scatter onion evenly in dish and top with scrod fillets, arranging them, skinned side down, in one layer. Brush fillets evenly with mustard and season with salt and pepper.

In a skillet cook bacon over moderate heat until browned and crisp, transferring with metal tongs to paper towels to drain and reserving drippings in skillet. Cool bacon and crumble.

Pour off all but 2 tablespoons bacon drippings or if desired use oil and cook bread crumbs over moderate heat, stirring, until lightly browned. In a bowl stir together bread crumbs, bacon, parsley, and salt and pepper to taste.

Pat crumb mixture evenly on top of fillets and scatter tomatoes over fish. In a measuring cup whisk together cider and vinegar and pour around fillets. Bake fillets, uncovered, in middle of oven about 30 minutes, or until just cooked through. Serves 6.

Dingle Pie
(Lamb, Turnip, and Parsnip Pie)

For filling
2 medium turnips, peeled and cut into ½-inch
  cubes
3 medium parsnips, peeled and cut into ½-inch
  cubes
1 medium onion, chopped
½ stick (¼ cup) unsalted butter
2½ pounds boneless lamb shoulder or leg of lamb,
  cut into 1-inch pieces, plus bones and trimmings
  if making stock
1 tablespoon olive oil if necessary
1½ cups simmering lamb stock (recipe follows) or
  beef broth
2 to 3 tablespoons unbleached all-purpose flour
For dough
½ cup milk
1½ sticks (¾ cup) unsalted butter
2½ cups unbleached all-purpose flour
½ teaspoon salt

1 large egg, beaten lightly

Make filling:
In a heavy kettle cook turnips, parsnips, and onion in butter with salt and pepper to taste over moderate heat, stirring occasionally, until just tender, about 15 minutes. Transfer vegetables with a slotted spoon to a bowl. Add lamb to kettle, in batches, and brown over high heat, stirring occasionally, about 15 minutes, adding oil if necessary and transferring lamb, as browned, to bowl.

In a measuring cup whisk together stock or broth and flour and add to kettle with lamb and vegetables. Simmer filling, covered, stirring occasionally, (adding water if necessary), 1 hour and cool completely. *Filling may be made 1 day ahead and chilled, covered. Bring filling to room temperature before proceeding.*
Make dough while filling is cooling:
In a saucepan heat milk and butter over moderately low heat, stirring occasionally, until butter is melted and cool. In a large bowl whisk together flour and salt and make a well in center. Pour milk mixture into well and stir into flour until mixture just forms a dough. On a lightly floured surface with floured

hands knead dough about 1 minute. Divide dough in half and flatten into two 1-inch-thick disks. *Chill dough, wrapped in plastic wrap, at least 30 minutes and up to 1 day.*

On a lightly floured surface with a floured rolling pin roll out 1 disk into a 12-inch round, keeping other disk wrapped in plastic wrap. Fit round into a 10-inch pie plate (1½-quart capacity) and trim edge, leaving a ½-inch overhang and reserving scraps. Spoon filling evenly into shell. On a lightly floured surface roll out remaining disk into a 13-inch round. Drape round over filling and trim, leaving a ½-inch overhang and reserving scraps. Fold overhang under bottom crust, pressing edge to seal, and crimp edge decoratively. Brush top crust with some egg and make three 1-inch slits in top crust, forming steam vents. Chill pie.

Preheat oven to 400° F.

Make leaf decorations while chilling pie:

Gather reserved dough scraps into a ball and on a lightly floured surface roll out into an ⅛-inch-thick round. With a 3-inch leaf-shaped cutter or by hand cut out leaf decorations and transfer to a baking sheet. Score leaves lightly with back of a knife to form veins and chill until firm, about 15 minutes. With a spatula carefully remove leaves from baking sheet and brush underside of leaves with egg. Arrange leaves, egg sides down decoratively on top of pie, pressing gently.

Bake pie in a shallow baking pan in middle of oven 15 minutes.

Reduce temperature to 375° F. and bake pie 20 to 30 minutes more, or until crust is golden brown. *Pie may be made 1 day ahead and cooled completely before chilling, covered.* Bring pie to room temperature and if desired reheat in a 350° F. oven, about 15 to 20 minutes. Serve pie hot or at room temperature. Serves 6.

Lamb Stock

1 pound lamb bones and trimmings reserved
   from dingle pie (recipe precedes)
2 carrots, cut into 1-inch pieces
2 small onions, each cut into eighths
⅔ cup water
1 fresh thyme sprig
1 fresh parsley sprig

Preheat oven to 450° F.

In a shallow flameproof roasting pan arrange bones and trimmings in one layer and roast in middle of oven, stirring occasionally, until bones are browned, about 15 minutes. Add vegetables and salt and pepper to taste and roast, stirring occasionally, until vegetables are browned, about 15 minutes. Transfer vegetables and bones with metal tongs to a kettle.

Pour off fat from roasting pan. Deglaze pan with water over moderately high heat, scraping up brown bits, and add mixture to kettle with water to cover vegetables and bones by 2 inches. Bring liquid to a boil, skimming froth. Add herbs and cook at a bare simmer 1½ to 2 hours, or until liquid is reduced to about 3 cups. Strain stock through a fine sieve into a heatproof bowl. *Stock may be made 2 days ahead. Cool stock completely, uncovered, and keep chilled or frozen in an airtight container.* Makes 3 cups.

Irish Soda Bread

4 cups unbleached all-purpose flour plus
   additional for sprinkling dough
½ cup toasted wheat germ
2 teaspoons baking soda
1½ teaspoons salt
1 stick (½ cup) cold unsalted butter, cut into bits
1½ cups dried currants
1 tablespoon caraway seeds
1¾ to 2 cups buttermilk

Preheat oven to 400° F. and sprinkle a baking sheet lightly with flour.

In a large bowl whisk together 4 cups flour, wheat germ, baking soda, and salt. Add butter and toss to coat with flour. With fingertips blend in butter until mixture resembles coarse meal. Add currants and caraway seeds and toss until coated. Stir in 1¾ cups buttermilk, adding more if necessary to moisten dough evenly (do not overwork dough).

On a floured surface knead dough with floured hands about 1 minute, sprinkling with some additional flour to prevent sticking. Divide dough in half and on baking sheet pat dough out into two 5-inch rounds. Sprinkle rounds lightly with more additional flour and with fingertips spread over round. With a sharp knife cut a shallow X in top of each round.

Bake bread in middle of oven 35 to 45 minutes, or until golden brown and cool on a rack 2 hours before slicing. Makes 2 loaves.

Creamed Mushrooms with Chives

½ stick (¼ cup) unsalted butter
2 pounds mushrooms, trimmed and quartered
1 cup chopped onions (about 1 medium)
½ cup heavy cream
½ cup chicken broth
1 tablespoon plus 1 teaspoon fresh lemon juice
   plus additional to taste
3 tablespoons chopped fresh chives

In a large heavy skillet melt butter over moderate heat until foam subsides and sauté mushrooms over high heat, stirring, until liquid mushrooms give off is evaporated and mushrooms begin to brown, 5 to 10 minutes. Stir in onions and sauté over moderately high heat, stirring, until softened, about 5 minutes. Add cream, broth, and lemon juice and simmer until slightly thickened, about 15 minutes. Stir in chives, salt and pepper to taste, and additional lemon juice if desired. Serves 6.

Champ
(Mashed Potatoes with Leeks)

3 pounds russet (baking) potatoes (about 6),
   scrubbed
1½ cups milk
1 stick (½ cup) unsalted butter, cut into bits
6 small leeks, trimmed, halved lengthwise,
   sliced thin crosswise, and washed well
   (about 3 cups)

In a kettle cover potatoes with salted cold water by 2 inches and boil until tender, about 30 minutes.

While potatoes are cooking, in a saucepan heat milk and half of butter over moderate heat until butter is melted. Add leeks and simmer until tender, 5 to 10 minutes. Strain leek mixture through a sieve into a bowl. Transfer leeks to another bowl and keep milk mixture warm, covered.

When potatoes are cool enough to handle, peel and in a bowl mash, adding enough milk mixture, one-third at a time, to reach desired consistency. Fold in leeks and salt and pepper to taste. *Champ may be made 2 days ahead and chilled, covered. Reheat champ, covered, in a 350° F. oven until hot.*

Serve champ topped with remaining 4 tablespoons butter. Serves 6.

Sorrel, Watercress, and Beet Salad

3 medium beets, scrubbed and trimmed, leaving
    about 1 inch of stems attached
For dressing
2 hard-cooked large egg yolks,
    mashed
1 small garlic clove, minced
2 tablespoons malt vinegar* or cider vinegar
1½ tablespoons firmly packed brown sugar
1 teaspoon English dry mustard
½ teaspoon salt
1 teaspoon freshly ground black pepper
¼ cup plus 2 tablespoons heavy cream
¼ cup plus 2 tablespoons sour cream
about 1 tablespoon water

2 large carrots, shredded (about 1 cup)
3 cups watercress (about 1 large bunch), coarse
    stems discarded, washed and spun dry
3 cups sorrel (about 2 large bunches), coarse
    stems discarded, washed and spun dry
3 hard-cooked large eggs plus 2 hard-cooked
    large egg whites, chopped

*available at specialty foods shops, some
    supermarkets, and by mail order from
    Balducci's, tel. (800) 225-3822

Preheat oven to 450° F.

Wrap beets tightly in foil and roast in middle of oven 1 to 1½ hours, or until tender. Unwrap beets carefully and cool until they can be handled. Discard stems and peel beets. *Beets may be prepared up to this point 1 day ahead and chilled, covered.*

Make dressing:

In a bowl whisk together dressing ingredients. *Dressing may be made 3 days ahead and chilled, covered.*

Cut each beet into 8 wedges. In a large bowl toss together carrots, watercress, sorrel, and half of chopped egg with two-thirds of dressing. In a large serving bowl arrange watercress mixture, beets, and remaining chopped egg and drizzle with remaining dressing. Serves 6.

Blackberry Fool

3½ cups blackberries
3 tablespoons water
1 tablespoon freshly grated lemon zest
¾ cup superfine sugar, or to taste
2 teaspoons fresh lemon juice,
    or to taste
½ cup vanilla yogurt
1½ cups well-chilled heavy cream

Garnish: fresh lemon zest, removed with a
    vegetable pceler and cut into julienne strips,
    and fresh blackberries

In a saucepan simmer berries, water, and zest, covered, until berries begin to break apart, about 10 minutes. In a blender purée mixture until smooth and stir in sugar and lemon juice. Strain berry mixture in a sieve over a glass bowl and cool. *Berry mixture may be made 2 days ahead and chilled, covered.*

In a bowl combine 1½ cups berry mixture with yogurt, reserving remaining mixture for topping. In another bowl with an electric mixer beat cream until it just holds stiff peaks. Fold yogurt mixture gently into whipped cream until combined well.

Divide blackberry fool among 6 short-stemmed glasses and top each with 2 tablespoons reserved berry mixture. Garnish fool with lemon zest and blackberries. *Chill fool, covered, at least 2 hours and up to 4.* Serves 6.

A SCOTTISH DINNER

Mussel Soup

•

Roast Pheasant

Bread Sauce

Baked Apples with Red Currant Jelly

Clapshot
(Mashed Potatoes and Rutabaga)

Buttered Carrots with Lemon Thyme

Château Sociando-Mallet Cru Bourgeois, Haut-Médoc 1985

•

Cheese Course, (pages 249-250)

Château Ducru-Beaucaillou Grand Cru Classé, Saint-Julien 1983

•

Typsy Laird

•

Serves 6

Tantallon Castle,
East Lothian, Scotland

Typsy Laird

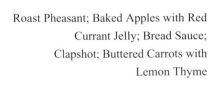

Roast Pheasant; Baked Apples with Red
Currant Jelly; Bread Sauce;
Clapshot; Buttered Carrots with
Lemon Thyme

274

about 5 minutes. (Do not let soup boil or it will curdle.) Stir in reserved mussels, parsley, and salt and pepper to taste and heat, stirring, until hot. Makes about 6 cups.

Ideally, 2-pound pheasants should be used in the following recipe. Due to seasonal changes, however, only larger birds may be available and allowance for a longer roasting time should be made.

Roast Pheasant

three 2- to 3¾-pound pheasants*
3 bay leaves
2 celery ribs, cut into 3-inch pieces
1 onion, cut lengthwise into 6 wedges
¾ stick (6 tablespoons) unsalted butter,
    melted
9 slices bacon

Garnish: fresh thyme sprigs
Accompaniment: bread sauce (recipe follows)

* available at many specialty foods and butcher
    shops and by mail order from D'Artagnan,
    tel. (800) 327-8246 or, in New Jersey,
    (201) 792-0748

Preheat oven to 400° F.
Season pheasants inside and out with salt and pepper and stuff cavities with bay leaves, celery, and onion. With kitchen string tie each pair of legs together and turn wings under. Cut 3 pieces of cheesecloth, each large enough to drape over a pheasant, and soak in butter. Cover each pheasant breast with 3 bacon slices and drape cheesecloth over each bird. In a large roasting pan arrange pheasants at least 1 inch apart and roast in middle of oven 10 minutes.
Reduce temperature to 350° F.
Roast pheasants, basting with pan juices about every 20 minutes, 50 minutes and discard cheesecloth and bacon to brown pheasants. Roast pheasants until juices run clear when fleshy part of a thigh is pierced with a skewer, about 30 minutes more for 2-pound pheasants.
Garnish pheasants with thyme sprigs and serve with bread sauce. Serves 6.

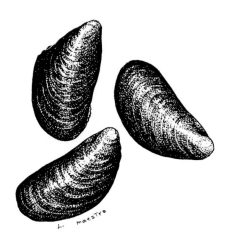

Mussel Soup

2 pounds mussels (preferably cultivated),
    scrubbed well and beards scraped off
1½ cups dry white wine
1 large onion, chopped fine
3 tablespoons unsalted butter
2 tablespoons all-purpose flour
2 cups milk, heated to lukewarm
1 cup heavy cream, heated to lukewarm
1 tablespoon finely chopped *dulse**
    (dried red seaweed)
¼ cup finely chopped fresh parsley leaves

*available at natural foods stores and some
    specialty foods shops

In a kettle combine mussels and wine. Bring wine to a boil over high heat and steam mussels, covered, shaking kettle occasionally, until shells have opened, 4 to 6 minutes. (Discard any unopened ones.) Drain mussels in a colander set over a bowl, reserving liquid, and strain reserved liquid through a fine sieve lined with a double layer of cheesecloth into a bowl. Remove mussels from shells, discarding shells, and reserve in another bowl.

In a 4-quart heavy saucepan cook onion in butter over moderately low heat until softened. Sprinkle flour over mixture and cook, stirring constantly, 3 minutes. (Do not let mixture brown.) Stir in reserved liquid, milk, cream, and *dulse* and cook over moderately low heat, stirring, until slightly thickened,

Bread Sauce

6 whole cloves
1 medium onion
1¾ cups milk, plus about 3 tablespoons
    additional if reheating
1 teaspoon whole black peppercorns
⅞ cup fine fresh bread crumbs
¼ cup heavy cream
1 tablespoon unsalted butter

Stick cloves into onion and in a heavy saucepan bring 1¾ cups milk, onion, and peppercorns to a boil. Let mixture stand off heat, covered, 30 minutes and strain through a fine sieve into another heavy saucepan. Stir in bread crumbs and simmer, stirring occasionally, until thickened, about 3 minutes. Stir in cream, butter, and salt and pepper to taste and cook over moderate heat, stirring, until butter is incorporated. *Bread sauce may be made 1 day ahead and chilled, covered. Reheat sauce in heavy saucepan, stirring, and thin with additional milk.* Makes 2 cups.

Baked Apples with Red Currant Jelly

6 small apples such as Empire, Red Delicious, or
    Granny Smith (about 1½ pounds)
½ lemon
6 tablespoons red currant jelly
½ cup hot water

Preheat oven to 400° F.
Core apples. Peel top third of each apple and rub peeled parts with lemon. In a baking dish just large enough to hold them arrange apples and spoon red currant jelly into cores. Pour hot water into baking dish and bake apples in middle of oven, brushing peeled parts twice with melted jelly, until just tender, about 45 minutes. *Baked apples may be made 1 day ahead and chilled, covered. Reheat baked apples in a 350° F. oven until warm, about 15 minutes.* Serves 6.

Clapshot
(Mashed Potatoes and Rutabaga)

1¼ pounds rutabaga or turnips
1¼ pounds boiling potatoes
1 large onion, cut into
    ½-inch pieces
3 tablespoons milk, plus 1 to
    2 tablespoons additional
    if reheating
½ stick (¼ cup) unsalted butter
¼ cup thinly sliced chives

In a 6-quart kettle bring 3 quarts salted water to a boil for vegetables.
Peel rutabaga or turnips and cut into ½-inch pieces. Peel boiling potatoes and cut into 1-inch pieces. Add rutabaga or turnips, potatoes, and onion to boiling water and simmer until potatoes are very tender, about 15 minutes. Drain vegetables well in a colander and transfer to a large bowl. In kettle heat 3 tablespoons milk and butter over moderate heat until butter is melted and pour over vegetables. With a potato masher mash vegetables coarse and stir in sliced chives and salt and pepper to taste. *Clapshot may be made 1 day ahead and chilled, covered. Reheat clapshot in heavy saucepan over low heat, stirring to avoid scorching, and thin with additional milk if necessary.* Serves 6.

Buttered Carrots with Lemon Thyme

10 medium carrots
2 tablespoons unsalted butter
1½ teaspoons lemon thyme or regular
   thyme leaves

Peel carrots and cut into 3- by ¼-inch sticks. In a kettle of boiling salted water cook carrots until just tender, about 4 minutes, and drain in a colander. *Carrots may be cooked 2 days ahead if plunged into a large bowl filled with ice and cold water to stop cooking and drained well. Chill carrots, covered.*

In kettle melt butter over moderate heat and add carrots, thyme, and salt and pepper to taste, tossing gently to combine. Serves 6.

Typsy Laird
(Scottish Trifle)

For sponge cake
3 large eggs
½ cup sugar
½ teaspoon vanilla
¾ cup all-purpose flour
½ teaspoon baking powder
¼ teaspoon salt

¼ cup sugar
½ cup seedless raspberry jam
For custard
¾ cup sugar
2 tablespoons cornstarch
8 large egg yolks
½ teaspoon freshly grated lemon zest
2⅓ cups milk
1 cup heavy cream
1 tablespoon Drambuie (Scottish liqueur)

¼ cup Drambuie
1 cup 1½-inch *amaretti** (Italian almond
      macaroons, about 16), crushed coarse
1 cup well-chilled heavy cream
3 tablespoons sugar

Garnish: sliced natural almonds, toasted until
      golden and cooled and glacéed cherries,
      quartered lengthwise if desired

* available at many specialty foods shops and by
      mail order from Perugina, tel. (800) 272-0500

Make sponge cake:
Preheat oven to 350° F. and line bottom of a buttered 13- by 9- by 2-inch baking pan with wax paper. Butter paper and dust pan with flour, knocking out excess flour.

In bowl of a standing electric mixer beat together eggs, sugar, and vanilla until thick and pale. Sift flour, baking powder, and salt over egg mixture and fold in gently but thoroughly. Spread batter evenly in pan and bake in middle of oven until a tester comes out clean, about 8 minutes.

While cake is baking, lay a clean kitchen towel on a work surface and sprinkle evenly with ¼ cup sugar.

In a small saucepan melt jam over moderately low heat, stirring.

Invert hot cake onto sugared kitchen towel and peel off wax paper carefully. Trim browned edges of cake with a knife and spread jam evenly over cake. Beginning with a long side and using towel as a guide, roll up cake jelly-roll fashion and transfer to a sheet of wax paper. Wrap cake in paper and cool completely.

Make custard:

In a large heatproof bowl whisk together sugar and cornstarch and whisk in yolks, zest, and a pinch of salt until combined well. In a heavy saucepan heat milk and cream until mixture just comes to a boil. Add hot milk mixture to egg mixture in a slow stream, whisking. In saucepan bring custard to a boil over moderate heat, whisking, and boil, whisking, 1 minute, or until thick and smooth. Whisk in 1 tablespoon Drambuie.

Cut cake into 16 slices and brush cut sides with ¼ cup Drambuie. Quarter 3 cake slices.

Assemble trifle:

In a 2- to 2½-quart straight-sided glass bowl arrange 6 whole cake slices in one layer around side of bowl. Arrange quartered cake slices in bottom of bowl and sprinkle with half *amaretti* crumbs. Pour 2 cups custard over quartered cake slices, spreading evenly and working into gaps between all cake slices with a wooden skewer. Arrange remaining 7 cake slices around side of bowl, trimming if necessary. Sprinkle remaining *amaretti* crumbs on custard and pour remaining custard into center, spreading evenly, and working into gaps between cake slices in same manner. *Chill trifle, its surface covered with plastic wrap, overnight.*

Just before serving, in a bowl with an electric mixer beat cream until it holds soft peaks and beat in sugar until cream holds stiff peaks. Transfer half of whipped cream to a pastry bag fitted with a decorative tip and spread remaining whipped cream over trifle. Pipe cream decoratively on trifle and garnish with almonds and cherries. Serves 6.

A GOURMET
ADDENDUM

QUICK AND EASY SOUPS AND SANDWICHES

The pairing of a special soup and sandwich offers casual fare that even the most rushed cook can prepare quickly and present with style. Here is a fresh look at this ever-popular food combination — 24 innovative recipes that bring together the newest foods found on today's brimming supermarket shelves with those we have enjoyed for years. For example, our corn chowder introduces spicy Spanish sausage, mellow saffron, and refreshing coriander to the sweetness of corn, while our BBLTs add a spread of peppered Boursin cheese to the classic bacon, lettuce, and tomato trio. We've developed recipes for both hot and cold soups and sandwiches that can be enjoyed on their own, or mixed- and- matched as you wish for seasonally appropriate snacks and meals.

Many people assume that soups take hours to prepare. Rest assured that all these recipes are designed with speediness in mind. When a stock is needed, we encourage you to use a premium-quality canned low-salt chicken or beef broth. We also suggest that you use a blender instead of a food processor to quickly purée soup ingredients: it simply produces a smoother soup.

For maximum flexibility, all our hot soups (except the Asian Chicken, Shrimp, and Noodle Soup, page 283) can be made ahead of time and refrigerated for a few days or frozen for weeks. The chilled soups must be refrigerated for at least 4 hours, but they will keep overnight.

As wonderful as soups are, when hunger strikes there is nothing like a satisfying sandwich. It all began one day in 1762, when the fourth Earl of Sandwich, an Englishman fond of playing cards, became peckish at the gaming table. Unwilling to leave an excellent hand, he ordered his manservant to bring him something to eat. This brilliant individual returned with a piece of beef between two slices of bread, and the rest is history.

Sandwiches have come a long way since the eighteenth century, and now, we've uncovered a few new condiments to jazz them up: *wasabi* powder (Japanese green horseradish), pickled ginger, *tahini* (sesame seed paste), Major Grey's chutney, Kalamata olives, honey mustard, and tomato salsa, to name a few. Also, we've included nontraditional cheeses, such as dill Havarti, Boursin, and feta; they really do make a remarkable difference.

But perhaps the most notable improvement in sandwich-making comes with the many forms of bread now readily available, and we have sampled several here. Whole-grain loaves, high in fiber and complex carbohydrates, are dense in texture and full of hearty flavor, making them ideal for substantial sandwiches. Whenever a white bread is needed, however, round loaves of crusty bread (peasant-style) should be considered, as well as *baguettes,* Portuguese rolls, and kaiser rolls; they are so much better than spongy white bread. Exciting flat breads such as Middle Eastern *lahvash* or Mexican tortillas make excellent rolled sandwiches, while Italian Boboli can hold a variety of toppings. Naturally, pita loaves can be cut into easy-to-use pockets and stuffed.

Next time you are looking for something special, give these delicious, easy recipes a try. As you are about to discover, "soup and sandwich" doesn't have to mean chicken noodle and grilled American cheese anymore. Go ahead and make yourself a memorable snack. Or, better yet, invite a few friends over for an impressive little lunch or dinner.

HOT SOUPS

Corn and Chorizo Chowder with Saffron

4 ears corn, shucked
8 cups cold water
1 pound cured *chorizo* (Spanish sausage)* or
    chourico (hot Portuguese sausage)*, quartered
    lengthwise and sliced ¼ inch thick
2 onions, chopped
2 russet (baking) potatoes (about 1 pound), peeled
    and cut into ½-inch dice
1⅔ cups low-salt chicken broth
¼ teaspoon crumbled saffron threads
⅓ cup finely chopped fresh coriander

*available at Hispanic markets

In a kettle combine corn and water. Bring water to a boil and simmer 5 minutes. Transfer corn to a cutting board and cooking water to a large heatproof bowl. On board cut kernels from cobs, scraping cobs with back of knife to extract corn milk. Discard cobs.

In kettle cook sausage over moderate heat, stirring, until lightly browned. Add onions and cook mixture, stirring, until onions are softened. Add corn cooking water, potatoes, broth, and saffron and simmer 20 minutes. With back of a wooden spoon mash about ½ cup potato against side of kettle. Add corn and salt and pepper to taste and simmer 15 minutes. Stir in coriander. Makes about 12 cups.

Curried Sweet Potato and Pear Soup with Roquefort Croutons

1 onion, chopped
2 tablespoons unsalted butter
1½ pounds sweet potatoes, peeled
    and cut into 1-inch pieces
1½ pounds pears (about 4), peeled, cored,
    and chopped
5½ cups low-salt chicken broth
1 cup dry white wine
2 teaspoons curry powder
1 bay leaf
six ¾-inch diagonal slices cut from
    a *baguette*
6 ounces Roquefort cheese,
    softened

In a kettle cook onion in butter over moderately low heat, stirring, until softened. Add sweet potatoes, pears, broth, wine, curry powder, and bay leaf and simmer 15 to 20 minutes, or until potatoes are very tender. Discard bay leaf and in a blender purée soup in batches. Return soup as puréed to kettle and season with salt and pepper.

Preheat broiler.

On a baking sheet lightly toast both sides of bread slices about 3 inches from heat until golden. Spread about 1 ounce Roquefort on one side of each toast and broil until melted. Cool toasts and with a sharp knife cut into 1-inch croutons.

Heat soup until hot and serve with croutons. Makes about 8 cups.

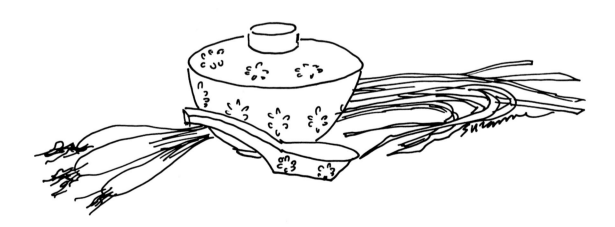

Vegetable Soup

white and pale green parts of 2 leeks, washed well,
    drained, and chopped
1 cup chopped carrot
1 cup chopped celery
2 tablespoons unsalted butter
5 cups beef broth
1 cup dry red wine
a 1-pound can whole tomatoes, drained and
    chopped
1 bay leaf
½ pound green and/or wax beans, sliced
    ¼ inch thick
1 cup chopped fresh parsley leaves

In a kettle cook leeks, carrot, and celery in butter over moderate heat, stirring, until leeks are softened. Add broth, wine, tomatoes, bay leaf, beans, and salt and pepper and simmer, covered partially, 30 minutes. Stir in parsley and discard bay leaf. Makes 8 cups.

Asian Chicken, Shrimp, and Noodle Soup

½ pound skinless boneless chicken breast, sliced
    across grain into very thin strips
½ pound (about 15) medium shrimp, shelled
1 tablespoon soy sauce
1 teaspoon Asian sesame oil*
2 teaspoons cornstarch
8 cups low-salt chicken broth
¼ cup thinly sliced scallion
1 tablespoon minced peeled fresh gingerroot
2 tablespoons fresh lemon juice
½ teaspoon dried hot red pepper flakes
¼ pound dried wide *lo mein* noodles* or
    fettuccine
5 ounces fresh spinach, washed well, coarse stems
    discarded, and leaves chopped coarse (5 cups)

*available at Asian markets

In a small bowl combine well chicken, shrimp, soy sauce, sesame oil, and cornstarch and marinate 15 minutes.

In a kettle simmer broth, scallion, gingerroot, lemon juice, and red pepper flakes, covered, 5 minutes. Add noodles and simmer, uncovered, 5 minutes. Add chicken mixture and spinach and simmer 5 minutes. Serve soup immediately. Makes about 10 cups.

White Bean, Swiss Chard, and Squash Soup with Bacon

½ pound bacon, chopped
1 onion, sliced
2 garlic cloves, minced
¾ pound butternut squash, seeded, peeled, and cut
    into ½-inch dice
½ pound Swiss chard, washed and chopped
    coarse
a 19-ounce can cannellini (white kidney) beans,
    drained
5½ cups low-salt chicken broth
1½ cups water
½ teaspoon dried thyme, crumbled

In a kettle cook bacon over moderate heat, stirring, until crisp and with a slotted spoon transfer to a bowl. Pour off all but 1 tablespoon fat from kettle and in remaining fat cook onion and garlic, stirring, until golden. Add remaining ingredients and salt and pepper to taste and simmer, uncovered, 20 minutes.

Serve soup sprinkled with bacon. Makes 11 cups.

Lentil Soup with Rice and Smoked Pork

1 large onion, chopped
1 cup chopped celery
1 cup chopped carrot
2 tablespoons vegetable oil
12 cups water
1 pound lentils, picked over and rinsed
1 pound boneless smoked pork butt or shoulder,
    cut into ½-inch pieces
⅓ cup long-grain rice
2 teaspoons ground cumin
¼ teaspoon ground allspice

In a kettle cook onion, celery, and carrot in oil over moderate heat, stirring, until browned. Add remaining ingredients and salt and pepper to taste and bring to a boil, stirring. Simmer soup, covered partially, 1 hour. Makes 14 cups.

Chilled Yellow Pepper Soup with Sour Cream Rouille

2 pounds yellow bell peppers, chopped coarse
1 pound potatoes, peeled and chopped coarse
3 garlic cloves
a 1-inch strip of fresh orange zest, removed
    with a vegetable peeler
5 cups low-salt chicken broth
1 cup half-and-half
For rouille
¾ cup sour cream
¼ teaspoon cayenne
2 garlic cloves, minced and mashed to a paste
    with ⅛ teaspoon salt
¼ teaspoon freshly grated orange zest

Garnish: 2 tablespoons finely chopped fresh
    chives

In a kettle simmer bell peppers, potatoes, garlic, zest strip, and broth, covered partially, 30 minutes. In a blender purée mixture in batches until smooth and strain as puréed through a fine sieve into a bowl. Stir in half-and-half and salt and pepper to taste. *Chill soup, covered, at least 4 hours or overnight.*
    Make rouille:
In a bowl stir together *rouille* ingredients and salt. *Chill rouille, covered, at least 2 hours or overnight.*
    Serve soup with a dollop of *rouille* and garnish with chives. Makes about 8 cups.

Chilled Celery and Crab Soup with Dill

1 onion, sliced
5 cups coarsely chopped celery
    including leaves
2 cups low-salt chicken broth
1 cup water
½ cup dry white wine
½ pound lump crab meat, picked over and
    crumbled slightly
1 cup heavy cream
1 tablespoon minced fresh dill
1 tablespoon fresh lemon juice

In a large saucepan simmer onion, celery, broth, water, and wine, uncovered, 30 minutes. In a blender purée mixture in batches until smooth and transfer as puréed to a bowl. Stir in remaining ingredients and salt and pepper to taste. *Chill soup, covered, at least 4 hours or overnight.* Makes about 6½ cups.

Chilled Beet Soup with Jícama and Mint

2 pounds beets, peeled and cut into
    ¼-inch dice
1 cup finely chopped onion
5 cups water
1½ cups ¼-inch dice peeled *jícama**
1 tablespoon fresh lime juice,
    or to taste

Garnish: sour cream and ¼ cup chopped fresh
    mint leaves

*available at specialty produce markets and
    some supermarkets

In a large saucepan simmer beets, onion, and water until beets are tender, about 20 minutes. Stir in *jícama*, lime juice, and salt and pepper to taste. *Chill soup, covered, at least 4 hours or overnight.*
    Garnish soup with sour cream and mint. Makes about 7 cups.

Chilled Cantaloupe and Apricot Soup

¾ cup dried apricots
1 cup dry white wine
½ cup water
1 cantaloupe, seeded and flesh
    scooped out
1 cup white grape juice
3 tablespoons honey,
    or to taste

Garnish: plain yogurt and ¼ cup sliced almonds,
    lightly toasted

In a small saucepan boil apricots, wine, and water 1 minute. Remove pan from heat and let stand 30 minutes.

In a blender purée apricot mixture and cantaloupe with grape juice and honey in batches until smooth and transfer as puréed to a bowl. *Chill soup, covered, at least 4 hours or overnight.*

Garnish soup with yogurt and almonds. Makes about 6 cups.

Chilled Vidalia Onion and Watercress Soup

2½ pounds Vidalia* or other sweet onions, chopped coarse
3 tablespoons vegetable oil
a ½ pound potato, peeled and diced
4 cups low-salt chicken broth
4 cups loosely packed watercress sprigs, coarse stems discarded
½ teaspoon dried sage, crumbled
1½ cups half-and-half

*available in the spring at specialty produce markets and some supermarkets and by mail order from Bland Farms, tel. (800) 843-2542

In a heavy kettle cook onions in oil, covered, over moderate heat, stirring occasionally, 30 minutes. Reduce heat to moderately low and cook onions, uncovered, stirring, until just pale golden, about 45 minutes. Add potato, broth, watercress, and sage and simmer, covered partially, 15 minutes. In a blender purée soup in batches and transfer as puréed to a bowl. Stir in half-and-half and salt and pepper to taste. *Chill soup, covered, at least 4 hours or overnight.* Makes about 8 cups.

Chilled Avgolemono with Oregano
(Greek Rice, Egg, and Lemon Soup with Oregano)

6 cups low-salt chicken broth
¼ cup long-grain rice
3 large eggs
¼ cup fresh lemon juice
1 cup whole-milk plain yogurt
1 tablespoon finely chopped fresh oregano

In a large saucepan simmer broth and rice, covered, 10 minutes. In a bowl whisk together eggs and lemon juice and add 1 cup hot broth in a stream, whisking. Whisk egg mixture into rice mixture and cook over moderate heat, whisking, until very hot and thickened slightly (do not let boil). Transfer soup to a bowl and whisk in yogurt, oregano, and salt and pepper to taste. *Chill soup, covered, at least 4 hours or overnight.* Makes about 6½ cups.

HOT SANDWICHES

Grilled Tuna and Onions on Pita with Tahini Parsley Pesto

For tahini parsley pesto
½ cup well-stirred *tahini* (sesame seed paste)*
¼ cup fresh lemon juice
5 tablespoons water
2 garlic cloves, chopped
2 cups loosely packed fresh parsley leaves
½ cup lightly toasted pine nuts

three 1½-inch-thick tuna steaks
  (2½ to 3 pounds total)
2 large onions, sliced ½ inch thick
vegetable oil for brushing tuna and onions
six 7-inch pita loaves, wrapped in foil and warmed

*available at natural foods stores and some
  supermarkets

Prepare grill.
Make tahini parsley pesto:
In a blender blend *tahini,* lemon juice, water, and garlic until smooth. Add parsley and blend just until chopped coarse. Add pine nuts and salt and pepper and pulse motor 2 or 3 times to distribute nuts evenly.

With a long sharp knife halve tuna steaks horizontally. Secure onion slices with wooden picks so they do not separate into rings. Brush tuna and onions with oil and season with salt and pepper. Grill onions on a rack set 5 to 6 inches over glowing coals 5 minutes on each side, or until softened. Grill tuna 2 to 3 minutes on each side, or until cooked through.

Cut 1 inch from edge of each pita loaf to form pockets and fill with tuna and onions, discarding picks. Drizzle onions with pesto and serve any additional pesto on the side. Serves 6.

Pastrami and Swiss on Rye with Caramelized Onions, Cabbage, and Carrots

3 onions, sliced ¼ inch thick (about 4 cups)
2 tablespoons vegetable oil
½ pound cabbage, sliced thin (about 4 cups)
1 cup coarsely grated carrot
⅓ cup white-wine vinegar
⅔ cup water
1 tablespoon Dijon mustard
1½ pounds thinly sliced pastrami
12 slices rye bread, lightly toasted
⅔ pound thinly sliced Emmenthaler cheese

Preheat oven to 350° F.
In a large skillet cook onions in oil over moderate heat, stirring, until golden. Add cabbage, carrot, vinegar, water, and mustard and simmer, stirring, until liquid is evaporated. Season onion mixture with salt and pepper and keep warm.

In a baking dish heat pastrami, covered, in oven until hot, about 15 minutes. Divide pastrami among 6 bread slices and top with Emmenthaler and onion mixture. Top sandwiches with remaining bread slices, pressing sandwiches together gently. Serves 6.

*Grilled Chicken Sandwiches with
Monterey Jack and Peperoncini*

3 whole skinless boneless chicken breasts, halved
¾ pound Monterey Jack cheese, sliced thin
6 teaspoons Dijon mustard, or to taste
12 teaspoons mayonnaise, or to taste
6 Portuguese rolls or kaiser rolls, halved
    horizontally and warmed
1¼ cups chopped seeded *peperoncini* (pickled
    Tuscan peppers)

Prepare grill.

Season chicken with salt and pepper and grill on
an oiled rack set 5 to 6 inches over glowing coals 8
minutes. Turn chicken and grill 3 minutes more. Top
chicken with Monterey Jack and grill 3 to 5 minutes,
or until cooked through. Spread mustard and
mayonnaise on cut sides of each roll and top bottom
halves of rolls with chicken and *peperoncini.* Top
sandwiches with top halves of rolls, pressing together
gently. Serves 6.

*Grilled Ham, Cheddar, and Spinach Sandwiches
with Chutney*

10 ounces fresh spinach leaves, washed well
¾ pound Cheddar cheese, sliced thin
12 large slices soft whole-grain bread such as
    Branola
1½ pounds thinly sliced baked ham
6 tablespoons Major Grey's chutney
unsalted butter for cooking sandwiches

Chop spinach coarse and in a large saucepan cook
in water clinging to leaves, covered, over moderately
high heat 3 minutes, or until tender. Drain spinach
and when cool enough to handle squeeze dry by
handfuls.

Preheat oven to 200° F.

Arrange half of Cheddar on 6 bread slices. Top
Cheddar with ham, chutney, spinach, and remaining
cheese and top with remaining bread slices, pressing
sandwiches together gently.

In a large skillet melt 1 teaspoon butter over moderately low heat and cook 2 or 3 sandwiches, covered,
until undersides are golden. Turn sandwiches over,
adding additional butter if necessary, and cook,
covered, until undersides are golden and cheese is
melted. Keep sandwiches warm on a baking sheet in
oven as cooked and cook remaining sandwiches in
same manner. Serves 6.

*Broiled Eggplant, Feta, Tomato, and
Olive Sandwiches*

2 large eggplants (about 2½ pounds total),
    sliced ½ inch thick
¼ cup extra-virgin olive oil
a 1-pound loaf French bread
    (about 18 inches long)
2 large vine-ripened tomatoes,
    sliced thin
½ cup chopped pitted Kalamata or other
    brine-cured black olives
½ cup chopped fresh mint leaves
6 ounces feta cheese

Preheat broiler.

Brush eggplant slices with oil and season with salt
and pepper. On a baking sheet broil eggplant in
batches about 2 inches from heat until tender and
browned, about 5 minutes on each side.

Halve loaf horizontally, leaving an edge uncut to
form a hinge, and arrange eggplant on bottom half of
loaf. Top eggplant with tomatoes, olives, and mint
and coarsely grate feta over mixture. On baking sheet
broil open sandwich about 8 inches from heat until
cheese is melted. Close sandwich, pressing together
gently, and with a serrated knife cut into 4 to 6 portions. Serves 4 to 6.

Capicola with Vegetables and Mozzarella on Boboli

six 7-inch Italian Boboli (pre-baked pizza crusts)
1½ pounds vine-ripened tomatoes, sliced thin
three 6½-ounce jars marinated artichoke hearts,
    drained and chopped
1 pound thinly sliced hot or sweet *capicola*
    (seasoned smoked ham) or salami
4 cups coarsely grated mozzarella (about 1 pound)

Preheat oven to 375° F.

With a long serrated knife halve Boboli horizontally. On bottom halves layer tomatoes, artichoke hearts, *capicola* or salami, and mozzarella and top with remaining Boboli halves. Bake sandwiches on baking sheets in middle and lower third of oven, switching position of sheets halfway through baking, 10 minutes, or until heated through. (Cover sandwiches loosely with foil if bread becomes too crisp.) Cut sandwiches into quarters. Serves 6.

COLD SANDWICHES

*Japanese-Style Smoked Salmon
and Cucumber Rolled Sandwiches*

1½ teaspoons *wasabi* (Japanese green horseradish)
    powder*
2 teaspoons water
8 ounces whipped cream cheese, softened
1½ tablespoons finely chopped pickled ginger*
2 tablespoons fresh lemon juice
3 large or six 7-inch *lahvash* loaves (mountain
    shepherd bread)** or six 7-inch flour tortillas
1 pound thinly sliced smoked salmon
1 large European cucumber, peeled, halved
    crosswise, halved lengthwise, and cut
    lengthwise into ¼-inch slices

*available at Asian markets, natural foods
    stores, and some supermarkets
**available at Middle Eastern markets,
    specialty foods shops, and some supermarkets
    and by mail order from Damascus Bakeries,
    56 Gold Street, Brooklyn, NY 11201, tel.
    (718) 855-1456

In a large bowl stir together *wasabi* and water and let stand 5 minutes. Add cream cheese and ginger and with an electric mixer beat until smooth. Beat in lemon juice and transfer to a small bowl. *Chill mixture, covered, at least 8 hours or overnight.*

Spread cheese mixture on *lahvash* or tortillas and arrange salmon and cucumber evenly on top. Roll up *lahvash* or tortillas, jelly-roll fashion. If using large loaves, halve sandwiches with a serrated knife. Serves 6.

Goat Cheese, Roasted Pepper, and Basil Sandwiches

1½ *baguettes*
7 ounces soft mild goat cheese such as Montrachet,
    at room temperature
2 red bell peppers, roasted (procedure on page 111)
    and chopped coarse
½ cup packed fresh basil leaves
3 teaspoons balsamic vinegar

Halve *baguettes* horizontally, leaving an edge uncut to form a hinge, and spread cut sides evenly with goat cheese. Scatter bell peppers and basil evenly over cheese and drizzle with vinegar. Season sandwiches with black pepper to taste and close loaves, pressing together gently. Cut sandwiches into 6 portions. Serves 6.

BBLT's
(Boursin, Bacon, Lettuce, and Tomato Sandwiches)

12 slices from a round loaf crusty bread
a 5.2-ounce package peppered Boursin cheese, cut
  into 6 wedges and softened
2 large vine-ripened tomatoes, sliced ¼ inch thick
1 pound bacon, cooked until crisp and drained
12 large romaine leaves, rinsed, spun dry, and torn
  into large pieces

Preheat broiler.

On a baking sheet lightly toast both sides of bread about 3 inches from heat until surface is crisp.

Spread 6 toasts with Boursin and top with tomatoes, bacon, and lettuce. Season filling with pepper to taste and top with remaining toast slices, pressing sandwiches together gently. Halve sandwiches with a serrated knife. Serves 6.

Mexican-Style Beef Grinders

1½ pounds thinly sliced cooked steak or roast beef
2 onions, sliced paper-thin
3 red bell peppers, sliced thin
¾ cup coarsely chopped fresh coriander
6 long Italian sandwich rolls, halved horizontally
1 cup tomato salsa

Divide meat, onions, bell peppers, and coriander evenly among bottom halves of rolls. Spread salsa on sandwiches and season with salt and pepper to taste. Top sandwiches with top halves of rolls, pressing together gently. Serves 6.

Turkey, Dill Havarti, and Celery Sandwiches

1¼ pounds thinly sliced baked turkey breast
5 to 6 ounces dill Havarti cheese,
  sliced thin
3 cups very thinly sliced celery
12 large slices whole-grain bread such as seven-
  grain, oatmeal, or wheat
honey mustard to taste

Divide turkey, Havarti, and celery among 6 bread slices and season with salt and pepper. Spread mustard on remaining bread slices and top sandwiches with bread, pressing together gently. Halve sandwiches with a serrated knife. Serves 6.

Avocado, Egg, and Sprouts with Cucumber Yogurt Sauce on Pita

1 cup plain yogurt
1 medium cucumber, peeled, seeded,
  and chopped
2 small garlic cloves, minced
six 7-inch pita loaves
6 hard-cooked eggs, sliced
3 ripe avocados (preferably California), pitted,
  peeled, and sliced
2 cups alfalfa sprouts

In a small bowl stir together well yogurt, cucumber, garlic, and salt and pepper to taste. Cut 1 inch from edge of each pita loaf to form pockets and fill with eggs, avocados, yogurt sauce, and sprouts. Serves 6.

GUIDES TO THE TEXT

GENERAL INDEX

Page numbers in *italics* indicate color photographs
◔ indicates recipes that can be prepared in 45 minutes or less
◔+ indicates recipes that can be prepared in 45 minutes but require additional unattended time
🍃 indicates recipes that are leaner/lighter

INDEX OF RECIPE TITLES

Page numbers in *italics* indicate color photographs

To avoid duplication below of table setting information within the same menu, the editors have listed all such credits for silverware, plates, linen, and the like in its most complete form under "Table Setting."

Any items in the photograph not credited are privately owned.
All addresses are in New York City unless otherwise indicated.

Front Jacket

Baked Scrod in Cider: All items in the photograph are privately owned.

Back Jacket

Tomato and Onion Tart: See Table Setting credits for Picnic among the Vines.

Frontispiece

Fancy Sandwich Cake (page 2): See Table Setting credits for English Afternoon Tea.

The Menu Collection

Fig, Ham, and Nectarine Salad (page 10): See Table Setting credits for Picnic among the Vines.

A Fondue Party

Table Setting (pages 12 and 13): "Rustico" earthenware dinner plates and bowls; "Stonehenge" unfinished metal flatware; cotton napkins; wooden cachepots (bread-sticks and flowers); bay-leaf candles—Pottery Barn, 117 East 59th Street. Venetian "Dotted" wineglasses—Bloomingdale's At Your Service, 1000 Third Avenue, (212) 705-3135. Fondue forks—Bridge Kitchenware Corp., 214 East 52nd Street. Fondue pot can be mail-ordered from Lamalle Kitchenware, 36 West 25th Street, New York, NY 10010, (800) 660-0750. English pine table, circa 1890; painted wood and glass four-panel screen—ABC Carpet & Home, 888 Broadway. Wicker chair—Palacek, (800) 274-7730. "Pinedale Plaid" cotton fabric (available by decorator) Schumacher, (800) 332-3384.

Dinner from the West Indies

Table Setting (pages 14 and 15): "Calypso" hand-painted earthenware soup bowls and dinner plates by Barbara Eigen—for stores call (201) 758-7310 or write Eigen Arts, 150 Bay Street, Jersey City, NJ 07302. "Green Ring" wineglasses—Pottery Barn, 117 East 59th Street. "Fish Batik" cotton napkins designed by Jane Krolik for Chateau • X—for stores call (212) 477-3123. Water glasses; reproduction Italian iron side chairs; twig stand, circa 1930—ABC Carpet & Home, 888 Broadway.

Supper in the Kitchen

Panettone Bread and Butter Pudding (page 18): French porcelain baking dish—Bridge Kitchenware Corp., 214 East 52nd Street.
Table Setting (pages 18 and 19): "Lima" porcelain dinner plates from the Switch II Collection—Villeroy & Boch Creation, 974 Madison Avenue. "Ramina" Italian hand-painted salad plates by Lucca—The Whitney Shop, 275 Greenwich Avenue, Greenwich, CT 06830. Italian acrylic-handled flatware—Bloomingdale's At Your Service, 1000 Third Avenue, (212) 705-3135. "Provenzale" water goblets; French cotton napkins by Martine Nourissat; straw place mats; napkin rings—ABC Carpet & Home, 888 Broadway. Hand-painted tin pitcher—Handblock, 860 Lexington Avenue. Beechwood stools with rush seats; iron fruit stands—Pottery Barn, 117 East 59th Street. Fruit and fern arrange-

ments—Castle & Pierpont, 401 East 76th Street.
Braised Veal Shanks with Green Olives and Capers; Parmesan Sage Polenta Sticks (page 21): French tin-lined copper roasting pan—Bridge Kitchenware Corp., 214 East 52nd Street.

Valentine's Day Dinner

Table Setting (pages 22 and 23): "Fruit" porcelain chargers; "Topkapi" cotton napkins; "Armor" fabric (tablecloth)—ABC Carpet & Home, 888 Broadway. French ceramic-handled flatware—Takashimaya, 693 Fifth Avenue. Union Street Glass "Spirals" wineglasses—for stores call (510) 451-1077. Tole candle-holders and vintage iron armchairs—Treillage Ltd., 418 East 75th Street. Flowers—Zezé, 398 East 52nd Street. Hand-painted three-panel screen—Lexington Gardens, 1011 Lexington Avenue.

America's Cup Countdown Picnic

Carrot Cupcakes with Molasses Cream Cheese Icing (page 24): "Perpignan" china plate—Villeroy & Boch Creation, 974 Madison Avenue.
Picnic Setting (pages 24 and 25): "Clearwater" bone china plates from the Ralph Lauren Home Collection—for stores call (212) 642-8700. "Toile de Jouy" acrylic-handled flatware by Sabre—William-Wayne & Co., 850 Lexington Avenue. Wineglasses, cotton beach towel—America[3] Foundation, (800) WOMEN-A3. "Star" crystal tumbler—Hermès, 11 East 57th Street. Cotton napkins and acrylic trays by

Laure Japy—Hoagland's of Greenwich, 175 Greenwich Avenue, Greenwich, CT, (203) 869-2127. Perrier "Sight Unseen" sparkling mineral water bottles designed by Jonathan Lund—Great Waters of France, (800) 937-2002.

A Wine Cellar Dinner

Table Setting (pages 26 and 27): Pewter flatware; French cotton and rayon throw—Frank McIntosh Shop at Henri Bendel, 712 Fifth Avenue. "Bacchus" wineglasses—ABC Carpet & Home, 888 Broadway. Pewter tumblers and glass hurricane lamps—Pierre Deux, 870 Madison Avenue. Cotton napkins with crocheted borders—William-Wayne & Co., 850 Lexington Avenue. Flowers—Tesoro, 649 Main Street, St. Helena, CA.
Smoked Pork, Sausage, and Vegetable Soup; Potato and Cheese Purée (page 28): "Cassis" soup bowl and dinner plate—Zona, 97 Greene Street.
Grape Custard Cake (page 29): "Strawberry" ceramic pie plate and dessert plates—ABC Carpet & Home, 888 Broadway.

Easter Dinner

Table Setting (pages 30 and 31): "Toscana" ceramic dinner plates by Grazia—Avventura, 463 Amsterdam Avenue. French acrylic-handled flatware; cotton napkins; bamboo place mats—William-Wayne & Co., 850 Lexington Avenue. "Perfection" crystal Rhine wineglasses; "Brummel" crystal water goblets—Baccarat, 625 Madison Avenue. Nineteenth-century tole monteith (one of a pair); artificial butterflies, dragonflies, and grasshoppers—Treillage, 418 East 75th Street. Flowers, grass, and quail eggs—Castle & Pierpont, 401 East 76th Street.

Antipasto Buffet

Octopus, Cannellini, and Arugula Salad (page 34): Glass bowl in metal stand—Pottery Barn, 117 East 59th Street.
Tomato and Olivada Crostini; Orange,

Fennel, and Garlic Marinated Olives (pages 34 and 35): Majolica platter and olive bowl; terra-cotta olive jar—Ceramica, 59 Thompson Street, (800) 228-0858. "American Originals" wineglasses—Pfaltzgraff, (800) 999-2811. Majolica pitcher—Cottura, (800) 348-6608. Flower arrangement—Zezé, 398 East 52nd Street.
Buffet Spread (pages 36 and 37): Wilton Armetale "Acanthus" metal platter—Strauss Christeson, (800) 356-4244. Cake stand (with *frittata* wedges); majolica rectangular platter and dinner plates—Ceramica, 59 Thompson Street, (800) 228-0858. Wire basket—Interieurs, 114 Wooster Street. "Providence" stainless-steel flatware—Pfaltzgraff, (800) 999-2811. Cotton napkins—Ad Hoc Softwares, 410 West Broadway. Nineteenth-century American Arts & Crafts oak table (46½ by 30¼ by 31 inches) with stretcher base—William-Wayne & Co., 850 Lexington Avenue. Portrait plates—Cottura, (800) 348-6608.

Picnic among the Vines

Buffet Spread (pages 38 and 39): "Grape Garland" stoneware dinner plates; "Elderberry Scallop" oval stoneware platter—for stores call Fioriware, (614) 454-7400. Twig-handled flatware; cotton napkins; ceramic stand; cotton tablecloth—Wolfman • Gold & Good Company, 116 Greene Street. "Grapevine" handmade silver-plated serving pieces—Fischer Designs 121 East 83rd Street, (212) 794-0040 (by appointment only). Wineglasses—Pottery Barn, 177 East 59th Street. Wire wicker baking dish holder (Pyrex bowl not included)—for stores call Palecek, (800) 274-7730. Ceramic urn (with flowers)—ABC Carpet & Home, 888 Broadway. Flowers—Tesoro, 649 Main Street, St. Helena, CA, (707) 963-3316.

Dinner at a Grand House

Table Setting (pages 40 and 41): "Tobacco Leaf" porcelain plates—for stores call Mottahedeh, (800) 242-

3050. Cobalt laquerware chargers—for stores call Sasaki, (212) 686-5080. "American Garden" sterling flatware; "Brittania" crystal wineglasses and water goblets—Tiffany and Co., 727 Fifth Avenue. Engraved wineglasses, circa 1820—Bardith, 901 Madison Avenue. Hemstitched linen napkins by Leslie Pontz; ceramic napkin rings—ABC Carpet & Home, 888 Broadway. French majolica urn, circa 1870—Yale R. Burge Antiques, 305 East 63rd Street. Votive candle holders—Carriage House Gift Shop, Biltmore Estate, Asheville NC, (704) 274-6353. Flowers—Zezé, 398 East 52nd Street. "Les Roseaux Tropicaux" cotton fabric (available through decorator)—Brunschwig & Fils, 979 Third Avenue
Strawberry Rhubarb Napoleon and Lemon Cream (page 43): Cut-glass wineglasses, circa 1820—Bardith, 901 Madison Avenue.

Poolside Lobster Buffet

Raspberry Lime Rickeys, Tomatillo Salsa, Spicy Curly Tortilla Chips (page 44): Schott-Zwiesel "Conte" wineglasses—Wolfman • Gold & Good Company, 116 Greene Street. "Poolside" cotton fabric—for stores call Waverly, (800) 423 5881.
Buffet Spread (pages 44 and 45): "Caribbean Sea" Limoges platter by Philippe Deshoulières (with lobsters)—for stores call (800) 993-2580. "Delphi" porcelain plates designed by Loretta Agro—for stores call Sasaki, (212) 686-5080. "Pearl Pompadour" acrylic and stainless-steel flatware by SCOF—for stores call Mariposa, (800) 788-1304. Lobster crackers—Bridge Kitchenware Corp., 214 East 52nd Street. Wineglasses—Pottery Barn, 117 East 59th Street. Cotton and linen napkins; ceramic pitcher—Dean & DeLuca, 560 Broadway. "Diska" cotton fabric (for tablecloth, available through decorator)—Brunschwig & Fils, 979 Third Avenue.

Vietnamese Salad Supper

Table Setting (pages 46 and 47):

"Celadon" Handmade stoneware plates and bowls; wicker cooling trays—Simon Pearce, 500 Park Avenue. Chopsticks; Italian slate table on chestnut base—Zona, 97 Greene Street. Fossilglass wineglasses—Platypus, 126 Spring Street. Linen napkins with cotton trim by Angel Zimick—Frank McIntosh Shop at Henri Bendel, 712 Fifth Avenue. Brass napkin rings; "Raffles" hand-carved plantation hardwood armchairs—Equator, 98 Greene Street. Galvanized tin cachepot and votives—Design Ideas, (800) 426 6394. Bromeliads- Zezé, 398 East 52nd Street.

Jasmine Tea Sorbet and Lemongrass Mint Sorbet (page 49): "Garden" crystal sorbet bowls (from a set of 5) and "Yoshino" crystal plates (from a set of 4)—Hoya Crystal Gallery, 450 Park Avenue, (800) 462-4692. Peter "Torsade" hand-carved wood and silverplate teaspoons—Bernardaud, 783 Madison Avenue, (800) 884-775.

A Cycling Picnic

Picnic Setting (pages 50 and 51): "Alsace" enamel dinnerware from Bagatelle—for stores call (214) 630-8484. French stainless-steel and acrylic flatware by Sabre—Kitchen Classics, Main Street, Bridgehampton, NY 11932. Blue-and-white cotton napkin by April Cornell—Hand Block, 42 Main Street, Nantucket, MA 02554. Yellow check cotton tablecloth—Williams-Sonoma, 20 East 60th Street.

Fourth of July Dinner

Table Setting (pages 52 and 53): Fioriware earthenware dinner plates—Portico Home, 379 West Broadway. "Thai" stainless-steel flatware—Equator, 98 Greene Street. Water glasses and wineglasses; iron candelabra lanterns—Crate & Barrel, 650 Madison Avenue. Hand-stenciled linen napkins by Garrett Chingery and Wayne Mahler—Mascot Studio, 398 East 9th Street. Stone cachepot—Smith & Hawken, 394 West Broadway. Vintage stone garden table—Treillage, 418 East

75th Street. French iron chairs, circa 1940—Rooms & Gardens, 290 Lafayette Street. Wire trellis; Argentine ivy topiaries; wire and glass votive candles—Lexington Gardens, 1011 Lexington Avenue.

Lunch on the Porch

Cold Cucumber and Yellow Pepper Soup with Crab Meat and Chives (pages 56 and 57): Faience soup bowls and plates; "Balloon" wineglasses; cotton napkins and placemats—Solanée, 866 Lexington Avenue. Vintage hotel flatware—Bergdorf Goodman, 754 Fifth Avenue.

Campsite Cookout

Cookout Setting (pages 60 and 61): Portable charcoal grill; ceramic dinner plate; wood-handled forks; picnic knives—Williams Sonoma, 20 East 60th Street. Stainless-steel saucepans—Paragon Sporting Goods, 867 Broadway. Galvanized tin tray—Pottery Barn, 117 East 59th Street. Log tray—ABC Carpet & Homes, 888 Broadway. Fiskars ax—The MoMA Design Store, 44 West 53rd Street. "Woodlands #2" tent—L.L. Bean, (800) 341-4341. Cotton napkins—Dean & DeLuca, 560 Broadway. Wolfman • Gold & Good Company, 116 Greene Street.

A Weekend in the Country

Mascarpone Cheesecake Tart with Nectarines (page 62): Wicker tray—Treillage Ltd., 418 East 75th Street.

Friday Supper (page 65): Ceramic dinner plate; vintage hotel flatware; mosaic votive candle holders—Pottery Barn, 117 East 59th Street. Wineglass—Williams-Sonoma, 20 East 60th Street. Cotton napkin—Wolfman • Gold & Good Company, 116 Greene Street.

Saturday Breakfast (page 66, top): Gien "Pont aux Choux" faience plates—Baccarat, 625 Madison Avenue. "Ivoire" acrylic-handled flatware—Wolfman • Gold & Good Company, 116 Greene Street. Wedgewood "Countryware" bone china cups and saucers—The Waterford Wedgewood

Store, 713 Madison Avenue. Glasses—Crate & Barrel, 650 Madison Avenue. "Rose Trellis" linen napkins—for stores call Necessities, (718) 797-0530. Bodum coffeepot—Dean & DeLuca, 560 Broadway. "Rondeau" cotton and linen fabric (available by decorator)—for stores call Waverly, (800) 423-5881. Twisted-wire settee, circa 1920—Lexington Gardens, 1011 Lexington Avenue.

Saturday Lunch (page 66, bottom): "Willow" earthenware salad plates and platter; "Monet" glasses; over-sized glass cups—Crate & Barrel, 650 Madison Avenue. Wood-handled flatware; cotton napkins; "Heartland" wood tray with iron handles—Pottery Barn, 117 East 59th Street. Wire tray—Dean & DeLuca, 560 Broadway.

Saturday Dinner (page 67, top): "Bokara" porcelain dinner plates by Designers Guild—for stores call Rosenthal, (201) 804-8000, ext. 226. "Branches" bronze flatware—Pottery Barn, 117 East 59th Street. "Lars" wineglasses—for stores call Schott-Zwiesel, (914) 969-6100. Cotton napkins; laminated paper place mats—ABC Carpet & Home, 888 Broadway.

Sunday Brunch (page 67, bottom): Ceramic striped plates; Ceramic cups; cotton fabric (on chair cushions)—ABC Carpet & Home, 888 Broadway. Wineglasses; "Rivets" stainless-steel flatware—Pottery Barn, 117 East 59th Street. Cotton napkins; glass bowls—Crate & Barrel, 650 Madison Avenue. Glasses with Sangrita Bloody Marys from a crystal party set consisting of a pitcher (not shown) and 6 glasses—Tiffany & Co., 727 Fifth Avenue.

Cocktails in the Sky

Roasted Squash, Red Pepper, and Jack Cheese Quesadillas with Chipotle Lime Sour Cream Dip (page 68): Vintage milk glass and silver plate tray—Vito Giallo, 22 East 83rd Street. "Swag" crystal Old Fashioned glass—Tiffany & Co., 727 Fifth Avenue.

Cocktail Buffet Spread (pages 68 and 69): English three-tiered silver-plate stand; English oak and silver-plate gallery tray, circa 1870—S. Wyler, Inc., 941 Lexington Avenue. "Argos" crystal glasses—Lalique, 680 Madison Avenue. "Capri" pitcher—Baccarat, 625 Madison Avenue. Beaded coasters by Dransfield & Ross—Barneys New York, Madison Avenue at 61st Street. Orchids and decorative pots—Greenwich Orchards, 106 Madison Street, Greenwich, CT, (203) 651-5544.

A Haunted House Dinner

Witches' Brew; Poppy Cheddar Moon Crackers (page 70): Glass punch bowl—Simon Pearce, 500 Park Avenue at 59th Street. Juice glasses—Frank McIntosh at Henri Bendel, 712 Fifth Avenue. Hand embroidered linen cocktail napkins—Leron, 750 Madison Avenue. "Spider Web" silver-plate dish—Fischer Designs, (212) 794-0400 (by appointment only). Ebonized oak tray, circa 1875—James II Galleries, 11 East 57th Street. Ceramic skulls—Pan American Phoenix, 857 Lexington Avenue.
Table Setting (pages 70 and 71): "Vendome" porcelain plates designed by Ravage—for stores call Sasaki, (212) 686-5080. "Poudre Orange" porcelain service plates—Bernardaud, 783 Madison Avenue. "Boneware" silver-plate flatware and knife rests designed by Michael Aram—The LS Collection, 469 West Broadway. Italian wine glasses; Archipelago linen napkins—Frank McIntosh at Henri Bendel, 712 Fifth Avenue. Sugar cookie place cards—Sweet Lisa, 374 Greenwich Avenue, Greenwich, CT, (203) 896-9545. "Spider Web" silver-plate candlesticks and wine coaster—Fischer Designs, (212) 794-0400 (by appointment only). Arts & Crafts patinated copper jewelry box (with flowers), circa 1890; ceremonial spade, circa 1890—James II Galleries, 11 East 57th Street. Flowers—Zezé, 398 East 52nd Street. Limestone tabletop on wrought-iron base—Lexington Gardens, 1011 Lexington Avenue. "Skeleton" sand-cast aluminum and steel chairs designed by

Michael Aram—Z Gallerie, 2071 Union Street, San Francisco, CA, (415) 346-9000. "Sun, Moon and Stars" cotton fabric (available through decorator)—Brunschwig & Fils, 979 Third Avenue. Tin skeletons—Pan American Phoenix, 857 Lexington Avenue.
Braised Short Ribs; Roasted Golden Nugget Squash; Duchesse Potato Ghosts (page 72): French ceramic baking dish—Bridge Kitchenware Corp., 214 East 52nd Street. Handmade blackware ovenproof serving dish—Geomancy, 337 East 9th Street. "Boneware" silver-plate serving pieces designed by Michael Aram—The L S Collection, 469 West Broadway.
Devil's Food Cake with Chocolate Spider Web (page 73): "Spider Web" silver-plate server—Fischer Designs, (212) 794-0040 (by appointment only).

A Country Thanksgiving

Table Setting (pages 74 and 75): Coalport porcelain soup plates, circa 1820—Bardith, 901 Madison Avenue. Gien faience presentation plates—Baccarat, 625 Madison Avenue. "Cardinal" silver-plate flatware—for stores call Puiforcat customer service, (800) 993-2580. "Epoque" wine glasses and water glasses designed by Anna Ehrner—for stores call Kosta Boda (609) 768-5400. Archipelago linen napkins—Frank McIntosh Shop at Henri Bendel, 712 Fifth Avenue. Flowers—Zezé, 398 East 52nd Street. Eighteenth-century brass candlesticks; Victorian biscuit tin—Bob Pryor Antiques, 1023 Lexington Avenue. *Out the Lane*, tempera 1948 (over fireplace), and *Transition*, oil on canvas, circa 1975 (on wall), both by John McCoy.
Entrée and Accompaniments (pages 76 and 77): Mason's ironstone platters, circa 1810; English pearl-ware chamber candlestick, circa 1860; Dr. Wall Worcester "Pinecone" porcelain bowl (beets), circa 1770; English pearl-ware shell dish (vegetable purée), circa 1790;—Bardith, 901 Madison Avenue. Nineteenth-century Irish mahogany silver table; four-panel Belgian tooled

leather screen, circa 1820—Yale R. Burge Antiques, 305 East 63rd Street. Flowers—Zezé, 398 East 52nd Street.

Thanksgiving California Style

Table Setting (pages 78 and 79): Gien faience dinner plates, salad plates, and serving bowl—Baccarat, 625 Madison Avenue. "Harbor" stainless-steel flatware and serving pieces—for stores call Ralph Lauren Collection, (212) 624-8700. Wineglasses—Simon Pearce, 500 Park Avenue at 59th Street. Cotton napkins; short wrought-iron candlesticks; ramekin in wicker holder; (butter); ceramic platter (turkey)—Pier One Imports, 1550 Third Avenue. Tall wrought-iron candlesticks with crystal drops designed by Cyril Doudeau—for stores call Paradigm Exclusives, (212) 629-3955. Porcelain leaf plate (olives) designed by Laure Japy—Bloomingdale's, 1000 Third Avenue. Dried-flower arrangement—Zezé, 398 East 52nd Street. Glass bowl (stuffing)—Gracious Home, 1220 Third Avenue. Wüsthof-Trident carbon-steel carving knife and fork—for stores call (800) 289-9878. Square ceramic bowl and ladle; wicker trivet—MacKenzie Childs, 824 Madison Avenue. Wire bread basket—Katz & Co., 6770 Washington Street, Yountville, CA 94599.
Grilled Turkey (page 79): Grill—Weber-Stephen Products, (800) 446-1071.

Rocky Mountain Christmas

Table Setting (pages 80 and 81): Champagne flutes—Pottery Barn, 117 East 57th Street. Pewter wine cooler; horn-handled stainless-steel flatware by Kirk & Matz; tin candlesticks (on mantlepiece)—William Wayne & Co., 850 Lexington Avenue. Earthenware plates designed by Barbara Eigen—for information call Eigen Arts, (201) 798-7310. "Column" wineglasses; carafe—Crate & Barrel, 650 Madison Avenue. Etched-glass water glasses—Aris Mixon, 381 Amsterdam Avenue. Cotton napkins—ABC Carpet & Home, 888 Broadway. Flower arrangement—Zezé, 398 East 52nd Street. "Copper

Mountain" wool fabric designed by Ralph Lauren (on table; available through decorator)—Hinson & Co., 979 Third Avenue.

Almond and Chocolate Dacquoise with Cranberry Sauce (page 80): Dessert plates designed by Barbara Eigen—call Eigen Arts, (201) 798-7310.

Southern Christmas

Table Setting (pages 82 and 83): "Iris" bone-china soup and dinner plates from the William Morris Collection for the Victoria & Albert Museum—Avventura, 463 Amsterdam Avenue. "Carat" Limoges chargers—for stores call Philippe Deshoulieres, (800) 993-2580. "Queen Anne" sterling flatware by Kirk Stieff—Colonial Williamsburg, (800) 446-9240. Wineglasses; gold ball candles—Wolfman • Gold & Good Company, 116 Greene Street. Victorian goblets and rose bowls; steel mounted fire screen and fire tools, circa 1780—James II Galleries, 11 East 57th Street. Linen and lace napkins—Frank McIntosh Shop at Henri Bendel, 712 Fifth Avenue. Nineteenth-century cutglass dish and underplate (croutons); silver-plate candelabra, circa 1880—S. Wyler, 941 Lexington Avenue. Pewter salt and pepper shakers, circa 1900; faux bamboo tea cart, circa 1920—J. Gavin Mecking, 72 East 11th Street. "Lindhurst" cotton damask fabric (on table; available through decorator)—F. Schumacher & Co., 939 Third Avenue. Spanish bentwood armchair, circa 1920; Swedish mahogany chairs, circa 1890—ABC Carpet & Home, 888 Broadway.

Entrée and Accompaniments (pages 84 and 85): Apilco porcelain baking dish (corn chive pudding)—Lamalle Kitchenware, 36 West 25th Street, (800) 660-0750. Copper gratin dish (onion casserole)—Bridge Kitchenware Corp., 214 East 52nd Street. English tazza (brandied fruit), circa 1820; sterling and glass two-part relish dish, circa 1890; sugar spoon, circa 1900 (chutney)—ABC Carpet & Home, 888 Broadway. Victorian wine rinser and frosted-glass plate, circa 1870 (chutney)—James II Galleries, 11 East 57th Street. Cut-glass dish on silver-plate stand, circa 1875 (watermelon rind)—S. Wyler, 941 Lexington Avenue.

Dining on the Light Side

Beet and Asian Pear Salad with Baby Greens; Roast Pork Loin with Shiitake and Leek Compote; Scalloped Potatoes and Parsnips; Steamed Broccoli Rabe with Garlic (pages 86 and 87): Gien "Aurelie" faience plates—Baccarat, 625 Madison Avenue. "Madeleine" flatware; "Dappled" glass—Pottery Barn, 117 East 59th Street. Napkin and tablecloth—Frank McIntosh Shop at Henri Bendel, 712 Fifth Avenue.

Dining on the Light Side

Saffron Linguine with Spicy Shrimp and Vegetables; Caesar-Style Salad (pages 88 and 89): "Yo Han" ceramic plates and bowls; napkins—ABC Carpet & Home, 888 Broadway. "Wallis" stainless-steel flatware by Vincente Wolf—The L • S Collection, 765 Madison Avenue. French wineglasses—Pierre Deux, 870 Madison Avenue.

A Recipe Compendium

Roasted Peppers and Potatoes with Bagna Cauda (page 90): See Table Setting credits for Antipasto Buffet.

English Afternoon Tea

Buffet Spread (pages 256 and 257): Teapot and platter (with sandwiches)—The Teapot, Summit, NJ (908) 273-1655. Spode "Blue Colonel" cups, saucers, creamer and sugar bowl—Royal China and Porcelain Companies, Moorestown, NJ (609) 866-2900. "Burgundy" sterling flatware—Reed & Barton Silversmiths, Taunton, MA (508) 824-6611. Lemonade pitcher—available at Bloomingdale's, 1000 Third Avenue. Napkins—Necessities, Brooklyn, NY (718) 797-0530.

An Irish Country Supper

Baked Scrod in Cider; Blackberry Fool; Dingle Pie; Creamed Mushrooms with Chives; Champ; Irish Soda Bread; Sorrel, Watercress, and Beet Salad (pages 266 and 267): All items in these photographs are privately owned.

A Scottish Dinner

Table Setting (pages 274 and 275): "Napoleon Ivy" dinner plates and large platter; "Edme" serving bowl and platter (with carrots); "Curraghmore" Crystal—Waterford Wedgewood USA Inc., Wall, NJ (800) 677-7860. "Country French" sterling flatware—Reed & Barton Silversmiths, Taunton, MA (508) 824-6611. Tablecloth—Necessities, Brooklyn, NY (718) 797-0530. Flowers—Zezé, 398 East 52nd Street.

CREDITS

Grateful acknowledgment is made to the following for permission to reprint recipes previously published in *Gourmet* Magazine.

Jessica B. Harris: "Silver Dollar-Size Biscuits" (page 109). Copyright © 1995 by Jessica B. Harris. Reprinted by permission of the author.

Eileen Yin-Fei Lo: "Fried Rice with Tomatoes" (page 164). Copyright © 1995 by Eileen Yin-Fei Lo. Reprinted by permission of the author.

Lydie Marshall: "Osso Buco of Lamb Shanks with Tomatoes and Garlic" (page 138) and "White Bean Purée" (page 139). Copyright © 1995 by Lydie Marshall. Reprinted by permission of the author.

Leslie Glover Pendleton: "Blueberry Maple Oatmeal Muffins" (page 109). Copyright © 1995 by Leslie Glover Pendleton. Reprinted by permission of the author.

Zanne Early Zakroff: "Braised Pheasant with Red Cabbage Wild Rice" (page 147); "Herbed Mayonnaise" (page 203); "Spicy Saffron Mayonnaise" (page 203). Copyright © 1995 by Zanne Early Zakroff. Reprinted by permission of the author.

The following photographers have generously given their permission to reprint the photographs listed below. Most of these photographs have previously appeared in *Gourmet* Magazine.

Mark Ferri: "Easter Dinner" (pages 6, 30-32); "A Cycling Picnic" (pages 50 and 51); "Lunch on the Porch" (pages 56, 57, and 59); "A Weekend in the Country" (pages 7, 66, and 67, bottom). Copyright © 1995.

Julian Nieman: "A Young Piper in Kanturk Castle, County Cork, Ireland" (page 7); "Longueville's Cattle in the Morning Mist, County Cork, Ireland" (page 264). Copyright © 1994.

Mathias Oppersdorff: "Cottage off Steep Hill, Lincoln, England" (page 254); "Tantallon Castle, East Lothian, Scotland" (page 272). Copyright ©1992.

Adam Woolfitt: "Burnsall Village in Wharfedale, Yorkshire" (page 240). Copyright © 1995.

If you are not already a subscriber to *Gourmet* Magazine and would be interested in subscribing, please call *Gourmet's* toll-free number, 1-800-365-2454.

If you are interested in purchasing additional copies of this book or other *Gourmet* cookbooks, please call 1-800-245-2010.